DIETER KIENAST

DIETER KIENAST

Essays
Martin R. Dean, Udo Weilacher

Textbeiträge / Text contributions
Thomas Göbel-Groß, Dieter Kienast,
Erika Kienast, German Ritz, Artur Rüegg

Photos
Christian Vogt

Birkhäuser – Verlag für Architektur
Basel · Boston · Berlin

Orte gegen die Selbstvergessenheit 6	Places against Oblivion of the Self 6
Martin R. Dean	Martin R. Dean

Gärten / Gardens

Gärten		Gardens	
Eintritt in den autobiographischen Garten	12	Entering the Autobiographical Garden	12
Vielfalt und Dichte	22	Variety and Density	22
Wo ist Arkadien?	34	Where is Arcadia?	34
Grenzen und Zäune	46	Borders and Fences	46
Lob der Zweideutigkeit	52	In Praise of Ambiguity	52
Zwischen Tradition und Innovation	64	Between Tradition and Innovation	64
Neue Gärten zum alten Schloß	72	New Gardens for the Old Castle	72

Sehnsucht nach dem Paradies	84	Longing for Paradise	84
Dieter Kienast		Dieter Kienast	

Öffentliche Anlagen / Public Projects

Öffentliche Anlagen		Public Projects	
Stadtpark Wettingen	94	Urban Park in Wettingen	94
Gartenanlagen der Psychiatrischen Klinik Waldhaus, Chur	104	Garden of the Waldhaus Psychiatric Clinic, Chur	104
Friedhof Fürstenwald Chur	116	Fürstenwald Cemetery in Chur	116
Verwaltungsgebäude Swisscom, Worblaufen Bern	126	Swisscom Administrative Building, Worblaufen Bern	126
Expo 2000 und Messegelände Hannover	140	Expo 2000 Hanover and Fair Grounds	140
Kurpark Bad Münder	150	Bad Münder Spa Gardens	150
Tate Modern London	160	Tate Modern London	160
Die Freiflächen des Zentrums für Kunst und Medientechnologie, Karlsruhe	166	The Grounds of the Center for Art and Media, Karlsruhe	166
Stadtgarten am Neubau des Bundesarbeitsgerichts, Erfurt	176	Urban Garden for the New Building of the Federal Labour Court, Erfurt	176
Internationale Gartenschau 2000 Steiermark, Graz	188	International Garden Show 2000 Styria, Graz	188
Innenhofgestaltung Geschäftshaus der Swiss Re, Zürich	204	Courtyard Design: Offices of the Swiss Re, Zurich	204
Seminar- und Ausbildungszentrum Swiss Re, Rüschlikon	212	Training Centre of the Swiss Re, Rüschlikon	212
Umgebungsgestaltung Spar- und Landeskasse, Fürstenfeldbruck	220	Open Space Planning for the Spar- und Landeskasse, Fürstenfeldbruck	220
Stockalper Schloßgarten Brig	230	Stockalper Palace Gardens in Brig	230
Neubau Madagaskarhalle, Zoo Zürich	236	New Madagascar Hall, Zurich Zoo	236

Zwischen Poesie und Geschwätzigkeit
Dieter Kienast	246	Between Poetry and Garrulousness
Dieter Kienast	246
Wettbewerbe		Competitions	
Dornröschen am Mechtenberg	258	Sleeping Beauty at Mechtenberg	258
Straße der Nationen, Chemnitz	266	Strasse der Nationen, Chemnitz	266
Conrad Gessner Park Zürich Oerlikon	270	Conrad Gessner Park in Zurich-Oerlikon	270
Töölönlahtipark Helsinki	276	Töölönlahti Park in Helsinki	276
Fährtenlese
Udo Weilacher	284	Scanning Tracks
Udo Weilacher	284
Projektdaten	298	Project Data	298
Auswahlbibliographie	300	Selected Bibliography	300

Orte gegen die Selbstvergessenheit

«Die Kinder lärmen auf den bunten Steinen. / Die Sonne scheint und glitzert auf ein Haus. / Ich sitze still und lasse mich bescheinen / und ruh von meinem Vaterlande aus.»

Kurt Tucholsky: Park Monceau, 1924

Gärten sind keine Vaterländer. Ihrer Definition als Hortus Conclusus gemäß sind sie ein Stück Land, welches umzäunt und abgegrenzt von der «wilden» Natur Schutz und Zuflucht bietet. Ein Flecken kultivierter Natur freilich, der nie ganz in der Gegenwart liegt, sondern sich in die Vergangenheit wie in die Zukunft verzweigt. «Wir können,» schreibt Dieter Kienast, «den Garten als Metapher der Ursehnsucht des Menschen, der Rückkehr ins Paradies gebrauchen, zu jenem Ort, wo Friede und Geborgenheit, Nahrung und Schönheit sind.»[1]

Ich besuchte Gärten, bevor ich zum Schreiben kam. Als Student in Paris eilte ich an den hellen Sommertagen frühmorgens schon in die Parks – den Parc des Buttes Chaumont, den Jardin du Luxembourg –, um meinen Baudelaire oder Rilke zu lesen. Was ich später durch das Schreiben meines ersten Buches «Die verborgenen Gärten» vertiefte, durchlebte ich damals intuitiv: «Der Garten ist immer Utopie, Wunschbild und Projektion einer Epoche. Die Natur eines Gartens ist immer sedimentierte Geschichte,»[2] so sinniert Manuel, der Protagonist meines Romans.

Der einem Garten zugrunde liegende Plan vermittelte mir damals ein Lebensgefühl, in dem ich mich gleichzeitig aufgehoben und aus der Gegenwart weggetragen fühlte. Eingebunden in die strenge Geometrie der Wegachsen im «Luxembourg», eingenommen von den flackernden Farben und Lichteffekten der Buttes Chaumont. Ich benötigte Jahre des Studiums und des Schreibens, um genauer sagen zu können, was bei diesen frühen Gartenerlebnissen alles ineinander ging. Gewiß etwas, das über einen bloßen Naturspaziergang hinausführte, ein komplexes Zusammenspiel von Natur, Ästhetik und Geschichte, was Dieter Kienast so formulierte: «Ich habe nach einem Garten gefragt, nach jenem Kunstwerk, von dem Kant gesagt hat, daß es das

---

1 Dieter Kienast: Die Poetik des Gartens. Über Chaos und Ordnung in der Landschaftsarchitektur, hrsg. von der Professur für Landschaftsarchitektur ETH Zürich. Basel, Berlin, Boston 2002, S. 72
2 Martin R. Dean: Die verborgenen Gärten, München 1982

Places against Oblivion of the Self

Children make noise. A windowpane is gleaming. / The sun is warm and shines so bright today. / I'll let it shine on me while I lie dreaming, / And take a rest from my country far away.

Kurt Tucholsky: Park Monceau, 1924

Gardens are not fatherlands. Given their definition of hortus conclusus, they are a piece of land which, fenced and divided off from "untamed" nature, provides protection and refuge. Needless to say, a piece of cultivated nature is never quite part of the present, but has both past and future aspects. "We can understand," writes Dieter Kienast, "the garden as a metaphor for our longing to return to paradise, to that place of tranquility and certainty, nurture and beauty."[1]

I visited gardens before I came to start writing. When I was a student in Paris, I got up early during the light summer months to visits the parks - the Parc des Buttes Chaumont, the Jardin du Luxembourg - and read my Baudelaire or Rilke there. At that time, I intuitively experienced what was to assume deeper meaning for me when I wrote my first book "Die verborgenen Gärten" (The Hidden Gardens). "The garden is always utopia, the ideal and projection of an epoch. The nature of a garden is always history in layers;"[2] philosophises Manuel, my novel's protagonist.

The plan underlying a garden gave me a feeling at the time of being alive, in which I felt both in good hands and removed from the present. Part of the strict geometry of the layout of paths in the "Luxembourg", enraptured by the flickering colours and light effects of Buttes Chaumont. It took me years of study and writing to enable me to give more precise expression to the unifying aspect of all these early experiences of gardens. Certainly something which went beyond a simple walk through swathes of nature, a complex interaction of nature, aesthetics and history, which Dieter Kienast expressed as follows: "I asked about a garden, about the work of art that Kant said was the most perfect of all works of art. I asked about the Garden of Pe-

---

1 Diener Kienast: Die Poetik des Gartens. Über Chaos und Ordnung in der Landschaftsarchitektur, edited by the Professur für Landschaftsarchitektur ETH Zürich. Basel, Berlin, Boston 2002, p. 72
2 Martin R. Dean: Die verborgenen Gärten, Munich 1982

vollkommenste überhaupt wäre, ich habe nach dem Garten Petrarcas gefragt, nach Orsinis heiligem Wald, nach Le Nôtres Vaux und Lancelot Browns arkadischen Landschaften, nach Müllers Gartenzwerggruppe und Meiers Pflanzensammlung.»[3]

Ein Garten, wie ihn Kienast versteht, setzt unmittelbar ein synästhetisches Erlebnis in Gang, das auf den Spaziergänger eine tiefe Wirkung ausübt. Es ist nicht anders möglich, als daß sich die bestimmte Luftmischung, die Atmosphäre auf ihn überträgt. Der Gartenbesucher entwickelt, in Kants Worten, ein Interesse am Interesselosen.

Nachdem «Die verborgenen Gärten» abgeschlossen waren, verfiel ich einer seltsamen Obsession: wo immer ich hinkam, besuchte ich als erstes die Gärten. Sah, am frühen Morgen in einem verregneten Garten in Kopenhagen, einen Schwarm Vögel einem Haufen Laub entflattern. Ging in Berlin in der Hitze im Schatten des Tiergartens, in Herrenhausen in Hannover entlang einer Baumallee im Nebel. In Denver summte vor mir ein Teich voller Herbstgold, in der Villa d'Este in Tivoli fuhren meine Hände über die Statue der Fruchtbarkeitsgöttin und im Jardin de Kahn an der Porte de Versailles in Paris überschritt ich auf einer hölzernen Brücke zum ersten Mal einen Fluß aus nichts als Steinen.

Einmal im Pariser Parc de la Villette verließ mich, nach stundenlangem Gehen im hohen Ton einer Flöte im Bambuswald und neben einem modernen, in seinem Prospekt an den Renaissancegarten in Lante erinnernden Brunnen, in Sichtweite der «Folies», jegliches Gefühl für die Zeit. Verwirrung, Desorientierung, ein ästhetischer Schock, vom unablässigen Gemurmel des Brunnens umrauscht, ließen mich meiner selbst inne werden. Plötzlich entsann ich mich anderer Lebenszeiten, war gleichzeitig im Parco Celimontana in Rom und im Sacro Bosco in Bomarzo, in Vaux-le-Vicomte und in der Quinta da Regaleira in Sintra. Ich war im Garten meiner Kindheit ebenso wie in den großartigen Anlagen des Parc André Citroën, den ich zwei Jahre zuvor besucht hatte: ich erlebte alles so, als wäre es gleichzeitig, als wäre die Gegenwart der Fluchtpunkt aller meiner Vergangenheiten. Man darf dieses Erlebnis nicht als Metapher mißverstehen, denn es zeigt sich darin eine Wirkung, wie sie nur von Gärten – oder, in einem extremeren Maße von Rauschmitteln – ausgehen kann. Ein Garten sammelt Biographeme, also Kleinstbruchstücke des eigenen Lebens, in einer auf die Höhe der Gegenwart transponierten Schau. Der Gartenbesucher, der von

trarcas, about the Holy Forest of Orsini, about Le Nôtre's Vaux, and the Arcadian landscapes of Lancelot Brown, about Müller's collection of garden gnomes and Meier's collection of plants".[3]

A garden as understand by Dieter Kienast initiates a synaesthetic experience which has a profound effect upon the visitor. He has no way of resisting the effect the particular air, the atmosphere has on him. The visitor to the garden develops, in the words of Kant, interest in the uninteresting.

After "Die verborgenen Gärten" was completed, I fell prey to a strange obsession: the first thing I did wherever I went was to visit the garden. Saw a flock of birds emerge from a heap of leaves to take to flight in the early morning in a rainy garden in Copenhagen. Enjoyed the shade provided by Berlin's Tiergarten park in the heat of summer, walked along an avenue of trees on a misty day at Herrenhausen in Hanover. A pond humming with insects in Denver, my hands touched the statue of the goddess of fertility at the Villa d'Este in Tivoli, and at the Jardin de Kahn at the Porte de Versailles in Paris I walked across a wooden bridge spanning a river made up of nothing but stones for the first time in my life.

Once at the Parisian Parc de la Villette, after spending hours walking in a bamboo wood accompanied by the high-pitched sound of a flute when I came to a modern fountain with a vista reminiscent of the Renaissance Garden in Lante, and within sight of the "Folies", I lost all sense of time – confusion, disorientation, an aesthetic shock, the unceasing babbling of the fountain, made me stop and think. Suddenly, I remembered other times in my life, was at the same time in the Parco Celimontana in Rome, at Sacro Bosco in Bomarzo, at Vaux-le-Vicomte and the Quinta de Regaleira in Sintra. I was both in the garden of my childhood and in the magnificent grounds of the Parc André Citroën that I had visited two years previously: I experienced all of this at one and the same time as if the present were the vanishing point of all my pasts.

This experience should not be misunderstood as a metaphor as it reveals an effect that can only be produced by gardens or, to a more extreme extent, by intoxicants. A garden collects biographemes, in other words tiny fragments of its own life, in a display transported to the level of the present. The garden visitor who puts everything behind him and surrenders to the garden both forgets and gains himself.

---

[3] Kienast ebenda, S. 71

[3] Kienast ibid. p. 71

allem los- und sich auf den Garten einläßt, vergißt sich und gewinnt sich gleichzeitig.

«Der Garten», schreibt Dieter Kienast, «ist der letzte Luxus unserer Tage, denn er fordert das, was in unserer Gesellschaft am seltensten und kostbarsten ist: Zeit, Zuwendung und Raum.»[4] Sind es nicht genau diese Eigenschaften – Zeit, Zuwendung, Raum – die aus flüchtigen biografischen Bruchstücken, die uns in der beschleunigten Zeit entwirbeln, wieder etwas Homogenes werden lassen? Braucht man nicht Zeit und Zuwendung zur eigenen Geschichte ebenso wie den ausgreifenden Raum, um zu einem Bild seiner selbst zu kommen? Denn aus dem Lebenslauf wird ja nur insofern eine eigene Geschichte, wie wir sie imaginativ und erinnernd zusammenstellen und ordnen. Ohne an sich selbst zu denken – oder in einer älteren Formulierung: ohne seiner Selbst zu gedenken oder inne zu werden, gibt es keine Ich-Geschichte. Die große autobiographische Anstrengung, wie sie Jean Jacques Rousseau auf seinen Promenades – ein passionierter Gartengänger –, und später auch Elias Canetti in seiner ausschweifenden Autobiografie vorführt, hat mit dieser doppelten Bewegung des Ausholens und zu sich selbst Zurückkehrens zu tun.

Natürlich kann das Sich-selber-innewerden auch in einem Kino, bei der Lektüre, auf einer Zugfahrt, beim Einkaufen oder beim Joggen eintreffen. Doch gibt es meiner Meinung kein geeigneteres ästhetisches Medium, das uns besser zu Subjekten unserer Geschichte machen kann als den Garten. Das hängt damit zusammen, daß ein Garten, wie Dieter Kienast es formuliert, die «Gleichzeitigkeit von Natur und Kultur darstellt. Er ist nicht reine Kultur, weil das Naturhafte notwendiger Bestandteil ist, wie er auch nicht reine Natur sein kann, weil der tätige Mensch sonst ausgeschlossen wäre.»[5]
Kienasts Gartenanlagen belegen, daß er den Menschen wie den Garten als eine hybride, zwischen Natur und Kultur oszillierende Setzung verstand. Was ein Garten ist, nimmt man nicht nur durch seinen kulturell präfigurierten Verstand, sondern ebenso durch seine vegetative Seite wahr. Beide Erfahrungsschichten konvergieren im Begriff der «Atmosphäre», wie ihn Gernot Böhme versteht: «Atmosphären sind räumliche Gebilde, die in affektiver Betroffenheit erfahren werden. Jeder kennt Atmosphären aus der Naturerfahrung. Aber Atmosphären sind nicht subjektiv, vielmehr können sie Dingen oder Situationen, einem

"The garden," wrote Dieter Kienast, "is the last remaining luxury of our time, as it demands the rarest and most precious things in our society: time, attention and space."[4]

Are these not the very qualities – time, care and attention, space – which allow something homogenous to be recreated from the fleeting biographical fragments which provide tranquility in a time when everything is high speed? Does one not need time and attention for one's own biography as well as space to form an image of oneself? After all, a biography only becomes a personal history to the extent that we put it together and order it with imagination and recollection. Without thinking about oneself, or to use an older expression: without celebrating oneself, without being aware of oneself, there can be no self-history. The great autobiographical undertakings as demonstrated by Jean Jacques Rousseau – a passionate visitor of gardens – during his walks and later also by Elias Canetti in his elaborate autobiography are linked with this double act of breaking out and returning to oneself.

There is no denying that the process of self-realisation can occur watching a film at the cinema, reading a book, on a train journey, while shopping or out jogging. Yet, there is, in my opinion, no aesthetic medium better suited to making us subjects of our history than the garden. One of the reasons for this is that, as Dieter Kienast puts it, a garden represents the "simultaneity of nature and culture. It is not purely culture as nature is an integral part of it nor can it be purely nature as human beings as an intervening element would then have no place there."[5]

Kienast's gardens demonstrate that he understood both human beings and gardens as hybrids oscillating between nature and culture. We not only recognise what a garden is by our culturally prefigured understanding, but equally by its vegetation. Both levels of experience converge in the concept of "atmosphere", as defined by Gernot Böhme: "Atmospheres are spatial creations, experienced emotionally. Everyone is familiar with atmospheres arising from an experience of nature. But atmospheres are not subjective, rather they can be inherent to things or situations, a cliff or a landscape – which also allows intersubjective understanding."[6] Gardens are an excellent means of creating atmospheres and including the individual, who, after all, is himself always part of nature. Böhme returns to the English garden, writing that the theory of its "characters"[7]

---

4 Kienast ebenda, S. 76
5 Kienast ebenda, S. 137

4 Kienast ibid. p. 76
5 Kienast ibid. p. 137
6 Gernot Böhme: Für eine ökologische Naturästhetik, Frankfurt/M 1989, p. 148
7 Böhme, p. 46: "Characters are objective emotional qualities – such as serene, gently melancholic, serious – which are attributed to landscapes, scenes or individual objects taken from nature. Such characters are created in the English garden by deliberate composition."

Fels, einer Landschaft anhängen – worüber auch eine intersubjektive Verständigung möglich ist.»⁶ In ausgezeichneter Weise schaffen Gärten Atmosphären und beziehen den Menschen, der ja immer selber ein Teil Natur ist, mit ein. Böhme rekurriert auf den englischen Garten, aus dessen Theorie der «Charaktere»⁷ er den Begriff der Atmosphäre ableitet: «Der englische Garten war zum alltäglichen Gebrauch angelegt und sollte für das Leben des Benutzers, für seine psychische Ökonomie bestimmte Bedingungen schaffen und Möglichkeiten bereitstellen. Die englische Landschaftsgärtnerei war so gesehen nicht nur ein Zweig der Ästhetik, sondern der ... Humanökologie.»⁸

Damit wird deutlicher, was Dieter Kienast mit der Bedeutung des Gartens für unsere Zukunft im Auge hatte, wenn er schrieb: «Die Bedeutung des Gartens als Ort der Arbeit, der Muße, der Erholung, als Zeichen eines mehr oder weniger großen Überflusses wird in unserem Land weiter zunehmen.»⁹

Gärten sind Orte mit erhöhter Energie. Sie haben Schauplatzcharakter, was nicht nur zahllose Filme belegen, in denen in Gärten geliebt, gestritten und gemordet wird. Für den Besucher können solche Kunstwerke zum Ort höchst intensiver Selbsterfahrung werden. Erlebt wird dabei nicht nur, worauf das Erholungsargument – wenn auch stark verkürzt – stets anspielt: der eigene Leib und die eigene Psyche als Teil der Natur. Erfahrbar wird auch die geschichtliche Dimension der Existenz, die im Garten als Raum des Erinnerns aufscheint. Paradoxerweise können Gärten, die ja gern als abseitige oder «geschichtsfreie» Fluchtorte verstanden werden, die Einsicht in die eigene Geschichtlichkeit vorantreiben.

Die Zukunft des Gartens, um die sich Dieter Kienast besorgte, wird sich daran erinnern müssen, daß das Paradies (wie die eigene Geschichte) immer wieder neu hergestellt werden muß. Das führen gerade Kienast's Entwürfe mit ihren vieldeutigen, rätselhaften und an andere, vergangene Gärten erinnernde Schriftzüge mustergültig vor. Die zukünftigen Gärten werden noch mehr das sein, was sie unter der strengen Fuchtel der französischen Gartengeometer und der englischen Landschaftsmaler eingestandenermaßen nie sein durften: imaginäre Traumlandschaften. Daß der Mensch in den Gärten zu sich selber komme, wird man auch dann ganz wörtlich nehmen dürfen.

Martin R. Dean

serves as the basis of his conception of atmosphere: "The English garden was laid out with a view to everyday use and was intended to provide certain conditions and possibilities for the life of the user and his psychological needs. Seen this way, English landscape gardening was not only a branch of aesthetics, but of ... human ecology." ⁸

This well illustrates what Dieter Kienast had in mind regarding the meaning of the garden for our future when he wrote: "The meaning of the garden as a place of work, of time for leisure and relaxation, of recreation, as a sign of affluence to a greater of lesser degree will continue to increase in our country."⁹

Gardens are places of heightened energy. They have the character of a stage – something which is not only demonstrated by countless films in which a garden is a setting for romance, arguments, and murder. Such works of art can be a place of intensive self-experience for the visitor. This is not only a question – as alluded to constantly by the leisure argument, albeit in a greatly condensed form – of experiencing our own body and own psyche as part of nature. What is also experienced is the historical dimension of existence which appears in the garden as a place of memory. It is a paradox that gardens, which are frequently understood as esoteric or "history-free" places of refuge, can further understanding of our own historical dimension.

The future of the garden, a future which Dieter Kienast cared about, will have to remember that paradise (like our own history) has to be recreated anew every time. This is superbly demonstrated by Kienast's designs with their ambiguous, enigmatic traits and their reminiscence of other gardens of times past. The gardens of the future will be far more than what it must be admitted, they were never allowed to be under the thumb of the French garden geometricians and the English landscape painters: imaginary dream landscapes. And then we will be able to understand the statement that man finds himself in the garden quite literally.

Martin R. Dean

---

6 Gernot Böhme: Für eine ökologische Naturästhetik, Frankfurt/M 1989, S. 148
7 Böhme, S. 46: «Charaktere sind objektive Gefühlsqualitäten – wie beispielsweise heiter, sanft-melancholisch, ernst – die Landschaften, Naturszenen oder einzelnen Naturstücken zukommen. Solche Charaktere werden im englischen Garten durch bewußte Komposition erzeugt.»
8 Böhme ebenda, S. 93
9 Kienast ebenda, S. 76

8 Böhme ibid. p. 93
9 Kienast ibid. p. 76

Eintritt in den autobiographischen Garten

Die Autobiographie, diese Hybride aus einer ganz anderen Form der Kunst, erweckt eine seltsame Vorstellung bei einem Garten. Es gibt den Hausgarten, den privaten, intimen und «secreten» Garten, Abstufungen, die einen wachsenden Ausschluß der Betrachter bedeuten. Die intimste Form der Verborgenheit im geheimen Garten gibt den Blick frei, nicht zu einem privaten Inhalt, sondern nur zu einem privaten Raum. Ist das Private nur das Schweigen, das, was nach der Gestaltung kommt? In der Literatur reibt sich das Autobiographische mit der geschlossenen Gestaltung, so das Tagebuch mit dem Roman. Es tritt auf als Antiform, als Bruch mit der Konvention oder dem Tabu, als Quelle des Neuen und Reservat des Anderen. Das Autobiographische ist gewachsener Text, sich verändernde Form, es begleitet die Zeit und es ist offen. Es mißt und begrenzt sich nur gegenüber dem Tod und ruft von dieser Grenze aus nicht nach Ovids «Exegi monumentum», sondern bleibt anarchische Fülle und wendet sich dem Leben zu. Es hat keine Angst vor Aussagen, streift das Cliché, den Kitsch, es zitiert Fremdes, wiederholt Eigenes, es lebt vom Alltag, der Abfallhalde des Verschiedenen und Eigenen. Das Autobiographische betrat die Bühne, als reihum in der Spätmoderne die große Form unter lauter Klage zu Grabe getragen wurde. Für viele blieb das Autobiographische lange eine Ersatzkultur, ein Zeichen der Erschöpfung. Für alle war es jedoch eine Herausforderung. Die Postmoderne hat sich schließlich nur mehr gefreut an diesem ehrenwerten Vorfahren, der bis auf Augustinus zurückgeht. Sie befreit das Autobiographische vom Psychologischen und führt das Private auf den Platz.

Das Autobiographische wird im Garten an der Thujastraße in Zürich auf verschiedenen Ebenen manifest. Es ist zunächst ein Moment der räumlichen Konstellation. Die Stilpluralität ist keine Collage, in der der Heterostil gegenüber dem anderen als different erkannt wird. Die Stilmischung betont hier weniger das Konzeptionelle als vielmehr das Geschichtliche, das Lebensgeschichtliche des Gartens. Die Heterogenität verweist auf die Zeit und nicht auf den Raum. Die Abfolge der Räume gehorcht dem Alltag: der Arbeit, dem Wohnen, dem Ausblick auf

Entering the Autobiographical Garden

The autobiography, this hybrid from a totally different art form, evokes a strange idea when it comes to a garden. There is the house garden, the private garden, the intimate garden, and the "secret" garden, all of which are gradations representing increasingly the exclusion of the observer. The most intimate form of concealment in the secret garden opens up the view to a private space, not a private content. Is privacy just the silence following the design? In literature, the autobiographic creates a friction with the closed concept, as does the diary with the novel. It appears as an anti-form – a break with the convention or the taboo – as a source of the new and repository of the different. The autobiographic is a growing text, a changing form, it accompanies time and is open. It measures and limits itself only towards death, and from this threshold does not call for Ovid's "Exegi monumentum", but remains an anarchic fullness and turns to life. It is not afraid of statements – it touches on the cliché, kitsch; it quotes what is foreign and repeats the individual; it lives from every-day-life, the garbage dump of the different and unique. The autobiography entered the stage when, during the period of late modernism, the large form was buried with loud complaint. For many, the autobiography remained a substitute culture. It was a sign of exhaustion. To all, however, it was a challenge. Post-modernism only took plea-

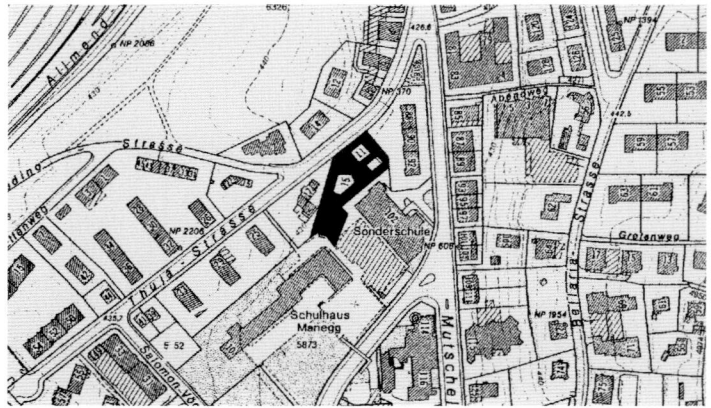

Projektplan 1991
Grundriß
Original 1:100, 84 x 90 cm; Tusche,
Farbstift auf Plandruck

Project plan 1991
Ground plan
Original 1:100, 84 x 90 cm; ink,
color pencil on plan print

die andere Mitwelt. Ältere Räume stehen in späteren, und wenn sie in ihrem Nebeneinander ästhetisch miteinander kommunizieren, ist das freies Spiel, das ihre eigene andere Bedeutung nicht überdeckt, so die autobiographische Erinnerung an Kindheit beim Spielplatz, an Familie im Gewächshaus. Postmoderne Existenz entdeckt sich als Teil einer Familiengeschichte.

Das Tor zur Familiengeschichte öffnet sich in der Kindheit, in unserem Garten in seinem autobiographisch wichtigsten Einzelmotiv, den Tierfiguren. Der Garten gestaltet die Erinnerung an die Kindheit nicht als formales Zeichen, sondern formt den Akt der Erinnerung plastisch nach. Die geschnittenen Baumtiere sind groteske Traumgebilde. Sie überragen alle andern Elemente des Gartens und sind doch nicht vertikale Raumorientierung, sondern erzählte Geschichte, die uns anzieht und die Metamorphose vom Erwachsenen zum Kinde, die sie erzählen, distanzlos miterleben läßt. Wer immer unter diesem phantastischen Federvieh wandert, kommt nicht umhin, weil er zwangsmäßig nach oben schaut, den Kinderblick zu wiederholen, der selbst die kleine Welt des Federviehs von unten sieht, das heißt von so tief unten hinaufschaut, daß der Blick nicht realer Kinderblick ist, sondern in der Erinnerung zu einem Grotesken verschoben wird. Das autobiographische Kind verschwindet in der unendlichen Kleinheit der Imagination.

Mit dieser Metamorphose sind wir vom öffentlicheren Raum in den privateren Raum getreten. Der private Raum ist freilich nun nicht der andere Raum, der nach der Metamorphose in das Kind erwartet wird, nicht das Ziel der Metamorphose. Die mythoide Geschichte bleibt als ritueller Akt in sich geschlossen. Die Fabeltiere sind ein Moment des autobiographischen Textes, nicht aber ihre Metageschichte. Der anschließende Raum mit dem Wasserbecken ist streng formal, nicht mehr existentielles, sondern nun mehr ästhetisches Zeichen. Er macht in seiner Abgeschlossenheit, als Raum im Raum, seine Immanenz deutlich und ist in seinem Streben nach Schönheit narzistisch, ähnlich wie das Baumgeviert gleich nach dem Eingang, in dem auf dem Grund die abwesenden Äpfel in einem abwesenden Spiegel sich rot betrachten.

Es sind ästhetische Leer-, besser Pausenzeichen, in deren Formalismus die Nähe zum Zitat spürbar wird. Ausgeformte Gestalt entdeckt sich leichter als Wiederholung, denn singuläre Lebenserfahrung.

sure in this honorable ancestor which goes back to Augustinus. It frees the autobiography from psychology and brings privacy into play.

In the garden at Thujastrasse in Zurich, the autobiographic is apparent on many different levels. First, it is a momentum of spatial constellations. The plurality in style is not a collage in which the hetero-style is recognized as different from the other. The mixture of styles enhances the conceptual less than the historical; i.e., the history of the garden's life. The heterogeneity points to time, not space. The sequence of spaces conforms to every-day-life: work, living, the outlook to the other coexisting world. Older spaces are placed into younger ones. And if they communicate esthetically in their side-by-side coexistence, it is free play which does not disguise different meanings, such as the autobiographic memory of childhood in the playground, and of family in the greenhouse.

The gate to family history opens up during childhood; in our garden it does so with its autobiographically most important single motif, the topiary figures. The garden designs the memory of childhood not as a formal sign, but it sculpturally reshapes the act of memory. The topiary animals are grotesque dream creatures. They surmount all other elements of the garden and yet are not a vertical spatial orientation. They are a narration of history which attracts us and lets us experience the metamorphosis from the adult to the child which they recount without distance. Whoever walks among this fantastic poultry can not help but have the look of a child because they are forced to constantly look up; even the small world of poultry is seen from below, from so far down that the view is not a true child's view, but is shifted into something grotesque in memory. The autobiographic child disappears in the eternal smallness of imagination.

With this metamorphosis we have stepped from the public space into the more private space. Certainly, the private space is not the other space which, succeeding the metamorphosis, is anticipated in the child. This is not the goal of the metamorphosis. The mythogenic story remains closed within itself as a ritual act. The fable animals are a mere moment of the autobiographic text; they are not its meta-history. The adjoining space with the water basin is strictly formal. No longer an existential symbol, it now becomes more of an esthetic one. It clarifies its

Die aufragenden Fabeltiere haben erst im nächsten zentralen Gartenraum ihr Gegenzeichen. Aus dem häuslichen, funktionalen Bereich führen «altväterische» Stufen in die Tiefe. Auf dem Grund verweist abwechselnd mooriges Wasser nicht in helle Höhe, noch dunkle Urtiefe, öffnet sich kein Urauge, das nach innen und nach außen schaut. Die Tiefe verweigert sich, zitiert nicht den artifiziellen Spiegel als ironisches Simulacrum, sondern bleibt bunte, glatte Oberfläche. Plaudern die luftigen Zeichen aus der Kindheit ungehemmt über Bedeutung, verweigert das Zeichen der Tiefe ironisch seine Aussage. Die beiden autobiographischen Symbole sind nicht optisch verbunden, die Beziehung schafft erst die autobiographische Erzählung.

Der Garten endet nicht in der Untiefe, sondern in seiner formal am stärksten herausgearbeiteten Begrenzung, dem Zaun, der die private Erzählung abschließt. Er ist selber schon nicht mehr nur eigener autobiographischer Text, sondern auch fremder, öffentlicher. Noch verweist der Zaun stark auf die andere Umwelt, aber die hoch angelegten Fenster zeigen, daß hier nicht Durchblick, sondern Anblick gemeint sein wird.

Die autobiographische Geschichte ist selber nur ein Moment in der unabgeschlossenen Geschichte. Sie muß immer neu erzählt werden, so wie der Erbauer und das Erbaute in diesem Garten immer neue Geschichten erzählen, ohne daß sie sich aber je ganz aus der Magie der privaten Mythologie werden befreien können und wollen.

German Ritz

immanence in its self-contentiousness as a space within the space and, in its striving for beauty, is narcissistic, similar to the square of trees right past the entrance where the non-existent apples watch themselves on the ground in the non- existent mirror. They are esthetic 'pause' symbols in whose formalism the closeness to a quotation becomes perceivable. The well-shaped design discovers itself more easily than repetition of a singular life experience.

The fable animals rising up from the ground receive their counter-symbol only in the following garden space. From the homey functional area, "old grandfather" steps lead into the depths. On the ground, changing moory water does not point into bright heights nor to the darkest age-old depths and no ancient eye opens up to look within, nor out. The depth denies itself. It does not quote the artificial mirror as an ironic simulacrum, but remains a colorful flat surface. Whereas the airy symbols from childhood speak uninhibitedly about meaning, the symbol of depth ironically refuses its statement. The two autobiographic symbols are not linked visually; the relation is created only by the autobiographic story.

The garden does not end in the shallow, but in its formally most strongly worked-out limitation – the fence – which ends the private recitation. It is no longer just its own autobiographic text. It is also a strange and public one. The fence still points to the other environment; however, the high windows show that it is not simply a view that is intended here, but rather a vision.

The autobiographic story is in and of itself only a moment in the unfinished story. It has to be constantly retold in the same way as the builder and the built in this garden constantly tell new stories without, however, ever being able nor wanting to free themselves from the magic of the private mythology.

German Ritz

Der anschließende Raum mit dem Wasserbecken ist streng formal, nicht mehr existentielles, sondern nun mehr ästhetisches Zeichen. Er macht in seiner Abgeschlossenheit, als Raum im Raum, seine Immanenz deutlich und ist in seinem Streben nach Schönheit narzistisch ...

The adjoining space with the water basin is strictly formal. No longer an existential symbol, it now becomes more of an esthetic one. It clarifies its immanence in its self-contentiousness as a space within the space and, in its striving for beauty, is narcissistic ...

Die geschnittenen Baumtiere sind groteske Traumgebilde.
Sie überragen alle andern Elemente des Gartens und sind doch nicht
vertikale Raumorientierung, sondern erzählte Geschichte ...

The topiary animals are grotesque dream creatures.
They surmount all other elements of the garden and yet are not
a vertical spatial orientation. They are a narration of history ...

Vielfalt und Dichte

Konzept und räumliche Zusammenhänge eines Gartens sind schwer darzustellen. So fällt es nicht leicht, den Garten des Hauses M. als Modell zeitgenössischer Gartenkultur zu begreifen, wenn man nur von Bildern ausgeht. Photographien der Südseite etwa zeigen ein traditionelles Parterre mit Buchseinfassung, das in regelmäßigen Stufen gegen den See hin abbricht. Diese sind ihrerseits mit Buchs vorgepflanzt. Rechts und links führen Treppen zur untersten Gartenebene, die von einem rechteckigen Wasserbecken besetzt ist und talseits von einer geschnittenen Ahornhecke begrenzt wird. Exotische Pflanzen in tönernen Töpfen verschiedenster Art sind vor dem dunkelgrünen Hintergrund der Buchskaskade arrangiert wie die Vasen vor den Brunnenterrassen der Villa d'Este in Tivoli. Der Blick zurück zum efeubewachsenen Haus vermittelt vollends einen Eindruck von Hierarchie, von klassischer Ordnung, eine Ahnung von italienischem Renaissancegarten und von jener Verwunschenheit, die nur ganz alten Orten eigen ist.

Die Erwartungen, welche die Bilder dieses homogenen, auf das Wohnhaus bezogenen Gartenstückes wecken, werden auf der Nordseite enttäuscht. Je nach Blickwinkel ergeben sich hier «malerische», jedenfalls asymmetrisch gefaßte Perspektiven mit ungebändigtem Pflanzenmaterial. Geometrische Elemente – eine platzartige Fläche aus metergroßen Zementplatten, sorgfältig geschnittene Eiben- und Ahornhecken – stehen in lockerer Beziehung zur Eingangsfassade des Hauses. Einige rosa blühende Fuchsien in Töpfen sind frei aufgestellt. Auf den ersten Blick erkennen wir keine logische Entsprechung zum Terrassengarten; es handelt sich offenbar um einen Gartentyp, der als Antithese zum ersten gesehen werden muß, nicht um einen «Naturgarten» allerdings; es könnte, angesichts des sorgfältigen Arrangements, um die Natur als Inszenierung, um eine Demonstration der Künstlichkeit auch eines landschaftlichen Gartens, gehen.

Spätestens jetzt wird es nötig, entweder den Plan zu Rate zu ziehen oder besser – die ganze Anlage abzuschreiten. Schon das Haus ist eine Kuriosität: dem symmetrischen Quergiebel gegen den See entspricht auf der Bergseite eine aus der Mitte

Variety and Density

The concept and spatial relations of a garden are difficult to represent. Therefore, it is not easy to understand the garden of the M. house as a model of contemporary garden culture on the basis of photographs. For example, the photos of the southern side show a traditional parterre with a frame of box, which break up towards the lake in regular steps. The steps are also framed with box. On the right and left side, steps lead to the lowest garden level which is occupied by a rectangular water basin and limited towards the valley by a trimmed maple hedge. Exotic plants in an assortment of clay pots are arranged in front of the dark green background of the cascade of box like the vases in front of the fountain terraces of Villa d'Este in Tivoli. The view back to the ivy-covered house provides a final impression of hierarchy, of classical order, a sense of Italian Renaissance gardens and of that enchanting aura associated only with very old places.

The expectations raised by the images of this homogeneous piece of garden that refers to the house are let down when attention is turned to the northern side. Depending on the angle, "painterly" images or, at the very least, asymmetrically arranged perspectives with untamed plant material, arise. Geometric elements – a square-like surface formed by cement paving stones, carefully cut yew and maple hedges – take on a

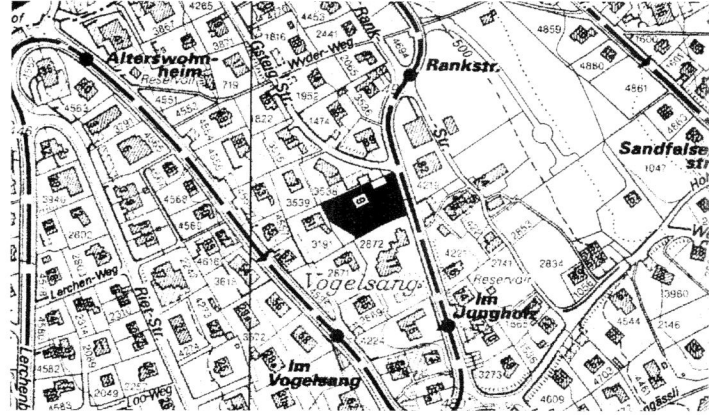

gerückte, dreieckige Lukarne. Diese bildete einst den Ansatz eines enormen Treibhauses, dessen Grundriß im längsrechteckigen Rasenstück vor dem Haus erhalten ist. Seine Position wurde durch eine parallel angelegte, an die Grundstückgrenze gerückte Remise bestimmt. Was wir heute vor uns haben, ist also lediglich das Fragment einer einst größeren Anlage, des Ökonomiekomplexes einer stattlichen Villa, die auf dem östlichen Nachbargrundstück liegt. Der Eingang des Gärtnerhauses lag ehemals beim Brunnen auf der Ostseite; beim Umbau wurde in jenem Bereich die Bade- und Schlafabteilung angeordnet und die Haustüre in die Achse des ehemaligen Treibhauses versetzt.

Kienast verzichtete nun darauf, den bestehenden Garten umzupflügen, dessen räumliche Ordnung noch auf die Existenz des Glashauses Rücksicht nimmt – wie übrigens auch auf eine Aushöhlung oder einen Neubau des Hauses verzichtet wurde. Bestehende Elemente wie Natursteinmauern und -sitzgelegenheiten wurden im Gegenteil freigelegt und ergänzt. Das rechteckige Rasenstück vor dem neuen Haupteingang erhielt bergseits einen Abschluß in Form einer doppelten Eibenhecke und eine Längenbetonung mit zwei Kugeleiben – räumliche Verstärkungen und Klärungen, die vor allem aus dem Eingangsbereich des Hauses wirksam sind. Dieser Längsentwicklung wurde unmittelbar vor der Fassade eine Querzone in der Form eines plattenbelegten Hartplatzes überlagert, die dem bestehenden Gartenstück eine völlig neue Dimension hinzufügt: den Blick von der mit Mauern und Remise verbauten Westseite – wo ein Sitzplatz geschaffen wurde – hinüber zum hohen Baumbestand gegen die benachbarte Villa hin: ein Blick, der ohne Inszenierung nicht erlebbar wäre. Vor dem ehemaligen Hauseingang beim Brunnen behindert ein erhöhter Vorplatz den unbefugten Zutritt; Kienast schuf hier einen intimen, abgeschlossenen Bereich, dessen Ahornhecke als Gegengewicht zur Remise gedacht ist.

Der Bestand des alten Gartens wird also bewertet, interpretiert, ergänzt und kommentiert. Kienast scheut sich nicht, selbst alte Tannen zu fällen, wenn dies für die Klärung der Raumbildung notwendig ist. Wenige wichtige Bäume werden belassen, schöne Exemplare – etwa ein Magnolienbaum – freigestellt. Die Eingriffe zielen darauf, Vorhandenes nicht abzuschotten, sondern aufzudecken und einzubeziehen. So zeigt dieser nördliche Gartenteil exemplarisch, wie mit Fragmenten gearbeitet werden kann. Bestehendes, mit kleinen Eingriffen ergänzt, erhält einen

loose relationship with the entrance facade of the house. Some pink-flowering potted fuchsias are freely distributed. At first sight, we can't seem to recognize any logical correspondence with the terrace garden. Obviously, we are dealing here with a garden type that must be seen as the antithesis to the first one, but not with a "natural garden". Given the careful arrangement, it could deal with nature as a production, a demonstration of the artificiality even of a landscaped garden.

Now, at least, it becomes necessary to either consult with the plan, or even better, to actually take a walk through the entire grounds. The house is already a curiosity: the symmetrical cross gable facing the lake is answered on the hillside by a triangular roof-window, placed off-center. It had at one time formed the beginnings of a huge greenhouse whose ground plan is preserved in the longitudinal rectangular piece of lawn in front of the house. Its position was determined by a parallel shed that had been moved to the property border. So, what we see today is merely a fragment of a once larger complex, the outbuildings of a stately villa on the neighboring property to the east. The entrance to the gardener's house was once at the fountain on the east side. During the conversion, the section containing the bathroom and bedroom was placed in this area and the house door was moved to the axis of the former greenhouse.

Kienast then dropped the idea of plowing up the existing garden which, through its spatial order, still considers the existence of the glass house. We also did not want to gut or rebuild the house. On the contrary, many existing elements, such as the natural stone walls and seating areas, were excavated and extended. The rectangular piece of lawn in front of the new main entrance was closed off towards the hill with a yew hedge and longitudinally enhanced with two sphere-shaped yews – spatial clarifications which have their greatest effect, above all, when viewed from the entrance area of the house. Immediately in front of the facade, this longitudinal development was overlapped by a transverse-zone in the form of a tile-covered court, adding a completely new dimension to the existing piece of garden: the view from the west side built-in with walls and the shed where a seating area was created to the high trees and the neighboring villa; a view which could not be experienced without this development. In front of the former house entrance at

Projektpläne 1989
Grundriß und Schnitte
Originale 1:100, 58 x 95 cm;
Bleistift und Farbstift
auf grauem Halbkarton

Project plans 1989,
Ground plan and sections
Originals 1:100, 58 x 95 cm;
pencil and colored pen
on gray illustration board

neuen Sinn, der zwar das Ganze umfaßt, nicht aber auf eine «Totale Architektur», auf die «Unverfrorenheit und Unzweideutigkeit» eines alles umfassenden Wurfes abzielt. Rowe und Koetter, die mit Recht die Architektur der Gärten als Kritik an der Architektur der Stadt auffassen[1], stellen in diesem Zusammenhang das Konzept von Versailles dem Modell der Villa Hadriana gegenüber. Deren «relativierend inszenierte Stücke» sind Musterbeispiele eines stückweise vorgeführten, komplexen, von Reminiszenzen bestimmten Entwurfes. Auch Kienast verwendet die Verfahren des «Weiterstrickens», des lokalen Eingriffes, der Überlagerung, der Collage. Es ist evident, daß er dabei seinerseits einem Muster folgt, das sich etwa 1965 in der Architektur- und Städtebaudiskussion abzuzeichnen begann und das sich – wenigstens in der Theorie – seither weitgehend durchgesetzt hat. Aus dieser Sicht gewinnt unser Garten eine erste Stufe von Aktualität und von Bedeutung.

Die stilistischen Mittel, die Kienast einsetzt, stützen sich vor allem auf den Kontrast von organisch bestimmter, freier Form zur geometrischen Setzung des Menschen. Diese umfaßt nicht nur das Gebaute, sondern auch Pflanzenmaterial, das gezähmt, geschnitten, künstlich in geometrische Form gebracht wird. Im großen Maßstab wird der geometrische Nahbereich des Hauses, der sich auf der Westseite an die baulich definierte Kante anlehnt, ausgespiegelt gegen die großzügige Baumkulisse, die zur «Verbergung der Grenzen» gegen den Garten der Villa hin dient (ein Begriff, den Peter Joseph Lenné bei der Beschreibung englischer Landschaftsgärten verwendet hat[2]). Im Kleinen wird das Prinzip etwa bei den Fugen der Zementplatten lesbar, die mit Duftkräutern ausgepflanzt sind: diese Pflanzen entwickeln sich, der Benützung des Platzes folgend, in der unregelmäßigen Geometrie des Fugennetzes.

Für seine baulichen Setzungen verwendet Kienast gerne Sichtbeton oder Zementwaren. Einerseits handelt es sich dabei um ein «armes» Material, dessen Oberflächenqualität nicht von der reinen Form ablenkt (Le Corbusier propagierte schon 1921 die «matériaux bruts» als Mittel zur Erzeugung von räumlichen Gebilden, die den Betrachter zutiefst bewegen[3]). Anderseits ist der Beton ein Baustoff, der zur Moderne gehört und eine zeitliche Zuordnung der neuen Eingriffe erlaubt (daher die Einfassung der Natursteinpflästerung vor dem Badezimmer). In dieser Beziehung haben es ja die Landschaftsarchitekten schwer: Ihr

the fountain, a raised entry court prevents unauthorized access; Kienast has created an intimately enclosed area here, whose maple hedge is thought of as a counterweight to the shed.

The population of the old garden is thus qualified, interpreted, extended and commented on. Kienast does not shy away from cutting down even the old pine trees if it's necessary for clarifying the spatial form. Only a few important trees are left standing. The most beautiful ones are liberated. One example would be the wonderful magnolia tree. The operations aim not at sealing off the existing, but at uncovering and integrating it. Thus, this northern part of the garden shows in an exemplary way how one can work with fragments. The existing, complemented with small operations, receives a new meaning which embraces the whole yet does not aim at an "unambiguous and unabashed" "total architecture" or of an all-embracing strike. Rowe and Koetter, who justifiably understand the garden architecture as a criticism of the urban architecture[1], compare, in this context, the concept of Versailles with the model of the Villa Hadriana. Its "relativistically produced 'bits'" are perfect examples of a partially staged, complex design determined by recollections. Kienast also uses the procedures of a further 'knitting together' of the local operation – the overlapping; the collage. It is evident that he follows a pattern which began to evolve in the architectural and urban architectural discussion from around 1965 which, at least theoretically, has asserted itself widely ever since. From this perspective, our garden gains a primary level of actuality and importance.

The stylistic means used by Kienast are based above all on the contrast of organically determined free form and the geometric placements by humans. This not only includes the buildings, but also the plant material which is trimmed, tamed and brought into an artificial geometric form. On a large scale, the close proximity of the house, which leans onto the architecturally defined edge on the west side, is reflected against the generous tree scenery serving the "concealment of the borders" towards the garden of the villa (this is a term used by Peter Joseph Lenné when describing the English landscape gardens[2]). On a small scale, the principle can be read; e.g., in the seams of the cement tiles which are filled with scented herbs: these plants develop following the irregular geometry of the seam network.

primärer Baustoff bleibt sich immer gleich, und auch die mit dem Pflanzenmaterial erzielbaren räumlichen Wirkungen sind längst erprobt – kein Wunder, daß Kienast «architektonischen» Formulierungen seines Gartens viel Aufmerksamkeit widmet.

Es lohnt sich nun, auch die Südseite, die uns zunächst als traditionelle, fast nostalgisch wirkende Oase erschien, auf die erwähnten Merkmale hin zu überprüfen. Hier ist anzumerken, daß Katharina Medici, eine gelehrte und passionierte Gartenliebhaberin, selbst das obere Gartenparterre mit den fünf von Buchshecken eingefaßten Staudenbeeten angelegt hat. Diese bilden also den «point de départ» für die weitere Arbeit. In die Böschung mit verwilderter Bepflanzug, die vor der Gartenumänderung zur Grundstücksgrenze vermittelte, wurden drei Stufen und eine Terrasse eingeschnitten, die mit Splitt belegt und wiederum mit Zementwaren begrenzt sind. Das elegante Wasserbecken auf der untersten Ebene ist ebenfalls mit schmalen Betonelementen eingefaßt. Es bildet von oben her gesehen den Abschluß des Gartens, einen horizontalen Spiegel, der hinführt zur breit gelagerten Perspektive des Zürichsees. Von unten gesehen führt es das Spiel mit Querbezügen weiter, die diesen Garten als Ganzes prägen: es verleiht dem Blick zur seitlichen Baumkulisse hin eine präzise Richtung und macht wiederum aufmerksam auf das Verfahren des Kontrastes, das auch diesem Grundstück zugrunde liegt.

Der Terrassengarten erscheint somit als Verstärkung eines bereits vorhandenen Fragmentes. Die Wahl dieses Typs ist aber auch von der Notwendigkeit her zu erklären, die Vielfalt der südlichen Pflanzen aus der Sammlung der Hausherrin zusammenzufassen und in einen größeren Zusammenhang einzubinden. Die Freude an der Exotik dieser Pflanzen ist zwar Bestandteil der Gartenkultur; deren unbedachte Verteilung im Garten führt aber zum Widerspruch mit dem Postulat, vom Charakter eines Ortes – letztlich von der Landschaftlichkeit – auszugehen und diesen zu verstärken. Durch die Geometrisierung der Terrassen erhält die Pflanzensammlung einen Rahmen und eine präzise Rolle im Plan des Gartens zugewiesen.

Zwei gegensätzliche Gartenstile finden sich also auf engstem Raum: auf den ersten Blick fast zuviel des Guten. Kienast meint aber, daß sich der Besitz eines Ortes nicht über die Grundstücksgröße definiert, sondern über die Intensität der Auseinandersetzung mit diesem Ort.[4] Von daher wird die Vision

For his constructive placements, Kienast likes to use fair-faced concrete or cement-wares. On one hand, the surface quality of this "poor" material does not distract from the pure form (in 1921, Le Corbusier had already propagated the "matérieaux bruts" as a means of creating spatial structures which deeply move the observer[3]). On the other hand, concrete is a building material which belongs to modernism and allows a chronological assignment of the new operations (therefore the framing of the natural stone tiles outside the bathroom). In this respect, the landscape architects are having a difficult time: their primary building material always remains the same and the spatial effects which can be created with the plant material have long ago been tried out – it is no surprise that Kienast devotes a lot of attention to the "architectural" composition of his garden.

It is now worth checking out the south side for the aforementioned characteristics, as it appeared at first to be a traditional and almost nostalgic oasis. At this point, it should be mentioned that Katharina Medici, herself an educated and passionate garden lover, laid out the upper garden parterre with the five shrub beds framed by box. These form the "starting point" for the further work. Three steps and a terrace covered with gravel and framed with cement ware were cut into the wildly overgrown slope which, before the change of the garden, mediated towards the property border. The elegant water basin on the lowest level is also framed with small concrete elements. Seen from above, it forms the enclosure of the garden, a horizontal mirror leading to the broad view of Lake Zurich. Seen from below, it continues the play with cross references which mark this garden as a whole: it provides the view of the lateral tree scenery with a precise direction and again points out the process of contrast which is the basis of this property.

Thus, the terrace garden appears as a reinforcement of an already existing fragment. The choice of this type, however, can also be explained through the necessity of summarizing the variety of southern plants from the lady of the house's collection and integrating it into a larger context. The joy in the exoticness of these plants may be a component of garden culture; however, their thoughtless distribution in the garden leads to a contradiction of the postulate of taking the character of a location – in the end, the landscape – as a starting point, and then to enhance it. By making the terraces geometric, the collection

von Dichte erklärbar, die das Konzept des Gartens ausmacht – Dichte nicht aus formaler, sondern zuerst aus inhaltlicher Begründung heraus. Zur Erzeugung von Vielfalt wird die Methode sowie Kontrastierung auf doppelte Weise eingesetzt: Maximale Geometrisierung im Westen (im Bereich des Hauses) versus maximale Freiheit in den östlichen Bereichen (beim Wäldchen an der Grenze zur Villa hin); asymmetrische Komposition und «Landschaftsgarten» im Norden gegen symmetrischen Aufbau und «geometrischen Terrassengarten» im Süden. Dabei entpuppt sich die Antithese als poetisches Verfahren, als Möglichkeit, nicht nur Vielfalt zu erzeugen, sondern auch dem Umgang mit der Natur ein geistiges Vergnügen abzugewinnen.

Daß man auf derart souveräne Weise mit allen möglichen Ausdrucksformen der Gartenkunst umgehen kann, ist relativ neu. Allzu oft erschienen während der letzten Jahrzehnte geometrische Elemente – etwa das ominöse «Bauerngärtlein» – als bloße nostalgische Versatz- und Dekorationsstücke ohne jede Verankerung und Funktion im räumlichen Konzept des betreffenden Ortes. Der Verlust an diesbezüglichem Wissen ließ sich bis in die Technik der Plandarstellung von Gartenprojekten hinein verfolgen. Es ist das Verdienst von Leuten wie Kienast, an die große Tradition der Gartenkunst wieder anzuknüpfen, ohne die überlieferten Elemente zu Versatzstücken abzuwerten. Geschichte wird nicht als Fundus gesehen, den es zu plündern gilt, deren Elemente man beliebig einsetzen und manipulieren kann. Hingegen erlaubt das exakte Wissen um die grundlegenden Ideen der Gartenkunst erst, Fundstücke überhaupt zu erkennen und Ihnen einen adäquaten Wert zuzuordnen in einer neuen, dichteren, aufregenderen Komposition, durch einen Prozeß, dem allerdings auch Teile des Bestandes geopfert werden müssen. So kann eine Geschichte sinnvoll fortgeschrieben werden, die in der Tat längst begonnen hat. Auf dieser Ebene löst der kleine Garten des Hauses M. das Versprechen von Rowe und Koetter ein, daß aus der Architektur der Gärten Anregungen für die Architektur der Stadt zu gewinnen seien.[5]

Arthur Rüegg

of plants is provided with a framework and precise role in the plan of the garden.

Two opposing garden styles, at first sight and in such a small area, seem to be almost too much. Kienast, however, feels that the richness of a place does not define itself by the size of the property, but by the intensity of preoccupation with this location.[4] Thus, the vision of density which defines the concept of the garden becomes explicable – density not for a formal reason, but, first and foremost, for a contextual reason. In order to create variety, method and contrast are used in two ways: a maximum of geometry in the west (in the vicinity of the house) versus a maximum of freedom in the eastern areas (close to the small forest towards the border of the villa); an asymmetrical composition and "landscape garden" in the north versus the symmetrical design and "geometric terrace garden" in the south. The antithesis turns out to be a poetic procedure; a possibility to not only create variety, but also to provide the handling of nature with a spiritual pleasure.

It is a relatively new thing to handle all possible expressive forms of the art of gardening in such a sovereign way. During the past few decades, geometric elements have appeared much too often – such as the ominous "small farmer's garden" – merely as nostalgic theatrical sets and decorative pieces without any roots or function in the spatial concept of the appropriate location. The loss of this kind of knowledge could be followed up to the technique of representing plans for garden projects. It is the accomplishment of people like Kienast to reconnect to the big tradition of the art of gardening without degrading the inherited elements into these theatrical sets. History is not viewed as an exploitable warehouse whose elements can be used and manipulated at will. Instead, the exact knowledge of the basic ideas in the art of gardening allows for the recognition of found objects and providing them with an adequate value in a new, denser and more exciting composition through a process that asks, however, for sacrifices in the existing population. Thus, a story which had begun long ago indeed can be continued sensibly. On this level, the small garden of the M. house fulfills the promise by Rowe and Koetter to gain ideas from garden architecture for urban architecture.[5]

Arthur Rüegg

---

1 Colin Rowe, Fred Koetter, Collage City, dt. Ausgabe Basel 1984, 5 1997
2 Vgl. Gerhard Heinz, Peter Joseph Lenné, Göttingen 1977, S. 21
3 In «L'Esprit Nouveau». Vgl. Le Corbusier, Vers une architecture, Paris 1923
4 Dieter Kienast, Die Sehnsucht nach dem Paradies, in: Hochparterre 7/1990
5 Vgl. Kienasts siegreiches Wettbewerbsprojekt für die Gestaltung von Waisenhausplatz und Bärenplatz in Bern, 1990.

1 Colin Rowe, Fred Koetter, Collage City, Cambridge Mass. and London 1978
2 See also Gerhard Heinz, Peter Joseph Lenné, Göttingen 1977, p. 21
3 In "L'Esprit Nouveau". See Le Corbusier, Vers une architecture, Paris 1923
4 Dieter Kienast, Die Sehnsucht nach dem Paradies, in: Hochparterre 7/1990
5 See Kienast's successful competition project for the design of Waisenhausplatz and Bärenplatz in Bern, 1990

Das rechteckige Rasenstück vor dem neuen Haupteingang erhielt bergseits einen Abschluß in Form einer doppelten Eibenhecke und eine Längenbetonung mit zwei Kugeleiben ...

The rectangular piece of lawn in front of the new main entrance was closed off towards the hill with a yew hedge and longitudinally enhanced with two sphere-shaped yews ...

... das Spiel mit Querbezügen weiter, die diesen Garten als Ganzes prägen: es verleiht dem Blick zur seitlichen Baumkulisse hin eine präzise Richtung und macht wiederum aufmerksam auf das Verfahren des Kontrastes ...

... the play with cross references which mark this garden as a whole: it provides the view of the lateral tree scenery with a precise direction and again points out the process of contrast ...

... unmittelbar vor der Fassade eine Querzone, in der Form
eines plattenbelegten Hartplatzes überlagert, die dem bestehenden
Gartenstück eine völlig neue Dimension hinzufügt ...

Immediately in front of the facade, this longitudinal development
was overlapped by a transverse-zone in the form of a tile-covered court,
adding a completely new dimension to the existing piece of garden ...

Exotische Pflanzen in tönernen Töpfen verschiedenster Art
sind vor dem dunkelgrünen Hintergrund der Buchskaskade arrangiert
wie die Vasen vor den Brunnenterrassen der Villa d'Este in Tivoli.

Exotic plants in an assortment of clay pots are arranged in front
of the dark green background of the cascade of box like the vases in front of
the fountain terraces of Villa d'Este in Tivoli.

Wo ist Arkadien?

Gärten zu bauen heißt Geschichten erleben. Geschichten mögen ein Ende haben, während Gärten nie fertig werden. So haben auch unsere Gartengeschichten – die guten wenigstens – kein Ende, sondern es werden ihnen neue Kapitel hinzugefügt. Diese Geschichte beginnt 1989. Das Ehepaar E. besitzt am Üetliberg ein riesiges Grundstück. Darauf steht ein einfaches Haus aus den Fünfzigerjahren mit einem belanglosen Garten, der nur einen kleinen Teil des Grundstückes beansprucht. Ein zweiter Teil wird als Weide genutzt, ein dritter Teil besteht aus einem 50 Meter steil abfallenden, alten Buchenwald. Die Aussicht ist gegen Westen beeindruckend weit über sanft gewellte Hügel bis zu den Alpen.

Die Kinder von Frau und Herrn E. sind längst «ausgeflogen», ihr Geschäft haben sie verkauft. Den Garten pflegen sie mit Umsicht, sind aber etwas unzufrieden, weil die angepflanzten Sträucher die Aussicht versperren. Sie geben uns den Auftrag, ihren Garten neu zu planen. Auch nach längerem Gespräch wird lediglich der Wunsch nach einem Stauden- und Kräuterbeet deutlich. Ansonsten wünschen sie sich einen schöneren Garten. Wir bleiben im Ungewissen, wieviel Umgestaltung aus ihrer Sicht möglich und notwendig ist.

Der Befund vor Ort führt uns zu folgenden Schlüssen: Der enge, sichtverhindernde Strauchgürtel muß entfernt, die steile Böschung abgeflacht und die markante Baumkulisse ins Blickfeld gerückt werden. Sie bildet zugleich die natürliche Grenze des kultivierten Gartens gegen Süden. An der Westgrenze steht eine hundert Meter lange Weißdornhecke, die allzu hoch aufgewachsen ist und dadurch die Aussicht vom Gebäude in die Hügel- und Alpenlandschaft versperrt, während sie von der unteren Gartenebene als Raumgrenze hohe Qualität aufweist. Eine schöne Obstbaumwiese steigt sanft zum Üetliberg an, ist allerdings von Haus und Garten isoliert. Der Waldrand markiert zugleich die obere Hangkante und würde einen beeindruckenden Blick in das 50 Meter tiefer liegende Bachtobel (das ebenfalls noch zum Grundstück gehört) bieten, wenn nicht dichtes Brombeergebüsch die Einsicht verhindern würde.

Where is Arcadia?

Designing gardens means experiencing stories. Stories may have an end while gardens are never completed. In this sense, our garden stories – at least the good ones – don't have an end, but new chapters are always being added to them. This story begins in 1989. The elderly couple E. owns a huge property at Uetliberg. On it stands a simple house dating back to the fifties with an unimportant garden which takes up only a small part of the property. A second part is used as a pasture and a third consists of an old beech forest sloping steeply down about 50 meters. The view towards the west is impressively broad and reaches from soft foothills up to the Alps.

The children of Mrs. and Mr. E. have long 'left the nest' and they have sold their business. They carefully tend their garden, but they are somewhat unhappy because the planted shrubs block the view. They have asked us to redesign their garden. Even after a longer conversation, only the wish for a shrub and herb bed becomes clear. Otherwise, they wish only for a more beautiful garden. We are left with the uncertainty about how much of a redesign is possible and necessary in their view.

The on-site diagnosis leads us to the following conclusions: the narrow view-blocking belt of shrubbery must be re-

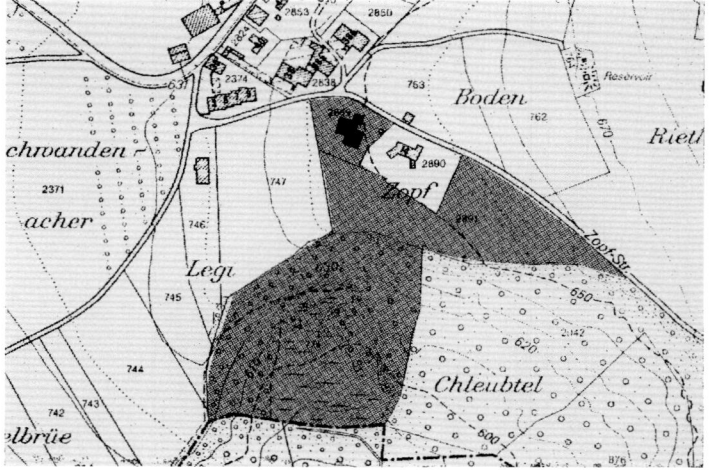

Unser erstes Projekt von 1989 konzentriert die Interventionen zwischen Gebäude und Waldrand. Die Topographie wird, dem früheren Gelände entsprechend, sanft abfallend planiert. Das Gebäude steht virtuell auf einem Betonplattenbelag mit weit gezogenen Fugen, in denen Mentha und Thymian eingesät werden. Die flankierende Eibenhecke bietet Windschutz und Rahmen für die vorgelagerte Staudenrabatte. Vom Sitzplatz und Gebäude aus wird der Blick durch Hecke und Eibenkegel auf den Waldrand und einen Teil des schmalen Wasserbeckens gelenkt. Die Buchstreppen hinuntergehend, wird das ganze Becken in seiner sich scheinbar verändernden Form sichtbar. Die Weißdornhecke ist neu beschnitten, unter den überhängenden Zweigen entdecken wir einen Treillagengang. Am Wasser sitzend, wird der Blick auf den vorher verborgenen Gartenteil der Obstbaumwiese frei. Der Waldrand und damit auch die Hangkante werden durch eine geschnittene Feldahornhecke präzisiert. Eine natürlich vorhandene Kanzel wird zum Aussichtspunkt gestaltet. Der Blick fällt hinunter, auf die im Hang entspringende Quelle, den Bach und das tief unten liegende Waldplateau oder auf die darüber ansetzende Lichtung zum Üetliberg. Der Aussichtspunkt wird zum bedeutungsvollsten Ort des Gartens, zu einem altbekannten Topos: dem inszenierten Aufeinanderprallen der lieblich gezähmten Natur des Gartens mit der wilden Natur des steil abfallenden Waldhanges. Ein Geländer, als Schriftzug ausgebildet, schützt vor dem Hinunterfallen und wird selber zum Gartenblickpunkt.

Schriften im Garten sind in der Gartengeschichte altbekannt. Erinnert sei an Orsinis «Heiligen Wald von Bomarzo», an die Inschriften in Englischen Landschaftsgärten wie Stowe, Wörlitz oder Ermenonville. In den letzten Jahren beobachten wir eine Wiederentdeckung der Schriften, selbstverständlich in der Werbung, aber auch in der Architektur und vor allem in der Kunst. Aus der bildenden Kunst nennen wir stellvertretend die Arbeiten von Jenny Holzer und Fischli/Weiss. Ian Hamilton Finlay hat den Brückenschlag zwischen Literatur und Gartenkunst erneut vollzogen und in vielen Gärten aufsehenerregende Arbeiten geschaffen. Die Gemeinsamkeit aller Schriftinstallationen ist der wechselnde Bedeutungsgehalt ihrer Rezeption.

Auch uns hat die ambivalente Lesart des Schriftzuges interessiert. «Differentia» war unser erster Vorschlag, womit wir auf die unterschiedlichen Naturformen von Garten und Wild-

moved, the steep slop needs to be flattened out and the striking tree scenery must be put into the center of perception. It also forms the natural border of the cultivated garden towards the south. On the western border, a one hundred meter long hawthorn hedge which has grown too high blocks the view from the building towards the landscape of the foothills and Alps; however, seen from the lower garden level, it has a high quality as a spatial border. A beautiful orchard softly raises up towards Uetliberg but is isolated from the house and the garden. The edge of the forest also marks the upper edge of the slope and would offer an impressive view into the ravine 50 meters lower down (which also belongs to the property), if it were not prevented by dense blackberry shrubs.

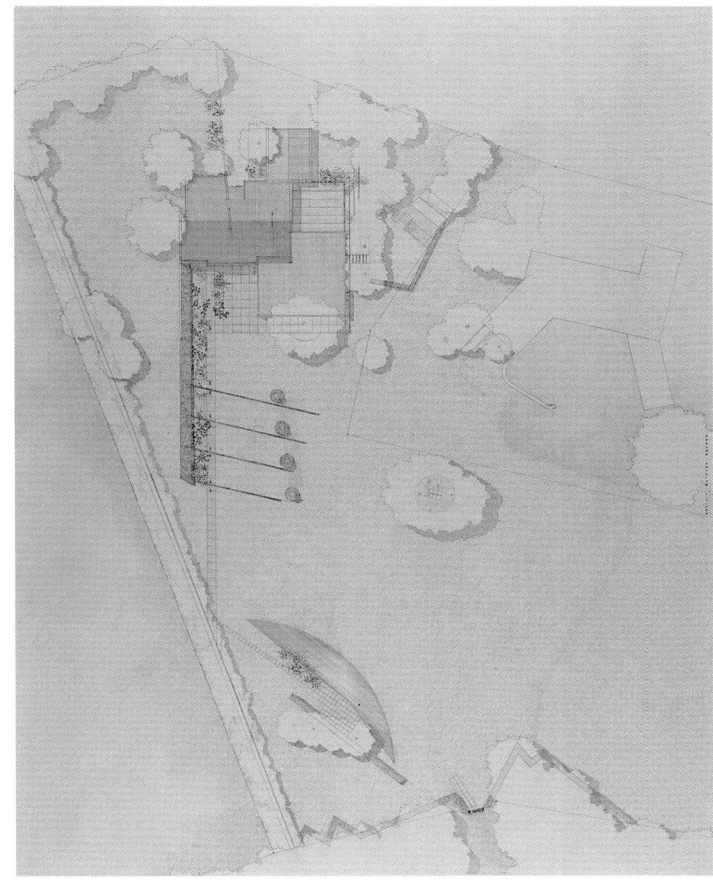

Projektplan 1. Phase 1989
Grundriß
Original 1:100, 87 x 118 cm;
Bleistift und Farbstift
auf grauem Halbkarton

Project plan 1st phase 1989
Ground plan
Original 1:100, 87 x 118 cm;
pencil and colored pencil
on gray semi-cardboard

nis, den versteckten Höhensprung oder den Wechsel von der früheren zur neuen Gartengestaltung gezielt haben.

Zu unserer Überraschung fand unser Projekt ungeteilte Zustimmung, mit der einzigen Ausnahme: die Wahl des «Brüstungswortes». Der Garten wurde gebaut und von den Besitzern nicht nur liebevoll in Pflege genommen. Vielmehr ist der Garten zu ihrer sinnstiftenden Lebensarbeit geworden. Auf unzähligen Gartenrundgängen haben wir über mögliche und notwendige Pflege- und Gestaltungsarbeiten gesprochen. Literatur wurde gewälzt, auf vielen Exkursionen im In- und Ausland neue Eindrücke gesammelt, Pflanzen mitgebracht und eingepflanzt. Und immer wieder neue Schriftzüge wurden erwogen, bis unser letzter Vorschlag «Et in Arcadia ego» ihre ungeteilte Zustimmung fand.

Arkadien, von Vergil erstmals beschrieben, ist weniger die reale Landschaft in Griechenland, sondern geistige Landschaft, die Metapher der glückseligen, naturverbundenen Hirtenidylle. Bekannt geworden ist die Inschrift erstmals auf einem Bild Guercinos (ca. 1621/23): zwei Hirten bei der Betrachtung einer Grabstätte mit einer Inschrift und einem großen Totenschädel. «Et in Arcadia ego» heißt nach Panofsky richtig übersetzt: «Auch ich bin da, ich existiere, sogar in Arkadien.» Gemeint ist der Tod, der auch im glücklichen Land Arkadien gegenwärtig ist. Populär geworden ist das Motiv

Nicolas Poussin
«Et in Arcadia ego»
(ca. 1638/39, 2. Fassung)
Musée du Louvre, Paris

Nicolas Poussin
"Et in Arcadia ego"
(approx. 1638/39, 2nd version),
Musée du Louvre, Paris

Our first project in 1989 concentrated the interventions between the building and the edge of the forest. The topography is planed down to be softly sloping, according to the former grounds. The building is situated on a concrete tile surface with wide seams in which mint and thyme are sowed. The adjoining yew hedge provides protection from the wind and the frame for the narrow shrub bed in the front. The vista from the sitting area and the building is guided through the hedge and the yew cone towards the edge of the forest and a part of the narrow water basin. When descending the box steps, the entire basin with its seemingly changing form becomes visible. The hawthorn hedge is trimmed back and beneath the overhanging branches we discover a covered walk. Sitting by the water, the view of the once hidden part of the garden with the orchard is now free. The edge of the forest, and thus the slope, is made more precise by a trimmed field maple hedge. A naturally existing pulpit is designed as a lookout point. The view descends to the spring with its source in the slope, to the brook and the forest plateau far below, or to the clearing towards Uetliberg starting above. The lookout becomes the most important place in the garden, a well-known topos: the produced collision of the rather tamed nature of the garden with the wild nature of the steeply sloping forest hill. A balustrade in the form of an inscription provides protection from falling off and becomes a center of interest in itself.

Inscriptions in the gardens have been well-known throughout their history. We recall Orsini's 'Holy Forest of Bomarzo' and the inscriptions in English landscape gardens such as Stowe, Wörlitz or Ermenonville. In recent years, we have observed a rediscovery of the script – certainly in advertising, but also in architecture and, above all, in art. For the latter, we name representatively the works by Jenny Holzer and Fischli/Weiss. Ian Hamilton Finlay has again built the bridge between literature and the art of gardening and has created works in many gardens which gain a lot of notoriety. What all script installations have in common is the changing meaning of their content in their reception.

We too were interested in the ambivalent way of reading the inscription. "Differentia" was our first proposal and with it we took aim at the different natural forms of garden and wilderness, the hidden change in altitude or the change from

the former to the new garden design. To our surprise, our project was met with undivided consent with only one exception: the choice of the 'balustrade word'. The garden was converted and taken over by the proprietors not only for care-taking, but also and perhaps more importantly, the garden has brought sense and meaning to their existence and has become their life's work.

On numerous garden tours we have discussed possible and necessary care and design work. We've pored over the literature and, on our many excursions both at home and abroad, have collected new impressions and brought back many plants and planted them. And ever new inscriptions were thought of, until finally our last proposal "Et in Arcadia ego" found the proprietor's complete approval.

Arcadia, once described by Virgil, is not so much the real landscape of Greece, but the spiritual landscape, the metaphor of the blissful shepherd's ideal close to nature. The inscription first became famous from a painting by Guercino (ca. 1621/23). It depicts two shepherds looking at a grave with an inscription and a large skull. According to Panofsky, "Et in Arcadia ego" means : 'I too am there, I exist, even in Arcadia'. What is meant is death, which is also present in the happy land of Arcadia. The motif has become popular only by two paintings by Poussin which he painted in ca. 1630 and ca. 1639. Lévi-Strauss shows in his sharp analysis how the relation with death gets lost in Poussin's paintings and the skull is missing in the second painting (see picture). In the 18th century, the inscription was finally completely detached from the grave scene and received a new meaning with various authors, such as Herder, Schiller and Goethe: 'I too have enjoyed bliss', or 'I too have lived in the blissful peaceful shepherd's land of Arcadia'.

In our garden at Uetliberg, the balustrade inscription becomes the strongest narrative element, allowing for a multitude of associations and interpretations: from the landscape painters, to the poets dealing with gardens, to the life story of the proprietors.

"Et in Arcadia ego" becomes the starting point and impetus for the second construction phase in 1994 during which the dramatic forest slope is 'discovered' – not by us, but first by Mr. E., who laid out a dangerously steep pathway, steps, and a bridge. Unconsciously, a classical pattern of behavior is

durch zwei Bilder Poussins (ca. 1630 und 1639 gemalt). Lévi-Strauss zeigt in seiner scharfsinnigen Analyse, wie die Verbindung zum Tod bei Poussin abnimmt und der Totenschädel im zweiten Bild fehlt (vgl. Abbildung). Im 18. Jahrhundert erfährt der Schriftzug seine endgültige Loslösung von der Grabstätte und erhält jetzt bei Autoren wie Herder, Schiller und Goethe eine geänderte Bedeutung: «Auch ich habe das Glück genossen» oder «Auch ich habe im glücklichen, friedfertigen Hirtenland Arkadien gelebt.»

In unserem Garten am Üetliberg wird der Brüstungsschriftzug zum stärksten, narrativen Element, das eine Viel-

Projektplan, Gesamtplan
2. Phase 1994
Original 1:200, 70 x 100 cm;
Tusche, Farbstift
auf Plandruck weiß

Project plan, entire plan
2nd phase 1994
Original 1:200, 70 x 100 cm;
ink, colored pencil
on white plan print

zahl an Assoziationen, Interpretationen und Deutungen zuläßt: Von der Landschaftsmalerei, den Dichtern, die sich mit Gärten befaßt haben, bis hin zur Lebensgeschichte des Besitzerpaares.

«Et in Arcadia ego» wird zum Ausgangspunkt und Generator der zweiten Bauetappe von 1994, in der der dramatische Waldhang ‹entdeckt› wird – nicht von uns, sondern zunächst von Herrn E., der einen gefährlich steilen Weg, Treppen und eine Brücke anlegt. Auch hier wird unbewußt einem klassischen Verhaltensmuster gefolgt: Nachdem der Garten ausreichend kultiviert worden ist, erfolgen die Ein- und Übergriffe in die Wildnis. Unsere geplanten Interventionen zielen nicht auf eine Gartenerweiterung, sondern beschränken sich auf wenige Eingriffe, mittels derer die wilde Natur besser erlebt werden kann. Wichtigstes Element ist ein intensiv blau eingefärbter Handlauf, der wegbegleitend ein einigermaßen sicheres Hinuntersteigen erlaubt. Zwei kleine Sitzplätze an markanten Orten und einige wenige, auf die vorhandene Waldvegetation abgestimmte Pflanzungen weisen auf die sanfte Inanspruchnahme der wilden Natur.

Wir sitzen auf der Waldbank und erinnern uns – Arkadien ist an einem anderen Ort.

Dieter Kienast

followed here, as well: after the garden has been sufficiently cultivated, the operations and infringements of the wilderness begin. Our planned interventions do not aim at an extension of the garden, but are limited to only a few operations through which the wild nature can be better experienced. The most important element is an intensively blue balustrade which accompanies a somewhat safer descent. Two small sitting areas in important places and a few plantings in harmony with the existing forest vegetation point to the gentle use of the wild nature.

We are sitting on the bench in the forest and remember – Arcadia is in a different place.

Dieter Kienast

Der Aussichtspunkt wird zum bedeutungsvollsten Ort des Gartens, zu einem altbekannten Topos: dem inszenierten Aufeinanderprallen der lieblich gezähmten Natur des Gartens mit der wilden Natur des steil abfallenden Waldhanges.

The lookout becomes the most important place in the garden, a well-known topos: the produced collision of the rather tamed nature of the garden with the wild nature of the steeply sloping forest hill.

40

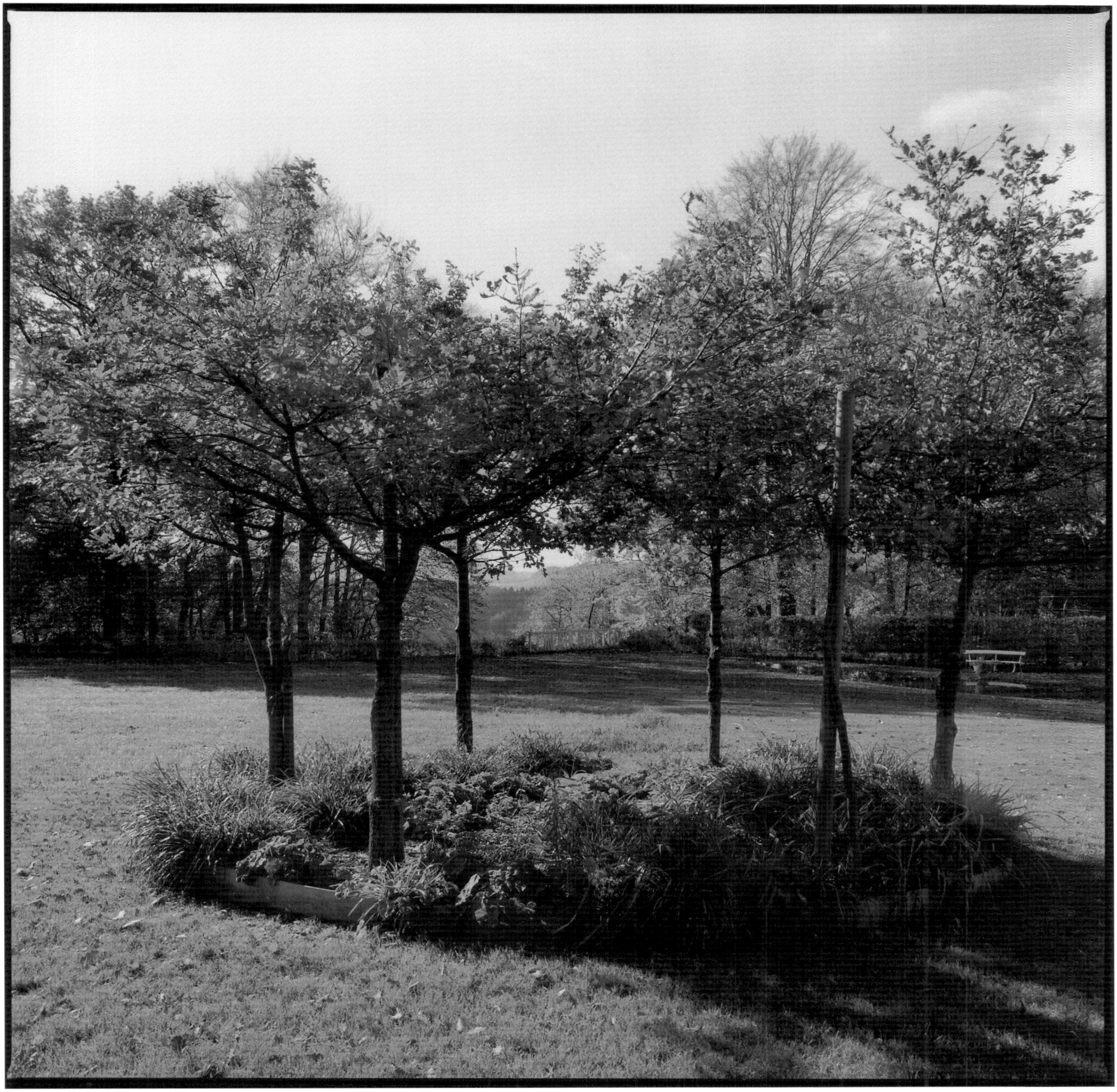

In unserem Garten am Üetliberg wird der Brüstungsschriftzug zum stärksten,
narrativen Element, das eine Vielzahl an Assoziationen, Interpretationen und
Deutungen zuläßt: Von der Landschaftsmalerei, den Dichtern ...

In our garden at Uetliberg, the balustrade inscription becomes the strongest narrative element, allowing for a multitude of associations and interpretations: from the landscape painters, to the poets ...

… wenige Eingriffe, mittels derer die wilde Natur besser erlebt werden kann.
Wichtigstes Element ist ein intensiv blau eingefärbter Handlauf, der wegbegleitend
ein einigermaßen sicheres Hinuntersteigen erlaubt.

... few operations through which the wild nature can be better experienced. The most important element is an intensively blue balustrade which accompanies a somewhat safer descent.

Grenzen und Zäune

Die Englischen Landschaftsgärtner des 18. Jahrhunderts haben mit der Erfindung des Aha's die sichtbaren Grenzen zwischen dem bewußt gestalteten Garten und der bäuerlich bewirtschafteten Landschaft versteckt, aber nicht aufgehoben. Das Bild der arkadischen Hirtenidylle wird im Landschaftsgarten inszeniert, wo es aus der Gebrauchsfähigkeit entlassen ist. Eine feinsinnige Art, Reichtum und Überfluß darzustellen, indem das ärmlich karge Hirtenleben als gebaute Metapher eines glücklich einfachen Daseins in Harmonie mit der Natur vorgezeigt wird. Und nur im Gebrauchsverzicht des Gartens kann die überhöht schöne Hirtenlandschaft Wirklichkeit werden. Zusammen mit dem Einbezug des angrenzenden Landwirtschaftslandes erhält der Garten eine bisher unbekannte inhaltliche und geographische Dimension, die die auf den ersten Blick zur Schau getragene Bescheidenheit der Landedelleute im Zwielicht erscheinen läßt. Mit Hilfe des Aha's wird Landschaft staffagenartig einbezogen. Sie bleibt sowohl als Bild wie als genutzte Landschaft Kulisse auf der Bühne des feinen Lebens im Garten selber. Und nur sie ist letztendlich von Bedeutung.

Obwohl unser Garten am ehemaligen Bauernhaus ebenfalls die Gunst einer weiträumigen bäuerlichen Umgebung zukommt, zeigt er mit den streng gefaßten Aussichtsfenstern eine – zum Englischen Landschaftsgarten – differente Gartenauf-

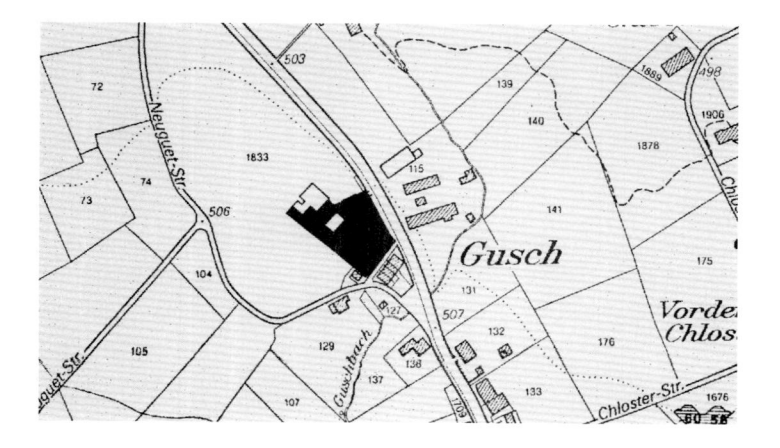

Borders and Fences

The English landscape gardeners of the 18th century, with the invention of the 'ha-ha', have hidden the visible borders between the consciously designed garden and the agriculturally used land. However, they did not entirely do away with them. The picture of the Arcadian ideal of the shepherd is 'staged' in the landscape garden where it is removed from usability. A subtle way to show wealth and surplus is to make the scarce shepherd's life a constructed metaphor of a happy and simple life in harmony with nature. And only by renouncing the usability of the garden can the exaggerated beautiful shepherd's landscape become a reality. Together with the adjoining agricultural land, the garden obtains a dimension, so far unknown in its contents and geography, which puts the modesty of the country noblemen – at first glance pretentious – into a twilight. With the help of the 'ha-ha', the landscape is included in a way of mere display. It remains, as a picture and as a used landscape, a prop on the stage of the noble life in the garden itself. And finally, only this is of any meaning.

Although our garden at the former farm house also has the advantage of a former wide agricultural surrounding, it shows – with its strictly framed vista windows – a garden approach different from that of the English landscape garden: with bushes, columns, and fence, the border is accentuated. The view of the adjoining orchard is framed by the striking columns and, thus, the difference between the unimportant vista into the landscape and the meaningfully produced outlook is created. Incidentally, the difference between the English and the Swiss landscapes becomes manifest. Whereas it is still widely spread and, therefore, quite ordinary in England, it has become rare in the agglomerate of a big city and is therefore precious because of the archaic style. Between the inside 'farmer's garden' and the outside orchard, the material and formal design of the border points to the new interpretation of the location, which searches for less harmony and more contrast with the agricultural rustic world: concrete columns painted gray with chrome steel wires for the different types of climbing clematis, and between them an industrially produced metal fence above a con-

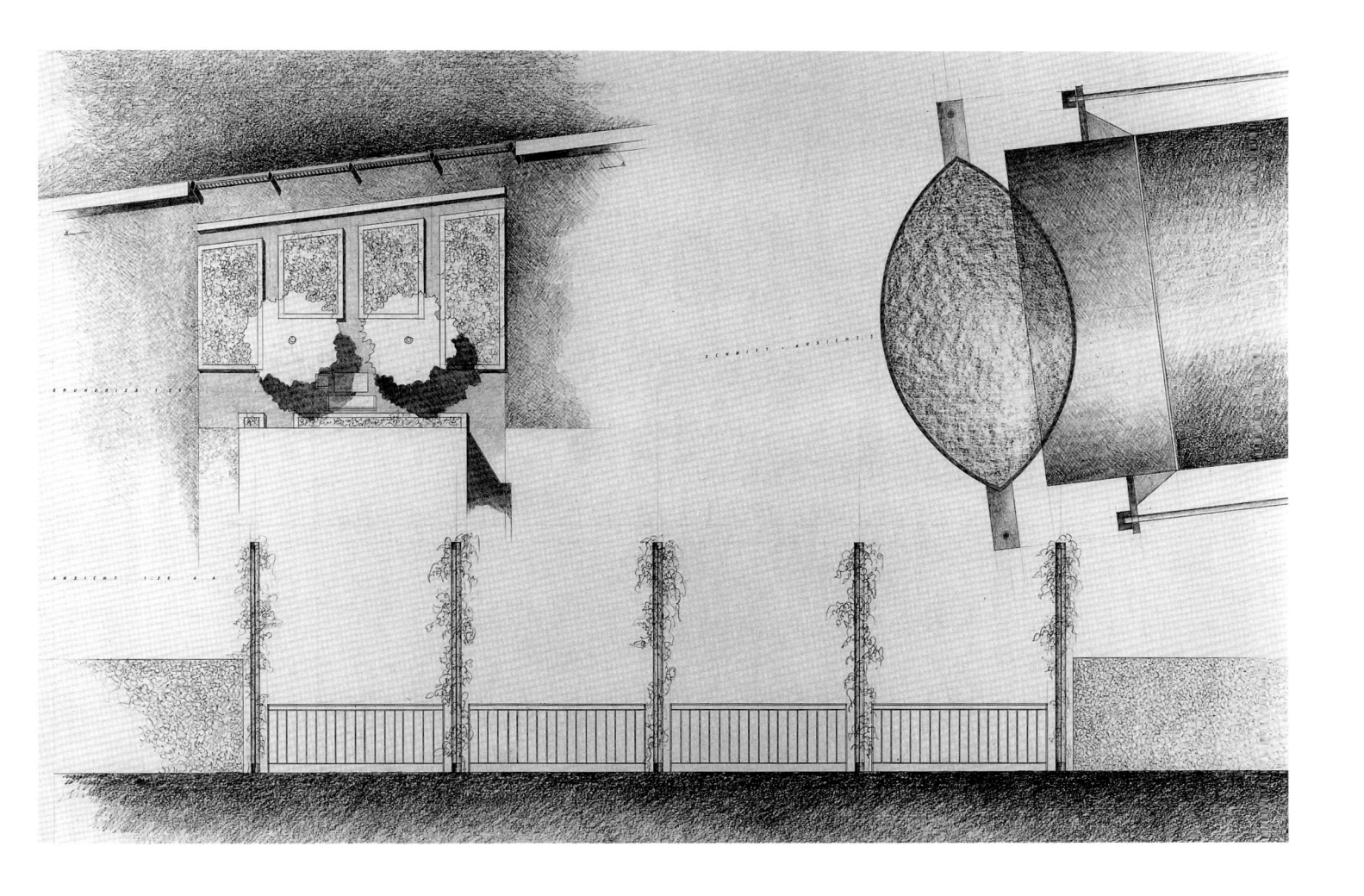

Projektplan 1994
Grundriß, Schnitte
Original 1:50/1:20/1:1, 70 x 100 cm;
Tusche, Farbstift, Ölkreide
auf Plandruck

Project plan 1994
Ground plan, sections
Original 1:50/1:20/1:1, 70 x 100 cm;
ink, colored pencil, oil crayon
on plan print

fassung: Mit Hecke, Säulen und Geländer wird die Grenze akzentuiert. Der Blick auf die angrenzende Obstbaumwiese wird mit den markanten Säulen gerahmt und damit die Differenz vom beiläufigen Blick in die Landschaft zur bedeutungsvoll inszenierten Aussicht festgeschrieben. Nebenbei wird damit auch die Differenz zwischen der englischen und schweizerischen Bauernlandschaft manifest. Während in England immer noch weitverbreitet und damit gewöhnlich, ist sie in der Agglomeration der Großstadt selten und gerade in der archaischen Ausprägung kostbar geworden. Zwischen dem inliegenden ‹Bauerngarten› und der außenliegenden Obstwiese verweist die materielle und formale Ausbildung der Grenze auf die neue Interpretation des Ortes, die weniger Harmonie als vielmehr Kontrast zur bäuerlich rustikalen Welt sucht: Grau eingefärbte Betonsäulen mit Chromstahldrähten für die Berankung mit unterschiedlichen Clematisarten und dazwischen ein industriell gefertigter Metallzaun über einer Betonplatte, als Schwelle und Begrenzung des Wieslandes zum sorgfältig gepflegten Gartenrasen.

Den gesamten Garten hat die Besitzerin im Verlauf von zwanzig Jahren Stück für Stück neu gebaut, umgestaltet und bepflanzt. Deutlich erkennbar sind die englischen Vorbilder des Edwardianischen Gartens mit der klaren, architektonischen Grundstruktur und den großflächigen, sorgfältig abgestimmten Staudenpflanzungen. Auf gemeinsamen Spaziergängen durch den Garten wurden Vorzüge und Probleme einzelner Bereiche diskutiert, nach Lösungen gesucht und anschließend umgesetzt. Im Verlaufe der Zeit hat sich Nicole Newmark von der begeisterten Hobbygärtnerin zur passionierten Gartenarchitektin entwickelt und sich ein eigenes Gartenreich geschaffen, dessen Pflanzungen den Vergleich mit ihren englischen Vorbildern nicht zu scheuen brauchen. Und so verspüren wir an diesem Ort etwas gleichermaßen Vertrautes und doch so wenig Selbstverständliches – Gartenkultur.

Dieter Kienast

crete platform, as a threshold and limitation from the meadow to the carefully tended garden lawn.

The owner has rebuilt, converted and planted the entire garden in the course of twenty years. The examples of the Edwardian garden with the clear architectural basic structure and the spacious, carefully chosen bushes are clearly visible. During our common walks through the garden we discussed the advantages and problems of various areas, looked for solutions and later on realized them. Within due time, Nicole Newmark has turned from an enthusiastic hobby gardener into a passionate garden architect and has created her own personal garden kingdom whose plantings do not have to shy away from a comparison with their English idols. Thus, we feel something familiar and yet not so self-understood in this place: garden culture.

Dieter Kienast

Grau eingefärbte Betonsäulen mit Chromstahldrähten für die Berankung mit unterschiedlichen Clematisarten und dazwischen ein industriell gefertigter Metallzaun über einer Betonplatte, als Schwelle und Begrenzung des Wieslandes zum sorgfältig gepflegten Gartenrasen.

Concrete columns painted gray with chrome steel wires for the different types of climbing clematis, and between them an industrially produced metal fence above a concrete platform, as a threshold and limitation from the meadow to the carefully tended garden lawn.

Der Blick auf die angrenzende Obstbaumwiese wird mit den markanten
Säulen gerahmt und damit die Differenz vom beiläufigen Blick
in die Landschaft zur bedeutungsvoll inszenierten Aussicht festgeschrieben.

The view of the adjoining orchard is framed by the striking columns and, thus, the difference between the unimportant vista into the landscape and the meaningfully produced outlook is created.

Lob der Zweideutigkeit

Unsichere Zeiten sind angebrochen. Es ist nicht mehr wie früher, sagen uns die alten Leute. Und auch wir spüren, daß scheinbar Unabänderliches, Festgefügtes, Eindeutiges aus den Fugen gerät: die politischen Machtverhältnisse, Religion, Gesellschaft, Familie, Kunst und Natur. Zweierlei Reaktionen sind möglich: das Herbeisehnen des Alten oder die Auseinandersetzung mit der rezenten Unsicherheit. Wir mißtrauen dem restaurativen Gedankengut und fassen das Zeitgeschehen auch in der beruflichen Arbeit als große Chance einer spannenden Entwicklung auf. Wir kultivieren die Freiheit der ambivalenten Wahrnehmung und Interpretation und sind gleichzeitig gegen die Beliebigkeit der Gestalt. Hier streben wir eindeutig Radikalität im Konzept und dessen Umsetzung an.

Der prototypische Garten als umgrenzter Ort definiert sich weniger über die gebaute Grenze als vielmehr durch seine Differenz zwischen Innen und Außen. War früher das Außen mit der Wildnis gleichgesetzt, so treffen wir heute nebenan einen ähnlichen Garten. Unser Grundstück zeigt noch die Nachbarschaft zur Wildnis, mehr noch, das Grundstück ist durch zehnjähriges Brachliegen selbst zur Wildnis geworden. Die vorgefundene Vegetation erzählt uns ihre Geschichte vom periodischen Wechsel zwischen intensivem Gebrauch und Wildwuchs: nitrophile Säume, Kahlschlagfluren, 10 Meter hoher Jungwald und dahinter der 100jährige Wald. Im Jungwald fanden wir verwilderte Gartenstauden, alte Rosenstöcke, Obstgehölz und Beerensträucher.

Die angedeutete Geschichte der Vegetation zeigt Kohärenz zur Kulturgeschichte des Ortes. Wir befinden uns an einem martialischen Ort, in unmittelbarer Nachbarschaft zur größten Festungsanlage Europas, am Rand der tieferliegenden Stadt und des Glacis, der sich zur hochliegenden Burg erstreckt. Das ehemals freie Schußfeld ist zum Wald herangewachsen, das 1877 erbaute Gebäude gehörte dem Wallmeister, der für den Glacisunterhalt zuständig war. Karljosef Schattner und Wilhelm Huber haben den Um- und Neubau für die kulturell engagierten Besitzer geplant. Der erste Gang durch den dornröschenhaften Garten zeigt alle Reize und Unzulänglichkeiten: Natur ist nicht

In Praise of Ambiguity

Uncertain times have begun. Older people tell us that things are no longer as they used to be. And we too can feel that something seemingly unchangeable, fixed and unequivocal is getting out of kilter: the political power structures, religion, society, family, art and nature. Two reactions are possible: the longing for the old or the confrontation of the recent insecurity. We mistrust the restorative ideas and consider the current events a big chance for an exciting development in our professional life, as well. We cultivate the freedom of ambivalent perception and interpretation and at the same time oppose the arbitrary design. Here, we clearly strive for radicalism in the concept and its realization.

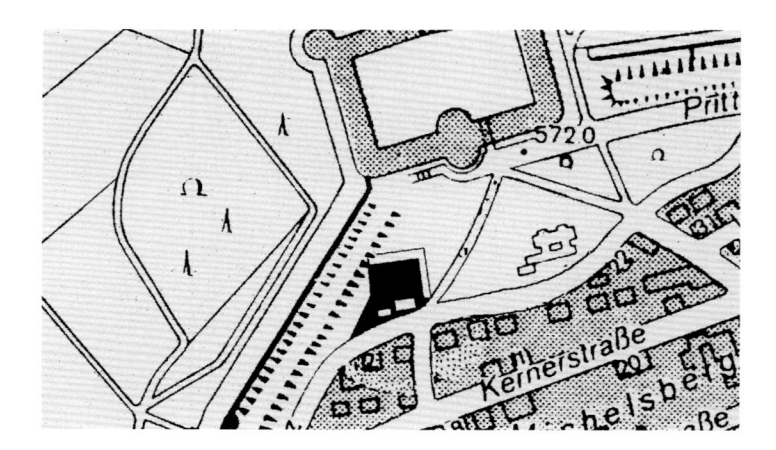

The prototypical garden as a fenced-in place defines itself less through the constructed border than through the difference between inside and outside. Whereas in former times the outside was equal to wilderness, today we meet a similar garden right next door. Our property still shows signs of the neighboring wilderness, and, moreover, the property itself has turned into a wilderness after having lain fallow for ten years. The existing vegetation tells us the entire story about the periodic change between intensive use and wild growth: nitrophilous seams, cleared open fields, the 10 meter high trees of the young forest and then behind it the century-old forest. In the young

nur schön, romantisch, vielfältig, sie kann auch banal, indifferent und unattraktiv sein. Der Blick auf die Stadt mit dem Kirchturm und zu den Alpen ist völlig zugewachsen, der Steilhang kaum begehbar.

Ziel und Thematik des Entwurfes ist die präzise Formulierung der drei differenten Erscheinungsformen von Natur, die in Korrespondenz oder Opposition zum Gebauten stehen. Auf der untersten Ebene prägt die gärtnerisch gestaltete Natur das Aussehen der gebäudenahen Gartenteile. Im Steilhang wechseln ruderalisierte und gepflegte Vegetation, während der alte Wald Grenze und Rahmen des inneren Gartens bildet und gleichzeitig den Übergang zur größtmöglichen Naturnähe des äußeren Gartens akzentuiert.

Entlang der Straße bildet die präzis geschnittene Eibenhecke auf der Mauer die Grenze zum Vorgarten und Gartenhof, den Einblick verhindernd und trotzdem Ausblick freilassend. Die Magnolienreihe leitet zum Hauseingang. Die Treppe hochgehend, verwehrt zunächst die Mauer den Einblick in den privaten Hofgarten, der erst nach dem Eintritt ins Treppenhaus überraschend inszeniert wird. In der fein planierten grünen Sandfläche ‹schwimmen› 14, in freien Formen geschnittene Pflanzenfiguren in unterschiedlichen Grüntönen. Beim Nähertreten erkennen wir Buxus, Ilex, Chaenomeles und Azaleen. Die ruhige Formenvariation kontrastiert mit der präzisen Sandebene und den Umgrenzungshecken. In dieser Reduktion wird die Nähe zu japanischen Zen-Gärten deutlich. Ein schmales Wasserbecken markiert die Trennung zwischen den Hausteilen und führt uns gleichzeitig auf die Hinterseite des Hauses, das hier auf einem grünen Andeersplitt-Teppich steht und Distanz zum Steilhang schafft.

Im Steilhang reihen sich Schichten unterschiedlichster Vegetationsbestände, mehrjähriger Ruderal- und Gehölzbestand wechselt mit Strauchreihen, die jeweils nur aus einer Pflanzenart gebildet werden. Diese heben sich in Form, Blüte und Duft deutlich von der Wildvegetation ab: Parkrosen, Flieder, Amerikanischer Blumenhartriegel, großblumiger Schneeball, Strauchpeonie, Schlehe oder Buchs ziehen sich über die ganze Hangbreite, ohne Rücksicht auf die Topographie und diese gerade dadurch betonend. Die Vegetationsschichten befinden sich im labilen Gleichgewicht zwischen Verwilderung und Kontrolliertheit. So wird manifest, daß unsere ungeteilte Wertschätzung dem Wilden und dem Kultivierten gehört. Auf

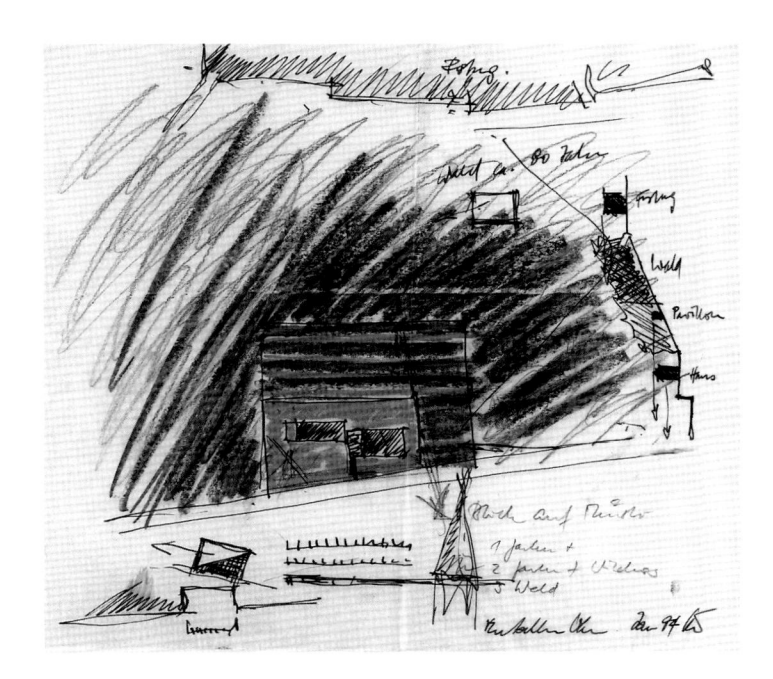

forest we found wild garden bushes, old rose bushes, fruit trees and berry bushes.

The mentioned history of the vegetation shows a coherency with the cultural history of the location. We are at a military place, in the immediate neighborhood of the largest fortress in Europe, at the edge of the lower-level city and the glacis stretching towards the castle on the hill. What was formerly an open shooting range has grown into a forest; the building dating back to 1877 belonged to the rampart master who was in charge of the maintenance of the glacis. Karljosef Schattner and Wilhelm Huber planned the conversion and new construction for the culturally engaged owners.

The first walk through the sleeping beauty-like garden reveals all the charms and shortcomings: nature is not only beautiful, romantic and diversified, it can also be banal, indifferent and unattractive. The view of the city with the church tower and the Alps has become completely overgrown and the slope is now hardly accessible.

The goal and theme of the design is the precise phrasing of the three different appearances of nature, which are in correspondence or opposition to the constructed. On the lowest

Konzeptskizze 1994 Conceptual sketch 1994

der Ostseite führt ein – im Plan auffälliger – Zick-Zackweg zum Aussichtspavillon am höchsten Punkt des Gartens. Die Wegführung ist nicht trendiges Design, sondern vor Ort im Gelände eingepaßt. Sie stellt die sanftest mögliche Höhenüberwindung sicher, analog den Wanderwegen im Gebirge. Der Weg durchschneidet die Vegetationsschichten im Rhythmus differenter Pflanzhöhen und Grüntöne.

Ziel unserer Neugierde ist der oben im Gebüsch leicht versteckte Pavillon mit seiner nicht lesbaren Buchstabenbrüstung. Wir nähern uns dem Pavillon. Eintretend erkennen wir einen einfachen Betonrahmen, verstärkt durch die hangseitige, hellgrün eingefärbte Mauer und den talseitigen Schriftzug aus hellblauen Betonbuchstaben. Das gerahmte Bild ist mit Bedeutung aufgeladen: Ganz hinten im Dunst die Alpen, die Stadt mit dem höchsten Kirchturm von Europa, die Pflanzen des Gartens und direkt vor uns «Ogni pensiero vola». Das Bild wirkt gleichzeitig modern und antiquiert. Es verkörpert das Credo visueller Kommunikation, die Gleichwertigkeit von Wort und Bild, erinnert uns aber auch an die Sinnsprüche alter Gärten.

level, the landscaped nature marks the looks of the parts of the garden close to the building. On the slope, the vegetation alternates between the ruderal and the tended, whereas the old forest forms the border and frame for the inside garden and, at the same time, accentuates the transition to the largest possible closeness to nature of the outside garden.

Along the street the precisely trimmed yew hedge along the wall forms the border to the forecourt and garden yard, blocking the view from the outside and yet leaving open an outlook. The row of magnolias leads towards the house entrance. Going up the stairs, the wall denies the view into the private yard garden which is produced, surprisingly, only upon entering the hallway. 14 plant figures trimmed in free forms and showing different shades of green 'float' in the finely leveled green sand surface. At a closer look we recognize Buxus, Ilex, Chaenomeles and azaleas. The calm form variation contrasts with the precise sand plane and the framing hedges. In this reduction, the closeness to Japanese Zen-gardens becomes clear.

A narrow water basin marks the separation between the different parts of the house and leads us at the same time to the back side of the house which stands here on a green Andeer granite gravel-carpet and creates a distance to the steep slope.

On the slope, there are alternating layers of various flora populations, several year old ruderal vegetation, and a copse with rows of bushes, which are also formed by just one type of plant. They clearly differentiate themselves from the wild vegetation in form, flowers and scent: park roses, lilac, American Cornus florida, large flowering snowball, tree peony, sloe and box are spread across the entire width of the slope without consideration for the topography and, in fact, enhancing it. The layers of vegetation are in an unstable balance between wild growth and control. It thus becomes manifest that our unanimous appreciation belongs to both the wild and the cultivated.

On the east side, a zigzag pathway – standing out on the plan – leads to the outlook pavilion at the highest point in the garden. The path is not a trendy design, but fits into the grounds in situ. It assures the easiest possible ascent of the heights, analogous to the hiking paths in the mountains. The path cuts through the layers of vegetation in the midst of the rhythm of different plant heights and shades of green.

Höllenschlund in Bomarzo;
Vicino Orsini, ca. 1560

Hell's gorge in Bomarzo;
Vicino Orsini, approx. 1560

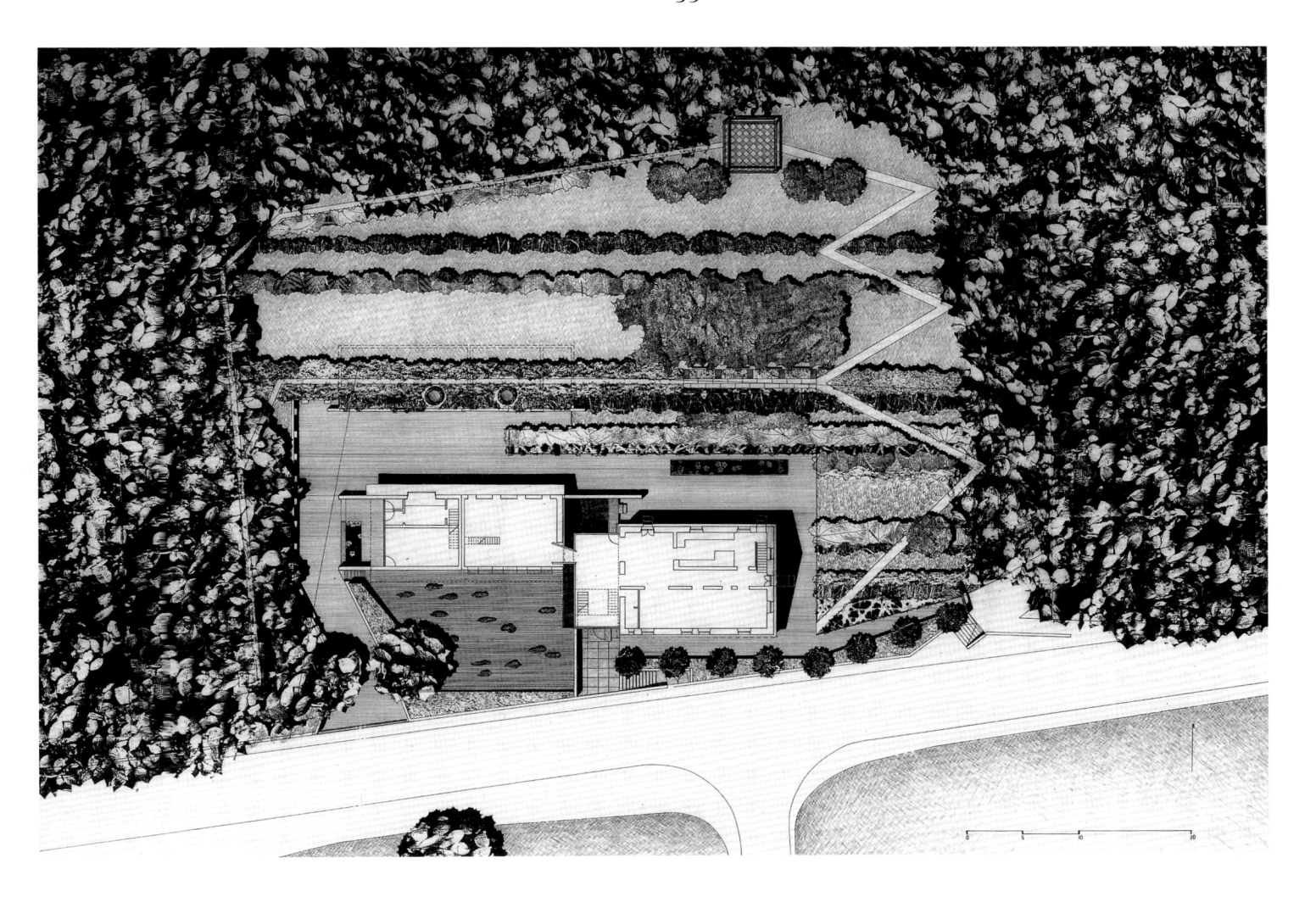

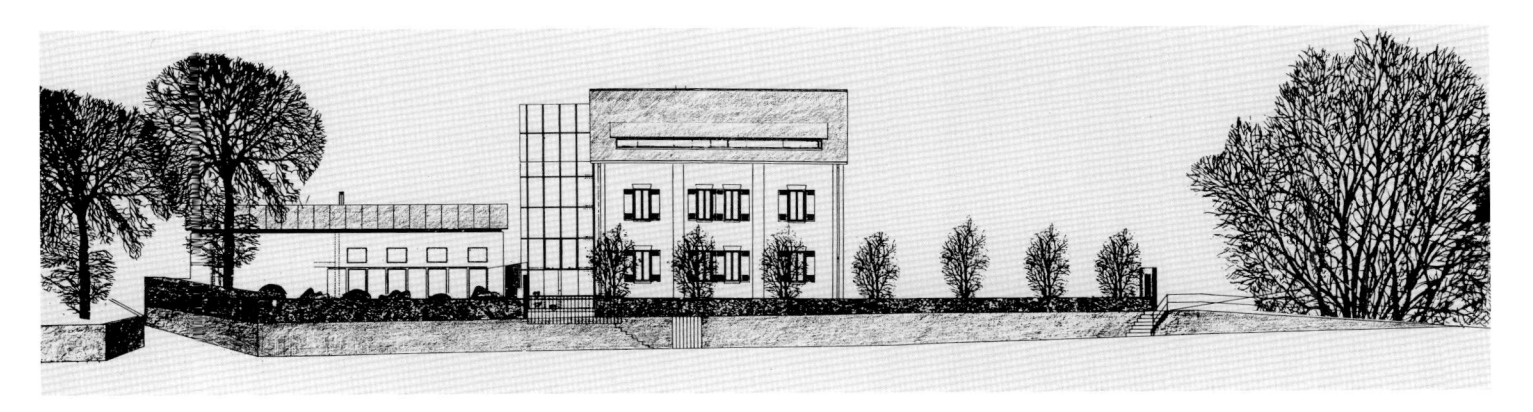

Projektplan 1994 (95)
Grundriß
Original 1:100, 80 x 110 cm; Tusche,
Folie, Farbstift auf Plandruck weiß

Ansicht von der Straße

Project plan 1994 (95)
Ground plan
Original 1:100, 80 x 110 cm; ink, foil,
colored pencil on white plan print

View from the street

Im heiligen Wald von Bomarzo finden wir die prominentesten Garteninschriften der Renaissance, die von Fürst Orsini als Rätsel und Prüfung der Gelehrtheit seiner Besucher entworfen wurden. Das bekannteste Beispiel findet sich um den Höllenschlund eingehauen – «Ogni pensiero vola». Ein rezenter Irrtum, wie die neuen Nachforschungen von Bredekamp darlegen. Orsini hat das Dante-Zitat aus der Göttlichen Komödie feinsinnig abgewandelt «lasciate ogni pensiero o voi che entrate» – Laßt, die ihr eintretet, jeden Gedanken (und nicht die Hoffnung, wie bei Dante) fahren. In Umkehrung zum fürchterlichen Aussehen des Höllenschlundes entpuppt sich die Höhle in Bomarzo als Ort gemeinsamer Lustbarkeit.

In unserem Garten wird der Irrtum zur Absicht, weil sich auch der Ausdruck nochmals gewandelt hat: Nicht mehr in Nachbarschaft zu steingehauenen Ungeheuern, sondern auf dem höchsten Punkt, über Garten und Stadt, schützt uns der Schriftzug vor dem Absturz und läßt die Gedanken fliegen.

Dieter Kienast

The object of our curiosity is the pavilion with its illegible letter balustrade which is slightly hidden between the shrubbery. We approach the pavilion. Upon entering it we recognize a simple concrete frame, reinforced by the light-green wall of the hillside and the inscription, in light blue concrete letters, on the side of the valley. The framed picture is charged with meaning: all the way back in the haze are the Alps, the city with the highest church tower in Europe, the plants in the garden and directly in front of us, "Ogni pensiero vola". The picture has both a modern and, at the same time, antique effect. It embodies the credo of visual communication, the equality of word and image. It also reminds us of the axioms of old gardens.

In the sacred forest of Bomarzo we find the most prominent garden inscriptions of the Renaissance, which were designed by count Orsini as an enigma and a gesture to the scholarship of his visitors. The most famous example is carved into the hell's gorge – "Ogni pensiero vola". As Bredekamp's new research findings show, this is a piquant error. Orsini has sensitively altered the quote from Dante's Divine Comedy "lasciate ogni pensiero o voi che entrate" – May those who enter let go of every thought (and not hope, as in Dante's case). As an antithesis to the terrible looks of the hell's gorge, the cave in Bomarzo turns out to be a place of common pleasures.

In our garden the error becomes an intention because the expression has changed yet again: removed from the neighborhood of stone-carved monsters, on the highest point above the garden and the city, the inscription protects us from the abyss and allows our thoughts to soar.

Dieter Kienast

... verwehrt zunächst die Mauer den Einblick in den privaten Hofgarten, der erst nach dem Eintritt ins Treppenhaus überraschend inszeniert wird.

... the wall denies the view into the private yard garden which is produced, surprisingly, only upon entering the hallway.

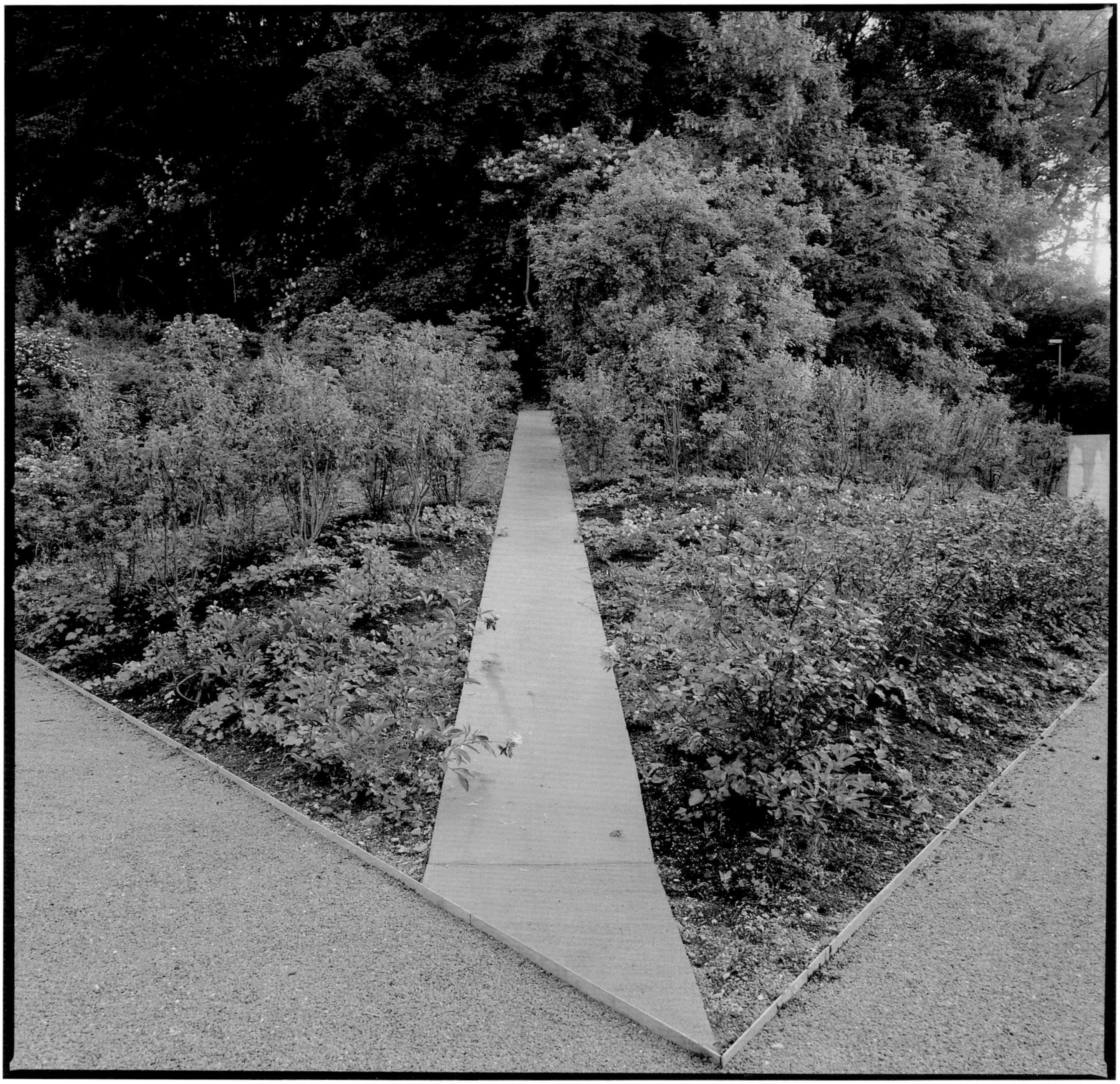

Ziel unserer Neugierde ist der oben im Gebüsch leicht versteckte Pavillon mit seiner nicht lesbaren Buchstabenbrüstung.

The object of our curiosity is the pavilion with its illegible letter balustrade which is slightly hidden between the shrubbery.

... wechseln ruderalisierte und gepflegte Vegetation, während der alte Wald Grenze und Rahmen des inneren Gartens bildet und gleichzeitig den Übergang zur größtmöglichen Naturnähe des äußeren Gartens akzentuiert.

... the vegetation alternates between the ruderal and the tended, whereas the old forest forms the border and frame for the inside garden and, at the same time, accentuates the transition to the largest possible closeness to nature of the outside garden.

Eintretend erkennen wir einen einfachen Betonrahmen, verstärkt durch die hangseitige, hellgrün eingefärbte Mauer und den talseitigen Schriftzug aus hellblauen Betonbuchstaben. Das gerahmte Bild ist mit Bedeutung aufgeladen ...

Upon entering it we recognize a simple concrete frame, reinforced by the light-green wall of the hillside and the inscription, in light blue concrete letters, on the side of the valley. The framed picture is charged with meaning ...

Die Wegführung ist nicht trendiges Design, sondern vor Ort im
Gelände eingepaßt. Sie stellt die sanftest mögliche Höhenüberwindung sicher,
analog den Wanderwegen im Gebirge. Der Weg durchschneidet die
Vegetationsschichten im Rhythmus differenter Pflanzhöhen und Grüntöne.

The path is not a trendy design, but fits into the grounds in situ. It assures the easiest possible ascent of the heights, analogous to the hiking paths in the mountains. The path cuts through the layers of vegetation in the midst of the rhythm of different plant heights and shades of green.

Zwischen Tradition und Innovation

Ökologie ist nicht nur ein vielzitiertes gesellschaftliches Schlagwort, sie ist auch eine wichtige Grundlage unserer Arbeit. Das Verständnis ökologischer Wirkungsweisen und deren Umsetzung gehört zur Grundlage verantwortungsvollen Bauens in unserer Zeit. Bei der Durchsicht unserer Projekte mag dies überraschen, weil man gewohnt ist, Ökologie mit bestimmten Eigenschaften oder Bildern gleichzusetzen: das Feuchtbiotop, die Ruderalvegetation, die artenreiche Blumenwiese, die Feldhecke, das Waldstück, den Wintergarten haben wir im Kopf und denken an Gesundes, Natürliches, vom Menschen wenig Beeinflußtes, Nachhaltiges. Dabei bedeutet Ökologie nur «die Lehre von den Beziehungen der Lebewesen zu ihrer Umwelt». Ökologisch ist demnach die Blumenwiese, aber auch die zunehmende Verbreitung der Malaria. Loslösen von den vordergründigen Bildern und nach der Funktionsweise, nach der Materialität, dem Herstellungsaufwand, der Nachhaltigkeit und Reziklierbarkeit fragen. Überrascht stellen wir dann vielleicht fest, daß das Alternativenergiehaus ökologisch schlechtere Werte zeigt als das einfache Backsteinhaus, daß das natürlich erscheinende Feuchtbiotop nur dank einer kaum entsorgbaren PVC-Folie funktioniert. Wir setzen auf ein vertieftes, hintergründiges Ökologieverständnis und betonen gleichzeitig, daß nicht nur Ökologie, sondern auch die Gestalt und der Gebrauch gleichberechtigte Parameter unserer Gärten sind.

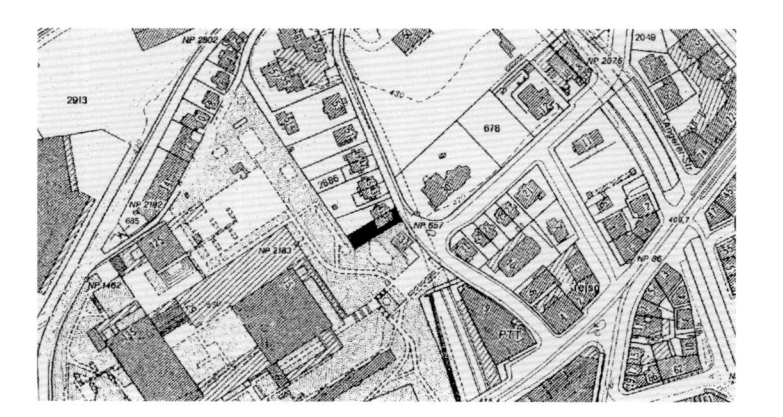

Between Tradition and Innovation

Ecology is not only a much quoted social slogan. It has also become an important basis for our work. Understanding ecological effects and realizing them is part of the basis for a responsible architecture in our days. This may come as a surprise when viewing our projects because we are accustomed to associating ecology with very specific characteristics or images: the damp biotope, the ruderal vegetation, the rich, flowering meadow, the field hedge, the forest, the winter garden. All these things are on our minds and we think of something healthy, natural, little influenced by man and enduring. Yet, all that ecology means is "the teaching of the relationships of the living beings with their environment". According to this, the flowering meadow is as ecological, as is the increasing spread of Malaria. One has to distance oneself from the obvious images and ask about the function, the material, the effort of production, the lifetime and the recyclability. Then we may be surprised to find that the alternative energy house has a worse ecological value than the simple brick house, that the seemingly natural damp biotope functions only due to an almost non-recyclable PVC foil. We count on a deeper knowledge of understanding of ecology and, at the same time, emphasize that not only ecology, but also the design and the use are equivalent parameters in our gardens.

The quarter is distinguished by the grid-like development dating back to the 'Gründerzeit' (years of rapid industrial expansion in Germany) and the single villas with larger gardens. Our property is located on a street with row houses from the turn of the century. The 11 m wide and 40 m long garden space shows, like the adjoining properties, a unified zoning pattern: walkway, wall and forecourt which is connected by a small passageway with the garden.

The building, which was successfully converted by the architects Romero & Schaefle, and the school yard with a beautiful old tree population on the south side become the starting point for the new garden concept. The four space-defining borders are designed differently. The forecourt is framed with a simple metal fence. It is oriented towards the street and is com-

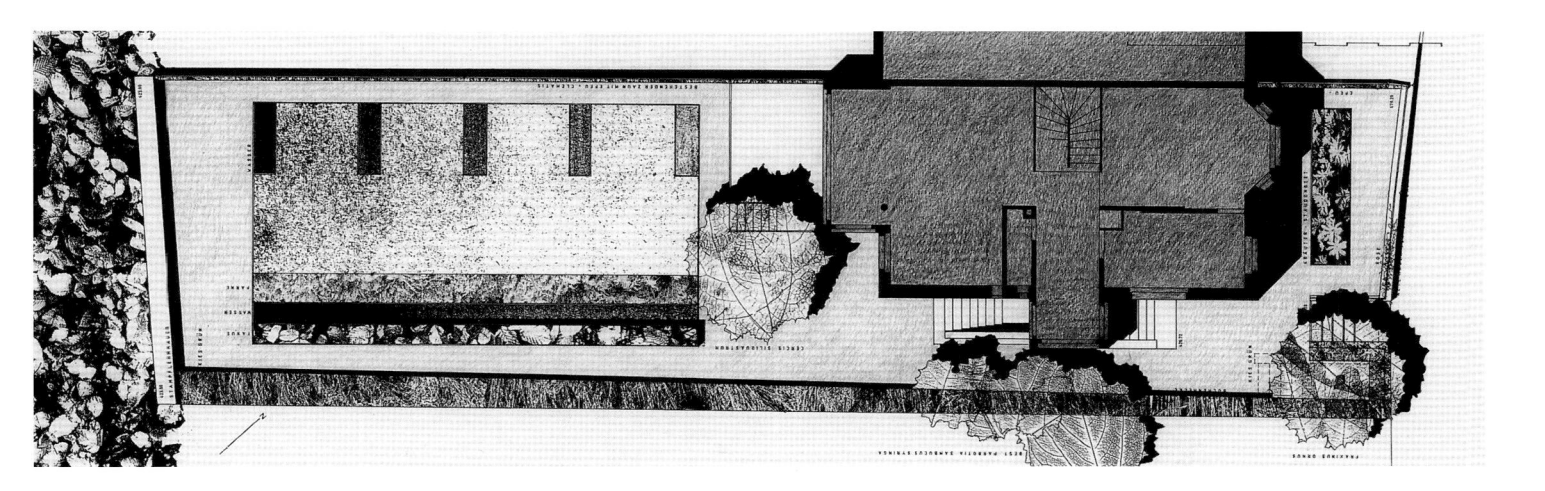

Das Stadtviertel wird durch die rasterartige Gründerzeitbebauung und einzelnen Villen mit größeren Gärten geprägt. Unser Grundstück liegt an einer Straße mit zusammengebauten Wohnhäusern aus der Jahrhundertwende. Der 11 Meter schmale und 40 Meter lange Gartenraum zeigt ebenso wie die angrenzenden Grundstücke ein einheitliches Zonierungsmuster: Gehsteig, Mauer und Vorgarten, der mit einen schmalen Durchgang mit dem Wohngarten verbunden ist.

Das Gebäude, von den Architekten Romero & Schaefle gekonnt umgebaut, und der südlich angrenzende Schulhausfreiraum mit schönem alten Baumbestand wird zum Ausgangspunkt der neuen Gartenkonzeption. Die vier raumdefinierenden Grenzen werden unterschiedlich ausgebildet. Der Vorgarten wird mit einem einfachen Metallzaun gefaßt. Er orientiert sich zur Straße und ist voll einsehbar. Der Vorgarten ist gleichermaßen Empfangsraum, Distanzhalter und ‹Visitenkarte› seiner Bewohner. Die 40 Meter lange, sich verdickende Buchenhecke auf der Ostseite, betont die Länge des Gartens und gibt den Ausblick in den anliegenden Schulgarten frei. Gegenüber wird der alte Zaun berankt und somit die Ungleichseitigkeit des Wohngartens verdeutlicht. Die südseitige Grenze steht, von Wohnzimmer und Terrasse aus betrachtet, im direkten Blickfeld und stellt das omnipräsente Abschlußbild mit 20 Meter hohen Buchen und vorgelagerten Eiben dar, das scheinbar auf dem Sockel einer neuen, 2.50 Meter hohen Stampflehmmauer steht. Die Stampflehmmauer ist ein archaisches, auch in unseren Brei-

pletely open to view. The forecourt is a reception area and, at the same time, creates a certain distance. It is, so to speak, the "business card" of the occupants. The 40 m long beech hedge on the east side enhances the length of the garden and reveals a view of the adjoining school garden. On the opposite side, the old fence is covered with climbing plants and the unevenness of the garden is thus made clear. The southern border, seen from the living room and terrace, is a view of central importance and represents the omnipresent terminating image with 20 m high beeches and yews, seemingly standing on the base of a new pressed loam wall of 2.50 m height.

The loam wall is an archaic building procedure which can be realized in our latitude, as well. It challenges the tradesmen to execute this kind of work once again. The 60 cm thick wall is framed like a concrete wall. The humus and slightly clayey earth material is filled into the frame in layers and then stomped down. The wall is then covered with a rusting steel plate to prevent water from draining into it. The layers of soil remain visible in their various shades of brown. The wall shows a 'lively' mutable picture which changes in color and structure depending on the time of day and year. It has thus become the bearer of the image of the ordinarily hidden earth and contrasts strikingly with the differing greens of the plants and the gravel.

Similar to colored carpets imbedded in the gravel, an herb bed is placed in the forecourt and a lawn bed in the garden. The lawn bed is framed on its longitudinal side by a tall yew hedge,

Projektplan 1994
Grundriß
Original 1:50, 40 x 90 cm;
Tusche, Folie, Farbstift
auf Plandruck weiß

Project plan 1994
ground plan
Original 1:50, 40 x 90 cm;
ink, foil, colored pencil
on white plan print

tengraden mögliches Bauverfahren, bei dem die handwerkliche Umsetzung neu erprobt werden muß. Die 60 cm dicke Mauer wird wie eine Betonmauer geschalt. Darin wird das vor Ort vorhandene, humose und etwas lehmhaltige Erdmaterial schichtweise eingebracht und festgestampft. Die Mauerabdeckung erfolgt mit einer rostenden Stahlplatte, die das Einsickern des Wassers verhindert. Die Erdschichten bleiben in ihren differenten Brauntönen sichtbar. Die Mauer zeigt ein ‹lebendig› wechselndes Bild, das sich in Tages- und Jahresverlauf, in Farbe und Struktur verändert. Sie ist damit zum Bildträger der normalerweise verborgenen Erde geworden und kontrastiert auffällig das unterschiedliche Grün der Pflanzen und des grünen Gartenkieses.

Farbigen Teppichen gleich, im Kies eingefügt, sind im Vorgarten ein Kräuterbeet und im Wohngarten ein Rasenbeet plaziert. Die Begrenzung des Rasenbeetes erfolgt auf der Längsseite mit einer hohen Eibenhecke, dem Wasserbecken und Farnstreifen. Diese spielen mit der ambivalenten Grundkonzeption des asymmetrischen Gartens. Wegeinfassungen und das Wasserbecken sind aus unbehandeltem Stahl angefertigt, der Rost ist selbstverständlicher Teil der Elemente, die Patina ansetzen und darüber hinaus dem Wasser einen schönen Farbton beigeben. An markanten Stellen des Vor- und Wohngartens betonen Cercidiphyllum japonicum und Cornus controversa die Raumhaltigkeit des Gartens und werden mit Laub, Blüte und Duft sinnlich erfahrbar.

Der kleine Garten für die Familie K. ist der Versuch, das Gefäß eines stimmungsvollen Gartens zu schaffen, dessen Weiterentwicklung oder Füllung sie selber übernehmen wollen und müssen, aber auch die Fortschreibung der Gartentypologie des anliegenden Stadtviertels.

Dieter Kienast

the water basin and strips of fern. They play with the ambivalent basic conception of the asymmetrical garden. The edges of the pathways and the water basin are trimmed with raw steel, the rust is a self-understood part of the elements which create a patina and, furthermore, provide the water with a nice hue. The spaciousness of the garden is marked in important places of the forecourt and garden by Cercidiphyllum japonicum and Cornus controversa and can be sensually experienced through their foliage, blossoms and scent.

The small garden for the K. family is an attempt to create a vessel for the creation of an atmospheric garden whose further development or filling-in, but also the continuation of the garden typology of the adjoining quarter, is and has to be effected by the family itself.

Dieter Kienast

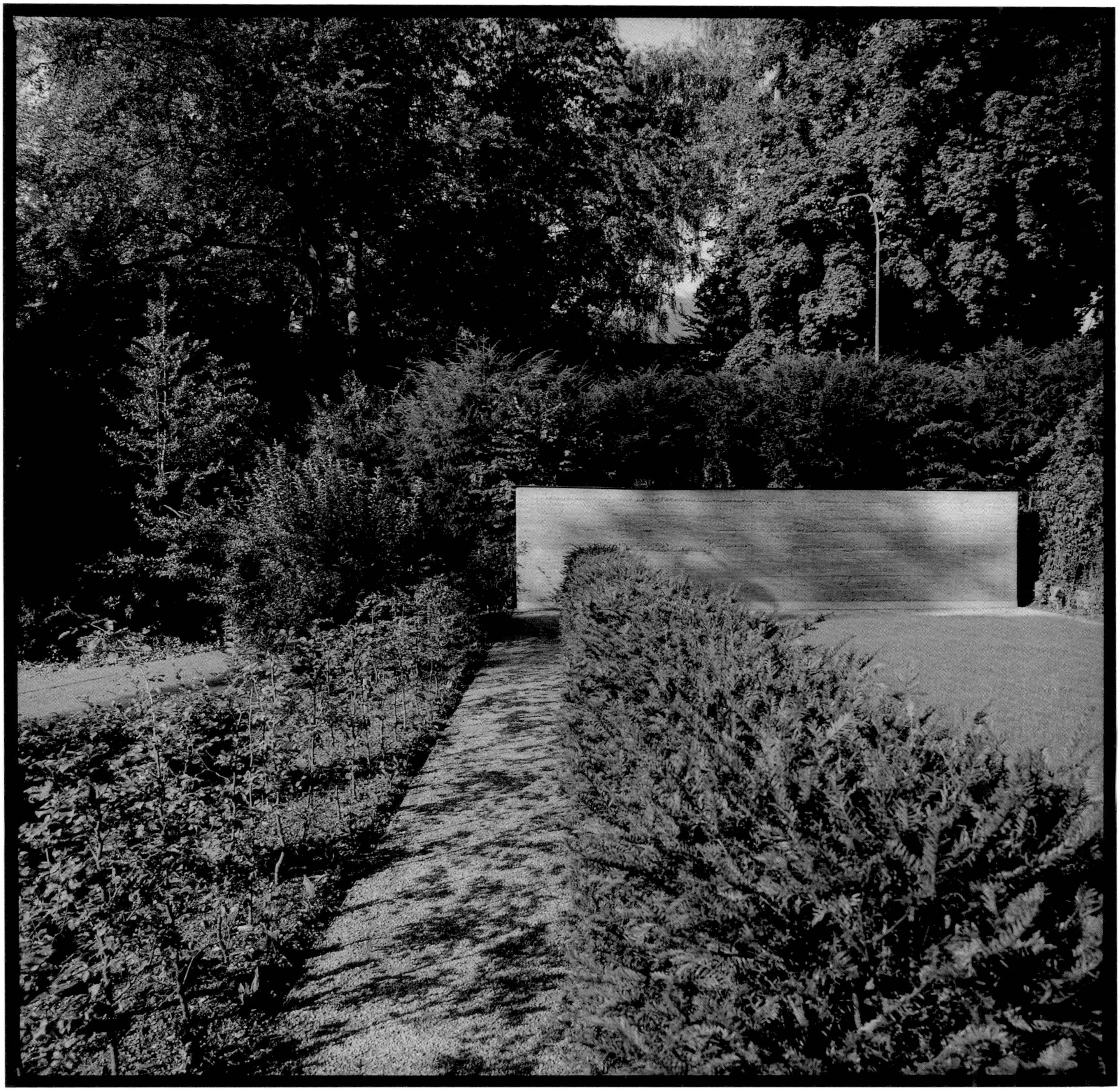

Die südseitige Grenze steht, von Wohnzimmer und Terrasse aus betrachtet, im direkten Blickfeld und stellt das omnipräsente Abschlußbild mit 20 Meter hohen Buchen und vorgelagerten Eiben dar...

The southern border, seen from the living room and terrace, is a view of central importance and represents the omnipresent terminating image with 20 m high beeches and yews ...

Die Erdschichten bleiben in ihren differenten Brauntönen sichtbar.
Die Mauer zeigt ein ‹lebendig› wechselndes Bild, das sich in Tages- und
Jahresverlauf, in Farbe und Struktur verändert. Sie ist damit
zum Bildträger der normalerweise verborgenen Erde geworden …

The layers of soil remain visible in their various shades of brown.
The wall shows a 'lively' mutable picture which changes in color and structure
depending on the time of day and year. It has thus become the bearer
of the image of the ordinarily hidden earth …

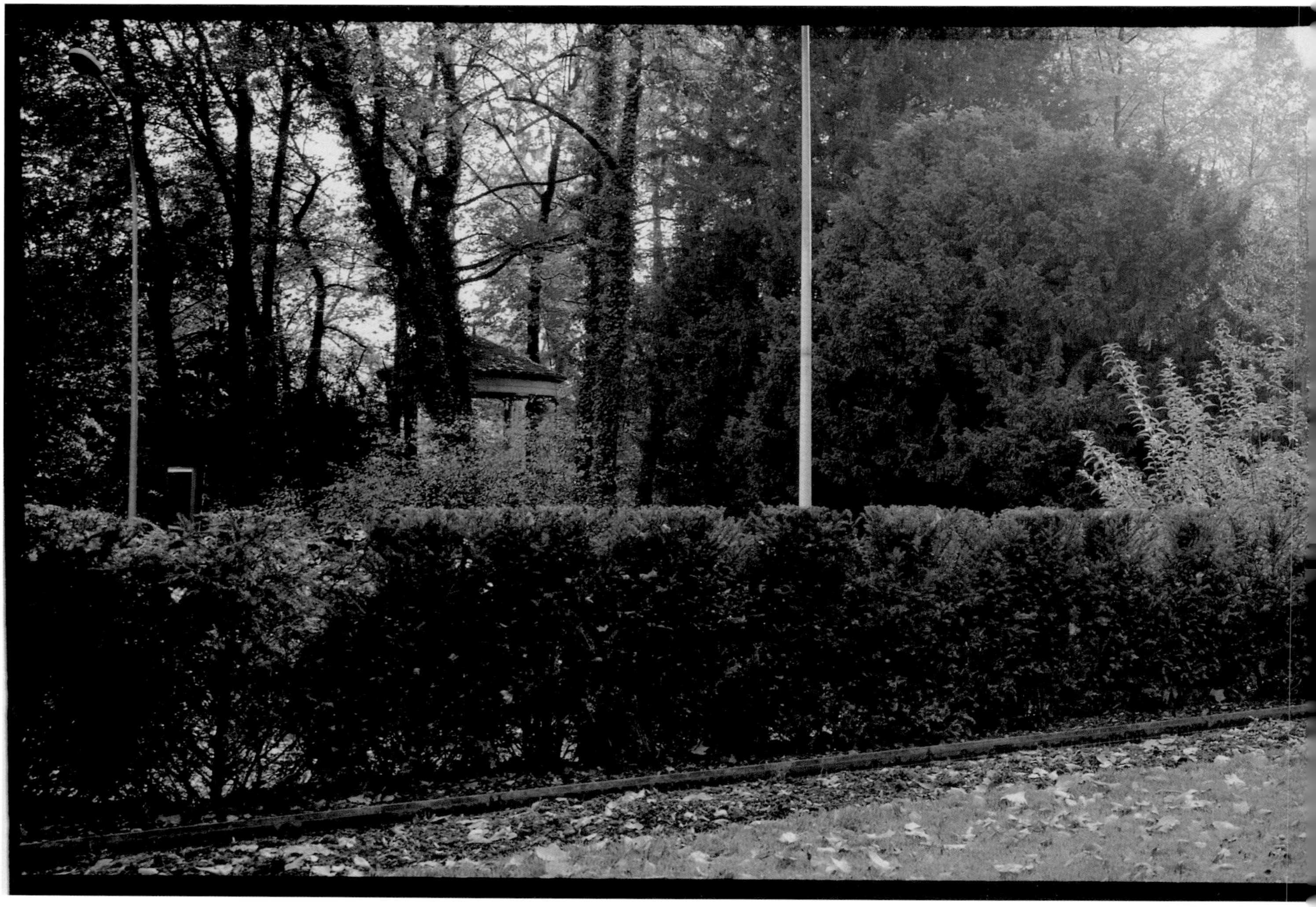

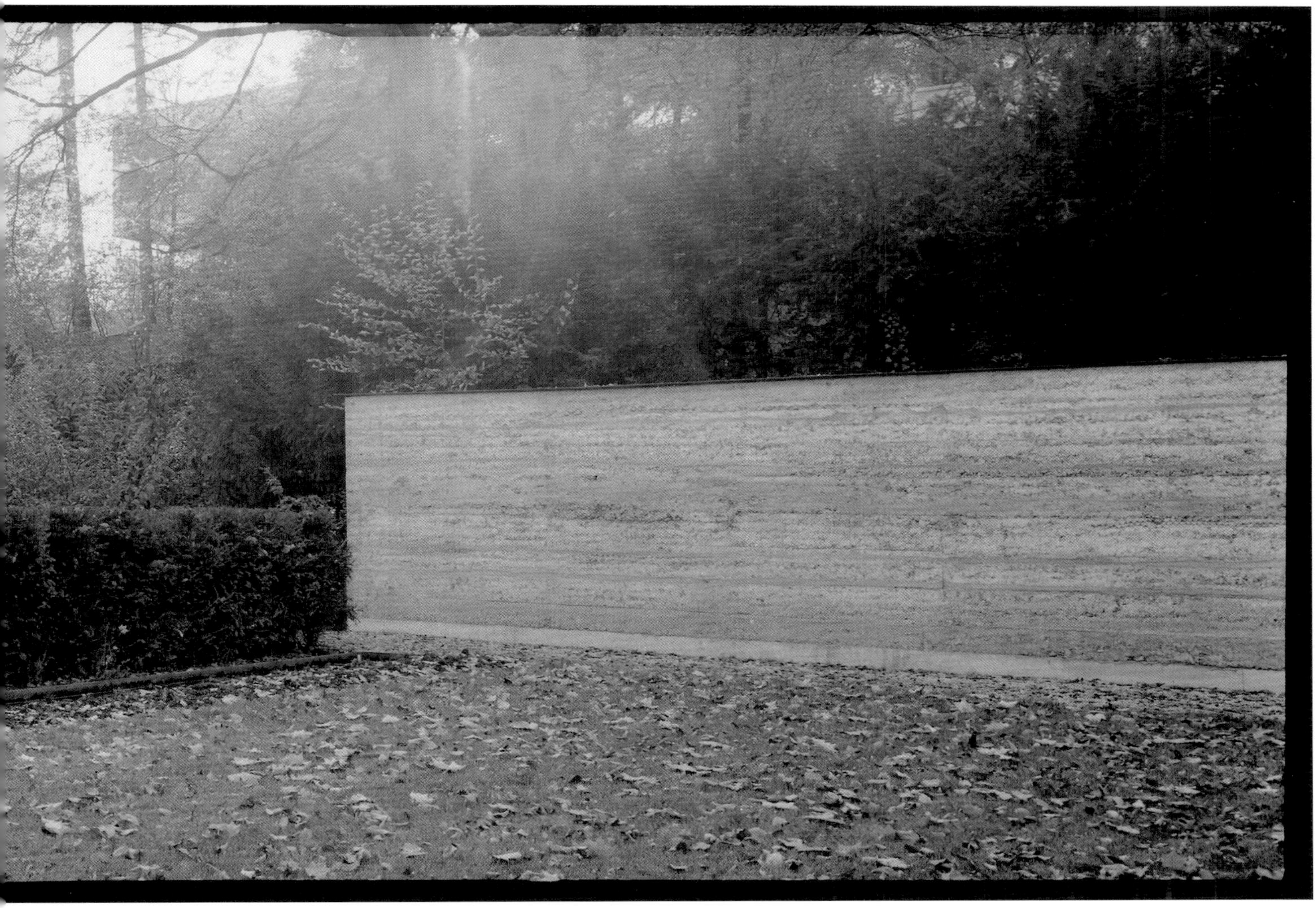

Neue Gärten zum alten Schloß

Die genuine Eigenschaft des Gartens ist seine – durch das Pflanzenwachstum bedingte – permanente Veränderung, die letztlich durch noch so intensive Pflege nicht aufgehalten werden kann. Darin begründen sich die bis in die jüngste Zeit anhaltenden Zweifel über den Wert des Kulturgutes Garten und damit auch über die Notwendigkeit seines Schutzes vor der Zerstörung. Das Nachdenken über den Umgang mit unserem historischen Erbe beschränkte sich deshalb lange Zeit auf die Bauten, während die Gärten erst in den 60er und 70er Jahren zum Gegenstand fundierter wissenschaftlicher Untersuchungen geworden sind. In der Gartendenkmalpflege hat die Denkmalpflege eine Diversifikation gefunden, deren Grundsätze 1981 in der Charta von Florenz festgelegt und seither in zahllosen Publikationen verfeinert diskutiert werden. Es liegt im Trend der Zeit, daß das Alte in der Fachdiziplin und der Gesellschaft eine zunehmende Wertschätzung erfährt. So hat sich die Gartendenkmalpflege zumindest in den deutschsprachigen Ländern relativ rasch emanzipiert und verteidigt selbstbewußt das neu gewonnene Terrain. Der sorgsame Umgang mit vorhandenen Gärten ist zweifelsohne wichtig. Trotzdem stimmen zwei Aspekte in der Praxis nachdenklich:

Trotz der, in der Fachliteratur eindeutig ablehnenden Haltung gegenüber Rekonstruktionen beobachten wir gerade in jüngster Zeit eine Vielzahl von Rekonstruktionen oder, noch problematischer, historisierende Neuschöpfungen. Zum Zweiten stellen wir eine große Skepsis gegenüber dem Weiterbauen, dem Neubauen in alten Gärten fest. Damit wird aber gerade verhindert, was die moderne Denkmalpflege propagiert: nicht ein bestimmter Zustand ist erhaltenswert, sondern die unterschiedlichen Sedimentationen der Geschichte. Dies schließt bewußt auch neueste Bauteile mit ein unter der Bedingung, daß das Neue als solches erkennbar bleibt. Ist dies bei den Bauten durch die Verwendung aktueller Baumaterialien und entsprechender Anwendung signifikant herstellbar, so stellt sich im Garten beim wichtigsten Element ‹Pflanze› die Frage nach der Ablesbarkeit in höchster Brisanz: der Buchs, die Buche, der Holunder haben auch heute das gleiche Aussehen wie vor 300 Jah-

New Gardens for the Old Castle

Because of the plant growth, which can not be stopped no matter how intensive the care may be, one genuine characteristic of the garden is its permanent transformation. This is a basis for doubts about the value of the cultural good of the garden and the necessity of its protection from destruction. Therefore, thoughts about the handling of our historic heritage were for a long time limited to buildings, whereas gardens became the object of scientific research only in the '60s and '70s. Monumental preservation has found a diversification in the garden preservation whose principles were set in 1981 by the charter of Florence and have been discussed in many publications ever since. It is the trend of our times for the traditional to experience increased attention and appreciation in special disciplines and society as a whole. Thus, garden preservation has emancipated rather quickly, at least in the German speaking countries, and it self-consciously defends its newly found territory. The careful handling of existing gardens is, without any doubt, important. Still, two aspects in practice make you think:

Despite what is clearly an attitude of refusal in specialized literature towards reconstruction, we can observe, especially in recent times, an abundance of reconstruction activity. Or – and this may be even more problematic – new creations from a

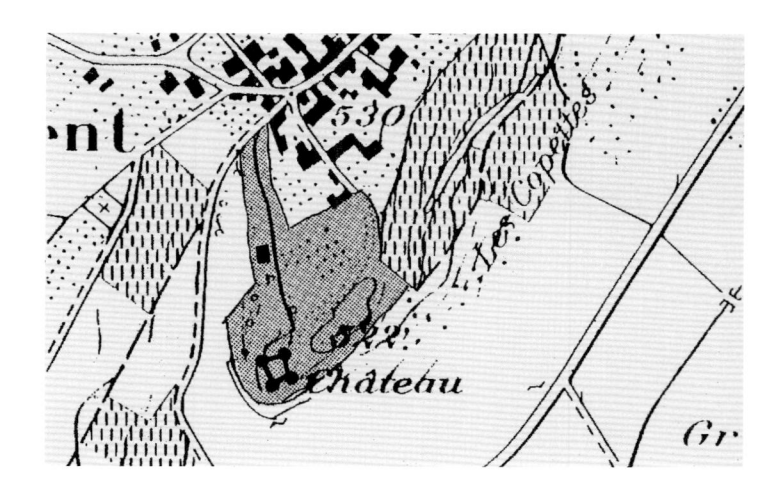

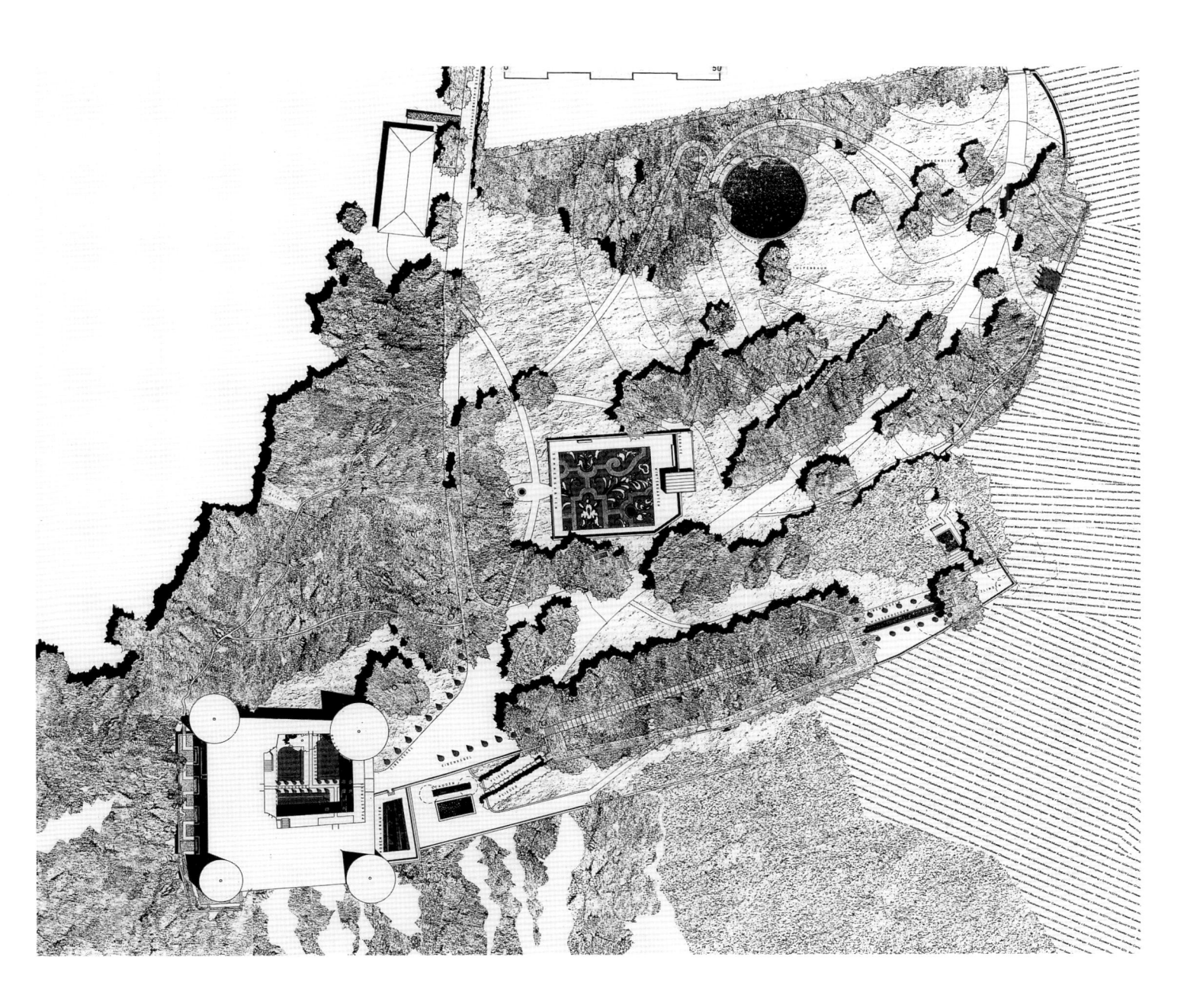

Projektplan 1995
Grundriß
Original 1:250, 87 x 102 cm;
Tusche, Folie
auf Plandruck weiß

Project plan 1995
Ground plan
Original 1:250, 87 x 102 cm;
ink, foil on
white plan print

ren. Die Verwendung ‹moderner› Baumaterialien ist zwar möglich, erscheint im Hinblick auf das Ensemble jedoch meist nur Notbehelf zu sein. Neues Bauen in alten Gärten wird deshalb immer eine heikle Gratwanderung zwischen dem angestrengten ‹Sichtbarmachen› des neuen Eingriffes, dem selbstbewußten Weiterbauen und der Rekonstruktion sein. Entscheidend scheint, daß in Raumkonzeption, Material, Vegetation für veränderte Nutzungsansprüche und Rahmenbedingungen zeitgemäße Lösungen entwickelt werden, die im Dialog oder vielleicht auch in Opposition zur historischen Substanz stehen.

Mitte des 13. Jahrhunderts wurde mit dem Bau des Schlosses durch Henri von Ch. begonnen. Eine wehrhafte Burg mit vier Türmen entstand in der Waadt, markant am Rand des Hochplateaus gelegen, mit beeindruckender Sicht ins Tal nach Süden und Osten. 1478–1505 erfolgte unter dem Bauherrn Erzherzog Maximilian der Umbau zum Schloß, so wie es heute noch im wesentlichen besteht. Dendrochronologische Untersuchungen belegen, daß alle Deckenbalken vom Ende des 15. Jahrhunderts stammen. Das Château de Ch. und die dazugehörigen Ländereien haben im Verlauf der Geschichte viele wechselnde Eigentümer erlebt, bis es 1989 von den jetzigen Besitzern erworben wurde. Vielleicht sind die vielen Handänderungen verantwortlich dafür, daß relativ wenig Pläne und Schriften vom Schloß vorhanden sind. Ein Stich aus dem 18. Jahrhundert zeigt, daß der Schloßhügel vollständig mit Weinterrassen bedeckt war, während im flacheren Teil nordöstlich des Schlosses Obstbäume und Gemüsebeete sichtbar sind.

Von dieser intensiven Landwirtschaftsnutzung sind bis heute wichtige Teile geblieben. Der Weinanbau am Schloßosthang ist großflächig erhalten, der jetzt mit Mauern eingefriedete Schloßpark wird zur Hälfte beweidet. In den Steilhängen der Süd- und Westseite stockt ein 100 jähriger Wald, während auf der Ostterrasse eine ca. 150 Jahre alte Lindenallee vom Schloßeingang zu einem zugewachsenen Aussichtsplatz führt. Inmitten des Wieslandes liegt ein – wohl im letzten Jahrhundert angelegter – Hofgarten mit einem kleinen, verfallenen Gewächshaus. Lindenallee, Hofgarten und Zedern im Wald zeigen, daß im letzten Jahrhundert die ersten Anstrengungen zur Anlage eines Parkes um das Schloß herum unternommen worden sind. Die neu geplanten Interventionen stellen die Weiterführung der Gestaltung des 19. Jahrhunderts dar. Dabei geht es um die

reemerging history. Secondly, we can perceive a marked skepticism towards the extension – new building in old gardens. This, however, prevents exactly what modern preservationism propagates: it's not a specific condition that is worth preserving, but rather the various sedimental layers of history. This consciously includes the newest building sections under the premise that the new can be recognized as such. Whereas, in the case of buildings this can, to a high degree, be attained by using current materials and an appropriate application, in the case of a garden and its most important element, the plant, the question of readability becomes highly incendiary: box, beech or elder still have the same appearance as they had 300 years ago. The use of 'modern' building materials is possible; however, with respect to the ensemble it seems to be just an expedient in most cases. Therefore, new construction in old gardens always becomes a tricky act of balance between the goal of making the new operation 'visible' and the self-confident continuation of the building and reconstruction. What seems to be decisive is that, when it comes to the spatial concept – material, vegetation, changed utilization expectations and framework conditions – new contemporary solutions are developed which stand in a dialogue or, perhaps, in opposition with the historic substance.

In the middle of the 13th century the construction of the castle was started by Henri of Ch. A weir-like castle with four towers was created in the Waadt, strikingly situated at the edge of the high plateau with an impressive view of the valley towards the south and east. From 1478 to 1505 the archduke Maximilian had the castle converted to what, essentially, can be seen today. Dendrochronological research proves that all ceiling rafters date back to the end of the 15th century. The 'Château de Ch.' and the estates have seen many changes of owners in the course of history until it was bought in 1989 by its current owners. Perhaps the many changes of hands is responsible for the existence of relatively few plans and historical writings of the castle. An 18th century etching shows that the castle hill was entirely laid out as vineyard terraces, whereas, on the flatter part northeast of the castle grounds, fruit trees and vegetable beds are visible.

Important parts of this intensive agricultural utilization have been preserved up to this day. The viticulture on the east-

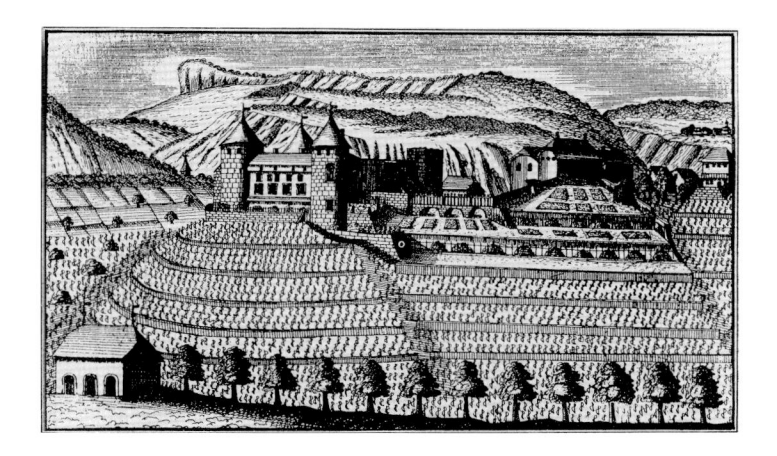

Präzisierung bestehender Anlageteile, ohne die historische Substanz anzutasten, sowie um die Neuschaffung von Gartenteilen, die bisher landwirtschaftlich genutzt wurden.

Der Bereich der Vorfahrt und Ostterrasse ist im Verlauf der letzten hundert Jahre vor allem durch den Vegetationsbewuchs und Pflanzungen verunklärt worden. Im Schloßhof werden die vorhandenen Rasenkompartimente entlang der Wege mit Buchshecken gefaßt, der Hauptweg ist von Buchskegeln begleitet. Die Heckenbänder sind gegenüber den historischen Vorbildern vergleichbarer Anlagen überdimensioniert breit und gegen die Hofmauern offen gehalten. Der große Eingangsplatz wird seitlich durch breitgezogene Eibenkegel gefaßt. Dem Schloßeingang vorgelagert ist ein kleiner, tiefer gelegener Garten, der neu mit Rosen und Stauden bepflanzt ist.

Die Lindenalleeachse wird zur Landschaft geöffnet, der Weg wiederhergestellt und mit einem Wasserbecken abgeschlossen. Dieses wird von Eibenkugeln flankiert und endet auf dem Aussichtsplatz. Linkerhand führt eine Treppe in den ‹verborgenen Garten›. Ein unter Erde und Laub verdecktes Wasserbecken wurde instand gesetzt und bildet den Mittelpunkt des verborgenen Gartens. Die vorgefundene Durchmischung angepflanzter Sträucher und Stauden mit Wildwuchs wird fortgeschrieben.

Die nachfolgenden Gartenteile befinden sich zur Zeit in der weiteren Plandetaillierung. In den 60er Jahren wurde auf der Ostseite eine unschön ins Terrain gelegte Straße mit direktem Zugang zum Dorf gebaut. Die Straße ist Anlaß einer neuen

ern side of the castle hill still covers a large surface, and half of the castle park, which is now enclosed by walls, is used as pasture grounds. A century-old forest is situated on the steep slopes of the south and west sides, whereas, on the eastern terrace an approximately 150 year old alley of lime trees leads from the castle entrance to an overgrown outlook. In the midst of the pasture lies a garden court – probably laid out during the last century – with a small, dilapidated greenhouse. The lime tree alley, the garden court and the cedars in the forest reveal that, during the past century, the first efforts for laying out a park around the castle were undertaken.

The area of the access road and eastern terrace has become unclear during the past hundred years. This is due, above all, to the growth of the vegetation and new plantings. In the courtyard of the castle, the existing lawn sections are framed with box along the pathways, the main pathway is accompanied by box cones. Compared to the historic examples of similar complexes, the hedges are dimensionally too wide and they remain open towards the court walls. The large entrance area is framed laterally by trimmed yew cones. In front of the castle entrance there is a small garden on a lower level which has recently been planted with new roses and shrubbery.

The lime tree corridor axis is opened up towards the landscape and the pathway has been reestablished and terminated with a concrete water basin. The water basin is framed by yew balls and ends at the outlook. To its left, a staircase leads in to the 'secret garden'. A water basin that was covered up by soil and foliage was renovated and now forms the center of the secret garden. The existing mix of planted shrubbery and wild bushes is continued.

During the '60s, a new road with a direct access to the village was built into the terrain on the eastern side with quite unfavorable results. This street is the reason for a remodeling of the terrain of the adjoining pasture grounds, which are transformed into a landscaped garden with a water-lily basin. Groups of trees and lone trees define the new part of the garden, which is accessed by a circular pathway.

The wish for a 'historic' garden was made for the vegetable garden yard enclosed by walls. With the present project, we intend to quote a prospect from a baroque parterre by distorting the scale because, as we all know, history can't be repeated. At

Stich Beginn 18. Jahrhundert, Ansicht von Süden

Etching, 18th century, view from the south

Terrainmodellation des angrenzenden Weidelandes, das in einen landschaftlich gestalteten Garten mit Seerosenbecken übergeführt wird. Baumgruppen und Einzelbäume definieren den neuen Gartenteil, der mit einem Rundweg erschlossen wird.

Für den mauerbegrenzten Gemüsegartenhof wurde der Wunsch nach einem ‹historischen› Garten geäußert. Weil Geschichte bekanntlich nicht wiederholt werden kann, beabsichtigen wir im vorliegenden Projekt, durch Maßstabszerrung einen Prospekt aus einem Barockparterre zu zitieren, das bei flüchtiger Betrachtung vertraut wirkt, bei genauerem Hinsehen jedoch die Transformation verrät. Dezallier d'Argenville hat in seinem weitverbreiteten Buch ‹La théorie et la pratique du jardinage› eine bedeutendes Werk geschaffen, das wesentlich zur Verbreitung des barocken Gartenkonzeptes in ganz Europa beigetragen hat. Gut zweihundert Jahre später greifen auch wir auf eine seiner Vorlagen zurück und zeigen das stark vergrößerte Teilkompartiment eines Broderieparterre-Entwurfes. Der Vergrößerungsausschnitt ist so gewählt, daß die Axialität bzw. Symmetrie verweigert, wohl aber das prägnante Formenspiel erhalten bleibt. Der Rahmen mit den dreiseitigen Mauern und dem Metallzaun auf der Vorderseite soll erhalten bleiben.

So werden unterschiedlich alte Sedimentationen gestalterischer Eingriffe und des natürlichen Wachstums offengelegt und/oder weiterentwickelt. Wahrgenommen und gelesen werden die verschiedenen Gärten als neue, vielleicht hybride Parkanlage zum alten Schloß.

Dieter Kienast

first glance it will look familiar; however, it will reveal the transformation on a closer look. Dezallier d'Argenville has created an important oeuvre in his widely known book 'theory and practice of gardening' which contributed greatly to the spreading popularity of the baroque garden concept throughout Europe. Almost two hundred years later, we go back to one of his designs and show the strongly enlarged partial compartment of a broderie parterre design. The enlargement is chosen in order to reject the axis and symmetry while at the same time preserving the impressive play with the forms. The frame with the walls on three sides and the metal fence in the front remains.

In this way, the sedimental layers of different ages of design operations and natural growth are revealed and/or further developed. The different gardens are perceived and read as the new and perhaps hybrid park complex of the castle.

Dieter Kienast

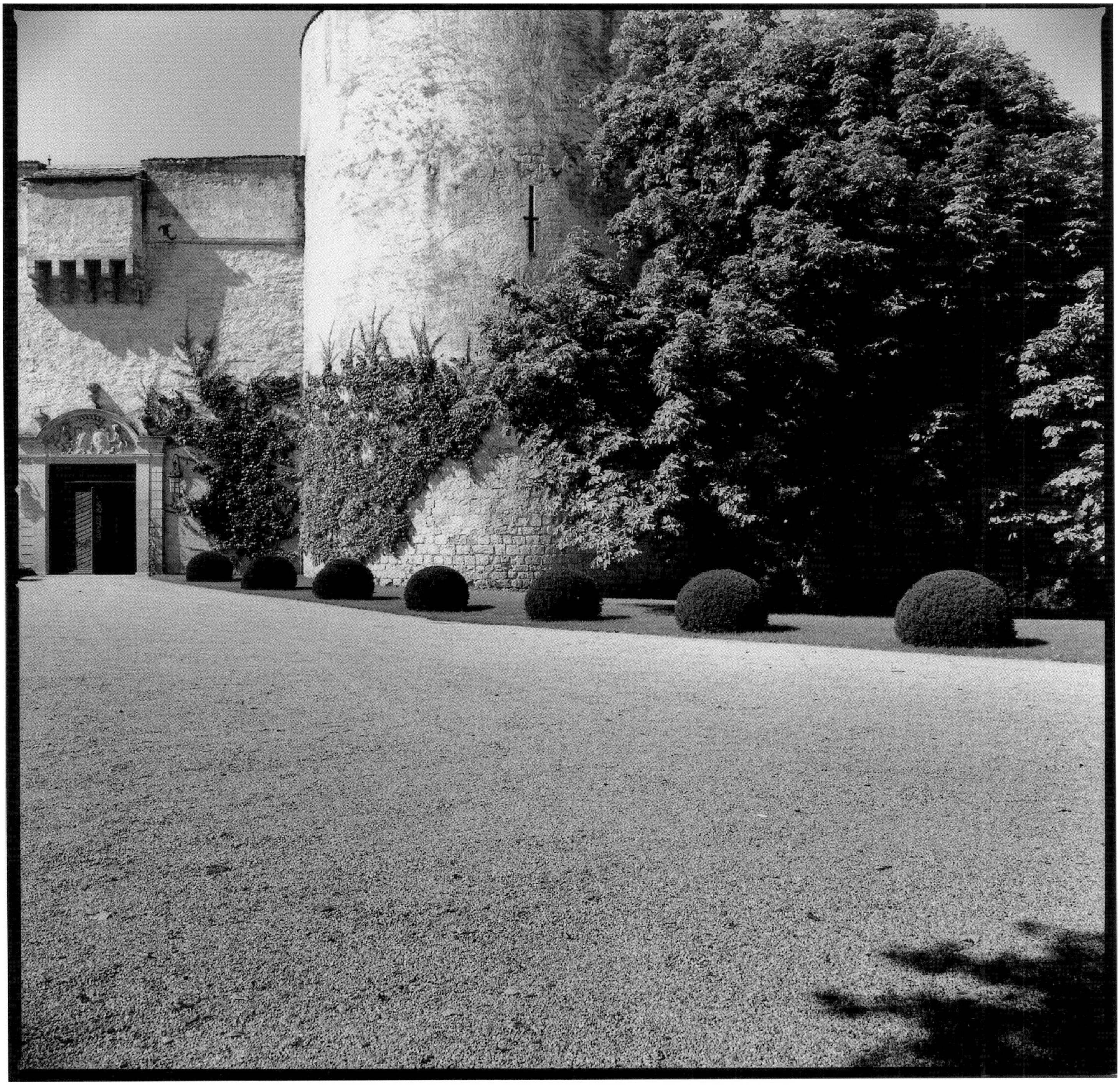

Im Schloßhof werden die vorhandenen Rasenkompartimente entlang der Wege
mit Buchshecken gefaßt, der Hauptweg ist von Buchskegeln begleitet.

In the courtyard of the castle, the existing lawn sections are framed
with box along the pathways, the main pathway is accompanied by box cones.

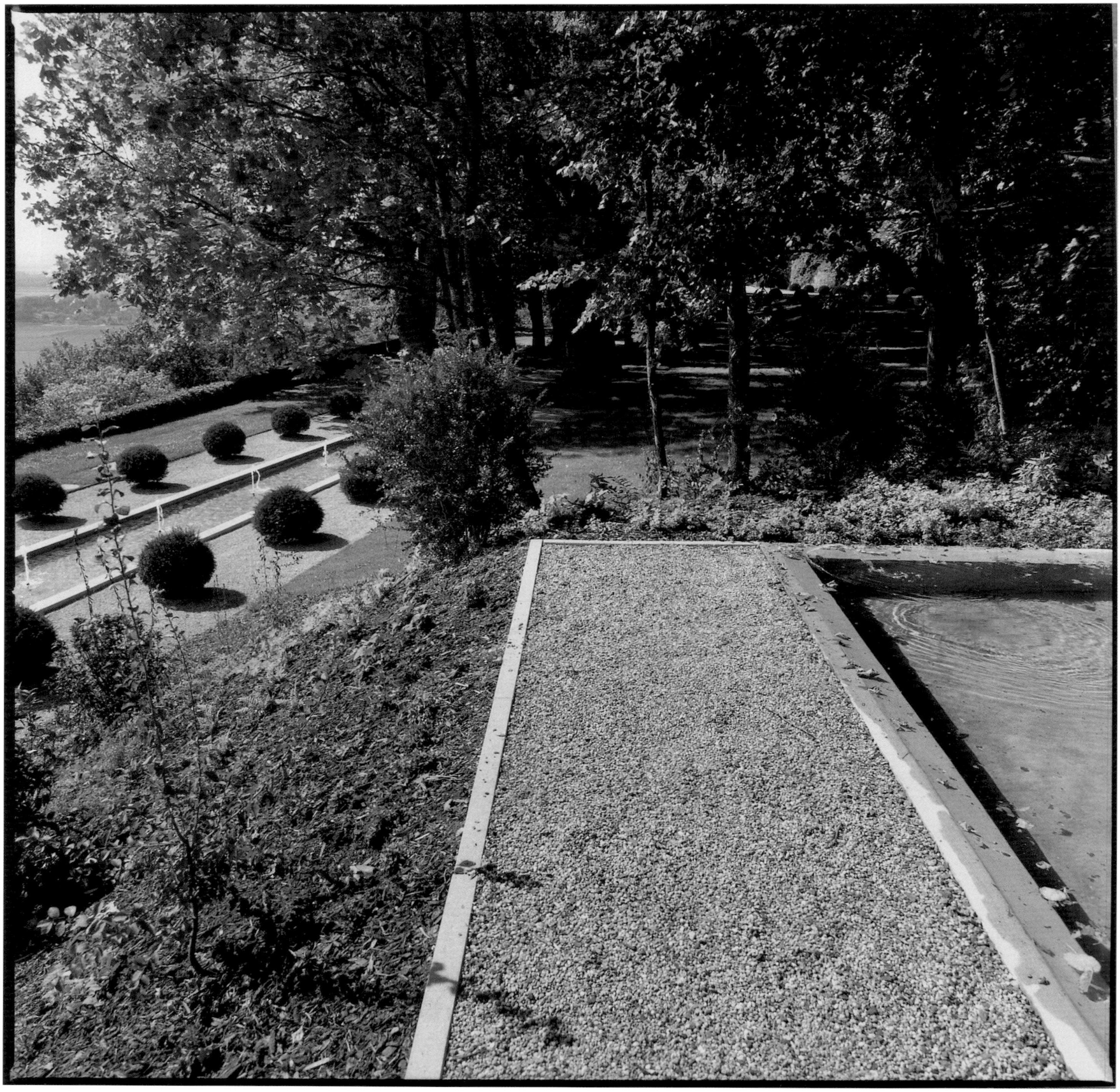

... Landschaft geöffnet, der Weg wieder hergestellt und mit einem Wasserbecken abgeschlossen. Dieses wird von Eibenkugeln flankiert und endet auf dem Aussichtsplatz.

... is opened up towards the landscape, the pathway has been reestablished and terminated with a water basin. The water basin is framed by yew balls and ends at the outlook.

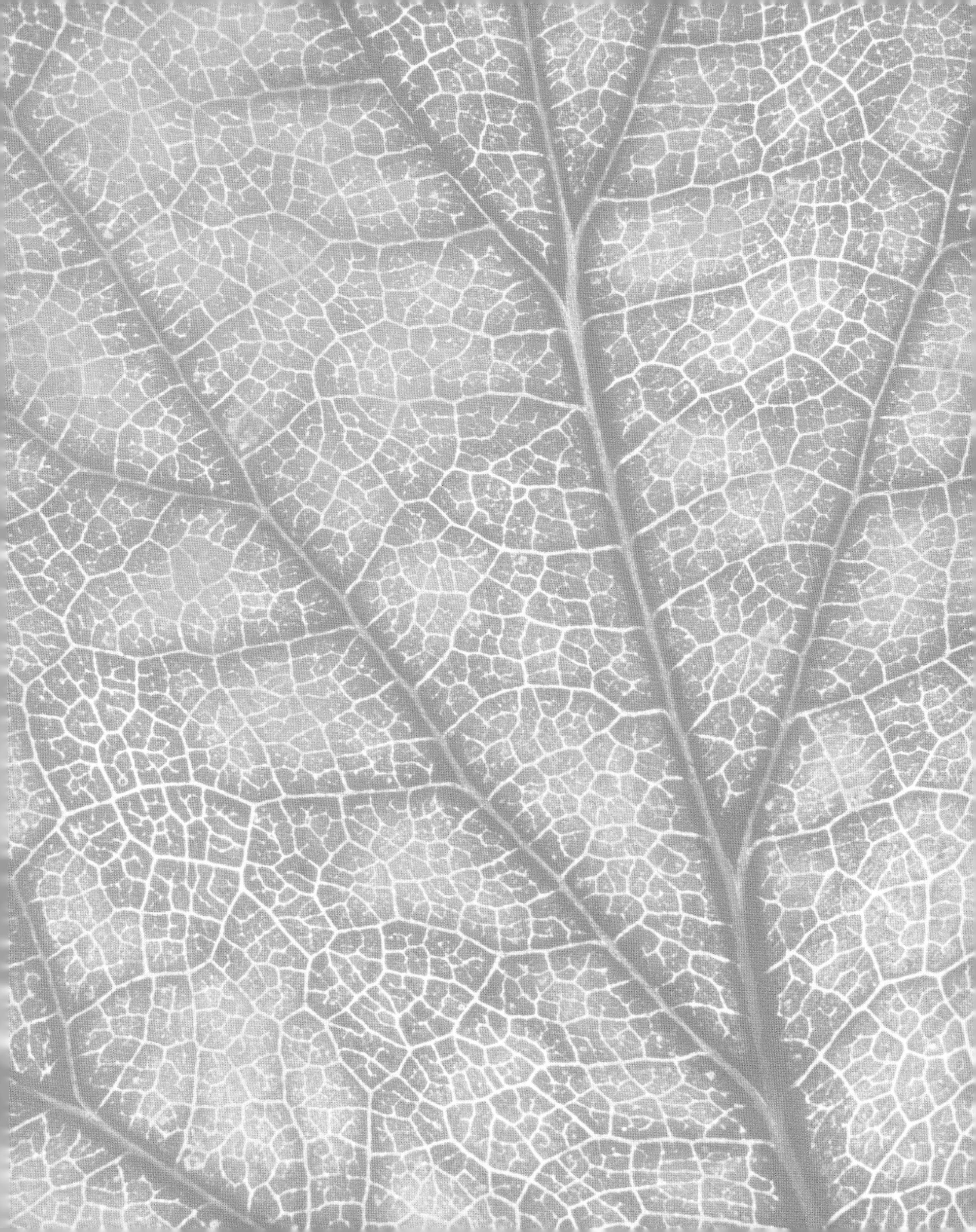

Sehnsucht nach dem Paradies

«Haben Sie einen Garten?»

«Ja, natürlich haben wir einen Garten mit schönem Rasen, sogar ein Biotop gibt es, mit einem Holzbohlensteg darüber, Forsythien und Hibiskus, einige Koniferen, damit auch im Winter etwas Grünes da ist. Den Sitzplatz haben wir mit braun einfärbten Pflastersteinen belegt, die Böschungen sind mit Bodenbedeckern bepflanzt. Anstelle von Betonmauern haben wir Eisenbahnschwellen versetzt, und der Container wird von einem grünen Plastikzaun verdeckt. Nur der Nachbar ärgert uns ein wenig mit seinem Unkrautgarten. Wir haben ja nichts gegen die Natur – sehen Sie unser Biotop an –, aber alles ist eine Frage des Maßes! Ich selber mähe den Rasen, meine Frau jätet, steckt im Herbst die Blumenzwiebeln, und im Winter kommt der Gärtner und schneidet unsere Sträucher.»

«Ich sehe, wir haben uns völlig mißverstanden. Ich habe nach einem Garten gefragt, nach jenem Kunstwerk, von dem Kant gesagt hat, daß es das vollkommenste überhaupt wäre, ich habe nach dem Garten Petrarcas gefragt, nach Orsinis heiligem Wald, nach Le Nôtres Vaux und Lancelot Browns arkadischen Landschaften, nach Müllers Gartenzwerggruppe und Meiers Pflanzensammlung. Ihr Garten und mein Garten haben soviel gemeinsam wie ein Nachtessen bei ‹Burger King› und ‹Chez Max›.»

So wollen wir uns denn, wie Colin Rowe und Fred Koetter[1] empfehlen, auf die Suche nach der suggestiven Kraft der Gärten begeben. Der Garten ist in seiner Form komprimiertes Wunschbild der Welt und somit Versuch der Annäherung an den ersten Garten, das Paradies. Nach Wolfgang Teichert wird jeder, der einen Garten in der realen Welt oder der phantastischen Innenwelt gestaltet, teilhaftig eines mikroskopisch kleinen Bereichs der Weltenschöpfung.[2] Dieser etwas schwülstigen Erklärung wollen wir zunächst die sachliche Tatsache beistellen, daß der Gartenbesitz, die Gartenpflege und -gestaltung immer Zeichen des Besonderen, des kleineren oder grösseren Überflusses, gewesen sind. Denn auch in den düstersten Perioden war er nie ausschließlich der Nützlichkeit, sondern immer auch der Schönheit verpflichtet. Wir können den Garten als Metapher der Ursehnsucht des Men-

---

1 Rowe, Colin und Koetter, Alfred: Collage City. Schriftenreihe gta ETH Zürich. Basel, Boston, Berlin 1984
2 Teichert, Wolfgang: Gärten – Paradiesische Kulturen, Stuttgart 1986

Longing for Paradise

"Do you have a garden?"

"Yes of course, our garden has a well-cared for lawn, even a biotope spanned by a wooden bridge, forsythia and hibiscus, a conifer or two so that there is something green to look at in the winter months. The seating area is laid out with brown-dyed paving stones, the slopes are planted with hardy herbaceous perennials. We have used railway sleepers instead of concrete walls and the refuse container is hidden by a green plastic fence. Of course, our neighbour's garden of weeds is a bit of a nuisance. Not that we have anything against nature – after all we have a biotope – but everything within reason! I mow the lawn, my wife does the weeding, plants bulbs in autumn, and in winter the gardener comes to prune the bushes."

"I see that we have completely misunderstood each other. I asked about a garden, about the work of art about which Kant said that it was the most perfect of all works of art. I asked about the Garden of Petrarcas, about the Holy Forest of Orsini, about Le Nôtre's Vaux and the Arcadian landscapes of Lancelot Brown, about Müller's collection of garden gnomes and Meier's collection of plants. Your garden and my garden have as much in common as dinner at Burger King or Chez Max.

So we want to follow up the suggestion of people such as Colin Rowe and Fred Koetter[1] and embark on a quest to find the suggestive power of gardens. A garden is a condensed ideal of the world, making it an attempt to intimate the first garden ever, namely The Garden of Eden. According to Wolfgang Teichert, anyone who designs a garden in either the physical world or in the world of the imagination is blessed with playing a role in a microscopic part of creation.[2] We would like to begin by accompanying this somewhat pompous interpretation by the far more sober observation that owning a garden, looking after and designing it has always been a sign of having something special, of abundance, be it on a small or large scale. A garden was never, even in darker periods of history, entirely something useful, but always also a matter of aesthetic considerations. We can understand the garden as a metaphor for our longing to return to paradise, to that place of tranquillity and certainty, nurture and

---

1 Rowe, Colin and Koetter Alfred: Collage City, Cambridge Massachusetts 1978
2 Teichert, Wolfgang: Gärten – Paradiesische Kulturen, Stuttgart 1986

schen, der Rückkehr ins Paradies gebrauchen, zu jenem Ort, wo Friede und Geborgenheit, Nahrung und Schönheit sind.

«Gewähre» – so heißt es in einem ägyptischen Totengebet –, «daß ich ein- und ausgehe in meinem Garten, daß ich Wasser trinke aus meinem Teiche jeden Tag, daß ich lustwandle am Ufer ohne Unterlaß, daß meine Seele sich niederlasse auf den Bäumen, die ich gepflanzt, daß ich mich erquicke unter meinen Sykomoren.»

Seit der Vertreibung aus dem Paradies ist der Garten auch Arbeitsort geworden. Es muß gepflanzt, gesät, gegossen, der Garten muß kultiviert werden. Es ist bezeichnend, daß das Wort «Kultur» in seinem etymologischen Ursprung erstmals in Verbindung mit dem Garten auftaucht. In ihm ist also vereint, was der Weltentwurf definiert – Natur und Kultur. Und die Geschichte des Gartens berichtet von nichts anderem als dem wechselhaften Primat von Künstlichkeit oder Natürlichkeit.

Während für Sokrates und Plato der Garten lediglich Hintergrund, Staffage für ihre philosophischen Gespräche bedeutet, wird er spätestens im 18. Jahrhundert selber zum wichtigsten Gegenstand nicht nur der zeitgenössischen Philosophie, sondern auch der gehobenen Gesellschaft. Doch bereits 1661 ist La Fontaine Berichterstatter eines der gewaltigsten Gesamtkunstwerke, des Eröffnungsfestes des Schlosses Vaux-le-Vicomte, von Le Nôtre als Gartenarchitekt, Le Vau als Architekt und Le Brun als Maler gestaltet für Fouquet, den Finanzminister des Königs Louis XIV. Zu diesem Anlaß wurde im Garten Molières «L'Ecole des maris» uraufgeführt. Diese absolutistische Macht- und Prachtentfaltung wird – von England ausgehend – im 18. Jahrhundert durch eine neue Gesellschaftsordnung in Frage gestellt und bekämpft. Und die neue Gartengestaltung – der Englische Landschaftsgarten – stellt diese neue Ordnung dar. Pflanze, Baum und Strauch werden nicht mehr gezähmt, geschnitten, in Formen gepreßt, sie sollen sich ebenso wie der Mensch frei entfalten und wachsen können. Rousseau betreibt in seinem Roman «Julie ou la Nouvelle Héloïse» radikale Gesellschaftskritik und entwirft eine Utopie, in der Gesellschaft und Natur miteinander ausgesöhnt sind und ein arkadisches Ideal seine Verwirklichung findet. Und Goethes Wahlverwandtschaften, eine Auseinandersetzung mit der Sittengeschichte, wird bildhaft eingebettet in den Widerstreit zwischen Barockgarten und Englischem Landschaftsgarten. Durch das unangefochtene Primat der «Englischen Landschafts-

beauty. "Grant" – an Egyptian prayer for the dead says – "that I enter and leave my garden, that I drink water from my pond every day, that I stroll along river banks as I please, that my soul rests on trees that I have planted, that I find refreshment under my sycamores."

The garden has become a workplace since the expulsion from Paradise. Planting, sowing, watering – in other words, the garden is a place in need of constant care. It is indicative that the etymological origin of the word "culture" first occurs in connection with the garden. In other words, it combines the universal definition, namely nature and culture. And all history of gardens bears witness to the changing primacy of the artificial and the natural.

Whereas Socrates and Plato only see the garden as a backdrop, "window dressing" for their philosophical discourse, it becomes a major subject not only of contemporary philosophy but also of sophisticated society by the 18th century at the latest. And even earlier, in 1661, La Fontaine gives an account of one of the most magnificent gesamtkunstwerk, the opening of Vaux-le-Vicomte with Le Nôtre as its garden architect, Le Vau as the architect and Le Brun as the painter – designed for Fouquet, the finance minister of King Louis XIV. The occasion was marked by the first performance of Molière's "L'Ecole des maris" in the garden. This absolutist display of power and pomp is – England led the way – called into question and challenged in the 18th century by a new social order. A new form of garden design – the English landscape garden – embodies this new order. Plants, trees and shrubs are no longer tamed, clipped, forced into forms – they are, just like human beings, to be able to develop and grow freely. Rousseau's novel "Julie ou la Nouvelle Héloïse" is highly critical of society and develops a utopia in which society and nature are at one and an Arcadian ideal is realised. And Goethe's "Wahlverwandtschaften", a discourse on the history of life and customs, has the conflict between the Baroque garden and the English landscape garden as its vivid setting. The undisputed primacy of the "English landscape garden" in the 19th century means the end of society's interest in the garden. Its magnificent peak gives way to a slumber – and we cannot today say whether this is still its state or it has indeed been awakened by the "gardens of the hundreds of thousands". Industrialisation and urbanisation are the causes of the miserable housing condi-

gartenkonzeption» im 19. Jahrhundert bedingt, versiegt das gesellschaftliche Interesse am Garten. Sein glanzvoller Höhepunkt geht über in einen Dornröschenschlaf, von dem wir nicht genau wissen, ob er bis heute anhält oder ob er doch geweckt wurde von den «Gärten der Hunderttausend».

Industrialisierung und Verstädterung haben das Wohnungselend der breiten Bevölkerung verursacht. Gartenstadt-, Schrebergartenbewegung und Volksparke werden zu Hoffnungsträgern und Heilmitteln erkoren. Die «Gärten der Hunderttausend» fordert Leberecht Migge und liefert zu Beginn des 20. Jahrhunderts bemerkenswerte ökologische und gestalterische Beispiele. Aus Gartenbau und Gartenkunst entwickelt sich – so Migge – eine neue Gartenkultur, die Laie und Fachmann gemeinsam vorantreiben müssen. Der intensiv genutzte architektonische Garten einerseits und die großen, einfach gestalteten Volksparke anderseits sind nicht nur zur Selbstversorgung, zu Spiel, Sport und Erholung, sondern auch zu einer neuen politischen Bestimmung geeignet.

Nach den vielversprechenden Gärten, die Gustav Ammann bei den Bauten der Moderne (z.B. Werkbundsiedlung Neubühl oder Kunstgewerbeschule Zürich) gestaltet hat, verbreitet sich schnell der beliebige, heimattümlerisch angehauchte Wohngartenstil mit seinen weiten Rasenflächen, den locker verteilten Bäumen, Blumen und den Goldfischteichen. Der Bauerngarten erlebt seine Wiedergeburt an der Schweizerischen Landesausstellung, Landi 1939.

Vor diesem Hintergrund bedeutet die G|59, die Erste Schweizerische Gartenbauausstellung, einen gewaltigen Paukenschlag. Allen voran Ernst Cramers «Garten des Poeten», eines der ersten Beispiele einer Kunstrichtung, die wir mittlerweile unter dem Namen Land Art kennen. Cramer bricht mit der eigenen Vergangenheit und erreicht mit der extremen Reduktion von Formen und Materialien – Betonplatten, Rasenpyramiden und Wasserbecken – ein bemerkenswertes Gartenkunstwerk. Das oberste Prinzip der Garten- und Landschaftsgestaltung – die Harmonisierung der Welt, die Eingliederung und Verschönerung von Bauwerken in Garten und Landschaft – wird in Frage gestellt. Cramers nachfolgende Arbeiten bestätigen seine Radikalität. Die Plätze werden hart, die Pflanzenvielfalt auf wenige, dafür massenweise eingesetzte Arten reduziert. Sein Beispiel macht Schule bei Gärtnern und Gartenarchitekten, die darin je-

tions of the masses. Hopes are pinned on remedies in the form of the garden city and garden colony movements, and the volksparks (people's parks). Leberecht Migge calls for the "gardens of the hundreds of thousands" and provides remarkable ecological and design examples at the beginning of the 20th century. According to Migge, horticulture and garden art give rise to a new garden culture which both amateurs and experts are called upon to develop. The garden which is elaborate architecturally and is used intensively, on the one hand, and the swathes of the volksparks, simple in their means of design, on the other hand, are not only suited to self-sufficiency, play, sport and recreation but also to a new political definition.

The promising gardens which Gustav Ammann designed in connection with modernist buildings (e.g. the Neubühl Werkbund estate based on reformist aesthetic principles or the Zurich School of Crafts) are rapidly followed by an arbitrary, domestic garden style with sentimental tendencies, with expanses of lawn, scattered trees, flowers and goldfish ponds. The cottage garden experiences its renaissance at the Swiss Exhibition in Landi in 1939.

It is against this background that the G|59, the first Swiss Horticultural Show, comes as a thunderbolt. Above all, Ernst Cramer's Poet's Garden is one of the first examples of what has become known as Land Art. Cramer abandons the tradition of garden art and uses an extreme reduction of forms and materials – concrete slabs, lawn pyramids and water pools – to achieve a remarkable work of garden art. The overriding principle of garden and landscape design – harmonising the world, enhancing buildings by incorporating them into gardens and landscape – is called into question. Cramer's subsequent works confirm his radical approach. The surfaces become hard, the diversity of plants reduced to just a few species, which are used en masse.

His example is followed by gardeners and garden architects, who, however, are not so much interested in realising his artistic ideas but see them as a way of saving time and effort, and covering up their lack of knowledge of plants. Architects have also recognised the advantages: absence of horticultural knowledge is glossed over by references to the new garden idea when it comes to designing the surroundings. And tree nurseries abandon the wide range of plants requiring intensive care in favour of just a few robust, mass-produced species. The result is that

doch weniger das künstlerische Konzept, sondern die Ersparnis an Aufwand, Zeit und Pflanzenkenntnissen verwirklichen zu können meinen. Auch die Architekten haben die Gunst der Stunde erkannt, mangelnde Pflanzenkenntnisse bei der Gestaltung der Umgebung werden mit dem Hinweis auf die neue Gartenkonzeption überdeckt. Und in den Baumschulen wird das gärtnerisch anspruchsvolle, vielfältige und aufwendige Sortiment zugunsten der robusten Massenware weniger Pflanzenarten aufgegeben. Und somit pervertierte die ehemals hervorragende gartenkünstlerische Konzeption zur Landplage des pflegeleichten, aseptischen Einheitsgrüns von Balkonkiste, Garten und Park.

Wir haben gelernt, daß Gärten Zustandsbeschreibungen gesellschaftlicher Situationen sind. Sie geben uns Aufschluß über das Verhältnis des Menschen zur Natur. Und so ist auch die «Ökologiebewegung» mit ihrem Beginn in den siebziger Jahren in die Diskussion der Gartengestaltung eingeschlossen. Der Garten hat einmal mehr als bildhaftes Zeichen einer gesellschaftlichen Veränderung Vorreiterstellung eingenommen. Zu einer Zeit, als das Waldsterben noch kein Thema war, wurde bereits leidenschaftlich über das Für und Wider des «Naturgartens» diskutiert.

Von alters her ist der Schutzgedanke immer ein prägendes Element des Gartens gewesen. Das Gewöhnliche außerhalb, das Besondere innerhalb des Gartens wird von Naturgärtnern wie Urs Schwarz oder Louis Le Roy zeitgemäß interpretiert. Außerhalb sind die bedrohlich naturferne Land- und Forstwirtschaft, der Asphalt und Beton unserer Städte und Dörfer, und innerhalb des Gartens finden wir die geschützte Natur. Magnolie, Blautanne und Bambus sind die neuen Feinde des Gartens, während Brennessel, Wegerich und Schlehe als schützenswert erklärt werden.

Natur ist in unserer hochtechnisierten Welt zur begehrten Rarität geworden. Die «gute Form» als höchste Auszeichnung wird abgelöst durch das Prädikat «Natürlichkeit». Und damit läßt sich einiges anfangen. In der Werbung beispielsweise. Der natürliche Föhrenduft aus der Dose schafft Frische auf der Toilette, das Vogelgezwitscher in der Autobahnunterführung beglückt uns auf dem Weg zur Raststätte, Camel schmeckt unvergleichlich im wilden Canyon. Die unbefriedigte Sehnsucht nach Natur, nach Zeugnissen vergangener Lebens- und Arbeitsformen verlangt offenbar nach dieser Scheinwelt, die wir im Hochhausre-

what had once been an excellent garden art idea is degraded to the bane of the easy-care, aseptic standard greenery of window boxes, gardens and parks.

We have leant that gardens reflect the state of society. They reveal the relationship of human beings to nature. And the "ecology movement", which had its beginnings in the nineteen-seventies is also part of the discussion on garden design. Once again, the garden assumes a pioneering role as a visible sign of a change in society. There was passionate discussion on the pros and cons of the "natural garden" at a time when nobody was talking about forests dying from pollution.

The notion of protection has always been a central element of the garden. Creators of natural gardens such as Urs Schwarz or Louis le Roy give contemporary interpretation to what is ordinary outside the garden and what is special inside. What is outside is the menacingly unnatural in the form of agriculture and forestry, the asphalt and concrete of our towns and villages, and within the garden we find protected nature. Magnolia, blue spruce, and bamboo are the new enemies of the garden, whereas the stinging nettle, plantain, and sloe are considered to be worthy of protection.

Nature has become a sought-after rarity in our highly technological world. "Good form" as the highest accolade is replaced by "naturalness". And this opens the door to a number of things. For example in the world of advertising. The natural smell of pine in an aerosol creates a pleasant odour in the WC, the twittering of birds in the motorway underpass makes us feel happy as we make our way to the service area. A Camel smoked in a remote canyon tastes so much better. The unfulfilled yearning for nature, for testimony to past forms of living and working evidently requires this pretend world which we find in the highrise restaurant with cow-shed ambience, in the dryer decorated with geraniums or in the artificially created picture of naturalness in the garden.

Whereas the artificiality of naturalness was a central theme of the English landscape garden and in a figurative sense was shown and discussed in a new way, natural gardening contents itself with a direct representation of the image of nature. Good old mother nature provides the new beauty ideal of the garden. If this is not possible due to technical considerations, rustic processing methods of "natural" materials are resorted to. Visible

staurant mit Kuhstallambiente, in der geranienbepflanzten Wäscheschleuder oder eben im künstlich erstellten Bild von Natürlichkeit im Garten wiederfinden.

Während im Englischen Landschaftsgarten die Künstlichkeit der Natürlichkeit thematisiert und im übertragenen Sinne neu dargestellt und diskutiert wird, begnügt sich die Naturgärtnerei mit der direkten Darstellung des Naturbilds. Mütterchen Natur liefert das neue Schönheitsideal des Gartens. Wenn dieses aufgrund technischer Randbedingungen nicht ausreicht, wird auf rustikale Verarbeitungsmethoden «natürlicher» Materialien zurückgegriffen. Sichtbare Künstlichkeit, Gestaltgebung, ist verpönt, die Gerade gottlos und Beton das Grundübel der Welt. Wert gelegt wird auf die Zurschaustellung besonders exquisiter Naturbilder: die Wildnis des Urwalds, der plätschernde Bach, der schilfbestandene See, die blühende Alpwiese. Weil die natürlichen Voraussetzungen fehlen, müssen sie künstlich hergestellt werden. Und gleichzeitig gilt es, diese Künstlichkeit möglichst gut zu verdecken. Als «Öko-Design» wollen wir diese Art der Gartengestaltung bezeichnen, die sich am Bild der Natur orientiert, ohne daß das Bild etwas mit der Wesenhaftigkeit der Situation zu tun hat.

Das liebliche Feuchtbiotop auf der unterirdischen Tiefgarage, der malerisch plazierte, abgestorbene, von weither geholte Baumstamm und der versteckte Zufluß von Leitungswasser widersprechen dem Prinzip der Lesbarkeit der Welt, sind entgegen ihres natürlichen Aussehens von hoher Künstlichkeit.

Es ist ein Gemeinplatz, daß das Auskernen von Häusern keinen Beitrag zum Architektur- bzw. Geschichtsverständnis zu leisten vermag, weil die Fassade nichts mehr mit den Strukturmerkmalen des Gebäudes zu tun hat. Öko-Design, z.B. in Form des Feuchtbiotops auf der Tiefgarage, ist dem ausgekernten Haus gleichzusetzen. Es zeigt uns eine Fassade bzw. ein Bild, das nicht mehr mit der Wesenhaftigkeit der Situation übereinstimmt. Und damit wendet sich der vorerst lobenswerte Ansatz der Naturgärtnerei – die Bevölkerung zu einem neuen Umweltbewusstsein zu führen – gegen sich selbst.

Die strikte Ablehnung nicht einheimischer oder gar gezüchteter Pflanzen im Garten stellt letztlich die Arbeit des jahrhundertealten Gärtnerhandwerks und damit auch die Gartenkultur selbst in Frage. Daß die Züchtungen auch – im eigentlichen Wortsinn – seltsame Blüten hervorgebracht haben, sei damit kei-

artificiality, design is frowned upon, a straight line is sacrilege and concrete the root of all evil in this world. What is considered important is displaying particularly exquisite images of nature: the wildness of the jungle, the babbling brook, the pool surrounded by reeds, the carpet of alpine flowers. As the natural pre-conditions are lacking, they have to be created artificially while, at the same time, concealing this artificiality as far as possible. Let us call this way of creating a garden the "eco-design", a design which takes nature as its model without it having anything to do with the essence of the situation.

The charming wet biotope on the underground garage, the dead tree trunk, obtained from somewhere quite different and placed with loving care, and the concealed supply of mains water are in conflict with the comprehensibility of the world, are, contradicting with their semblance of being natural, actually highly artificial.

It is a commonplace that removing the interior structures of buildings does not contribute anything to understanding of architecture or history as the façade no longer has anything in common with the structural features of the building. Eco-design, e.g. in the form of a wet biotope on the underground garage, is tantamount to the building from which the core has been removed. It shows us a façade, i.e. an image that has nothing more whatsoever in common with the essential character of the situation. And what this means is that the initially so laudable approach adopted by natural gardening – namely giving people a new awareness of their environment – is directed against itself.

Strict rejection of non-native, let alone cultivated plants in the garden ultimately calls into question the work of centuries of the art of gardening and, by the same logic, garden culture itself. This is by no means to say that the strains have not produced strange flowers not only figuratively but also literally. Nobody will call into question the advantages of a "Bernese rose apple" over a wild apple. The robinia introduced into Europe from America by Vesbasian Robin in 1635 is a better tree for urban streets than the native beech. And, to be honest, most of us enjoy eating potatoes from time to time.

When we reflect on these matters, we arrive at the conclusion that a good deal of restorative body of thought belongs to the progressiveness of natural gardening. Incidentally, an equiv-

neswegs negiert. Es wird jedoch niemand den Vorzug eines «Berner Rosenapfels» gegenüber dem Wildapfel in Zweifel ziehen. Die von Vespasian Robin 1635 aus Amerika eingeführte Robinie eignet sich in unseren Stadtstraßen besser als die einheimische Buche. Und gelegentlich essen wir ganz gern Kartoffeln.

Über diese Dinge nachdenkend, kommen wir zur Einsicht, daß sich zur Fortschrittlichkeit der Naturgärtnerei auch ein gehöriges Stück restaurativen Gedankenguts gesellt. Eine Entsprechung übrigens, die wir bei der Ökologiebewegung auch in ihrem Verhältnis zur zeitgenössischen Kunst wiederfinden. Hier steht der zukunftsorientierten Gesinnung in gesellschaftlichen Fragen eine durch Unkenntnis und unkritische Rezeption gekennzeichnete, konservative Haltung in kulturellen Fragen gegenüber.

Die Bedeutung des Gartens als Ort der Arbeit, der Muße, der Erholung, als Zeichen eines mehr oder weniger großen Überflusses wird in unserem Land weiter zunehmen. Er ist Gegenwelt zu einer immer weiter technisierten, fremdbestimmten Gesellschaft. Wie das Bild im Zimmer nicht unbedingt notwendig ist, wir es aber trotzdem brauchen, so wird der Garten verstärkt zum Sinnbild unserer aktuellen Bedürfnisse, Sehnsüchte und Hoffnungen.

Die Zeichen dafür gewinnen an Kontur. Trotz alarmierender Schadstoffmeldungen ist die Nachfrage nach Kleingärten groß. Die Künstler verlassen das Atelier und setzen sich mit Garten-Kunst-Natur auseinander. Bei Schriftstellern und Philosophen wird der Garten zum Gegenstand ihrer Arbeit, seit den neuen Plätzen und Gärten in Barcelona, seit La Villette und Castel Grande ist die Gartengestaltung auch bei Architekten wieder hoffähig geworden. Die Ausbildungsstätten für Landschaftsarchitekten erreichen Höchstzahlen, und, last but not least, auch Hochparterre, worin dieser Beitrag erscheint, beginnt sich für den Garten zu interessieren.

Eine Erneuerung der Gartenkultur ist nicht ein formales, sondern ein inhaltliches Problem. Den Unterschied zwischen banalem, pflegeleichtem Abstandsgrün, sich selbst überlassener Urwüchsigkeit und Garten macht dessen tragfähiges Konzept, seine Partitur oder Vision aus. Der Garten muß wieder zum Bedeutungsträger werden, er soll unser Bewußtsein schärfen und die Sinne wecken. Nicht die Pflegeleichtigkeit, sondern die Pflegebedürftigkeit steht im Vordergrund. Dabei ist die physische

alent that we also find in the ecological movement in its relationship to contemporary art. Here, a forward-looking way of thinking in terms of societal questions is confronted by a conservative attitude on cultural questions marked by ignorance and uncritical adoption.

The significance of the garden as a place of work, of contemplation, of relaxation, as a sign of abundance will continue to increase to a greater of lesser degree in our country. The garden is the counter-world to a society which is increasingly influenced by technology and factors over which it has no control. Just like the picture in a room is not really necessary, but we need it nonetheless, the garden is increasingly becoming a symbol of our present needs, yearnings and hopes.

The indications of this are increasing. The demand for small gardens is great despite all the alarming reports about pollutants. Artists are leaving their studios to enter into dialogue with the questions posed by garden-art-nature. The garden is becoming part of the work of writers and philosopher; since the new squares and gardens in Barcelona, since La Villette and Castel Grande garden art has again become acceptable for architects. The training institutions for landscape architects are recording records and, last but not least, Hochparterre, where this article has been published, is beginning to be interested in the garden.

Revival of garden culture is not a formal problem but one of content. A viable idea, its score or vision are what make the difference between banal, easy-care, partitioned areas of greenery, an area of "nature" left to its own devices, and a garden. What matters is that the garden once again becomes a place of meaning, it should sharpen our awareness and arouse our senses. Emphasis should be on its need for attentive care not easy care. Physical work is only one aspect, the other is dialogue, one is tempted to say sympathy for and involvement with this strange object that we call a garden. Having a garden is not primarily defined by the size of the plot of land but also by the extent of the approach to it. This can take place just as well as in a public urban garden as in a front garden, a small garden or the prestigious garden of a detached house.

The garden is the last remaining luxury of our time as it demands something which has become rare and precious in our society: time, attention and space. It is the representative of na-

Arbeit nur ein Teil, der andere ist die Auseinandersetzung, man könnte auch sagen die Anteilnahme mit oder an diesem merkwürdigen Ding, zu dem wir Garten sagen. Dessen Besitz definiert sich nicht primär über eine bestimmte Grundstücksgröße, sondern auch über den Grad der Auseinandersetzung mit ihm. Das ist im öffentlichen Stadtgarten ebenso möglich wie im Vorgarten, dem Kleingarten oder dem repräsentativen Einfamilienhausgarten.

Der Garten ist der letzte Luxus unserer Tage, denn er fordert das, was in unserer Gesellschaft am seltensten und kostbarsten geworden ist: Zeit, Zuwendung und Raum. Er ist Stellvertreter der Natur, in dem wir Geist, Wissen und Handwerk wieder gebrauchen im sorgsamen Umgang mit der Welt und ihrem Mikrokosmos, dem Garten. Veränderte gesellschaftliche Wertvorstellungen bewirken die Gartenrenaissance. Anstelle der Ferienreise auf die Seychellen wird der Vorgarten umgestaltet. Auf die maximale Grundstücksausnutzung wird zugunsten des Freiraums verzichtet. Die Vernissage findet im Garten statt. Und anstelle von small talk wird über die Keramikgrotte oder die besonders gelungene Farbkombination des Staudenbeets diskutiert.

Und so flanieren wir im Garten, geniessen die schattige Kühle der alten Bäume, die verzauberte Wildnis von Holunder, Sommerflieder und Natternkopf, lassen uns vom unvergleichlichen Jasminduft betören, lauschen dem plätschernden Springbrunnen, kosten von der taufrischen Traube, träumen unter dem Apfelbaum, durchschreiten den Rosenbogen, betreten die sonnige Terrasse und atmen kräftig durch.

«Möchten Sie einen Garten?»

Dieter Kienast

ture, where we again use mind, knowledge, and manual skills in a careful approach to the world and its microcosm, namely the garden. Changes in social values are bringing about the renaissance of the garden. Redesigning the front garden replaces the holiday on the Seychelles. Maximum utilisation of the plot is waived in favour of open space. The gallery preview takes place in the garden and small talk is replaced by a discussion on the ceramic grotto or the particularly successful colour combination of the herbaceous borders.

And it is on this note that we stroll through the garden, enjoy the shade provided by the mature trees, the fascinating wilderness created by elderberries, buddleiea and echium, are almost overpowered by the unbelievable scent of mock orange, delight in the patter of the water from the fountain, enjoy grapes fresh from the vine, dream as we sit under the apple tree, stride through the rose-tree trellis, sit down on a sunlit terrace and take a deep breath of fresh air.

"Do you want to have a garden?"

Dieter Kienast

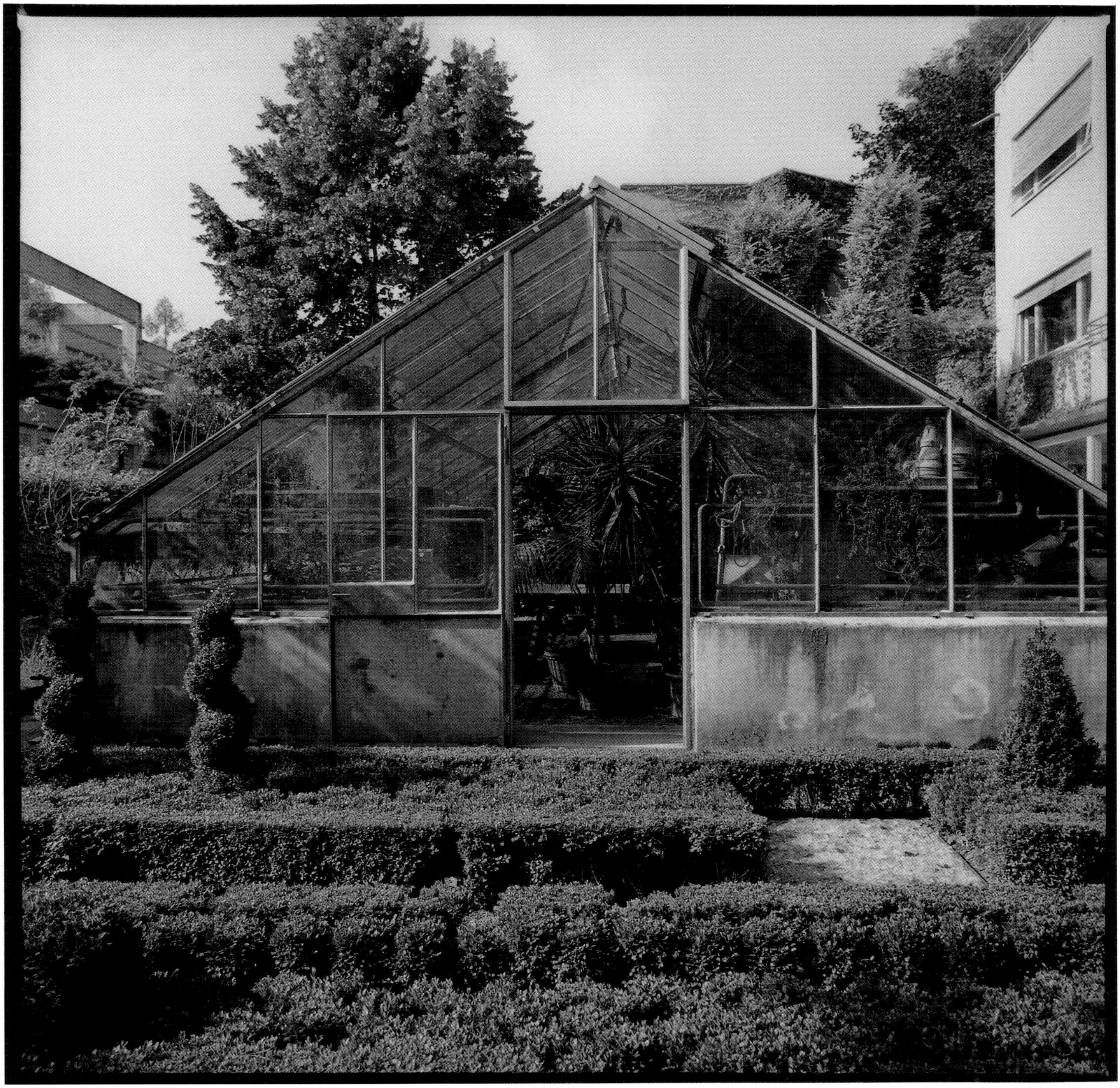

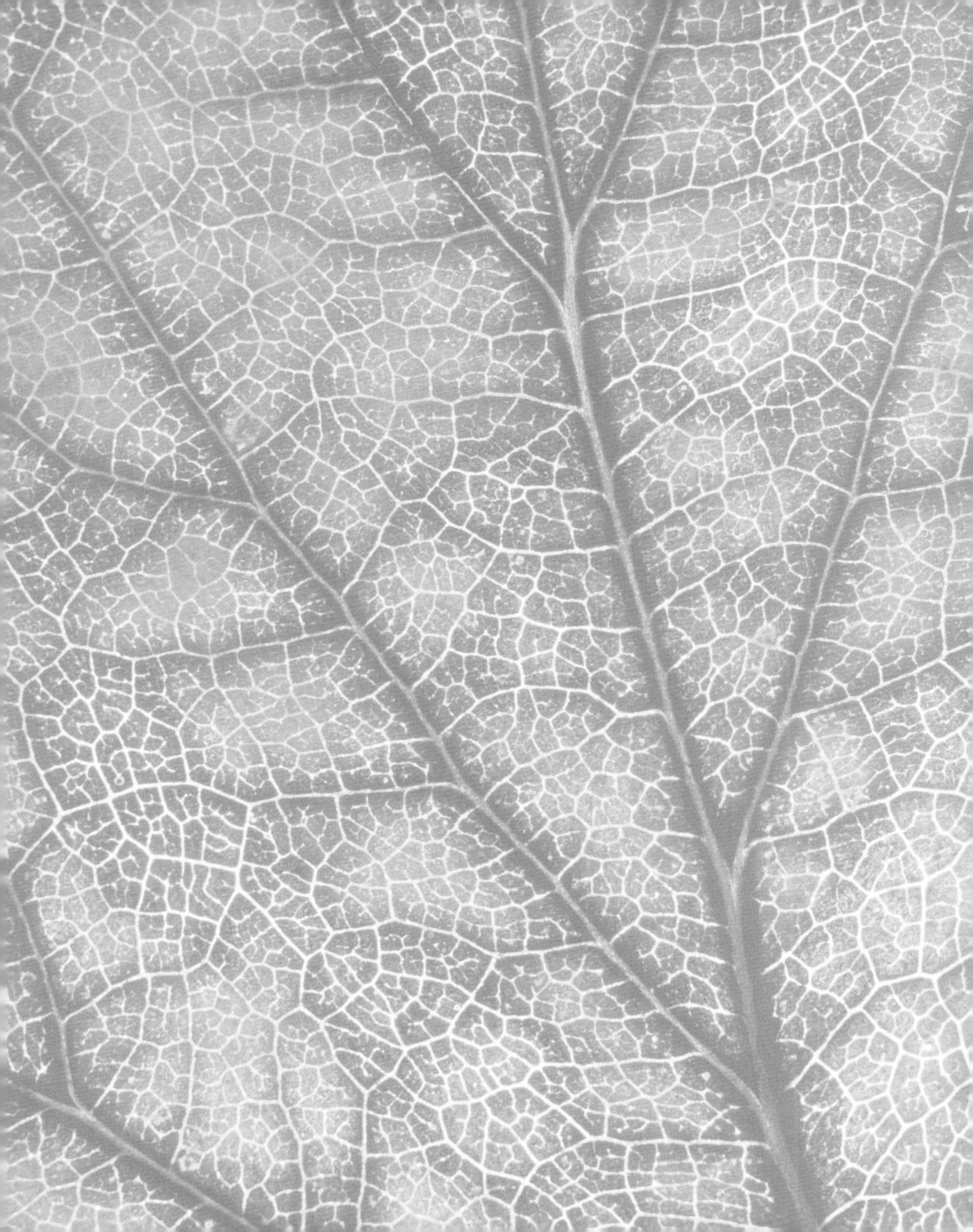

Stadtpark Wettingen

Der öffentliche Garten

Bei der Gestaltung des Stadtparks wird an die Konzeption des Volksparks zu Beginn des 20. Jahrhunderts angeknüpft. Diese zielt auf eine einfache und markante Raumbildung, die mit ihrer Ausstattung intensive, spielerische und sportliche Aktivitäten ermöglicht. Der Park entwickelte sich so vom Ort des sonntäglichen Lustwandelns zu einem Ort alltäglichen Gebrauchs und zur aktiven Erholung.

Die Einfachheit und Kraft der wenigen eingesetzten Elemente im Stadtpark Wettingen bestimmt die Raumfolge und Stimmung des zentral im Siedlungsgebiet und direkt neben dem Rathaus gelegenen Areals, das vorher als Fußballplatz genutzt wurde. Während für die gleichzeitig an anderer Stelle errichtete Sportanlage viel Geld bereitgestellt wurde, standen für den Stadtpark nur knapp bemessene Finanzierungsmittel zur Verfügung. Wir nahmen dies weniger als unangenehme Einschränkung, sondern vielmehr als Leitlinie zum sorgsamen Umgang mit dem Bestand und sparsamen Einsatz der gartenarchitektonischen Interventionen.

Die vorhandene Ebene mit dem Grasteil des ehemaligen Fußballfeldes wurde unverändert belassen. Dem Wunsch nach einer Rodelgelegenheit ist mit geometrisch geformten Erdhügeln entsprochen worden, die im Dialog zum sichtbaren «Lägernrucken» stehen. Auf den Erdhügeln entwickelt sich langsam eine Magerwiese. Die Hügel werden so auf verschiedenen Ebenen «lesbar». Durch die geometrische Ausformung wird das Artefakt deutlich, die naturnahe Vegetation überlagert die künstliche Hügelgestaltung und stellt unter Beweis, daß naturnahe Vegetation nicht auf eine naturalisierende Topographie angewiesen ist.

Der Parkwald bildet den raumdefinierenden Abschluß, das Gegenüber zum Rathaus. Unter dem forstmäßig angepflanzten Mischwald entwickelt sich in Übereinstimmung mit Standort und Nutzung eine Waldbodenvegetation. Aus dem Schatten und der Kühle des Wäldchens tritt der Besucher auf den hellen, zentralen Platz. Das runde Wasser- und Planschbecken liegt im Schnittpunkt der Rathaus- und Parkachse. Auf Blumenbeete

Urban Park in Wettingen

The public garden

The design of the urban park is based on the concept of the "Volkspark" as it existed at the beginning of the 20th century. This was a design aimed at achieving simple and distinctive space, with facilities permitting intensive use, play and sports activities. The park was transformed from a place for Sunday walks to a place of daily use and active recreation.

The simplicity and expressiveness of the few elements used in the Wettingen Urban Park determine the spatial sequence and atmosphere of this area – a site which once served as a football pitch – located in the centre of the settlement directly adjacent to the town hall. Whereas substantial amounts of money were made available for the sports facilities built elsewhere, only modest sums were set aside for the urban park. We conceived this not so much as an unwelcome restriction, but more as a guideline for a conservative approach to existing stocks and sparing use of interventions in the garden architecture.

The existing level consisting of the grass area of the former football pitch was not changed. The desire for a toboggan run was realised in the form of geometrical mounds forming a dialogue with the visible "Lägernrucken". A poor-nutrient meadow is developing slowly on the hillocks, making them "readable" on a number of different levels. The artefact is given definition by its geometrical shape, the semi-natural vegetation covering the artificial hill design is proof that semi-natural vegetation does not depend upon naturalising topography.

The park's wood provides spatial definition, forming the counterpoint to the town hall. Woodland floor vegetation reflecting location and use is developing under the mixed wood that has been planted as a forest. Visitors emerging from the shade and cool of the small wood arrive at the light, central area. The circular pool and wading area lies at the intersection of the town hall and park axes. Flowerbeds were dispensed with and, instead, columns of climbing roses and clematis placed at the main entrance. Hedges framing areas set aside for play and games complete the park, making this an inviting place for recreational activities.

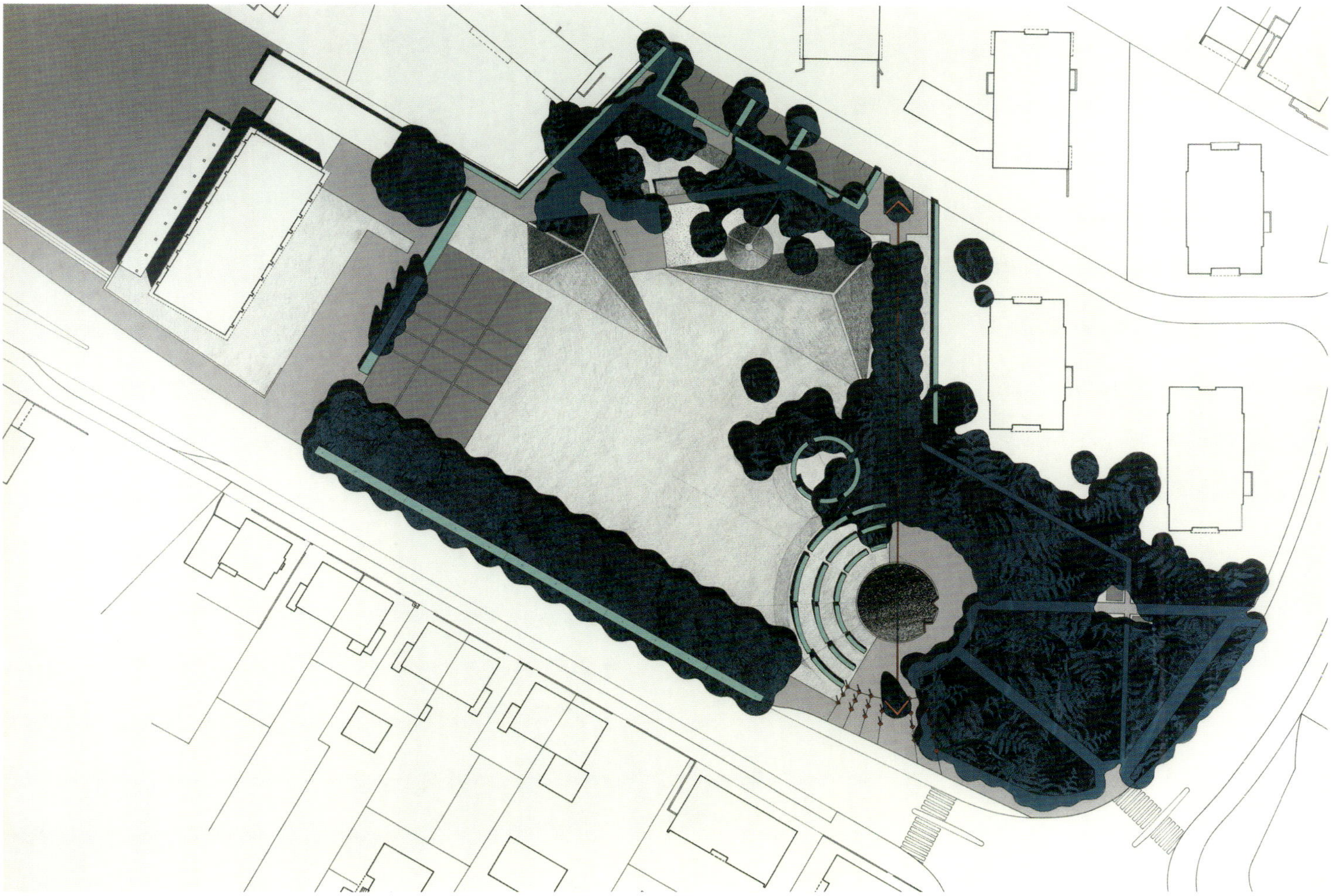

wurde verzichtet. Anstelle dessen wurden beim Haupteingang Pflanzsäulen mit Kletterrosen und Clematis plaziert. Hecken gegen die Spielwiese bilden den räumlichen Abschluß und reizen zum Spiel.

Eine dreistämmige Lindenallee entlang dem Gehweg grenzt den Park gegen die Straße ab. Eine Pappelschicht vor dem Rathaus verhindert den direkten Sichtkontakt. Es war unser Bestreben, einen alterungsfähigen, einfachen Stadtpark zu gestalten, der vielfältige Nutzungen ermöglicht. Der Beginn war wenig ermutigend: Bereits beim Bau wurde in Zeitungsartikeln die Unbrauchbarkeit der Hügel prophezeit und eine naturalisierende Ausformung verlangt. Fehlende Blumenfülle wurde ebenso beklagt wie die Baumalleen und Hecken Mißfallen erregten.

Nach 15jährigem Gebrauch haben sich die anfänglichen Aufregungen gelegt. Der Park hat sich dem Alltagsgebrauch geöffnet und ist, trotz einigen unnötigen nachträglichen Applikationen, zu einem einprägsamen Ort im diffusen Siedlungsraum geworden.

Dieter Kienast

A three-row avenue of lime trees along the paths separates the park from the road. A direct view of the town hall is obscured by the poplar trees planted in front of it. It was our aim to design a simple urban park capable of aging and useable for a wide variety of purposes. The beginnings of the project were not very encouraging. During the building phase, newspaper articles were published predicting that the hillocks would be unusable and calling for a naturalising approach. The lack of extensive flowerbeds was criticised as were the avenue of trees and the hedges.

The park has now been in existence for fifteen years and initial scepticism forgotten. The park is a place available for day-to-day use and has, despite a few superfluous subsequent additions, become a distinctive place in a diffuse settlement area.

Dieter Kienast

Hecken bilden den räumlichen Abschluß gegen die Spielwiese.

The grassy areas intended for games and play are framed by hedges.

Die geometrisch geformten Erdhügel stehen im Dialog zum Lägernrucken.

The geometrical earth-mounds address the Lägernrucken.

Im Schnittpunkt der Rathaus- und Parkachse liegt das runde Wasserbecken.

The circular pool is at the intersection of the town hall and parks axes.

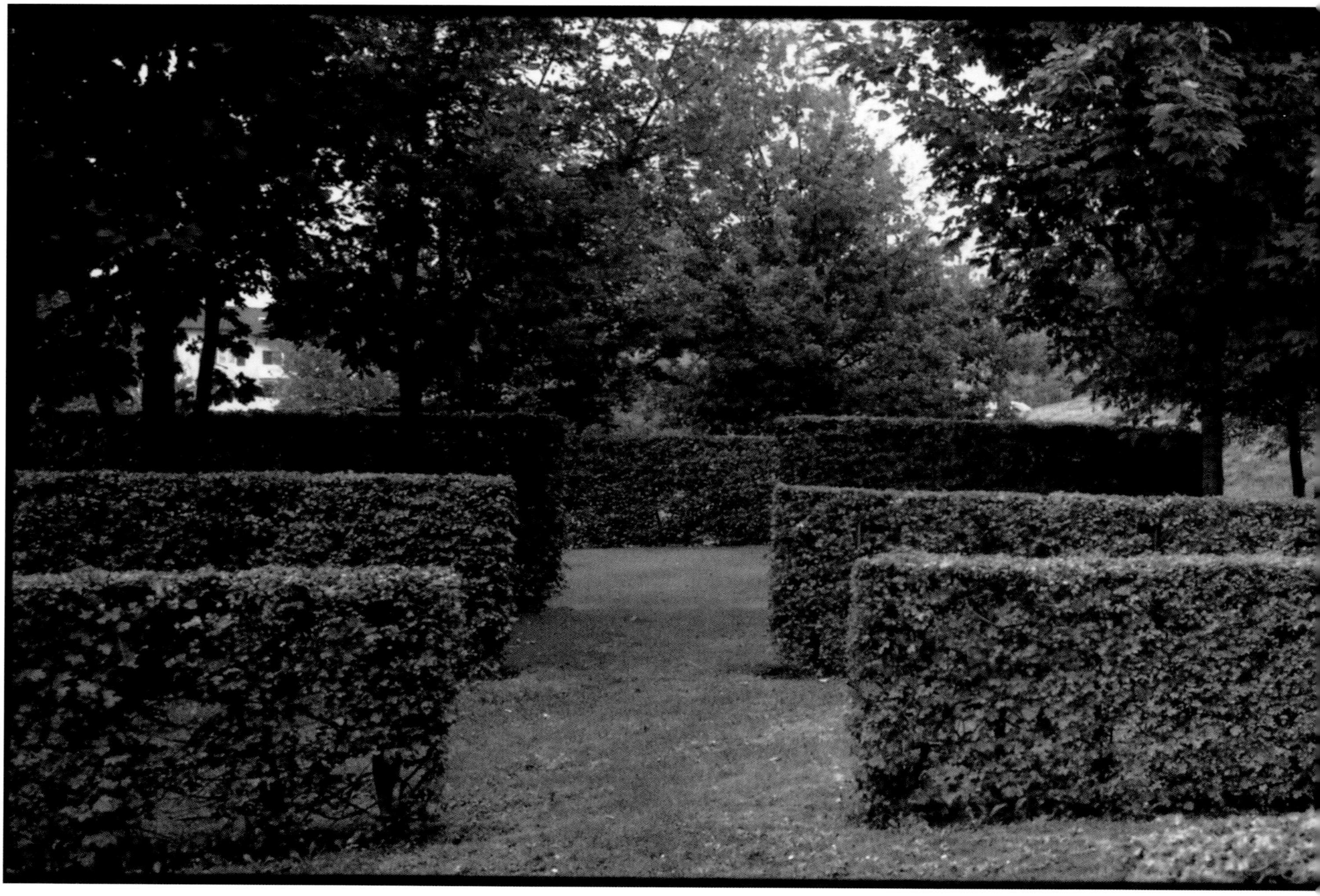

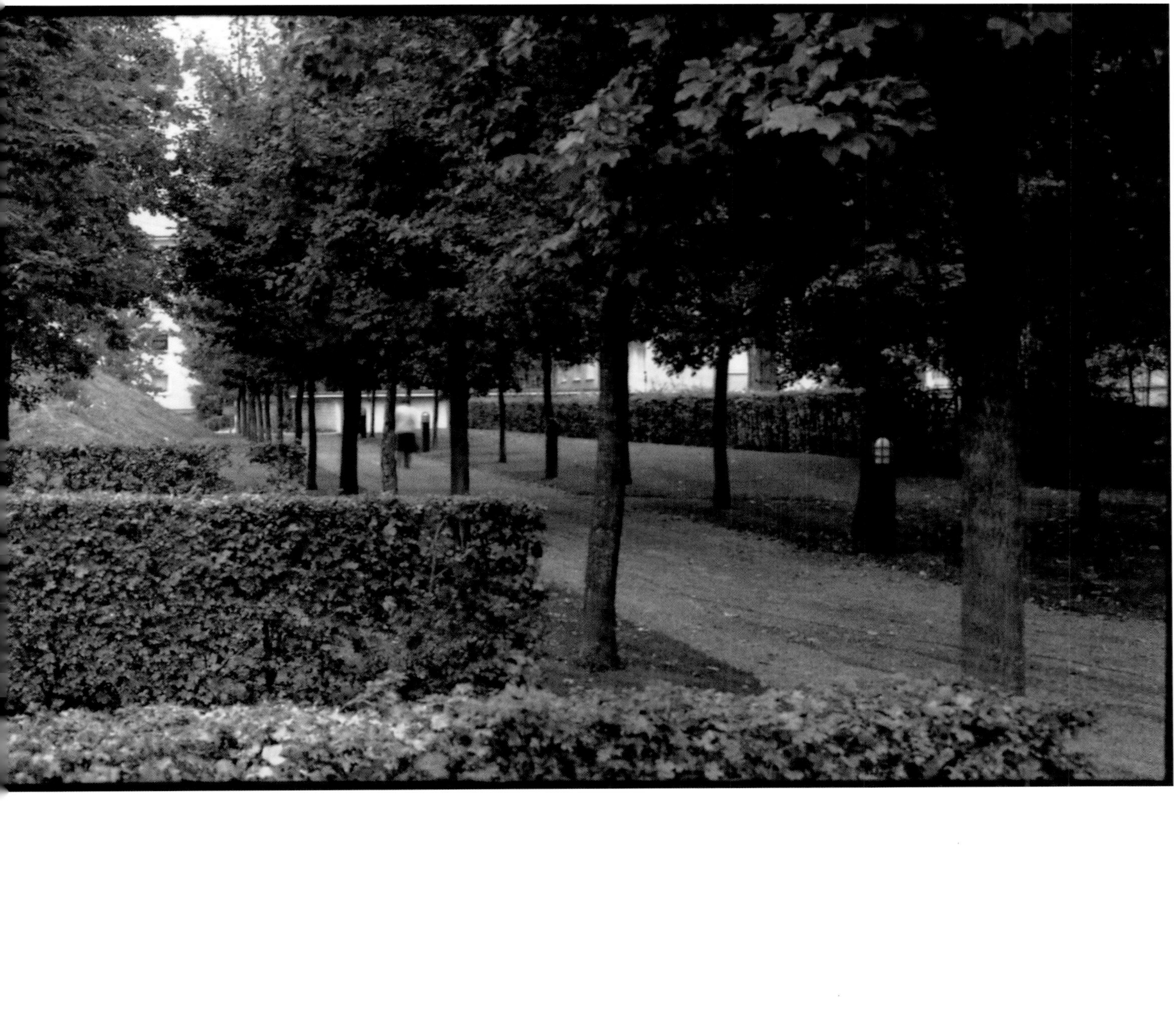

Gartenanlagen der Psychiatrischen Klinik Waldhaus, Chur

Einfach gesagt, stellt der Garten die Abstandsfläche zwischen den Gebäuden dar. Ein Zwischenraum, der die Tristesse grobklotziger Bauten kaschiert oder auflockert. Die Geschichte lehrt uns aber, daß der Garten weit mehr sein kann. In jeder kulturellen Hochblüte war die Gartengestaltung ein tragendes, gesellschaftliches Thema. Rousseau zitiert den Englischen Landschaftsgarten als Modell einer aufgeklärten, freiheitlichen Gesellschaft. Und heute finden Grüne Parteien im Naturgarten die Metapher einer ökologisch bestimmten Gesellschaft. So behaupten wir, daß der Garten gerade heute bedeutungsvoll sein kann.

Seit der Vertreibung aus dem Paradies zeigt der Garten zwei scheinbar widersprüchliche Charaktereigenschaften – Idylle und Utopie. Das idyllische Moment des Gartens findet seinen Höhepunkt im sentimentalen Garten des beginnenden 19. Jahrhunderts, dessen Leitbild die arkadische Hirtenlandschaft darstellt. Heute erkennen wir in der Forderung nach Naturgärten (Gärten, in denen nur wächst, was von «selbst» kommt) eine zeitgemäße Idyllensehnsucht. Der Idylle entgegengesetzt steht die Utopie. Sie ist im Wesensmerkmal des Gartens begründet. Er ist nicht reine Kultur, weil das Natürliche notwendiger Bestandteil ist, wie er auch nicht reine Natur sein kann, weil der tätige Mensch somit ausgeschlossen wäre und er sein Charakteristikum verloren hätte. Utopisch wäre demnach die Vorstellung, daß wir im Garten lernen und üben, mit der Natur auf eine sorgsame Art umzugehen. Der Garten wird so zum Modell für den Umgang unserer Gesellschaft mit Natur, denn Natur erhalten wir nicht durch unser Nichtstun, sondern durch die Beschäftigung mit ihr.

Es gehört zum Wunschbild der Gartenarchitekten, daß Gärten und Parkanlagen intensiv genutzt werden, wie wir dies vor allem in mediterranen Ländern kennen. Der unter Platanen Pétanque spielende Südfranzose, ebenso wie die italienische Großfamilie bei einem fellinischen Gelage im Freien, sind zu berufsständischen Metaphern geworden. Meistens bleibt es in unseren Breitengraden bei einem bescheidenen, alltäglichen Gebrauch des Gartens: der Gang zum Ab-

Garden of the Waldhaus Psychiatric Clinic, Chur

To put it simply, the garden represents the space between the buildings. An intervening area which conceals or detracts from the monotony of large buildings. However, history teaches us that the garden can be far more. Garden design was always a central theme of society in every golden age of culture. Rousseau quotes the English landscape garden as the model of an enlightened, liberal society. And today Green parties see the natural garden as a metaphor of a society based on ecological principles. And so we claim that today in particular the garden can be meaningful.

Since the expulsion from Paradise, the garden has had two seemingly contradictory character traits – idyll and utopia. The idyllic element of the garden reached its climax in the sentimental garden of the early 19th century, epitomised in an Arcadian pastoral setting. This can be equated with the contemporary desire for a natural garden (gardens where whatever grows, grows of its own accord). The idyll is in contrast to utopia. Its roots form the essence of the garden. It is not entirely a product of civilisation as nature is one of its essential features, neither can it be nature pure as this would imply the preclusion of human intervention and the garden would have lost its characteristic features. Consequently what is utopian is the notion that the garden helps us to learn how to adopt and put into practice a careful approach to nature. In this way the garden serves as a model for the way our society approaches nature: we cannot conserve nature by doing nothing, but by giving it our attention.

One of the ideals of garden architects is that gardens and parks are used intensively in the way which we are familiar with in Mediterranean countries in particular. The Frenchman playing pétanque under the plane trees and the Italian extended family feasting al fresco in true Fellini style have become metaphors in the profession. In our latitudes, use of the garden tends to be confined to modest, routine activities: carrying rubbish to the bin, hanging out washing or minding children at play. A different kind of climate, relatively comfortable apartments with balconies and different social pat-

fallcontainer, das Wäschehängen oder Kinderhüten auf dem Spielplatz. Andere Klimaverhältnisse, relativ komfortable Wohnungen mit Balkon und differentes Sozialverhalten, sind wesentliche Gründe für den geringen Gebrauch des Außenraumes.

Ganz anderes haben wir vor und auch während der Bauzeit im Waldhaus beobachtet und erfahren. Die Gartenanlagen werden intensiv genutzt, sie gehören wie selbstverständlich zum Klinikalltag: Gartenarbeiten, Gruppentherapie im Schatten einer alten Kastanie, Spazieren. Immer wieder haben wir gesehen, daß das einfache Sitzen und dabei in den Garten und in die Landschaft Blicken zum wichtigsten gehört.

Seit 1988 haben wir die Gartenanlagen zur Psychiatrischen Klinik Waldhaus geplant. Wir sind froh über diese lange Bearbeitungszeit. Sie gab uns Gelegenheit, mit dem Ort vertraut zu werden und Wünsche und Anforderungen von Patienten, Pflegepersonal, den Ärzten, der Verwaltung und der Baukommission kennenzulernen.

Die neu geschaffene Gartenanlage zum Waldhaus ist der vorläufig letzte Teil einer sozialen, geologischen, architektonischen und gartengestalterischen Geschichte, die dem Ort seine Identität gegeben hat. Ehemals ein Schuttkegel, dann Wald, später Weiden und Äcker und dann wurde im letzten Jahrhundert die Psychiatrische Klinik Waldhaus errichtet. Bergseits abgegraben und talseits aufgeschüttet, wurde eine architektonisch symmetrische Gebäudeanlage errichtet. Nach dem Geschmack der Zeit wurde der Außenraum konzipiert: eine kleinräumige, dem miniaturisierten Landschaftsgartenprinzip folgende Gartenanlage mit brezelförmig geschwungenen Wegen und locker verteilten Parkbäumen. Kennzeichnend für das ursprüngliche Gartenprinzip waren die additiven «mit Mauern und Hecken gefaßten Gartenräume», die ein Erleben der gesamten Gartenanlage verhindert haben. Hier setzt unsere Konzeption zur neuen Gartenanlage an.

Der Außenraum wird als Parkanlage aufgefaßt, die durchgehend erlebbar wird. Ein bogenförmiger Rundweg erschließt den Park und führt zwischen den mächtigen Parkbäumen hindurch zu den wichtigsten Teilen der Anlage, dem Haupteingang, zu den Patientenhäusern, den Personalhäusern, Sitzplätzen, Wasserbecken, Gartenpavillons und Brunnen. Die alten Parkbäume kontrastieren Licht und Schatten, Offenheit

terns are principal reasons for the little use made of outside space. We observed and experienced something entirely different both before and during the construction period at the Waldhaus Clinic. The gardens are used intensively, they are, as a matter of course, part of the daily life of the clinic: gardening, group therapy in the shade of an old chestnut tree, walks. On numerous occasions, we observed that one of the most important things was just to sit and contemplate the garden and the landscape.

Planning of the garden of the Waldhaus Psychiatric Clinic began in 1988. We welcomed this long period of preparation. It gave us the opportunity to become familiar with the location, to get to know the wishes and needs of patients, nursing staff, doctors, management and the building commission.

The redesigned garden of the Waldhaus is, for the time being, the final part of a social, geological, architectural and garden design history, which has given the place its identity. Once a cone of scree, then woodland, later on pasture and fields, it became the site of the Waldhaus Psychiatric Clinic in the 19th century. An architecturally symmetrical complex of buildings was created by levelling the ground. Outside space was designed according to tastes prevailing at the time: a small-scale garden in keeping with the principle of the miniaturised landscape garden – paths with pretzel-shaped curves and scattered park trees. Typical of the original principle of the garden were the additive "garden areas enclosed by hedges and walls", which made experience of the garden as a whole impossible. This was the point of departure of our design of a new garden.

Outside space is understood as a park, which can be experienced as a whole. A curved circular path provides access through the park and passes between the stately trees to the most important parts of the garden – the main entrance, the buildings for patients, the staff buildings, places to sit, pools, garden pavilions and fountains. The mature trees create contrasts between light and shadow, openness and seclusion, while the lawn is the unifying element. The spaciousness of the park is in contrast to the clearly defined garden courts of the buildings for patients. Their small scale permit different kinds of use and, at the same time, define the private areas which are directly aligned to the rooms. The entire complex is,

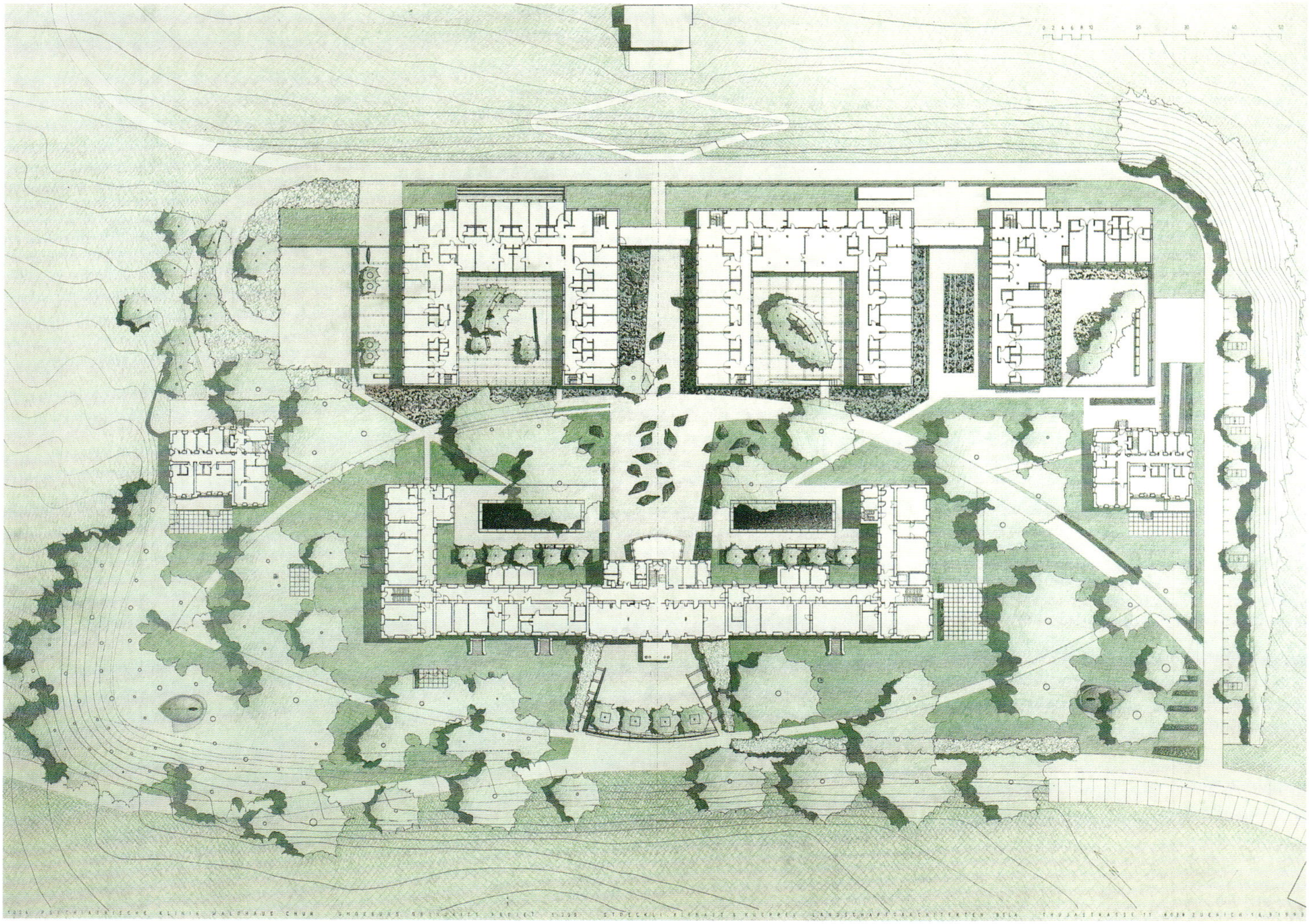

107

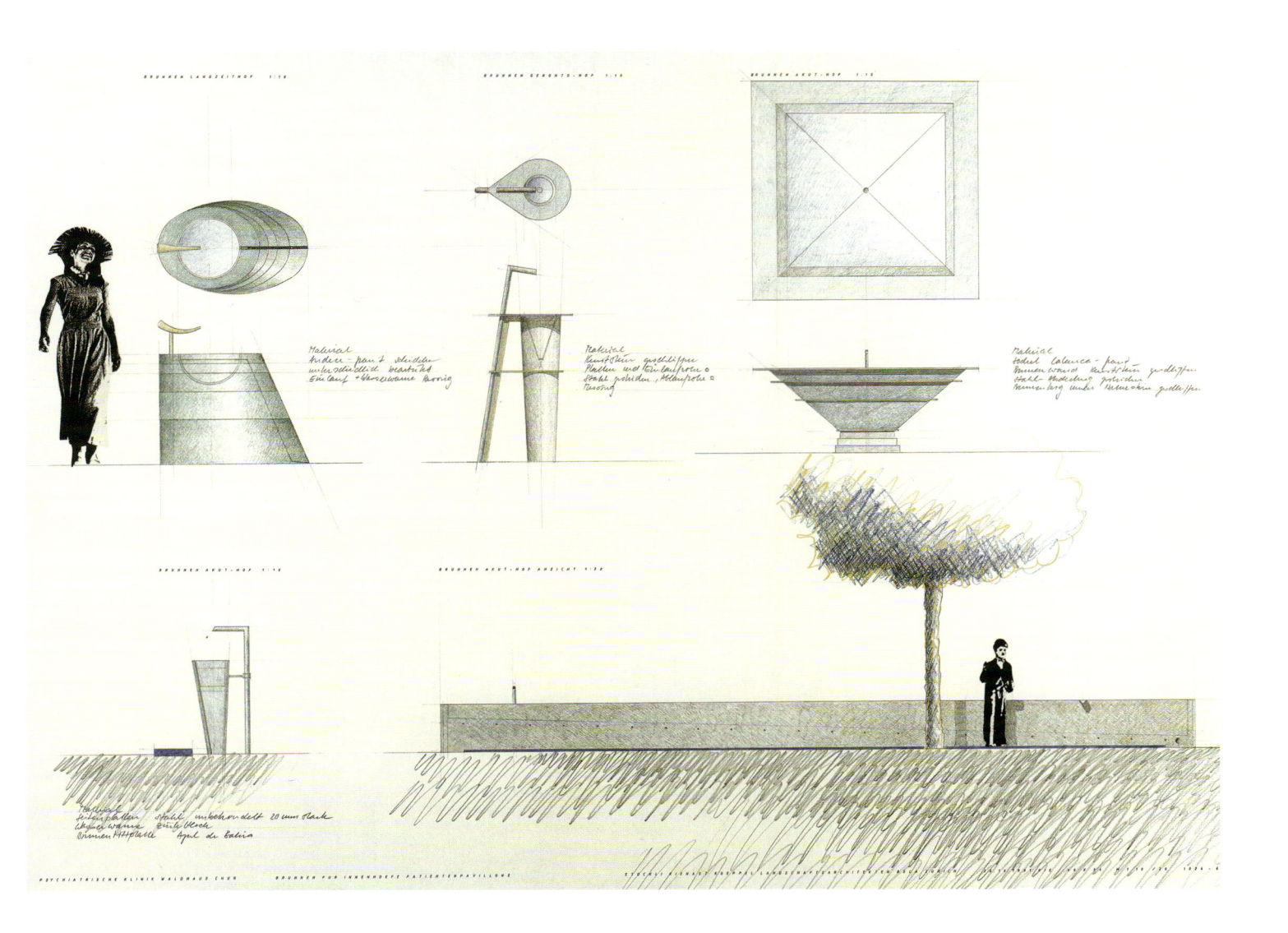

und Geschlossenheit, während der Rasenteppich das verbindende Element darstellt. Der Großräumigkeit des Parkteiles stehen die klar abgetrennten Gartenhöfe der Patientenhäuser gegenüber. Die Kleinteiligkeit läßt einen differenzierten Gebrauch zu und bestimmt gleichzeitig die intimen, den Zimmern unmittelbar zugeordneten Bereiche. Entsprechend dem neuen therapeutischen Prinzip ist die Gesamtanlage nicht mehr burghaft abgeschlossen. Verschiedenste Wegeverbindungen signalisieren den angestrebten Einbezug einer größeren Öffentlichkeit.

An der Südostseite sind die Parkplätze platzsparend angeordnet. Der steile Hang ist mit einheimischen Bäumen und Sträuchern bepflanzt. Er bildet die seitliche Raumdefinition und den Auftakt der Gesamtanlage. Ein Gartenpavillon lädt zum Verweilen ein. Ankommende und Vorübergehende werden beobachtet, ein kurzes Gespräch, ein Gruß ausgetauscht. Der Hauptweg führt uns in sanftem Schwung entlang an Hecken, blühenden Gartenstauden und vorbei an einzelnen Parkbäumen zum Eingangsplatz. Wie heruntergefallene Kastanienblätter sind geschnittene Eibenkuben locker auf dem Hauptplatz verteilt. Im Schatten des hohen Hauptgebäudes liegen zwei große, mit Seerosen bepflanzte Wasserbecken. Darin sehen wir die Spiegelung von Bäumen, Häusern und Menschen. Auf den seitlichen Bänken sitzend, blicken wir auf die Gartenhöfe der Patientenpavillons und erkennen den Maßstabswechsel zwischen Park und Höfen, der durch räumliche Definition und wechselnde Baumarten seinen Ausdruck findet. In jedem der vier Höfe charakterisieren gleichartige, aber unterschiedlich ausgeformte Elemente sowohl Einheitlichkeit wie auch Differenz. Es sind dies kleinkronige, blühende Bäume (Felsenbirne, Blumenesche, kleinkronige Kastanie, Zierkirsche), ein Brunnen und mehrere Bänke. Die formale Ausgestaltung und Anordnung dieser Elemente nimmt Bezug auf die Geometrie der Häuser und kontrastiert diese gleichzeitig mit freien Einlagerungen. Entlang der rückseitigen Erschließungsstraße erinnern Birnenspalierwände an die alte – ebenfalls mit Spalierobst – berankte Mauer und bilden die Überleitung zum angrenzenden Obsthain.

Dem Rundweg folgend, gelangen wir zur Nordwestseite des Hauptgebäudes. Das immer wieder auftretende Spiel mit Symmetrie und Asymmetrie wird hier durch das vorhandene

in keeping with new approaches to therapy, no longer cut off like a fortification. A variety of different systems of paths indicates the intention to involve a wider public.

Parking spaces on the south-east side are arranged in an economical way. Indigenous trees and shrubs are planted on the steep slope. It provides lateral spatial definition and is the prelude to the entire complex. A garden pavilion is an invitation to sit for a while, to observe those arriving and passing by, engage in a brief conversation or just pass the time of day. The gentle curve of the main path takes us past hedges, flowering perennials and free-standing park trees to the forecourt. Tubs of clipped yew are scattered over the main area like fallen leaves of chestnuts. Two large pools with water lilies lie in the shade of the tall main building. Trees, buildings and people are reflected in the water. From the vantage point of the benches placed on the side, we can see the garden courts of the patients' pavilions and become aware of the difference in scale between the park and the courts, which is expressed by spatial definition and differing kinds of trees. Each of the four courts is characterised by similar yet differently shaped elements, expressing both uniformity and difference – small-crown, flowering trees (shad bush, flowering ash, small-crown chestnut, ornamental cherry), a fountain and a number of benches. The formal design and arrangement of these elements addresses the geometry of the buildings while, at the same time, providing a contrast to the free-standing elements. Espalier pear trees bordering the rear access road are reminiscent of the old wall – along which fruit trees were also trained – and form the transition to the adjacent orchard.

Following the circular route, we arrive at the north-west side of the main building. The recurrent interplay of symmetry and asymmetry is emphasised here by the existing small area of woodland. A second garden pavilion lies in the midst of a dense foliage of trees. A small aperture in the wood provides us with a view of the surroundings of Chur as well as a close-up view of the pavilion. The leaf-shaped roof is covered in sheet metal, its underside consists of a fan-shaped structure of light-coloured plywood. The roof is supported by a black concrete pillar and a slender steel tube, painted red. Matching the roof, the floor is made of concrete, dyed pale blue. As this pavilion is located in woodland, it is surrounded

Waldstück thematisiert. Ein zweiter Gartenpavillon steht inmitten dunkler Bäume. Durch eine schmale Öffnung im Wald blicken wir auf die Umgebung von Chur oder sehen uns den Pavillon aus der Nähe an. Das blattförmige Dach ist abgedeckt mit Blech, seine Unterseite ist mit hellem Sperrholz ausgefacht. Eine schwarz gefärbte Betonsäule und ein feines, rot angemaltes Stahlrohr tragen das Dach. Korrespondierend mit dem Dach ist der Boden mit einer hellblau eingefärbten Betonplatte versehen. Der mitten im Wald stehende Pavillon ist rundherum mit Bärlauch, Maiglöckchen, Farn und Anemone bewachsen. Form, Pflanzen- und Materialverwendung zeigen, daß der Pavillon sich auf den Ort einläßt, ohne sich unterzuordnen, er ist gleichzeitig herausgehoben und in den Wald integriert. Dem Rundweg folgend, gelangen wir talseitig an den Fuß einer mächtigen, zum Gebäude mittig liegenden Bastion. Der blaue Mauervorsprung überdeckt die Holzsitzbank. Es ist heiß, wir sind ein bißchen müde. Über uns hören wir die unverwechselbaren Geräusche eines Gartenrestaurants. Vom Duft des blühenden Flieders leicht betäubt, steigen wir die Stufen hoch auf die Terrasse, sehen erleichtert einen freien Tisch und setzen uns hin. Im Schatten der flach gezogenen Linden genießen wir eine fast überwältigende Sicht auf die Stadt, das Rheintal und den – im nachmittäglichen Dunst – leicht verdeckten Calanda, der dem vor mir stehenden Getränk seinen unverwechselbaren Namen geliehen hat.

Dieter Kienast

by allium ursinum, lilies of the valley, ferns and anemones. Its form and the choice of plants and materials show that the pavilion addresses the location without subordinating itself to it, it is both external to and a part of the wood. We proceed further along the circular route and on the valley side arrive at the foot of a large bastion in line with the middle of the building. The blue projection covers the wooden bench. It is hot, we are a little tired. Above us we can hear the unmistakable sounds of a garden restaurant. Somewhat overcome by the heady smell of lilac, we ascend the steps to the terrace and, relieved to find an empty table, we sit down. In the shade of the low lime trees, we enjoy an almost overwhelming view of the city, the Rhine valley and – partly obscured by the afternoon haze – the Calanda after which the drink in front of me is named.

Dieter Kienast

Der Besucher wird auf einem Waldweg an den höchsten
Aussichtspunkt der Anlage geführt, den Pavillon – eine Blattform
in hellblauem Beton – als Ruheort.

A woodland path takes the visitor to the highest
vantage point in the grounds, the pavilion – leaf-shaped in
pale blue concrete – a place to sit and rest.

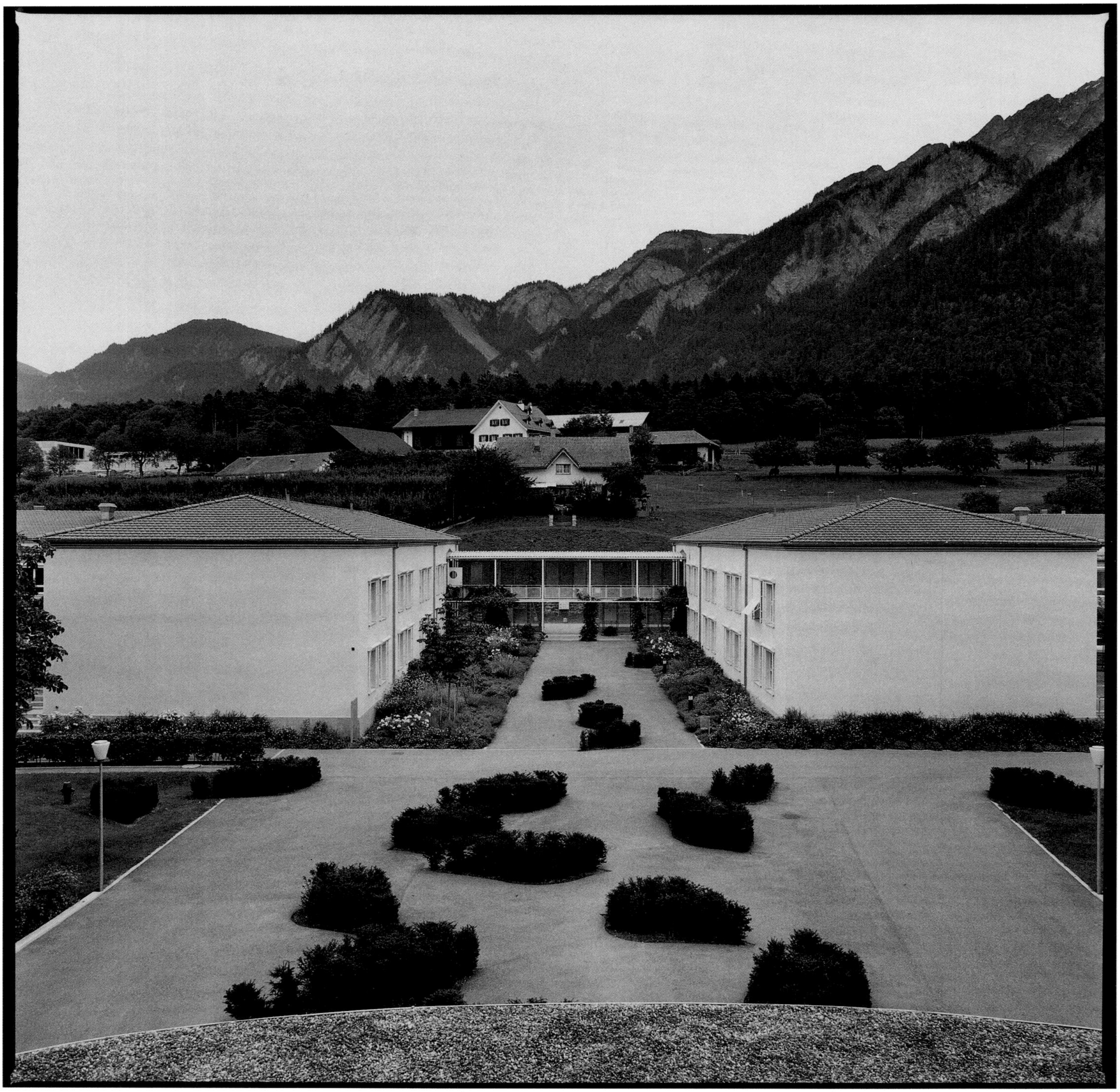

Die vier differenten Patientengärten sind mit kleinkronigen Blütenbäumen, Brunnen und einladenden Sitzbänken ausgerüstet.

The four different patients' gardens have small-crowned, flowering trees, fountains and inviting benches.

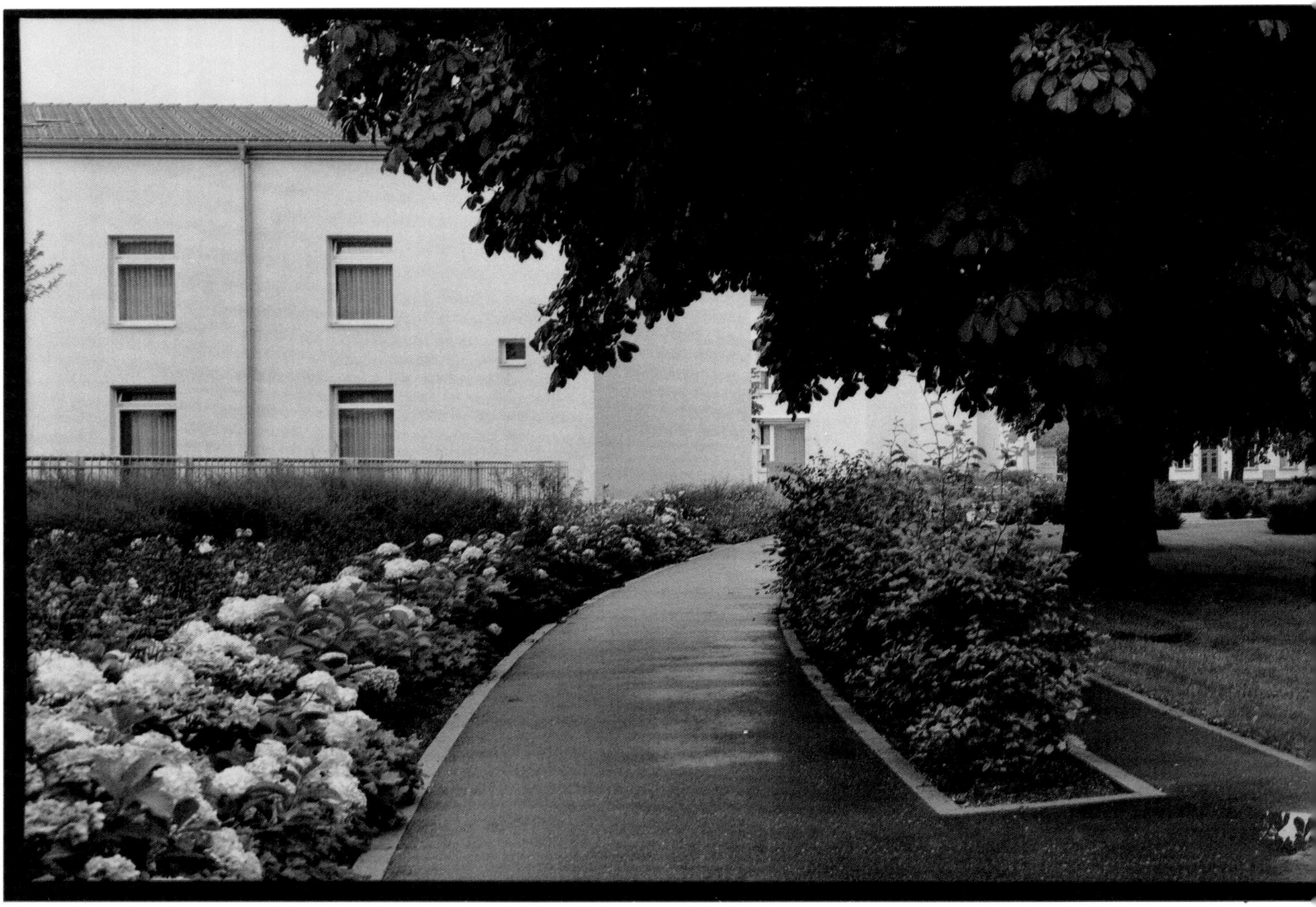

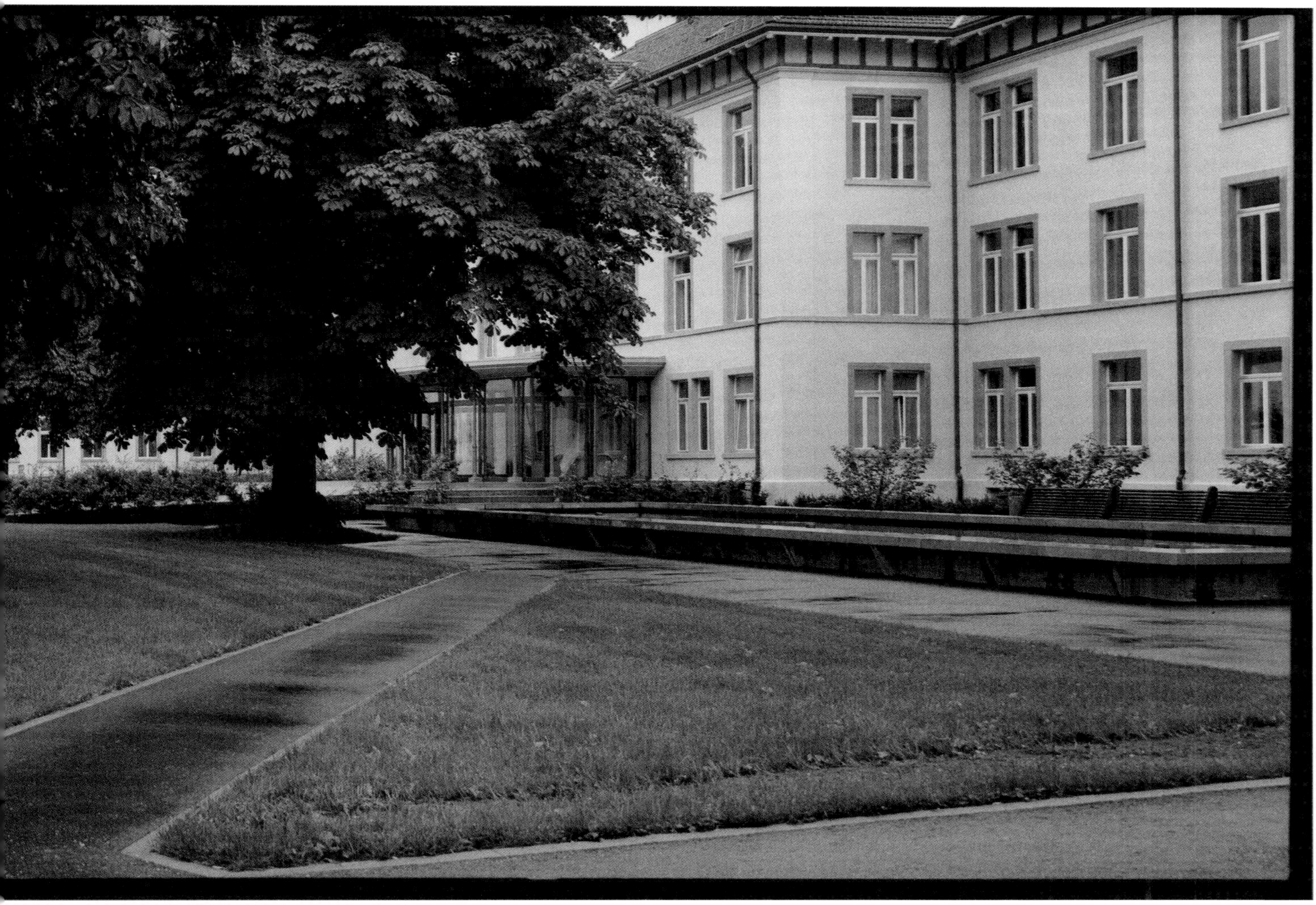

Friedhof Fürstenwald Chur

Rose, oh reiner Widerspruch
Lust
niemandes Schlaf zu sein
unter soviel
Lidern

Rainer Maria Rilke

Diese Inschrift steht auf dem Grabstein Rilkes in Raron. Er selbst hat bestimmt, daß dieser Vers dereinst auf seinem Grabstein stehen soll.

Rilke hat uns nicht nur vollendete Poesie hinterlassen. Wir lernen auch, daß der Friedhof ein Ort der Toten, vielmehr noch Ort der Lebenden sein muß. Mit dem Lesen des Gedichtes gedenken wir des Toten, lauschen dem Klang der kunstvoll gefügten Worte und denken nach über den Sinngehalt seiner hinterlassenen Botschaft. Mit dem Nachdenken verlassen wir das rein gefühlsbetonte Gedenken und sind auf dem Weg zur nachhaltigen Trauerarbeit. Der Friedhof erfüllt die Notwendigkeit der schicklichen Bestattung der Toten, ist aber auch prädestinierter Ort für die Hinterbliebenen, zu lernen, mit dem Verlust weiterzuleben.

Mit dem Standort Fürstenwald hat die Stadt Chur eine der schönsten Friedhofslagen weit und breit ausgewählt. Ruhig und erhaben liegt er über dem Rheintal und läßt den Blick auf die Stadt und die imposante Berglandschaft frei. Es war unsere Planungsabsicht, die landschaftliche Lagegunst auszunutzen und sie ortstypisch weiterzuentwickeln. Der Friedhof ist kompakt in die vorhandene Waldkammer eingepaßt und hat damit eine drei-

Fürstenwald Cemetery in Chur

Rose, o pure contradiction,
love
to be nobody's sleep
under so many
eyelids

Rainer Maria Rilke

This is the inscription on Rilke's gravestone in Raron. Rilke himself decided that this verse was to be inscribed on his gravestone.

Rilke did not just leave us perfect poetry. We also learn that a cemetery is not only to be a place for the dead, but also a place for the living. In reading the poem, we remember Rilke, listen to the sound of his artistically composed words, and ponder on the meaning of the message he left. We leave this purely emotional level of remembering in a reflective mood and move on to reflection on death and mourning expressed on a more lasting basis. The cemetery serves the purpose of a fitting place to bury the dead, but is also predestined as a place where the bereaved can come to terms with living with their loss.

In chosing Fürstenwald, the town of Chur has one of the finest cemetery locations in the region. Its tranquil and lofty position overlooks the Rhine valley does not obscure the view of the town and the imposing mountain scenery. It was an intention of our planning to exploit the advantages of the surrounding countryside and develop them in keeping with the locality. The cemetery fits into the existing woodland clearing compactly and, consequently, has clear spatial definition on three

seitige, klare Raumdefinition. Die talseitige Grenze wird durch die lange Stützmauer markiert, die eine präzise Abgrenzung zum Landwirtschaftsgebiet darstellt und trotzdem die Sicht offenläßt. Diese Stützmauer ist das Rückgrat der gesamten Friedhofsanlage, aus der die verschiedenen Bauten – Eingang, Aufbahrungsgebäude, Kapelle und Pavillon – herauswachsen. Das Gelände des Friedhofes erwies sich als sehr steil. Um eine rollstuhlgängige Erschliessung zu erreichen, mußte die Mauer hochgezogen werden. Mit dieser Maßnahme konnten flachere Grabstellen eingerichtet werden.

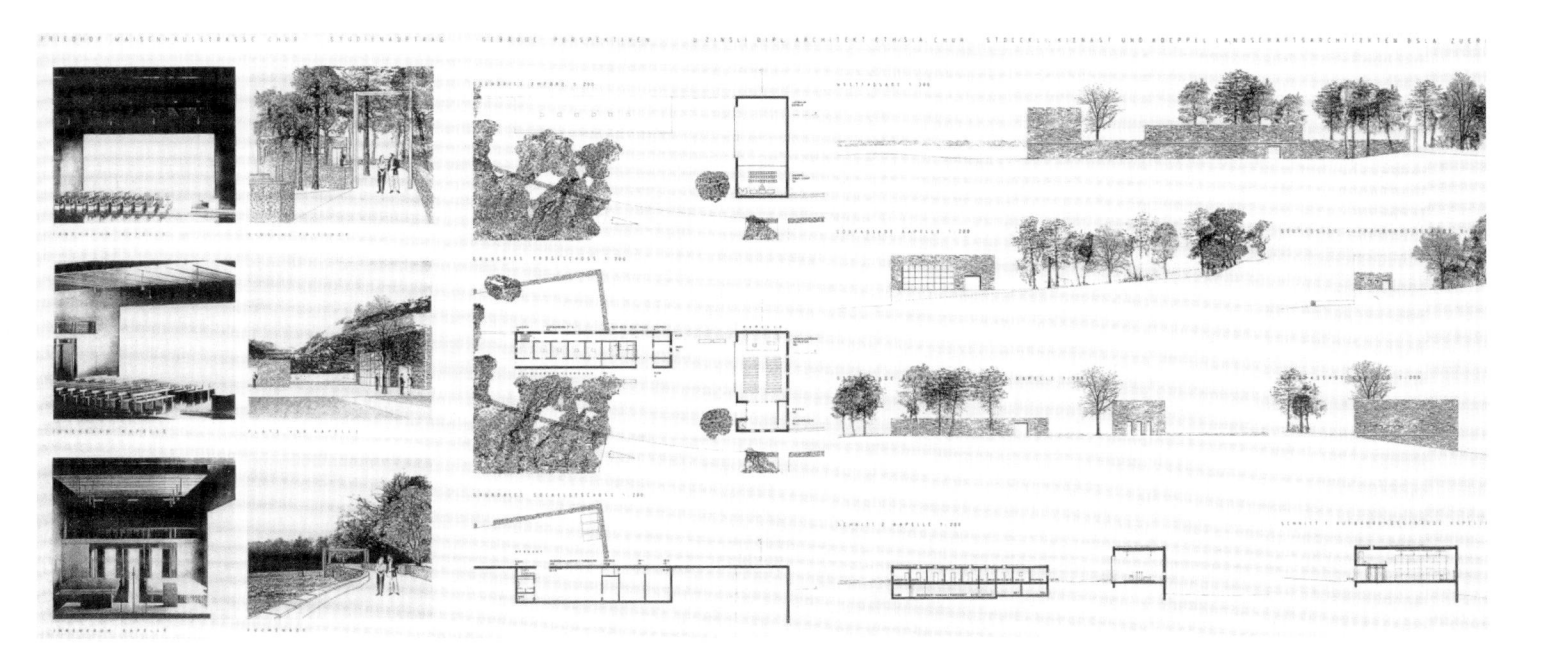

Von der Bushaltestelle her kommend, begleitet uns eine seitliche Hecke zum Eingang. Die Hecke wird geometrisch geschnitten, besteht aber aus unterschiedlichen Pflanzenarten wie Hainbuche, Liguster und Weißbuche, die wir auch im angrenzenden Wald wiederfinden. Diese Mischhecke ist ökologisch wertvoll und mit den variierenden Grüntönen gestalterisch interessant. Das Eingangstor thematisiert das Bauen in und mit der Natur weiter. In die Schalung wurden Föhrennadeln eingelegt. Damit erhält der künstliche Beton den Eindruck (im wörtlichen Sinn) von der Natur der nachbarlichen Föhren. Die Mittelschicht des Tores ist aus Holz gefertigt. Durch die lichte

sides. The boundary facing the valley is marked by the long wall; it forms a precise demarcation to the agricultural area, without obscuring the view. This wall forms the backbone of the entire cemetery complex, from which the various structures – entrance, chapel of rest, chapel and pavilion – ensue. The terrain of the cemetery was too steep. The wall had to be erected in order to make access for wheel-chair users possible. This made it possible to create more level burial plots.

The approach from the bus stop to the entrance is bounded laterally by a hedge. The hedge is clipped to create a geometrical form, but consists of such different plants as hornbeam, privet, and white hornbeam, all being plants that occur in the adjacent wood. This mixed hedge is ecologically valuable and, with its different shades of green, is of interest from the design point of view. The entrance gate takes up and continues the theme of building in and using nature. Pine needles were inserted in the formwork. This gives the artificial concrete the impression (in the literal sense) of the nature of the adjacent pines. The central section of the gate is made of wood. We enter the forecourt via the tongue of sparse pine trees. The courtyard is framed by buildings and has four lime trees at its centre.

Föhrenwaldzunge treten wir in den Empfangshof. Der Hof ist von Gebäuden gerahmt und zeigt im Zentrum vier Linden.

Mit dem horizontalen Höhenweg werden die Grabfelder einfach und direkt erschlossen. Die Grabfelder sind mit querliegenden Strauch- und Baumgürteln sowie Längshecken räumlich gefaßt. Die Baumgürtel sind in gleicher Artenzusammensetzung, wie sie im angrenzenden Wald zu finden sind, bepflanzt. In den Strauchgürteln wachsen Flieder, die im Frühjahr auffallend blühen und duften. Die Längshecken zeigen verschiedene Pflanzenarten: Von vorne nach hinten entdecken wir Buche, Hainbuche, Liguster und Linde, während die Abschlußhecke zum Gemeinschaftsgrab wieder als breite Mischhecke konzipiert ist.

Die Grabfelder sind für unterschiedliche Bestattungsarten vorgesehen. Neben den Reihengräbern für Erd- und Urnenbestattung, den Familien- und Kindergräbern ist oberhalb der Ka-

Access to the burial plots is simple and direct by means of the horizontal mountain path. Spatial definition of the burial plots is provided by transverse belts of bushes and trees as well as hedges on the long sides. The belts of trees are made up of the same trees existing in the adjacent wood. Lilacs, with their attractive springtime flowers and scent, grow in the belt of bushes. The hedges are made up of different plants: moving from front to back, we discover beech, hornbeam, privet and lime, whereas the rear hedge to the communal grave is conceived as a broad mixed hedge.

The burial plots are intented for different forms of burial. In addition to rows for graves and urns, family and child graves, a grass burial plot lies above the chapel. As the name would suggest, the site is dominated by grass. There are neither paths nor grave plants; no grave stones can be used, only horizontal memorial slabs. We ascend to the highest part of the cemetery,

pelle ein Rasengrabfeld vorgesehen. Wie der Name sagt, dominiert der Rasen. Es gibt weder Wege noch Grabbepflanzung und als Grabstein können nur liegende Grabplatten verwendet werden. Wir steigen hinauf zum höchsten Ort des Friedhofes, zum Gemeinschaftsgrab. Auf der Hochfläche liegen – leicht zueinander verschoben – ein schmales Wasserbecken und ein Plattenband. Das Gemeinschaftsgrab signalisiert das Zusammensein, gerade auch im Tod. Die bergseitige Stützmauer ist als Urnennischenwand ausgebildet. Wie bereits beim Eingangstor, wird hier das Bauen mit Natur weiter variiert. Die Natursteinwand ist durch die Grabplatten klar strukturiert, während die «versteinerten» Äste die rationale Ordnung und Schichtung der Mauersteine und Grabplatten kontrastieren.

Der Weg führt uns den Waldrand entlang zu einer Treppe, die den Anschluß zu den Wanderwegen des Fürstenwaldes herstellt. Vorbei an Grabfeldern, die erst in der zweiten Etappe weiter ausgebaut werden, gelangen wir zur Aussichtskanzel am Ende des Höhenweges. Angelehnt an eine Waldecke und zwei alte Eichen, markiert die einfache Betonkonstruktion einen ausgezeichneten Ort: Aufbahrungsraum, Kapelle und Grabfelder sind bereits auf weite Distanz gerückt. Langsam vermischt sich das Gedenken an den Verstorbenen mit dem sinnlichen Wahrnehmen der Gegenwärtigkeit von Landschaft und Natur.

Dieter Kienast

to the communal grave. There is a slender pool of water and a strip of slabs – not quite parallel to each other – on the plateau. The communal grave signals community, particularly also in death. The side of the wall facing the mountain is conceived as a wall with niches for urns. As at the entrance gate, building involving nature is further varied here. The natural stone wall is clearly structured by the grave slabs, whereas the "petrified" branches are in contrast to the rational order and stratification of the wall stones and grave slabs.

The path takes us along the edge of the wood to a flight of steps which provides a link to the Fürstenwald woodland trails. Passing the burial plots that are not to be developed further until the second stage, we arrive at the lookout platform at the end of the mountain path. Adjacent to a corner of the wood and two old oaks, the simple concrete structure marks a special place: the hall of rest, chapel and burial plots have already receded into the distance. Gradually, thoughts of the dead mingle with our experience of the immediacy of landscape and nature.

Dieter Kienast

Im Zentrum des Empfangshofs – mit Kapelle und Aufbahrungsgebäude –
stehen vier Linden.

There are four lime trees in the centre of the forecourt – with its chapel and laying-in-hall.

Die Stützmauer bildet das Rückgrat der gesamten Friedhofsanlage.

The wall forms the backbone of the entire cemetery complex.

Am Ende des Höhenweges erreicht man eine Aussichtskanzel – eine einfache Betonkonstruktion an einem ausgezeichneten Ort.

The ascending path leads to a look-out platform – a simple concrete structure that marks a special place.

Die bergseitige Stützmauer dient gleichzeitig als Urnennischenwand. Wie bereits am Eingangstor, wird hier das Bauen mit Natur weiter variiert.

The side of the wall facing the mountain is conceived as a wall with niches for urns. As at the entrance gate, building involving nature is further varied here.

... die versteinerten Äste kontrastieren die rationale Ordnung und Schichtung der Mauersteine und Grabplatten.

... "petrified" branches are in contrast to the rational order and stratification of the wall stones and grave slabs.

Verwaltungsgebäude Swisscom, Worblaufen Bern

Die Gärten der Swisscom

Eine neuere Swisscom-Taxcard zeigt den Plan des Bürobaus in Worblaufen als graphisches Signet – als rotblaues Streifenmuster, das wegen des dreieckförmigen Umrisses zur graphisch einprägsamen Figur wird. Man denkt bei seinem Anblick an die enormen Dimensionen eines solchen Baukomplexes, an die funktionellen Bedingungen des zeitgenössischen Bürobaus – aber kaum an Gartenkunst. Genügt eine solche Anlage nicht sich selbst? Oder umgekehrt: Was hat Gartenkultur mit Großbauten zu tun, die mit mindestens einem Geschoß großflächig unterkellert sind?

Selbst wenn wir uns erinnern, daß das Wort «Garten» weder auf die Blumen noch auf das Gemüse Bezug nimmt, sondern an das altnordische «Gart» erinnert – den Zaun, das Gitter, die feste Einfriedung jedenfalls, im Gegensatz zum Grenzstein, der den Acker oder die Wiese markiert –, will die Verbindung noch nicht gelingen. Eher noch vermitteln Begriffe wie derjenige des «Giardino segreto» (des abgeschlossenen Privatgartens) oder des «Hortus conclusus» die Vorstellung von Abgeschlossenheit durch schützende Umfassungsmauern. Vollends offensichtlich ist das Bedürfnis, Gartenflächen architektonisch zu fassen, im Lustgarten der Barockzeit. Allerdings werden dort die mit Rasen und Blumen orchestrierten Parterres nicht mit Mauern aus Backstein oder Bruchstein gefaßt, sondern mit einer grünen Architektur, welche auf die Masse der geschnittenen Bäume zählt. Das «Relief» ist der Schlüsselbegriff für diesen Typus des Gartens: «Boskett, Laubengang und Gartengebäude, alles was geschlossene Masse, aufstrebende vertikale Form bedeutet, setzt sich zur offenen Parterrefläche in einen Gegensatz, der durch seine architektonische Formulierung zugleich eine festere Verkettung zwischen den Quartieren herbeiführt.» (August Grisebach, Der Garten, 1910). Dieser barocke Gartentyp kann somit aufgefaßt werden als Folge von Räumen, die aus einer grünen Laubmasse gewissermaßen herausgeschnitten sind, oder umgekehrt als Folge von Raumkörpern, die mit Baummaterial satt hinterfüllt sind.

Swisscom Administrative Building, Worblaufen Bern

The gardens of Swisscom

A recent Swisscom Taxcard shows the plan of the office building as a graphic sign – a red and blue stripe pattern, which is a distinctive figure on account of its triangular contours. It brings to mind the enormous dimensions of such a building complex, the functional conditions of building contemporary offices – and scarcely seems to have anything to do with garden art. Isn't such a complex sufficient in itself? Or conversely: what does garden culture have to do with large buildings which extend underground over most of their area by at least one storey?

Even if we recall that the German word "Garten" neither refers to flowers nor to vegetables, but comes from the Old Nordic "gart" meaning fence, grille, a permanent enclosure, in contrast to the boundary stone marking the field or meadow, the connection is still a difficult one to follow. Concepts such as the "giardino segreto" (secret garden) or the "hortus conclusus" seem more able to convey the idea of seclusion in the form of protective surrounding walls. The need to give architectural design to garden space is ultimately reflected in the pleasure garden of the age of Baroque. However, its parterre designs of lawn and flowers were not enclosed by walls of brick or rough stone but by green architecture, which depends on the volume of the clipped trees. "Relief" is the key concept in this type of garden: "small woods, pergolas and garden buildings, everything which entails volume, a soaring vertical form, is in contrast to the openness of the parterre, which, due to its architectural nature, also creates clearer links between the individual quarters." (August Grisebach, Der Garten, 1910). Hence, this type of Baroque garden can be seen as a sequence of areas which have, as it were, been cut out of a green mass of foliage, or conversely as a sequence of spatial structures, set in ample tree material.

The same is true of the cities of the age: streets and squares form spatial sequences, which the imagination has no difficulty seeing continued in the prestigious areas of their

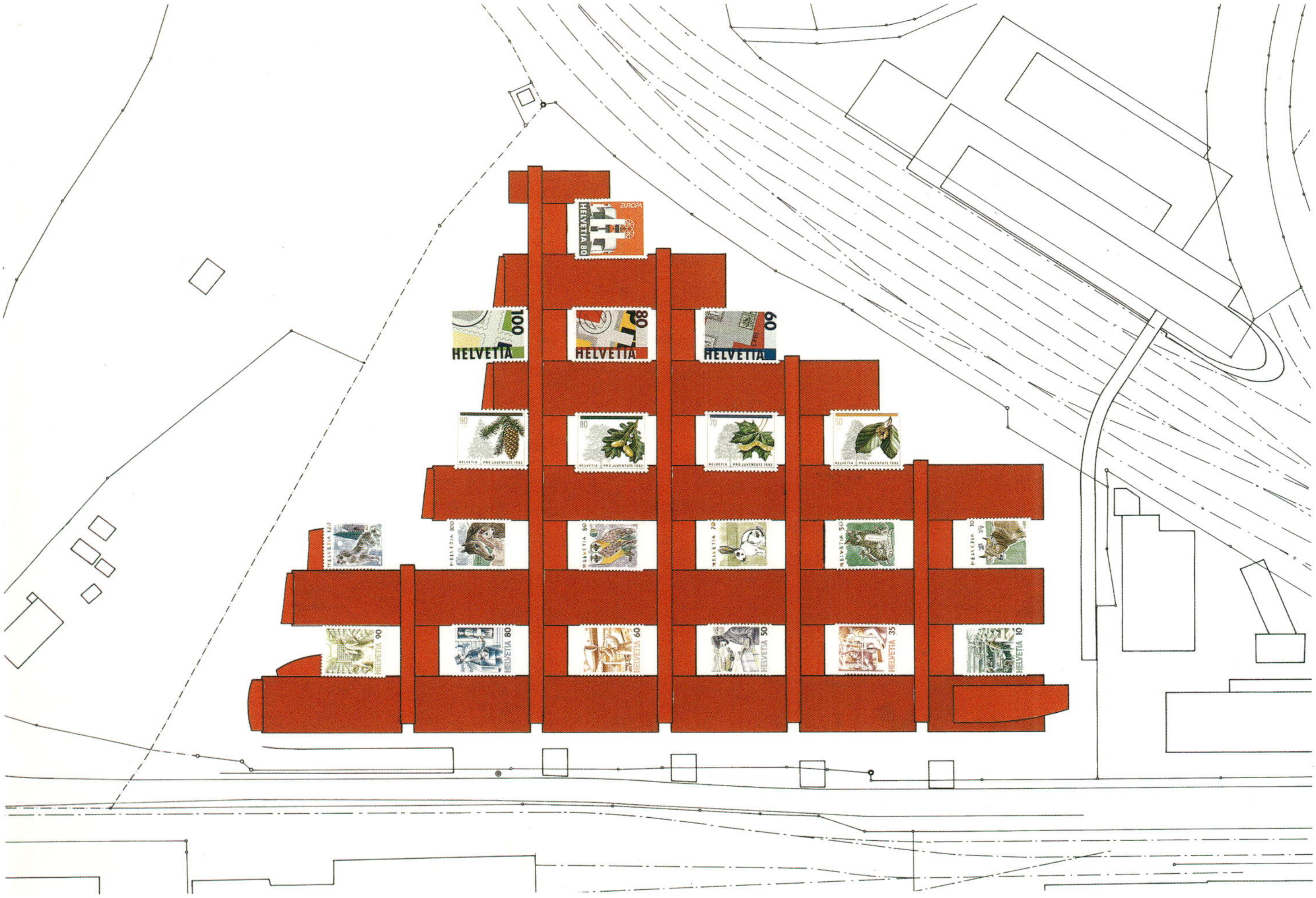

Ähnliches gilt für die Städte jener Zeit: Straßen und Plätze bilden Raumfolgen, die man sich bis in die Repräsentationsbereiche der Bauten hinein fortgesetzt denken kann. Diese Raumfolgen sind herausgeschnitten aus dem Teig der Stadt oder umgekehrt satt hinterstopft mit Baumasse, welche die Mauern und alle Nebenräume enthält («Poché» nannte man an der Ecole des Beaux-Arts die schraffierten oder dunkel angelegten Flächen, welche auf den Plänen die entsprechenden Flächen bezeichneten). Der barocke Garten und die barocke Stadt können durchaus als Modellvorstellung zum Verständnis der Swisscom-Anlage herbeigezogen werden: Die Masse der Gebäude ist die Gußform für das Muster der rechteckigen Hofräume, die gleichzeitig als Salons, als Stadtplätze oder aber als Gartenparketts interpretierbar sind. Diese Höfe stellen jedenfalls die eigentlichen Repräsentationsräume der Anlage dar, deren Möblierung im uniformen Muster der Anlage spezifische Orte zu definieren vermag.

Ein früher schematischer Grundriß des Swisscom-Gebäudes zeigt eine kleinmaßstäbliche Darstellung mit rechtwinklig sich überlagernden roten Bändern. Die Landschaftsarchitekten haben diesen Plan 1993 für die Präsentation ihrer Gestaltungsidee vor der Bauherrschaft verwendet. Die Zwischenräume des Bandrasters haben sie mit Briefmarken überklebt. Diese Marken passen nicht genau, überlappen ein bißchen den roten Bereich. Daraus ergibt sich eine doppelte Lesbarkeit: einerseits «möblieren» sie gewissermaßen die vorgegebenen Flächen, andererseits erscheinen sie als autonomes Muster auf rotem Grund. Einmal erscheinen sie als Füllung, als Hintergrund, das andere Mal machen sie die Hauptsache, den Vordergrund aus.

Bei näherem Hinsehen gehören die einzelnen Marken jeweils einer Serie mit ganz unterschiedlichen Motiven an. Sie bilden gewissermaßen Familien, die jeweils von Nord nach Süd – parallel zur Grundlinie der dreieckförmigen Anlage – aufgereiht sind. Verschiedene Postberufe zuerst, Tiere dann, schließlich Baumzweige, Variationen zum Thema Schweizerkreuz und zuletzt eine Marke aus der Europa-Serie mit modernen Schweizer Bauten (ein Einfamilienhaus von Mario Botta).

Dieses Konzeptblatt ist großartig. Die eingesetzten Materialien stammen vom Architekten und vom Bauherrn (zu dem

buildings. These spatial sequences are cut out of the fabric of the city or, conversely, set in ample building volume consisting of the walls and all the ancillary areas ("poché" was the name which the Ecole des Beaux-Arts gave the hatched or blackened areas to designate such areas on plans). The Baroque garden and the Baroque city can certainly serve as a model to understand the idea of the Swisscom complex: the volume of the buildings is the mould for the model of the rectangular courts, which can also be interpreted as salons, urban squares or as garden parquet. At all events, these courts are the real prestigious areas of the complex, furnishing of which is capable of defining specific location.

An earlier schematic outline of the Swisscom building shows a small-scale representation with pieces of red tape superimposed on each other at right angles. The landscape architects used this plan for their presentation of their design idea to clients in 1993. They stuck stamps on the spaces between the pattern composed of pieces of tape. The stamps do not fit exactly and slightly encroach on the red areas. This leads to dual readability: on the one hand they "furnish", as it were, the given areas, on the other hand, they appear as an autonomous pattern on a red base. They act both as filling, as background and as the principal element, the foreground.

On closer inspection, the individual stamps each belong to a series composed of entirely different motifs. They form, so to speak, families, which are each lined up from north to south parallel to the baseline of the triangular site. First various professions within the postal service, then animals, followed by branches of trees, variations of the theme of the Swiss cross and, finally, a stamp forming part of the Europe series with modern Swiss buildings (a one-family house designed by Mario Botta).

This conceptual collage is ingenious. The materials used were provided by the architect and the client (at the time the latter still operated the postal service). Minimal means are used to outline the idea, without making it necessary to reveal details at such an early stage. Each layer of space to be traversed from the baseline is assigned to an immediately recognisable theme, varied from court to court, so that clearly identifiable places are created. The individual courts still have to be designed, but – as the preliminary projects also dating

damals auch die Briefpost gehörte). Mit minimalen Mitteln wird die Idee umrissen, ohne daß in diesem frühen Stadium schon Auskunft gegeben werden muß über Detaillösungen. Jede der von der Grundlinie aus zu durchquerenden Raumschichten ist einem sofort erkennbaren Thema zugeordnet, das von Hof zu Hof so variiert wird, daß eindeutig identifizierbare Orte entstehen. Die Entwürfe der einzelnen Höfe sind noch zu erfinden, aber – wie die ebenfalls 1993 entstandenen Vorprojekte zeigen – sie sind aufgrund des klaren Konzeptes sehr rasch konkretisierbar.

Der Vergleich zwischen den ersten Skizzen und der Ausführung verblüfft. Scheinbar mühelos werden jeweils verschiedene Themen variiert oder – wenn man den Vergleich des Sprachlichen beizieht – dekliniert. Kienast Vogt Partner schöpfen offensichtlich aus einem Repertoire, in dem eine jahrzehntelange Erfahrung kondensiert ist. Dabei beziehen sie wie selbstverständlich die Künstlichkeit des Vorhandenen in ihr Kalkül ein. Wie alles von Menschen Geschaffene sind auch die Gärten künstlich, und im Kontext dieses Bürokomplexes wäre auch die leiseste Illusion des Gegenteils wohl unmöglich zu erreichen. Kein Zweifel, daß dieser Umstand den Vorlieben der Landschaftsarchitekten zutiefst entspricht: Sie setzen auf die Konfrontation von freier und geometrisch präziser Form, sie lieben die mit rohen Flachstahlbändern erzeugten messerscharfen Rasenränder, sie verwenden gerne Sichtbeton oder Zementwaren: «arme» Materialien, deren Oberflächenqualität nicht von der reinen Form ablenken und die zudem ihre Kompositionen als zeitgenössisch datieren lassen.

So zweifelt man keinen Augenblick an der Aktualität der ersten Serie von Hofgestaltungen, die sich am Thema der «Geformten Natur» orientiert, obwohl hier auch klassische Motive verwendet sind. Auf Rasen gesetzte, geometrisch geschnittene Buchs- und Eibenkörper werden konfrontiert mit kristallinen Glasprismen. Rollende Pflanzenkübel aus Eisen schaffen Raumkonstellationen auf einem Rasen, der durch Schienenbänder rhythmisch gegliedert ist. Berankte Metallstangen sind nach den Gesetzen des Zufalls über eine Fläche gestreut, die je etwa zur Hälfte mit Rasen und Chaussierung belegt ist. Alle diese Installationen sind den Fassaden entlang gerahmt mit streifenförmigen Betonplatten; sie werden zu «Bildern», die – aus den oberen Geschossen betrachtet – dem jeweiligen Qua-

from 1993 show – they can, thanks to the precise idea, readily be given concrete form.

The comparison between the initial sketches and execution is amazing. Different individual themes are varied seemingly effortlessly or – to use the language of linguists – declined. Kienast Vogt Partner are clearly able to draw on a repertoire which represents decades of experience. They incorporate, as if a matter of course, the artificiality of what exists in their calculations. Just like everything else created by human beings, gardens are artificial and in the context of this office complex it would probably be impossible to achieve even the slightest illusion of anything else. There is no doubt that this is a circumstance which is very much appreciated by the landscape architects: they seek the confrontation between free forms and those of geometrical precision, they love razor-sharp lawn edges, they are happy to use fair-faced concrete or cement, i.e. "poor" materials whose surface quality does not detract from the pure form and which have the additional advantage of showing their compositions to be contemporary.

Hence, there is no reason to cast doubt on the contemporary value of the first series of court designs, which, while based on the theme of designed nature, also includes classical motifs. Geometrically clipped shapes in box and yew, placed on lawns, are confronted with crystalline glass prisms. Moveable iron plant tubs create spatial constellations on a lawn which has been given a rhythmic structure by strips of metal. According to the principle of chance, plant-covered metal rods are strewn over an area, which is approximately half lawn and half hard surface. All these installations are framed by strips of concrete slabs along the facades; they become "pictures" which – seen from the upper stories – give each individual quadrant of the complex its unique identity. The declination of the "picture" motifs addresses the phenomenon of series in contemporary art. But even more important than the composition principle it is the direct experience of the sensuous qualities of surfaces and plants which makes these compositions so special.

The following series can be seen in the same way. The water gardens show the element of water in various manifestations. A pond framed by grating is home to a giant alu-

dranten der Anlage ihr unverwechselbares Gepräge geben. Die Deklination der «Bild»-Motive macht auf entsprechende Phänomene des Seriellen in der zeitgenössischen Kunst aufmerksam. Mehr noch als das Kompositionsprinzip ist es die unmittelbare Erfahrung der sinnlichen Qualitäten von Oberflächen und Pflanzen, welche diese Kompositionen zum Ereignis werden lassen.

Ähnliches läßt sich bei den folgenden Serien anmerken. Bei den «Wassergärten» geht es um die Darstellung des nassen Elementes in verschiedenen Erscheinungsformen. Ein mit Gitterrosten gerahmter Teich ist von einem riesigen Seerosenblatt aus Aluminium besetzt, das von mehreren Stellen aus mit echten Seerosen bedrängt werden wird. Anderswo findet sich etwa eine mit einer schimmernden Mischung aus grünem Andeersplit und gebrochenem Glas belegte Fläche mit einem Bambusstrauch und einem linealartigen metallgefaßten Wasserbecken, das mit einer geschnittenen Hecke hinterpflanzt ist.

Die «Blühenden Gärten» sind über das Pflanzenmaterial einerseits und über die Geometrie der mit Kalktuffsteinplatten belegten Wege andererseits differenziert. Mit den «Bewegten Gärten» schließlich unternehmen Kienast Vogt Partner den Versuch einer Synthese von gebauter plastischer Form, Pflanzenmaterial und assoziativ wirkenden Wortelementen. Eigentlich gibt es nur einen einzigen geschlossenen «Hof», der diesem Thema gewidmet werden konnte: Auf einem mit gelben Narzissen gesprenkelten Rasenrechteck ist schräg eine beidseits konkave, auf- und absteigende – mit andern Worten keinen rechten Winkel aufweisende – Form eingespannt, die mit einem in den Beton eingelegten Schriftzug an das «Poème de l'angle droit» Le Corbusiers und darüber hinaus an die omnipräsente Rechtwinkligkeit der Bürostruktur erinnert. Die beiden übrigen Gestaltungen zu diesem letzten Thema betreffen einseitig zur Umgebung hin offene Räume; gegen Norden ein einfaches Rasenstück mit dem großen Schriftzug «nature», gegen Süden ein rhythmisch gewelltes Rasenband, dessen Wellenkämme eine Folge von Wörtern tragen, die durch die amerikanische Künstlerin Jenny Holzer definiert wurden.

Diese Stelle macht auf den Umstand aufmerksam, daß es sich beim Swisscom-Center nicht etwa um einen an der dreieckigen Peripherie geschlossenen Komplex handelt, sondern

minium water lily leaf, which will be displaced at a number of points by real water lilies. Elsewhere there is, for example, a surface covered with a shimmering mixture of green Andeer stone chippings and broken glass together with a bamboo bush and a narrow, metalframed pool in front of a clipped hedge.

The "flowering gardens" are distinguished by the plants used, on the one hand, and by the geometry of the paths of tuff stone on the other hand. With their "ondulated gardens" Kienast Vogt Partner attempt a synthesis of built sculptural form, plant material and word elements which have an associative effect. Actually, there is only one enclosed "court" which it was possible to devote to this theme: on a rectangular lawn dotted with yellow narcissi an ascending and descending form has been inserted concave on both sides diagonally – in other words it has no right angles – and with the words set in concrete it evokes the "Poème de l'angle droit" by Le Corbusier and, in addition, the omnipresent right angles of the office building. The two remaining designs on this theme consist of areas open to the surroundings on one side; facing north a simple piece of lawn bearing the word "nature" in large letters, facing south a rhythmically undulating strip of grass, its crests bearing a sequence of words which were defined by the American artist Jenny Holzer.

This place draws attention to the fact that the Swisscom Center is not a complex which is flush with the triangular periphery, but a structure which has been cut back relatively arbitrarily along the boundary. As a result, not only the enclosed courts had to be designed, but also those which were broken open, as well as the immediate surroundings bordering the complex.

While a solution could be found for the groundline of the complex along the old Tiefenaustrasse in the form of hedges and a progressively dense row of carefully selected trees similar in form, complete clearance followed by reforestation was necessary on the terrain to the north. It is this context which gives the court area containing the word "nature" its poetic effect. Towards the south-east, the site is intersected by a broad stretch of railway tracks against which the undulating strip of grass, so to speak, "breaks". The result is a relentless confrontation of two entirely different worlds;

um eine Struktur, die entlang des Grenzverlaufes relativ willkürlich beschnitten wurde. Demzufolge waren nicht nur die geschlossenen, sondern auch aufgebrochene Hofräume zu gestalten und dazu die unmittelbare Umgebung im Grenzbereich des Areals.

Während die Grundlinie der Anlage entlang der alten Tiefenaustrasse mit Heckenkörpern und einer progressiv verdichteten Reihe von sorgfältig ausgesuchten Bäumen mit gleicher Form in den Griff zu bekommen war, mußte auf dem nördlich angrenzenden Gelände auf einen Kahlschlag mit anschließender Aufforstung reagiert werden. Vor diesem Hintergrund erhält der beschriebene Hofraum mit dem Wort «nature» erst seine poetische Wirkung. Gegen Südosten wird die Anlage hingegen von einem breiten Schienenstrang geschnitten, gegen den das gewellte Rasenband gewissermaßen anbrandet. Es resultiert eine unerbittliche Konfrontation zweier gänzlich verschiedener Welten; aus dem Gebäudeinnern gesehen werden sie als räumliche Schichtung wahrgenommen, die an eine Fotokomposition von Andreas Gursky erinnert.

Auf solche Weise versuchen Kienast Vogt Partner mit ihren Mitteln, den Mikrokosmos der Plätze im uniformen Bürokomplex anzubinden an den Makrokosmos der Außenwelt und ein Verhältnis zu finden zum Muster der gewachsenen Stadt, zu den Revieren mit «natürlichem» Bewuchs (zum kleinen Wald) und zu den weltumspannenden Systemen menschlicher Infrastrukturen (dem Netz der Eisenbahn).

Arthur Rüegg

from inside the building they are perceived as spatial layering reminiscent of a photo composition of Andreas Gursky.

It is in ways such as these that Kienast Vogt Partner use the means at their disposal to link the microcosm of the squares in the uniform office complex to the macrocosm of the outside world and seek to find a relationship to the pattern of the established city, to the areas with "natural" vegetation (the small wood) and to the all-embracing systems of man-made infrastructure (the rail network).

Arthur Rüegg

132

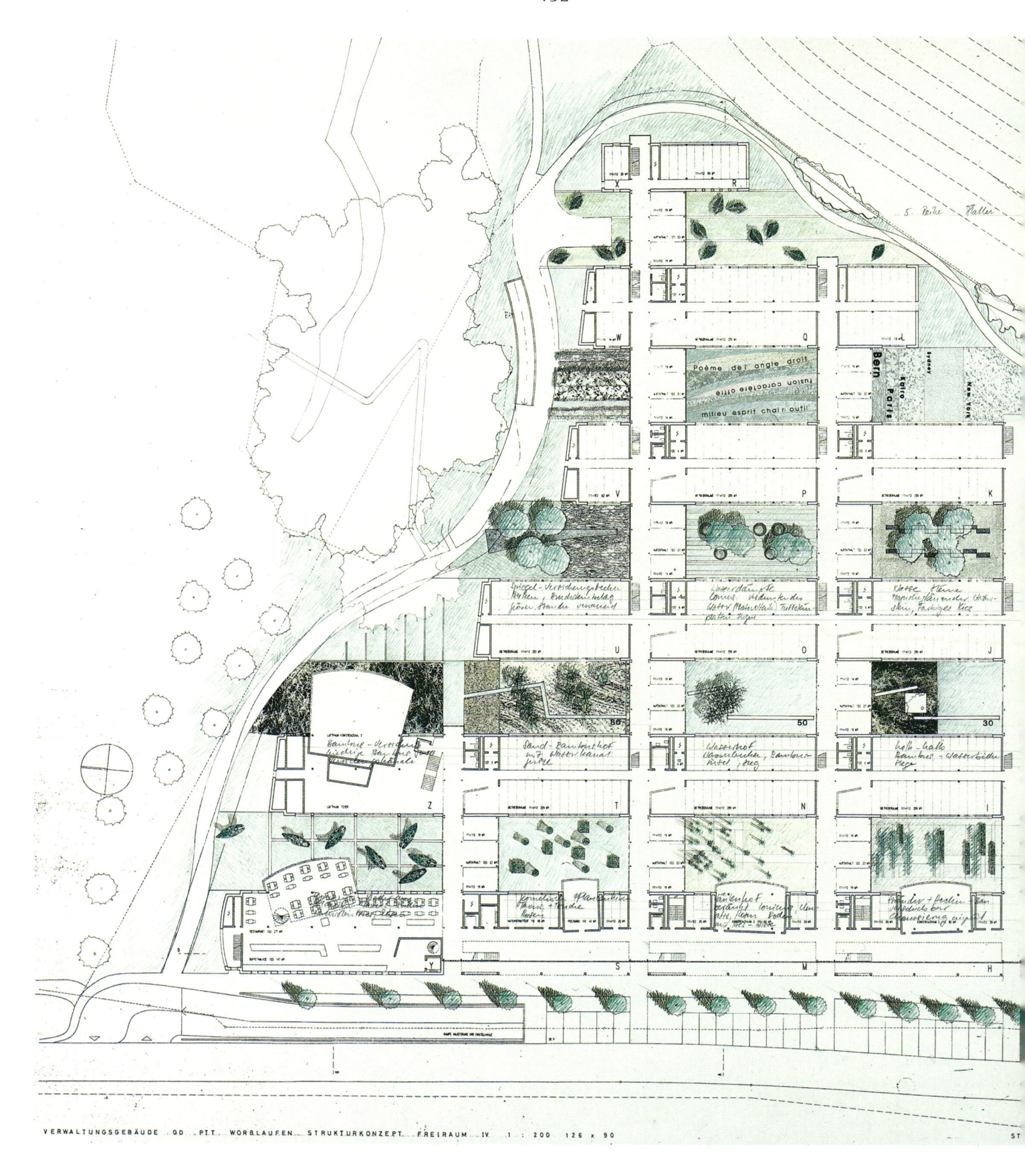

VERWALTUNGSGEBÄUDE GD PTT WORBLAUFEN STRUKTURKONZEPT FREIRAUM IV 1:200 126 x 90

133

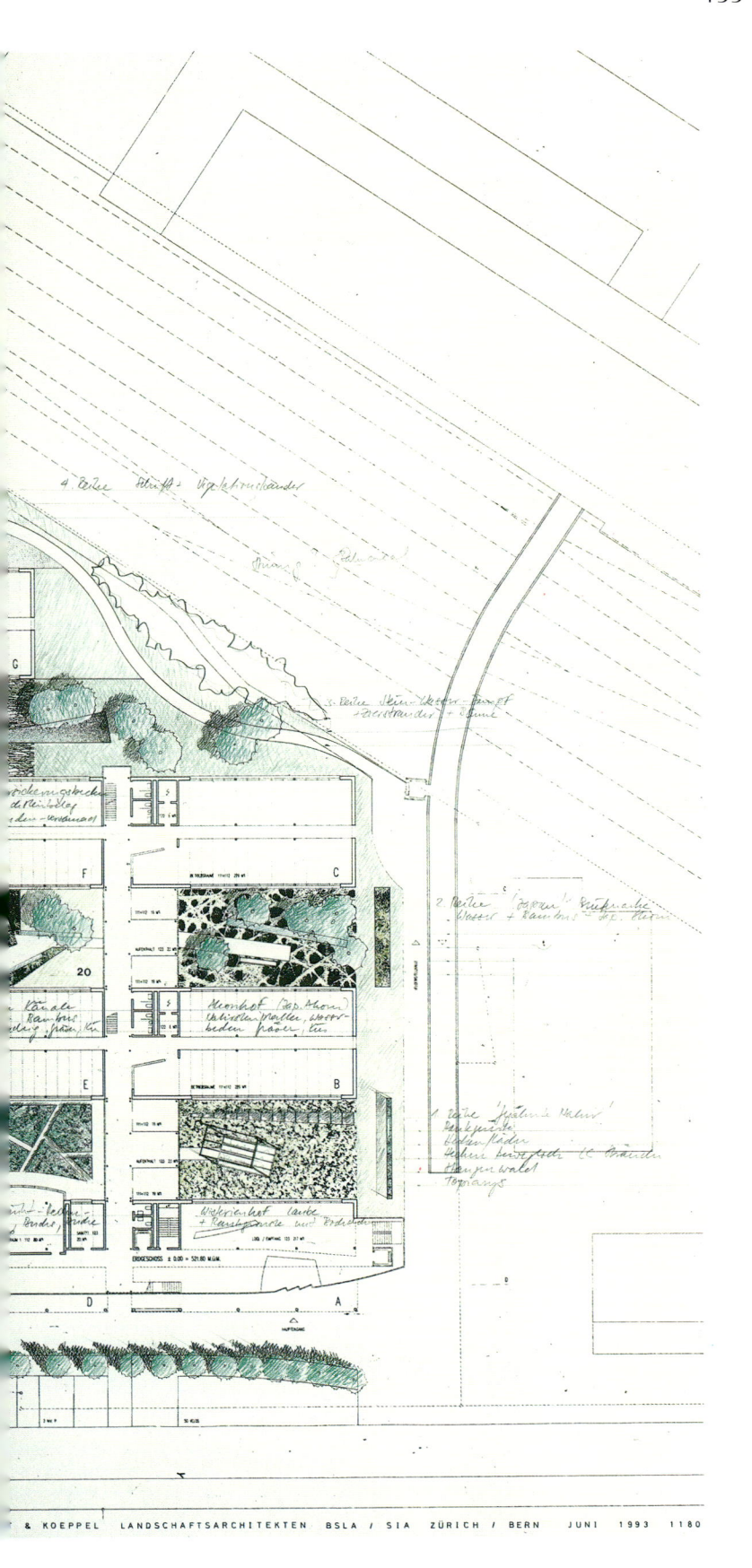

& KOEPPEL LANDSCHAFTSARCHITEKTEN BSLA / SIA ZÜRICH / BERN JUNI 1993 1180

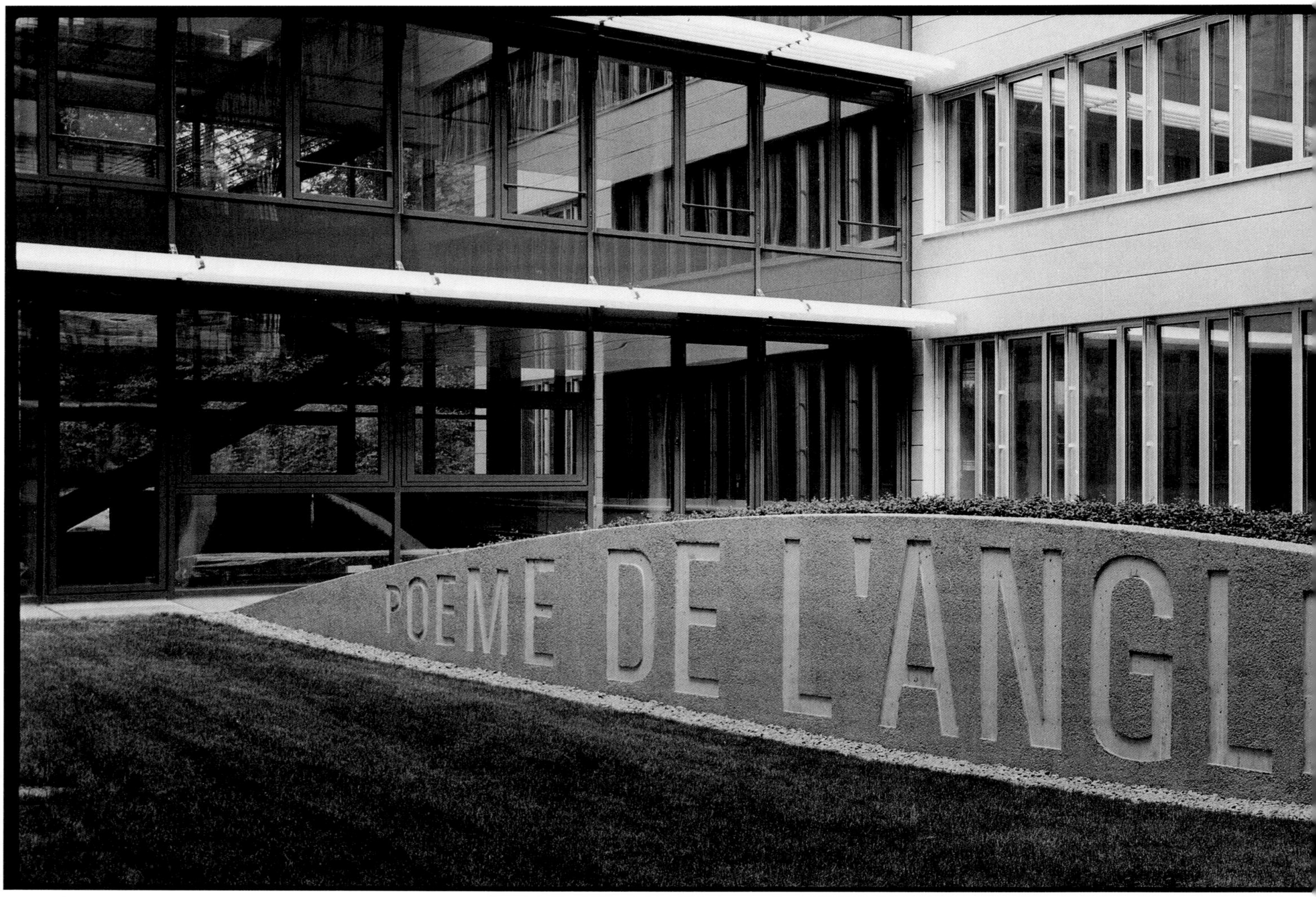
POEME DE L'ANGL

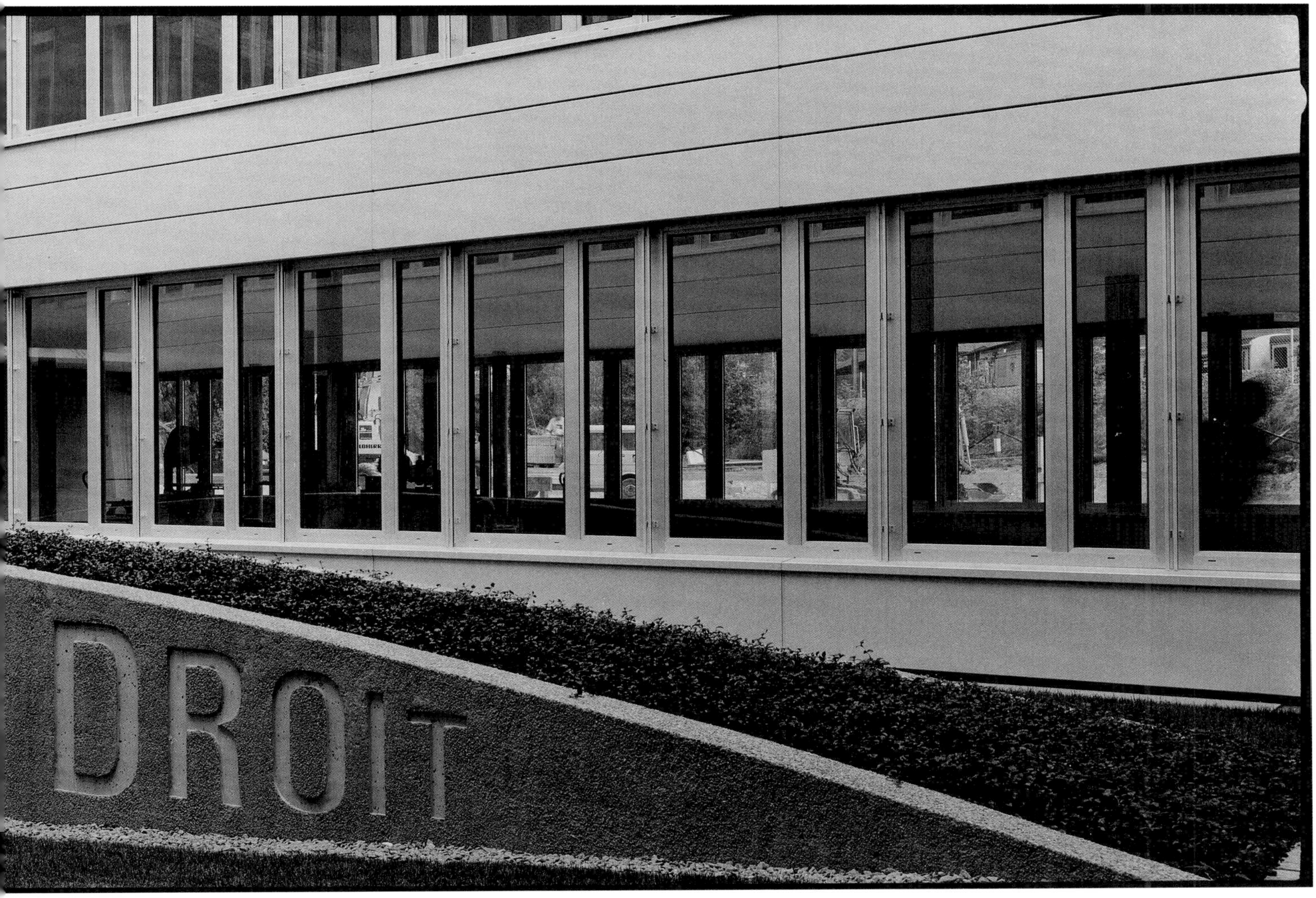
DROIT

Einem riesigen Seerosenblatt aus Aluminium
stehen weißblühende Seerosen gegenüber.

A giant waterlily leaf of aluminium is in contrast
to the pond of white water lilies.

Innerhalb kurzer Zeit werden die berankten Metallstangen zu einem undurchdringlichen Geflecht aus Rosen und Jasmin aufwachsen.

The metal rods will be covered in an impenetrable tangle of roses and jasmine within a short space of time.

Der sparsame Einsatz von Materialien wie Bambus, Sumpfiris, Wasser und Sand knüpft an die minimalistische Gestaltungstradition Japans an.

The sparing use of materials such as bamboo, marsh iris, water and sand is in the minimalist tradition of Japanese gardens.

Rollende Pflanzenkübel ermöglichen auf dem Rasen unterschiedliche Rauminstallationen.

Moveable tubs of plants make possible differing spatial constellations on the lawn.

Expo 2000 und Messegelände Hannover

Masterplan Expo 2000 Hannover

Die Grün- und Freiflächen sind von zentraler Bedeutung für das Weltausstellungsgelände. Ihre Gestaltung wurde entwickelt aus dem übergeordneten Freiflächenkonzept des Masterplans von 1994, der ein Netz aus rechtwinklig angeordneten, grünen Bändern vorsieht, die sich fingerartig zwischen die Ausstellungsbereiche schieben. Durch diese Anordnung wird das Gelände in überschaubare Teilbereiche gegliedert und eine in sich schlüssige Sequenz von Bauvolumen und offenen Freibereichen geschaffen. Gestalterische Zielsetzung waren offene Grünräume, die frei von Einbauten oder Gebäuden sind. Vorhandene Gebäude sollten in die Landschaftsgestaltung integriert werden.

Die Allee der Vereinigten Bäume
Die Allee der Vereinigten Bäume ist die grüne Verbindung zwischen den beiden Geländebereichen. Über eine Distanz von 900 Metern führt sie vom Eingang West direkt bis zur Expo-Plaza. Die Pflanzungen wurden bereits über ein Jahr vor der Expo 2000 abgeschlossen, um den Bäumen Zeit zur Entwicklung zu geben. Entstanden ist ein «Baumgarten» mit insgesamt 460 Bäumen aus 273 Gattungen. Auf einer Gesamtbreite von 26 Metern sind die Bäume in vier parallelen, zueinander versetzten Reihen angeordnet. Pflanzlücken schaffen unterschiedliche Raumsequenzen, die die Allee als Antipode zu einer regelmäßigen, barocken Allee erscheinen lassen. Abends wird die Allee von im Boden eingelassenen Scheinwerfern illuminiert, wodurch ein zusätzlicher Reiz geschaffen wird. Das Nebeneinander einheimischer und fremdländischer Baumarten ist Metapher für die Möglichkeit eines friedlichen Miteinanders unterschiedlichster Menschen.

Die Parkwelle
Mit ihrer stark modellierten Topographie erstreckt sich die Parkwelle entlang des Pavillongeländes West und wird auf der Ostseite begrenzt von verschiedenen Hallen. Im Süden lehnt sich die Bepflanzung aus dichtstehenden Eichen, Buchen und Mam-

Expo 2000 Hanover and Fair Grounds

Master plan Expo 2000 Hannover

The areas of vegetation and open space are of paramount importance for the grounds of the world's fair. Their design was developed from the superordinate open space concept of the 1994 master plan, which envisages a network of strips of green linked at right angles and extending like fingers between the individual exhibition areas. This arrangement divides the grounds into clearly defined sub-sections, creating a consistent sequence of building volumes and open outside areas. The aim of the design was to create open areas of vegetation without any installations or buildings. Existing buildings were to be integrated into the landscape design.

The Avenue of United Trees
The Avenue of United Trees provides a leafy link between the two parts of the grounds. From the west entrance, it extends over a distance of 900 metres to the Expo Plaza. Planting was completed over one year before Expo 2000 opened to allow the trees time to grow. The result is a "garden of trees" with a total of 460 trees representing 273 species. The trees have been planted in four parallel, staggered rows across a total breadth of 26 metres. Unplanted spaces create differing spatial sequences, giving the avenue an appearance antipodean to a regular, baroque avenue. The avenue is illuminated at night by spotlights set in the ground, giving it additional appeal. The juxtaposition of native and non-native species is a metaphor for the possibility of peaceful co-existence of very different people.

The Park Wave
With its undulating topography, the Park Wave extends along the west pavilion grounds and is bounded on the eastern side by halls 21, 24, and 25. To the south, the vegetation of closely planted oaks, beeches and sequoias is a reference to the adjacent Avenue of United Trees. The trees thin out along a slightly ascending incline and the visitor arrives at a gravel-covered plaza surrounded by tulip trees. The highest elevation in the

mutbäumen an die angrenzende Allee der Vereinigten Bäume an. Während eines leichten Anstiegs lichten sich die Bäume und der Besucher erreicht einen von Tulpenbäumen umgebenen, kiesbedeckten Platz. Die höchste Erhebung der Parkwelle wird durch einen Birkenwald markiert. An der tiefsten Stelle im Norden versteckt sich ein von amerikanischen Eichen eingefaßter See. Auf ihrer gesamten Länge ist die etwa drei Hektar große Parkwelle von Böschungen eingefaßt.

Der Erdgarten

Der von Hainbuchen gesäumte Erdgarten erstreckt sich westlich des Hallenkomplexes 14 bis 17 zwischen der Allee der Vereinigten Bäume und der Nordallee. Der Erdgarten ist in drei unterschiedliche Bereiche gegliedert. Im Süden bilden Zierobsthecken in geometrischen Grundformen kleine, geschlossene Räume. Im mittleren Bereich um den bestehenden Krupp-Pavillon, der während der Weltausstellung als Jugendtreff genutzt wird, stehen kastenförmig geschnittene Roßkastanien in einem regelmäßigen Raster. Einen markanten Blickpunkt bilden im nördlichen Bereich fünf bis zwölf Meter hohe, rasenbewachsene Erdkegel, die dem Erdgarten seinen Namen geben. Der Erdgarten ist ein in sich abgeschlossener Raum, der inmitten der Betriebsamkeit eine Insel der Ruhe darstellt.

Der Expo-See und das Expo-Dach

Eingerahmt von der Parkwelle, dem Erdgarten und der Allee der Vereinigten Bäume, bildet der 43 000 Quadratmeter große Expo-See einen stimmungsvollen Veranstaltungsbereich für bis zu 10 000 Besucher. Beispielsweise fand hier während der Weltausstellung allabendlich das «Flambée» statt. Auf dem Platz um den Hermesturm entstand eine Grachten- und Pontonlandschaft, die von der weltweit größten Holzdachkonstruktion überdacht wird. Das Großdach der Architekten Herzog & Partner besteht aus zehn 40 x 40 Meter großen Holzschirmen, die unabhängig voneinander stehend zu einer Gesamtfläche von 16 000 Quadratmetern zusammengesetzt wurden.

Dieter Kienast

Park Wave is marked by a grove of birch trees. A lake framed by American oaks lies hidden at the lowest point in the north. The approximately three-hectare Park Wave is defined by embankments extending along its entire length.

The Earth Garden

The Earth Garden, bounded by hornbeams, extends to the west of the complex made up of halls 14 to 17 between the Avenue of United Trees and the North Avenue. The Earth Garden is divided up into three different areas. Hedges of small ornamental fruit trees in basic geometrical shapes form small self-contained spaces. Horse chestnut trees clipped in box shapes stand in a regular grid in the central area around the existing Krupp Pavilion, used as a youth meeting place during Expo. Five to twelve-metre-high, grass-covered mounds of earth that have given the Earth Garden its name provide a striking focal point in the northern area. The Earth Garden is a self-contained area and an island of tranquility in the midst of the surrounding hustle and bustle.

The Expo Lake and the Expo Roof

Framed by the Park Wave, the Earth Garden and the Avenue of United Trees, the 43,000-square-metre Expo Lake is an exciting event area for up to 10,000 visitors. For example, the regular evening event "Flambée" took place here during the world's fair. A canal and pontoon landscape was created on the plaza around the Hermes Tower and is covered by the largest wooden roof structure in the world. The monumental roof, designed by the architects Herzog & Partner, consists of ten 40 x 40-metre wooden canopies which, standing independently of each other, span an overall area of 16,000 square metres.

Dieter Kienast

Der Erdgarten, ein in sich geschlossener Raum, stellt inmitten der Messebetriebsamkeit eine Insel der Ruhe dar.

The Earth Garden, a self-contained area, is an island of tranquility in the midst of the fair's hustle and bustle.

In stark modellierter Topographie verläuft die Rasenwelle rechtwinklig zur großen Allee.

The Park Wave is at right angles to the main avenue in the undulating topography.

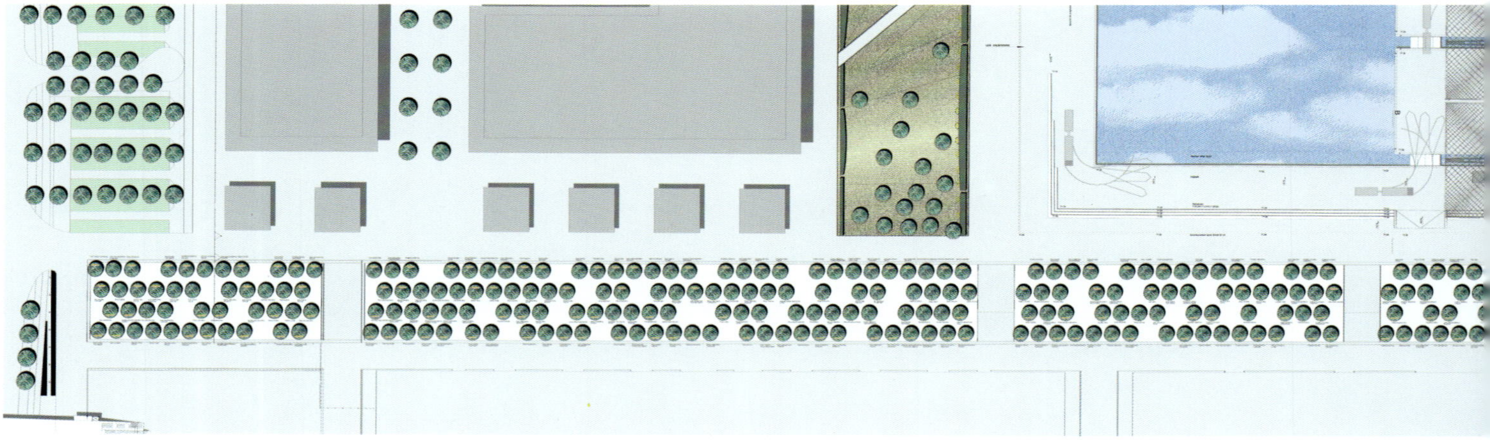

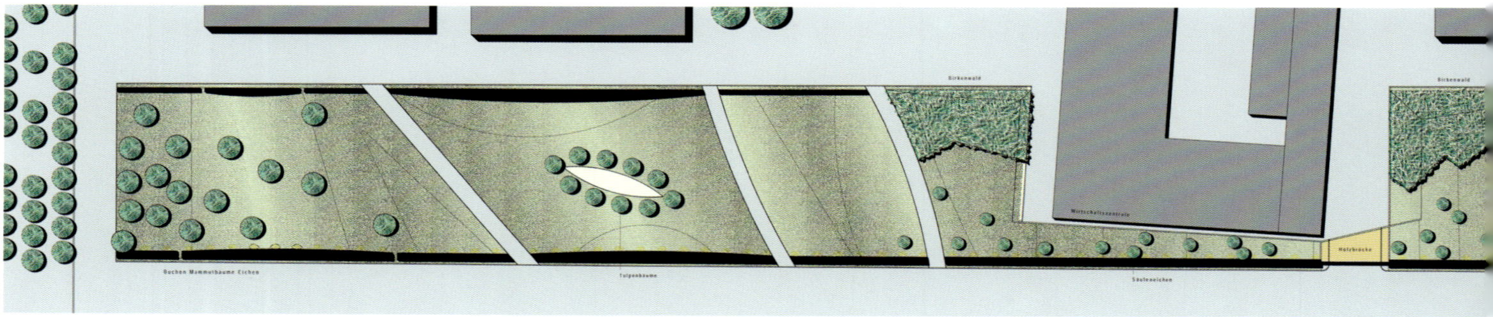
Birkenwald
Birkenwald
Wirtschaftszentrale
Holzbrücke
Buchen Mammutbäume Eichen
Tulpenbäume
Säuleneichen

SOLARGRAESER UND
FESTUCA GLAUCA
LEHMMAUER
HECKENRAEUME MIT
FREIER BESTUHLUNG
WASSERBECKEN UND
SCIRPUS
WASSERBECKEN UND
SEEROSEN
RASENBAENKE
HERBSTBLUEHENDE STAUDEN
SOMMERFLIEDER
SCHOTTERRASEN
HERBSTFLIEDER
FARNE
GESCHNITTENE
LINDEN
HORTENSIEN
BAMBUS
WASSERGEBUNDENE
DECKE

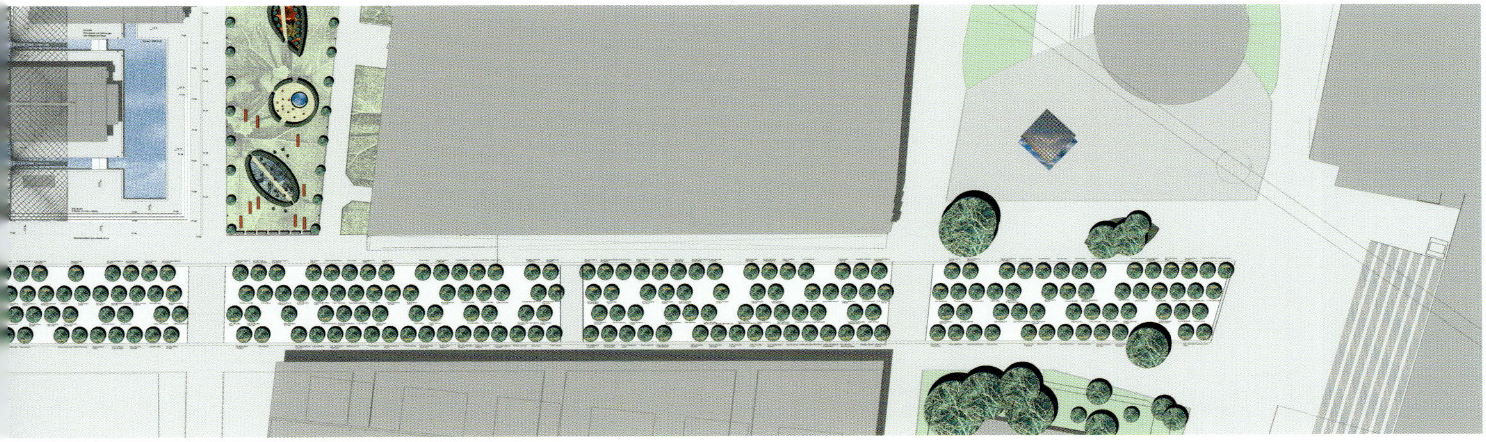

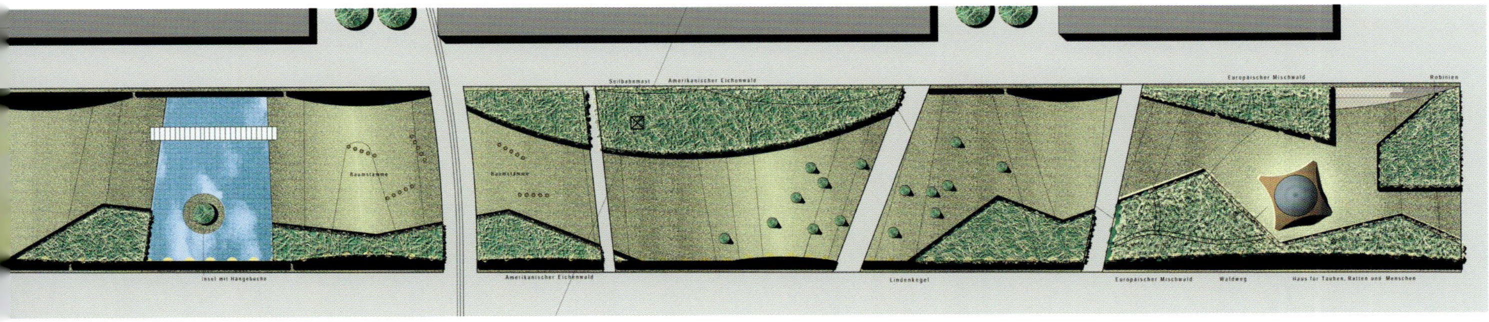
Seilbahnmast
Amerikanischer Eichenwald
Europäischer Mischwald
Robinien
Raumstämme
Raumstämme
Insel mit Hängebuche
Amerikanischer Eichenwald
Lindenkegel
Europäischer Mischwald
Waldweg
Haus für Tauben, Ratten und Menschen

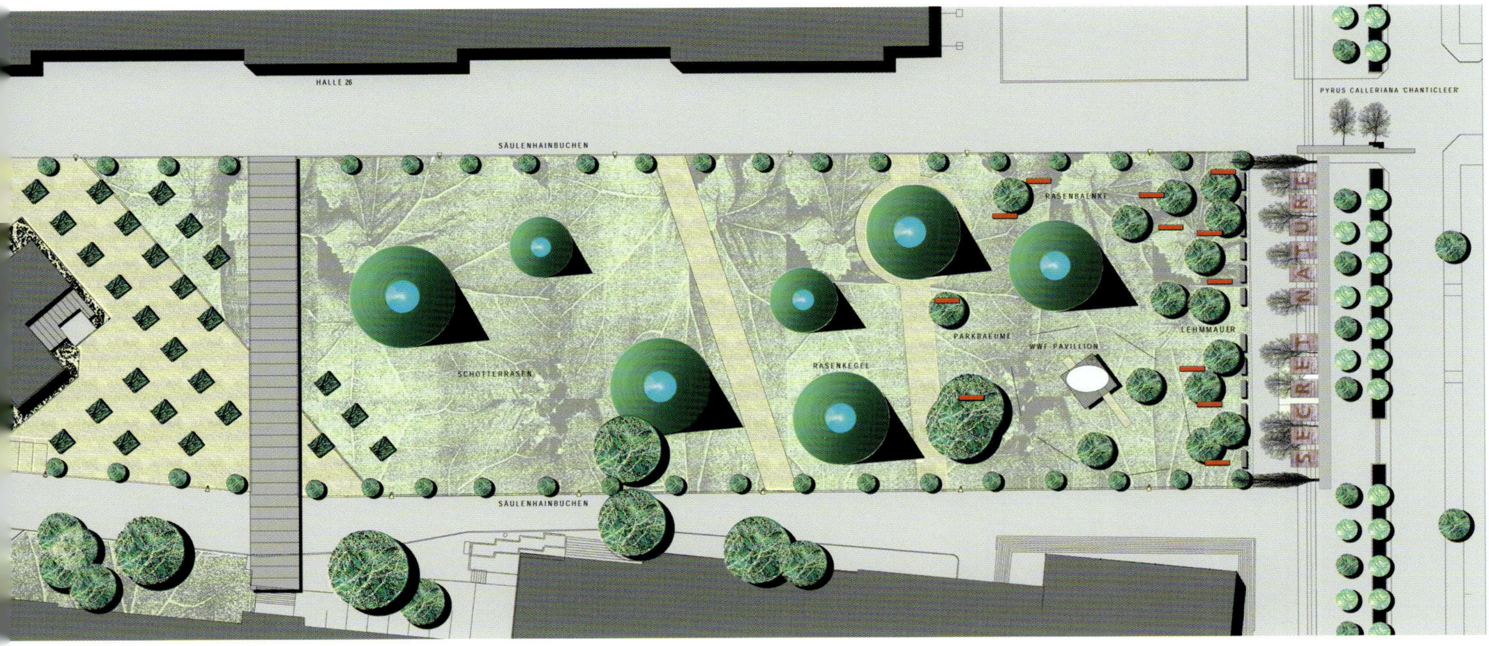
HALLE 26
PYRUS CALLERIANA 'CHANTICLEER'
SÄULENHAINBUCHEN
RASENBAENKE
PARKBAEUME
WWF-PAVILLION
LEHMMAUER
SCHOTTERRASEN
RASENKEGEL
SÄULENHAINBUCHEN
SECRET NATURE

Schnitt - Ansicht AA

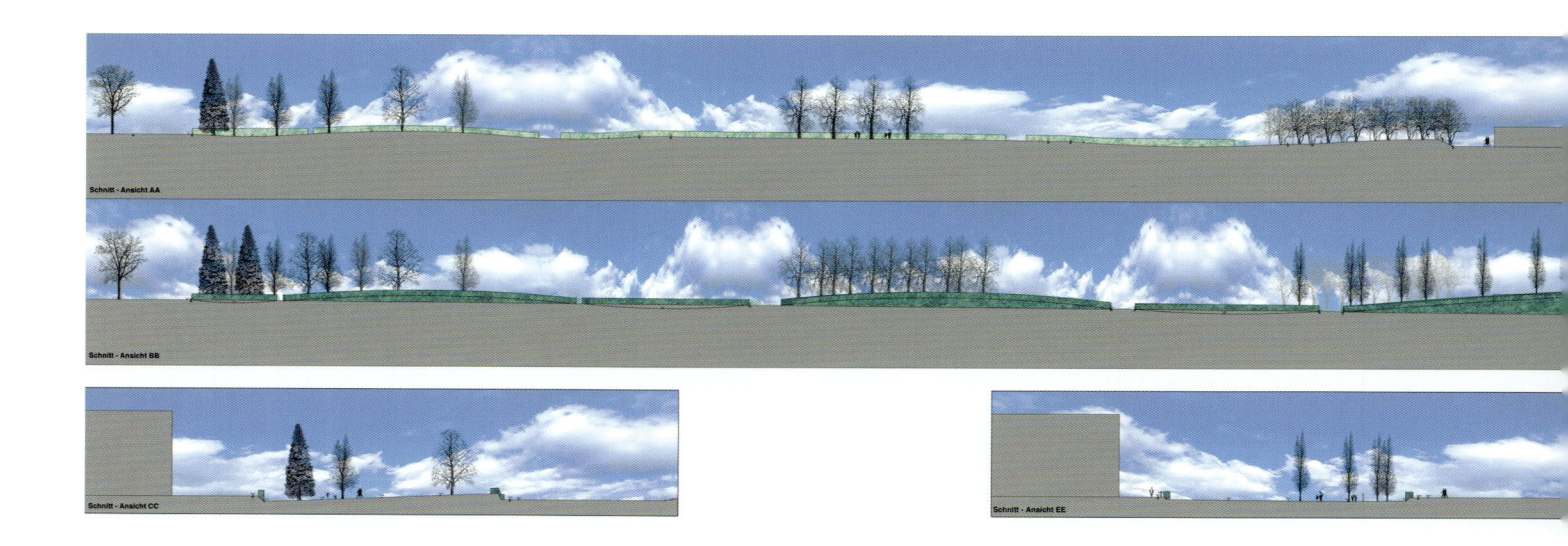

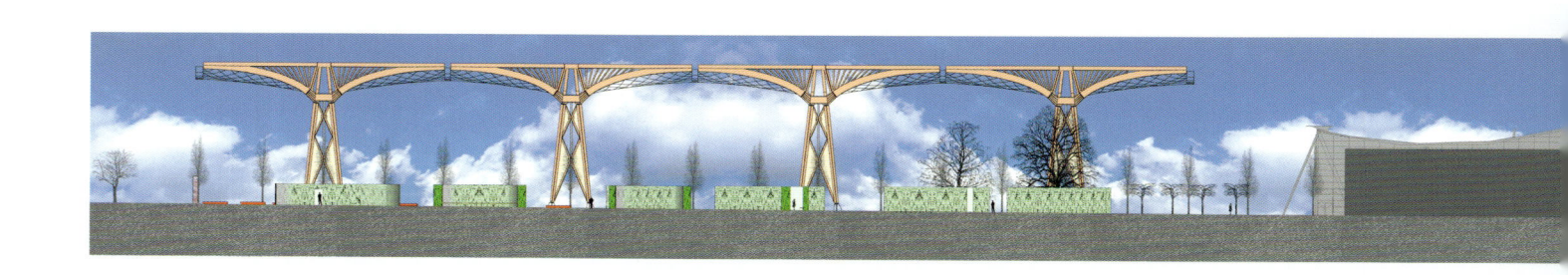

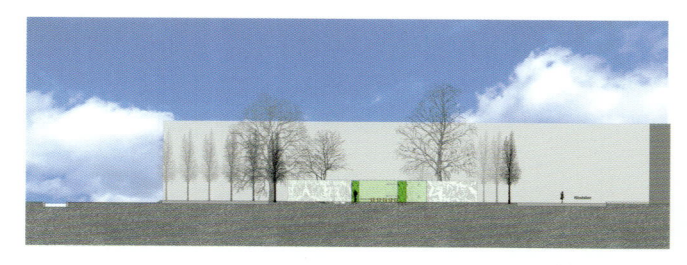

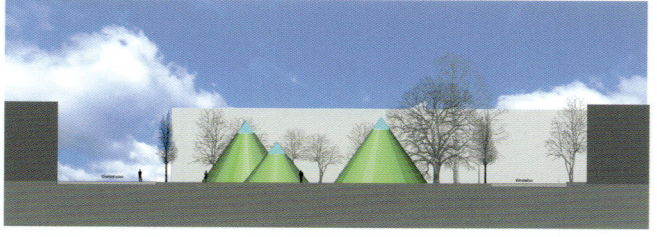

Schnitt - Ansicht BB

Schnitt - Ansicht CC

Schnitt - Ansicht EE

SCHNITT B-B M 1:250

SCHNITT A-A M 1:250

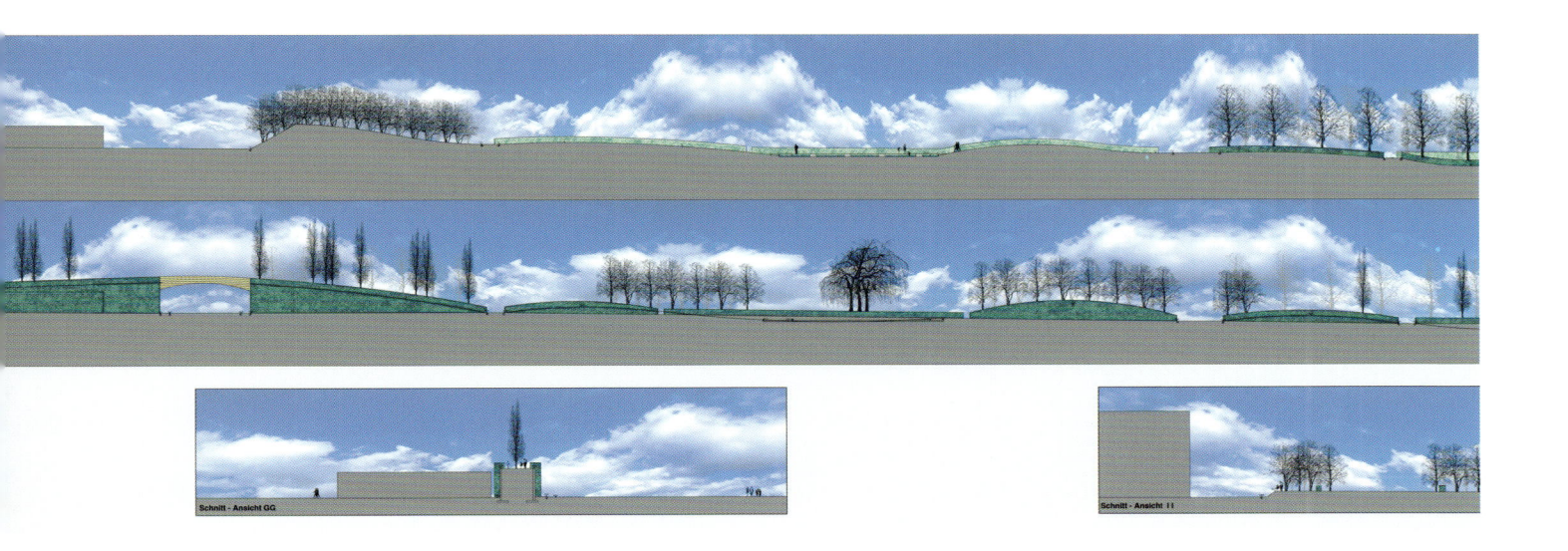

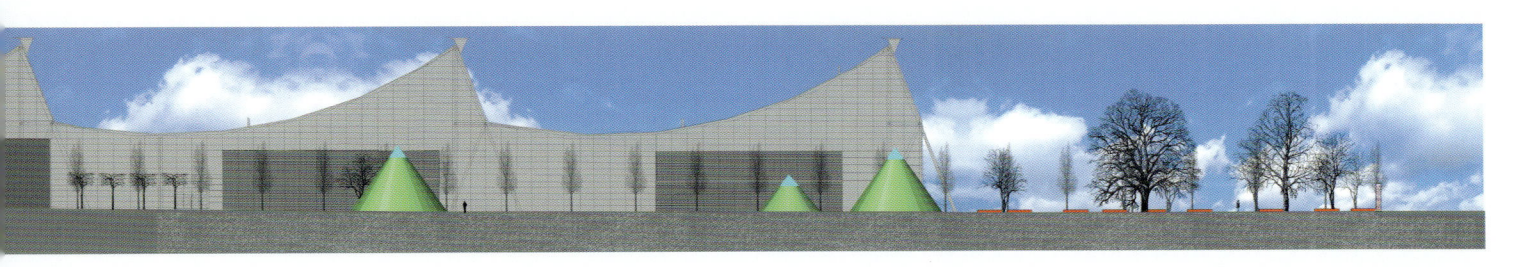

SCHNITT C-C M 1:250

PERSPEKTIVE HECKENRÄUME

PERSPEKTIVE RASENKEGEL

Die «Allee der Vereinigten Bäume»

Sophie, Kurfürstin von Hannover, übersiedelte 1680 von Osnabrück nach Hannover. Herrenhausen wurde ihr Leben. Sie plante die Erweiterung und Ausgestaltung des Herrenhäuser Gartens zu einem «großen Garten» gemeinsam mit dem Gärtner Martin Charbonnier und mit dem Bildhauer Pieter von Empthausen, der Skulpturen der griechischen Sage für das Gartenparterre schuf. Die Bauarbeiten wurden 1714 abgeschlossen und in ganz Europa – neben Versailles und Vaux le Vicomte – gepriesen als «Grand jardin de la Leine». Die barocke Gartenanlage ist bis heute erhalten. Dabei nehmen die großen Alleen einen breiten Bedeutungsraum ein.

Jahrhundertelang wurde die ungestaltete, agrarische Landschaft mittels Alleen messbar gemacht. Dabei haben die Alleen – weithin ins Zentrum der Macht führend – die Funktion der Lesbarkeit, der Hierarchisierung, sichtbar gemacht. Sie zeigen ein immergleiches Anordnungsmuster von regelmäßigen Abständen und gleicher Baumartenwahl. Lakaienhaft begleiten sie die Straßen und haben dadurch das absolutistische System über die Landschaft gelegt. Am Beispiel der Herrenhäuser Allee wird dies besonders deutlich sichtbar. Mit dem «Großen Garten», dem Georgengarten und der großen Allee war eine künstliche Welt geschaffen, die Natur als Herrschaftsinstrument ausgewiesen, subsumierter Gebrauchsgegenstand. Trotz ihrer Liebe zur Gartengestaltung wird Sophie die kilometerlange Allee nur als räumliches Gebilde gewertet haben. Begleitet vom Pferdeschweißgeruch war die Allee – mit Bäumen immer der gleichen Art und mit gleichem Pflanzabstand – nur der Weg zum Ziel: dem Schloß.

Die «Allee der Vereinigten Bäume» auf dem Messe- und Expo 2000-Gelände ist als eine Alternative zu dem historischen Bild der herkömmlichen Allee zu verstehen. Mit den unregelmäßigen Abständen und den unterschiedlichen Baumsorten und -arten – vier parallele Baumreihen aus 273 Baumarten und -sorten – wird die Allee nicht mehr nur zum schnellstmöglichen Durchgangsort und Ordnungsinstrument, sondern zeigt sich als Rückgrat einer «dominierenden Raumkonzeption» (Dieter Kienast) auf dem Hannoveraner Messegelände, verbindet den West- und Ostteil, wird zum Verteiler und Aufenthaltsort.

Indem die Baumarten und -sorten permanent wechseln, soll die Aufmerksamkeit geschärft auf das Individuum des Einzelbaumes mit seiner unterschiedlichen Wuchs- und Grünform

"Avenue of United Trees"

Sophie, Electoress of Hanover, moved from Hanover to Osnabrück in 1680. Herrenhausen became the centre of her life. She planned the extension and design of the Herrenhaus Gardens to create a "Grand Garden" with the assistance of the gardener Martin Charbonnier and the sculptor Pieter von Empthausen, who created sculptures of Greek myths for the garden parterre.

Building work was completed in 1714 and the result was lauded across Europe as "Grand jardin de la Leine" in the same breath as Versailles and Vaux le Vicomte. The baroque garden is still in existence, with the large avenues continuing to play a significant role. The undesigned, agricultural countryside was given structure by means of avenues. These avenues – largely leading to the centre of power- revealed the function of readibility, of hierarchy. The avenues have a repetitive pattern of regular spacing and same choice of types of tree. They line the roads in a subordinate way, thereby imposing an absolutist system on the landscape.

This is particularly revealed by the example of the Herrenhausen Avenue. The "Grand Garden" the Georgian Garden and the "Grand Avenue made up an artificial world, nature as an instrument to demonstrate power, a subsumed commodity. Despite her love of garden design, Sophie probably only saw the one-kilometre-long avenue as a spatial structure. Enveloped by the smell of horse sweat, the avenue – with its trees of one and the same kind, planted at equal intervals – was always only a means to an end, namely the palace.

The "Avenue of United Trees" at the fair site of Expo 2000 is to be understood as an alternative to the historical conception of the traditional avenue. With its irregular spacing and different kinds and species of trees – namely four parallel rows of trees made up of 273 kinds and species of trees – the avenue is not merely the most direct means of access and structure, but also reveals itself as the backbone of a "dominating spatial design" (Dieter Kienast) at the site of the Hanover Expo fair, creating a link between its eastern and western sections and functioning as a junction and lobby area.

The concept of ever-changing kinds and species of trees is designed to draw attention to the nature of the individual tree with its varying forms of growth and foliage. The "Avenue of

gelenkt werden. Die «Allee der Vereinigten Bäume» stellt den Versuch dar, das Arboretum des 19. Jahrhunderts in neuer Form zu fassen. Dennoch, die Scharen der Expo-Besucher – und später dann die Messegäste –, die teils lautlos auf dem Peoplemover durch die Allee gleiten, werden der differenten Narturerscheinung ebensowenig Aufmerksamkeit schenken wie der «großen Allee» zu Sophies Zeiten zuteil wurde. Die Beachtung der Natur wird durch das Ziel, welches auf dem Weg erreicht werden soll, konkurrenziert: Aufmerksamkeit wird der Besucher nur gerade den Pavillons widmen.

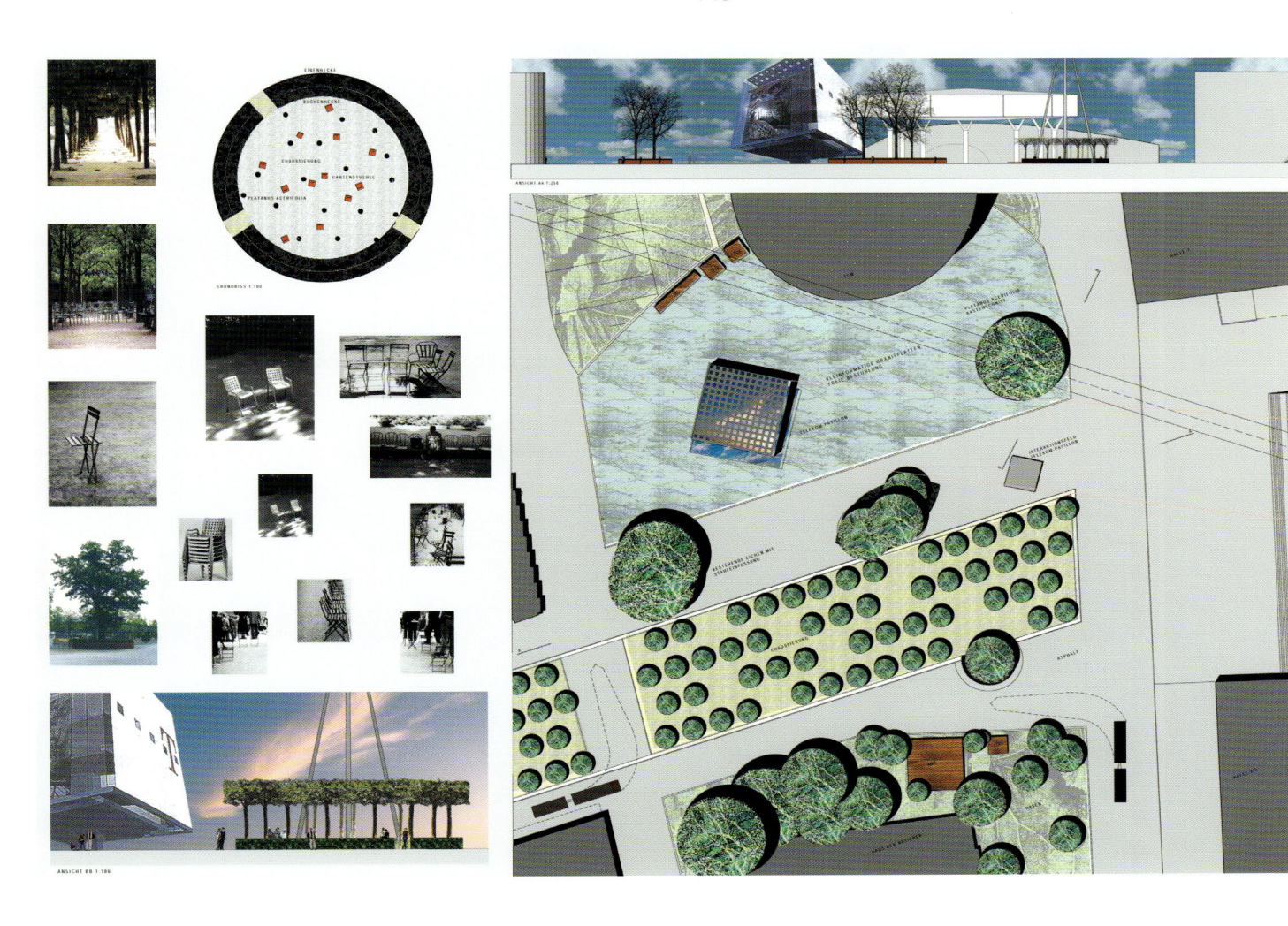

Erika Kienast

United Trees" is to be seen as an attempt to redefine the arboretum of the 19th century. Yet, despite this, the crowds of Expo visitors – and later on the fair visitors –, who in many cases will glide along the avenue noiselessly on the peoplemover, will pay as little attention to this expression of nature as was reaped by the "Grand Avenue" during Sophie's times. The contemplation of nature coincides with the destination of the path. The visitor's attention tends to be focussed on the pavilions.

Erika Kienast

Kurpark Bad Münder

Ein Kurort ist gemäß Lexikon ein Ort, der sich unter anderem durch besondere bioklimatische Verhältnisse oder durch das Vorkommen natürlicher Heilquellen auszeichnet. Eingebettet in die Höhenzüge zwischen Deister und Süntel ist Bad Münder ein aufstrebender Kurbad-Standort, der nach neuen Möglichkeiten sucht, das Kurwesen für zukünftige Besucher reizvoller zu gestalten.

Vitruv hat mit seinen Traktaten zur Bäderentwicklung ein Kompendium verfaßt, das heute noch in der Bädergeschichte eine zentrale Stellung einnimmt. Danach ist nicht nur die Beschaffenheit eines Ortes bei der Bädereinrichtung von Wichtigkeit, sondern insbesondere dessen Ausgestaltung.

Mit der Parkgestalt eines «Neuen Kurparks» und dem großen Angebot an gesundheitsfördernden Badeinrichtungen wird die größtmögliche Nutzungsoffenheit durch die unterschiedlichsten Benutzergruppen möglich. Die heute bereits vorhandenen Qualitäten des Landschaftsraumes werden behutsam im neuen Kurpark verstärkt. Erwähnenswert ist dabei die Respektierung der topographischen Verhältnisse wie auch die Anbindung an den alten Kurpark mit offengehaltenen Sichtachsen.

Das räumliche Gepräge des neuen Kurparks wird durch die kulissenartig angepflanzten Waldstücke bestimmt, deren Ausrichtung den Blickbezug zur Stadt betont. Die einzelnen Waldstreifen thematisieren den spezifischen Standort, so z.B. am großen Weiher der Birkenhain.

Wir beginnen unseren Spaziergang an der Musikmuschel und wenden uns gegen Osten. Auf dem alten Weg wird der Blick auf den am Hang liegenden Frühlingsgarten frei. Dem geschwungenen Weg folgend, sehen wir feine Linien von Hyazinthen, Krokus, Narzissen und Tulpen. Im Sommer erinnern nur die Blütenlinien im verfärbten Gras an diese bunt-blühende Frühlingspracht. Um den eingeschobenen Privatgarten herum gelangen wir zu einer in schillernden Farben ausgelegten Grotte, aus der Wasserdampf austritt. Seitlich sind Solarzellen angebracht, aus denen die notwendige Energie gewonnen wird. Wir erreichen den ersten Querweg, vorbei am Eingang der Minigolfanlage und gelangen zum Kinderspielplatz. Die skulptural ge-

Bad Münder Spa Gardens

Dictionaries define a spa as a place which, among other things, features particular bio-climatic conditions or the existence of natural medicinal springs. Bad Münder, embedded in the range of hills between Deister and Süntel, is an up-and-coming spa town seeking new ways of making spa facilities more attractive for future visitors.

With his tracts on the development of bathing, Vitruvius compiled a compendium that today still plays a central role in the history of bathing. According to what he wrote, not only the nature of a place is important for a bathing facility, but also, in particular, its design.

The design of the new spa gardens and the wide range of health-enhancing bathing facilities enable the greatest possible forms of use by very different groups. The qualities of the landscape that already exist today are gently intensified in the new spa gardens. Mention should be made of respect for existing topography, as well as the link with the old spa gardens by means of open vistas.

The spatial character of the new spa gardens is defined by portions of woodland planted like a backdrop, aligned in such a way that they emphasise the visual reference to the town. The individual strips at woodland specifically address the location, e.g. at the large pond at the grove of birch trees.

We begin our walk at the music pavilion and turn eastwards. As we proceed along the old path, the springtime gardens on the slope come into view. Following the curved path, we see delicate lines of hyacinths, crocuses, narcissi, and tulips. Their springtime splendour is recalled by faded lines in the grass during the summer months. By walking past the intervening private garden, we arrive at a highly colourful grotto from which steam rises. Solar cells providing necessary energy are placed along the sides. We reach the first intersecting path, pass the entrance to the mini-golf course and arrive at the children's playground. The shrubs at the east entrance, sculpturally clipped to form fabulous creatures, give the entrance an identity of its own and, along with the adjacent play area that announces itself on our walk by the noisy sounds of children at play, has an unmistake-

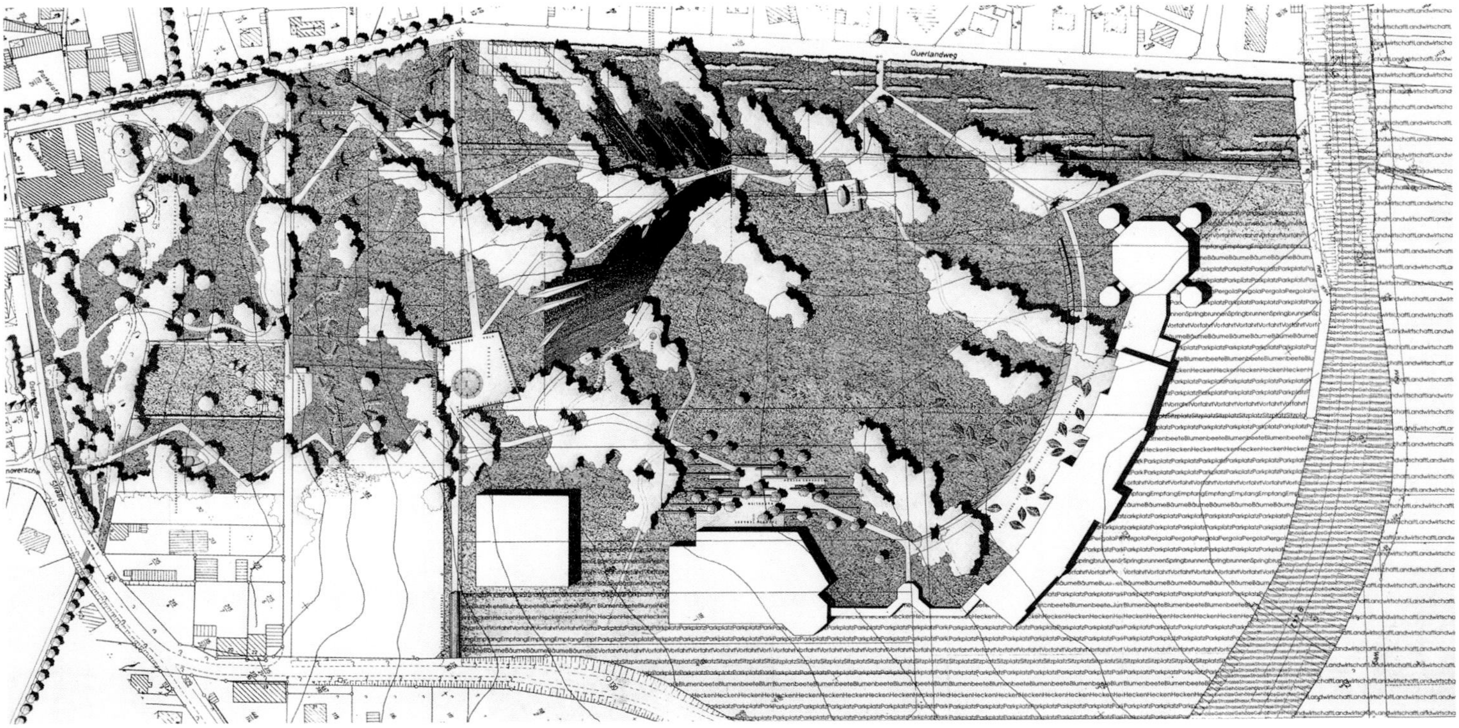
Querlandweg

schnittenen Pflanzenkörper in Form von Fabeltieren schaffen am Osteingang eine eigene Identität und geben mit dem angrenzenden Spielbereich, der sich auf unserem Spaziergang bereits durch laute Kinderstimmen ankündigt, ein unverwechselbares Gepräge. Um die teilweise beachtlichen Steigungen besser zu überwinden, sind Serpentinen angelegt. In einer Kurve erblicken wir eine große Muschel, in der das Bachwasser gesammelt und tosend der Unterwelt zugeführt wird. Wir meiden den steilen, rechts hochgehenden Weg zum Bellevue und gehen, sanft ansteigend, dem kaskadenförmig angelegten Rückhaltebecken entgegen. Es wird schattig und kühl. Künstliche Felsen aus Tuffsteinen sind mit grünen Algen überzogen. Zwischen den wasserüberspülten Felstreppen haben sich Moose und Farne angesiedelt. Rechterhand taucht der große Weiher auf. Über eine Stahlbrücke gelangen wir zu einem Platz und setzen uns auf die Bank. Direkt vor uns eine Balustrade, die aus den Buchstaben POCA DIFFERENZA gebildet wird. Über den Sinn der Worte grübelnd, fällt unser Blick auf den 150 Meter langen See. Schwarze Schwäne mit roten Schnäbeln steigen aus dem Wasser und recken sich flügelschlagend auf einer kleinen Insel, die uns an einen steingewordenen Fischrücken erinnert. Von Ferne ertönt das Gekreisch eines Beos, unterbrochen von Grillengezirpe. Hinter einer dichten Hecke versteckt, begrüßt uns der lachende Hans aus der Volière. Eine Amsel aus der nahegelegenen Wildhecke antwortet ihm. Wir durchqueren diesen wilden Vegetationsbestand mit wechselfeuchten bis trockenen Standorten, die durch längsgerichtete Wildhecken gegliedert sind. Es lockt die Hotelterrasse. Zwischen Stauden, Hecken und Blumenbeeten trinken wir Kaffee. Direkt vor uns ein flaches Wasserbecken. Zwischen glycinienberankten Säulen und Baumgruppen hindurch erkennen wir über dem Weiher die markante Kuppel der Stadtkirche. Der Weg führt uns hinab zu streifenförmig geschnittenen Hecken, die nicht nur aus Hainbuche, sondern auch aus blühenden Sträuchern wie Cornus, Chaenomeles, Forsythie oder Spirea bestehen. Locker verteilt wachsen stattliche Exemplare von großen Magnolien und Japanischem Ahorn. Die Großbäume – einzeln gepflanzt – bilden einen Kontrast zu den wald-

able character. Serpentines have been laid out to overcome the slopes that are in some cases steep. As we come to a curve, we see a large pool where the stream waters gather and disappear below ground in a thunderous roar. We avoid the steep, right-hand path leading to the belvedere and walk along the route that gently ascends to the retention basin with its cascading form. It becomes shady and cool. Artificial rocks of tuff are covered with green algae. Moss and fern have established themselves between the stone, water-washed steps. The large pond lies to the right. We cross a steel bridge and arrive at a clearing where we take a rest on a bench. Directly in front us, we see a balustrade containing the letters POCA DIFFERENZA. Reflecting on what these words mean, our gaze falls on the 150-metre-long lake. Black swans with red beaks rise out of the water and, beating their wings, come to rest on a small island that reminds us of the petrified back of a fish. The screetch of a beo can be heard from a distance, interrupted by the chirping of crickets. We are welcomed by the laugh of a kookaburra in the aviary, hidden behind a dense hedge. A blackbird from the nearby wild hedge answers. We cross this area of wild vegetation with its poikilohydric and dry locations that are structured by lateral hedges of wild bushes. The hotel terrace is inviting. We enjoy a cup of coffee between the shrubs, hedges and flower-beds. In front of us, a shallow pool of water. The striking dome of the town church is visible across the pond and between the glycinia-covered columns and groups of trees. The path we follow downhill leads us to austerely clipped hedges that not only consist of hornbeam, but also of flowering shrubs such as cornus, chaenomeles, forsythia and spiraea. There are scattered, magnificent examples of magnolia and Japanese maple. These large trees – planted at intervals – form a contrast to the woodland areas. A minor path with a waterbound surface branches off to the right. We pass the Kneipp pool by as we are riveted by the view of the belvedere and its rose-covered rotunda high above the lake. Climbing roses around the tower conjure up images of a well-known and frequently used park element. The scent of roses is evocative. Once again, the inscription: ET IN ARCADIA

artigen Bereichen. Ein kleiner Nebenweg mit wassergebundener Decke zweigt rechts ab. Die Kneipp-Station lassen wir unbenutzt, weil uns der Anblick des über dem See liegenden Bellevue mit seinem Rosenrondell fesselt. Kletterrosen am Rosenrondell rufen Erinnerungen an ein bekanntes und oft tradiertes Parkelement wach. Betört vom Duft der Rosen werden die Gedanken frei. Wieder eine Inschrift: ET IN ARCADIA EGO. Langsam dämmert es – war da nicht Goethe, der auch schon in Arkadien weilte? Das Bellevue – man nimmt es sofort wahr – ist das Herzstück des Kurparkes, der die unterschiedlichsten Durch- und Ausblicke in alle vier Himmelsrichtungen gewährt. Die nahe Klinik, der lange Weiher, die Stadt. Es ist dunkel geworden. Auf der südlichen Balustrade sitzend, blicken wir auf eine merkwürdig illuminierte Anordnung, die in den nächtlichen Himmel strahlt. Bodenlampen in der Minigolfanlage zeichnen ein Bild, das wir sonst über uns sehen – Aquarius, Cerus und Phoenix – der südliche Sternenhimmel.

Dieter Kienast

Gewähre, daß ich ein- und ausgehe in meinem Garten,
daß ich mich kühle in seinem Schatten,
daß ich Wasser trinke aus meinem Brunnen jeden Tag,
daß ich lustwandle am Ufer meines Teiches ohne Unterlaß,
daß meine Seele sich niederlasse auf den Bäumen,
die ich gepflanzt habe,
daß ich mich erquicke unter meinen Sykomoren.

Ägyptisches Gebet

EGO. Gradually, it dawns on us – dit not Goethe also sojourn in Arcadia? The belvedere – it is immediately perceptible – is the heart of the spa gardens, which permit very differing views in all directions of the compass. The nearby clinic, the elongated pond, the town. Darkness has fallen. Sitting on the southern balustrade, we see a curiously illuminated arrangement that lights up the night sky. Ground lights on the mini-golf course trace a picture that we normally see above us – Aquarius, Cerus and Phoenix – the southern sky.

Dieter Kienast

Grant that I may enter and leave my garden,
that I may cool myself in its shade,
that I may drink water from my well each day,
that I may wander along the banks of my pool at will,
that my soul may lay itself down on the trees I planted,
that I may refresh myself under my mulberry trees

Egyptian prayer

Gewähre, dass ich ein- und ausgehe in meinem Garten,
dass ich mich kühle in seinem Schatten,
dass ich Wasser trinke aus meinem Brunnen jeden Tag,
dass ich lustwandle am Ufer meines Teiches ohne Unterlass,
dass meine Seele sich niederlasse auf den Bäumen,
die ich gepflanzt habe,
dass ich mich erquicke unter meinen Sykomoren

Ägyptisches Gebet

Bad Münder am Deister wird sich in naher Zukunft wegen seiner geplanten grossmassstäblichen Bauten in sozialer, ökonomischer, städtebaulicher und landschaftlicher Sicht stark verändern. Allein ein Flächenvergleich zeigt, dass die drei grossen Bauvorhaben - Kurpark, Ferienpark und Golfplatz - etwa ein Drittel das bisherigen Siedlungsgebietes der Stadt belegen. Der Kurpark ist öffentlicher Raum Deshalb kommt ihm eine besondere Stellung zu. Bereits sind die vielfältigen Anforderungen und Erwartungshaltungen formuliert, die wir als Planer kaum erfüllen können. Zwischen Disneyland und ökologischer Ausgleichsfläche haben wir uns für eine Parkgestalt entschieden, die grösstmögliche Nutzungsoffenheit anstrebt und dadurch vielfältigen Gebrauch unterschiedlicher Besucher ermöglicht. Die Bezugnahme zum Ort wird auf verschiedenen Ebenen gesucht, wie zum Beispiel in behutsamer topographischer Integration, in der Anbindung an den Kurpark alter in offengehaltenen Sichtachsen (u.a. zur Stadtkirche).

Mit der Videokamera gehen wir durch den Park, erblicken die Besucher, erleben, die räumliche Gestalt, den Duft, die Farben und den Wind.

Zur Erinnerung haben wir vier Videostandbilder herausgenommen, die uns atmosphärisch beeindruckt haben.

Wir beginnen unseren Spaziergang an der Muslimuschel und wenden uns gegen Osten. Auf dem alten Weg wird der Blick auf den Hang liegenden Frühlingsgarten (1) frei. Dem geschwungenen Weg folgend, sehen wir feine, tanzende Linien (2) von Hyazinthen, Krokus Narzissen und Tulpen, während uns im Sommer nur das hier etwas verfärbte Gras an die Blütenlinien erinnert. Um den eingebetteten Pavillon herum gelangen wir zu einer in schillernden Farben ausgelegten Grotte (3), aus der Wasserdampf austritt. Seitlich sind Solarzellen angebracht, aus denen die notwendige Energie gewonnen wird. Wir erreichen den ersten Querweg. Kindergeschrei lockt uns an, vorbei am Eingang der Minigolfanlage (4) zum Kinderspielplatz (5). Einfache Spielgeräte - Sand- und Matschplätze - eine pneumatische Matte zwischen riesigen Kabel- und Terwesen aus geschnittenen Pflanzen erfreuen grosse und kleine Besucher gleichermassen. Um die teilweise beachtlichen Steigungen besser zu überwinden, sind Serpentinen (6) angelegt. In einer Kurve erblicken wir eine grosse Muschel (7), in der das Bachwasser gesammelt und tosend der Unterwelt zugeführt wird. Wir meiden den steilen, rechts hoch gehenden Weg zum Bellevue und gehen, sanft ansteigend, dem kaskadenförmig angelegten Rückhaltebecken (8) entgegen. Es wird schattig und kühl. Künstliche Felsen aus Tuffsteinen sind von grünen Algen überzogen. Zwischen den wasserüberspülten Felstreppen haben sich Moose und Farne angesiedelt. Rechterhand taucht der grosse Weiher und eine Stahlbrücke (9).

gelangen wir zu einem Platz (10), und setzen uns auf die Bank. Direkt vor uns eine Balustrade, die aus den Buchstaben POCA DIFFERENZA gebildet wird. Ueber den Sinn der Worte grübelnd, fällt unser Blick auf den 150 Meter langen See. Schwarze Schwäne mit roten Schnäbeln steigen aus dem Wasser, und recken sich flügelschlagend auf einer kleinen Insel, die uns an einen steingewordenen Fischrücken erinnert. Von Ferne ertönt das Geierisch eines Sees, unterbrochen von Grillengezirpe. Hinter einer dichten Hecke versteckt, begrüsst uns der lachende Hans aus der Volière. (11) Eine Amsel aus der nahegelegenen Wildhecke antwortet ihm. Wir durchqueren diesen wilden Vegetationsbestand (12) mit wechselfeuchten bis trockenen Standorten, die durch länggerichtete Wildhecken gegliedert ist. Die Hotelterasse lockt. Zwischen blattförmigen Stauden-, Hecken- und Blumenbeeten (13) trinken wir Kaffee. Direkt vor uns ein flaches Wasserbecken. Zwischen glycinienberankten Säulen- und Baumgruppen hindurch erkennen wir über dem Weiher, die markante Kuppel der Stadtkirche. Der Weg führt uns hinab zu streifenförmig geschnittenen Hecken, (14), die nicht nur aus Hainbuche, sondern auch aus blühenden Sträuchern wie Cornus, Chaenomeles, Forsythie oder Spirea, bestehen. Locker verteilt wachsen stattliche Exemplare von grossen Magnolien und Japanischem Ahorn. Ein kleiner Nebenweg mit wassergebundener Decke zweigt rechts ab. Die Kneipp-Station (15) lassen wir unberührt... weil uns der Anblick des über dem See liegenden Bellevue mit seiner Rosenrondells fesselt. Wieder eine Inschrift: ET IN ARCADIA EGO. Langsam dämmert es - war das nicht Goethe, der auch schon in Arkadien weilte? Das Bellevue (16) - man nimmt es sofort wahr - ist das Herzstück des Kurparkes. In allen vier Richtungen unterschiedliche Durch- und Ausblicke. Die nahe Klinik, die lange Weiher, die Stadt. Es ist dunkel geworden. Auf der südlichen Balustrade sitzend, blicken wir auf eine merkwürdig illuminierte Anordnung, die in den nächtlichen Himmel strahlt. Bodenlampen in der Minigolfanlage (17) zeichnen ein Bild, das wir sonst über uns sehen - Aquarius, Cetus und Phoenix - der südliche Sternenhimmel. Betört vom Duft der Rosen, werden die Gedanken frei.

JEDER GEDANKE IST FREI

ET IN ARCADIA EGO

AUCH ICH WAR IN ARKADIEN

BAD MÜNDER am Deister

VEGETATIONSKONZEPT

WALDSTREIFEN
Die kulissenartig angepflanzten Waldstücke bestimmen das räumliche Gepräge des neuen Kurparks. Die Ausrichtung betont die Blickbeziehung zur Stadt mit ihrem Wahrzeichen, dem Kirchturm. Die einzelnen Waldstreifen thematisieren den spezifischen Standort wie z.B.Birkenhain am grossen Weiher.
PFLANZENARTEN: z.B. Eiche, Esche, Ahorn, Weide,Birke, Vogelbeere

EINZELBAEUME
Einzeln gepflanzte Grossbäume stehen in Kontrast zu den waldartigen Bereichen. Sie thematisieren ein vom Prinzip des Landschaftsgartens bekanntes, räumliches Konstruktionsprinzip.
PFLANZENARTEN: z.B. Eiche, Ahorn, Säulenpappel,Magnolie,japanische Ahorn

BUCHENBLAETTER
Frei geschnittene Heckenkuben in Form von überdimensionierten Buchenblättern im Wechsel mit Staudenbeeten bestimmen den Terrassenbereich des neuen Kurhauses.
PFLANZENARTEN: Buche, Stauden

TOPIARY
Skulptural geschnittene Pflanzenkörper in Form von Fabeltieren schaffen am Osteingang eine eigene Identität und geben dem angrenzenden Kinderspielbereich ein unverwechselbares Gepräge.
PFLANZENARTEN: z.B. Buche, Eibe, Hainbuche

ROSENRONDELL
Kletterrosen am Rosenrondell rufen Erinnerungen an ein bekanntes und oft tradiertes Parkelement wach.
PFLANZENARTEN: Kletterrosen

TREILLAGE
Der Westeingang wird mit einem von Clematis überwachsenen Treillagegang ausgezeichnet.
PFLANZENARTEN: Clematis in verschiedenen Arten und Sorten.

HECKENGARTEN
Unterschiedliche Hecken aus blühenden und immergrünen Pflanzen zeigen im Lauf des Jahres ein fortwährend sich änderndes Bild.
PFLANZENARTEN: z.B. Cornus mas, Chaenomeles,Spiraea

PARKRASEN
Im Bereich des Kurparks soll sich im Verlauf des Jahres ein extensiv gepflegter Parkrasen entwickeln.

FELDHECKEN
Die Artenzusammensetzung orientiert sich an der potentiell natürlichen Vegetation. Grossbäume werden im Gegensatz zum Kurpark (Schattenwurf nicht gepflanzt.
PFLANZENARTEN: z.B. Hasel, Schwarzdorn, Schneeball,Holunder etc.

EXTENSIVER BEREICH
Differenzierte, feuchte bis trockene Standorte, die mit Feldhecken unterteilt sind.

OBSTBAEUME
Der Bestand an Obstbäumen wird mit hochstämmigen Bäumen ergänzt. Die Auswahl sollte sich auf regional bekannte Sorten beschränken.
PFLANZENARTEN: Apfelbäume

FRUEHLINGSGARTEN
Geometrisch ausgerichtete Pflanzenstreifen mit unterschiedlicher Zwiebelpflanzung ändern den Farbaspekt dieses bereits heute sehr stimmungsvollen Parkbereichs.
PFLANZENARTEN: z.B. Hyazinthen, Crocus,Narzissen,Tulpen

BEST. VEGETATION

WASSERKONZEPT

Der Bachlauf bleibt in seiner Lage unverändert. Das Bachbett wird ausgeflacht und mit kleineren Staustufen versehen.

Schmale Kanäle leiten das Dachwasser von den Gebäuden in den See bzw. den Park.

Das Wasserbecken auf der Hotelterrasse wird mit Dachwasser gespiesen.

Das Wasserrückhaltebecken ist in vier höhenabgestufte Becken unterteilt.

Wassermuschel

Dampfbrunnen

KLEINER UNTERSCHIED

KURHOTELTERRASSE

Das räumliche Gepräge des neuen Kurparks wird durch die kulissenartig angepflanzten Waldstücke bestimmt. Deren Ausrichtung betont den Blickbezug zur Stadt.

The spatial character of the new spa gardens is determined by the woodland areas planted like a backdrop. Their alignment emphasises the visual link to the town.

Langgezogene Tuffsteine, die mit grünen Algen überzogen sind, begrenzen den neuen künstlichen See.

Elongated artificial rocks of tuff, covered with green algae, define the boundary of the new lake.

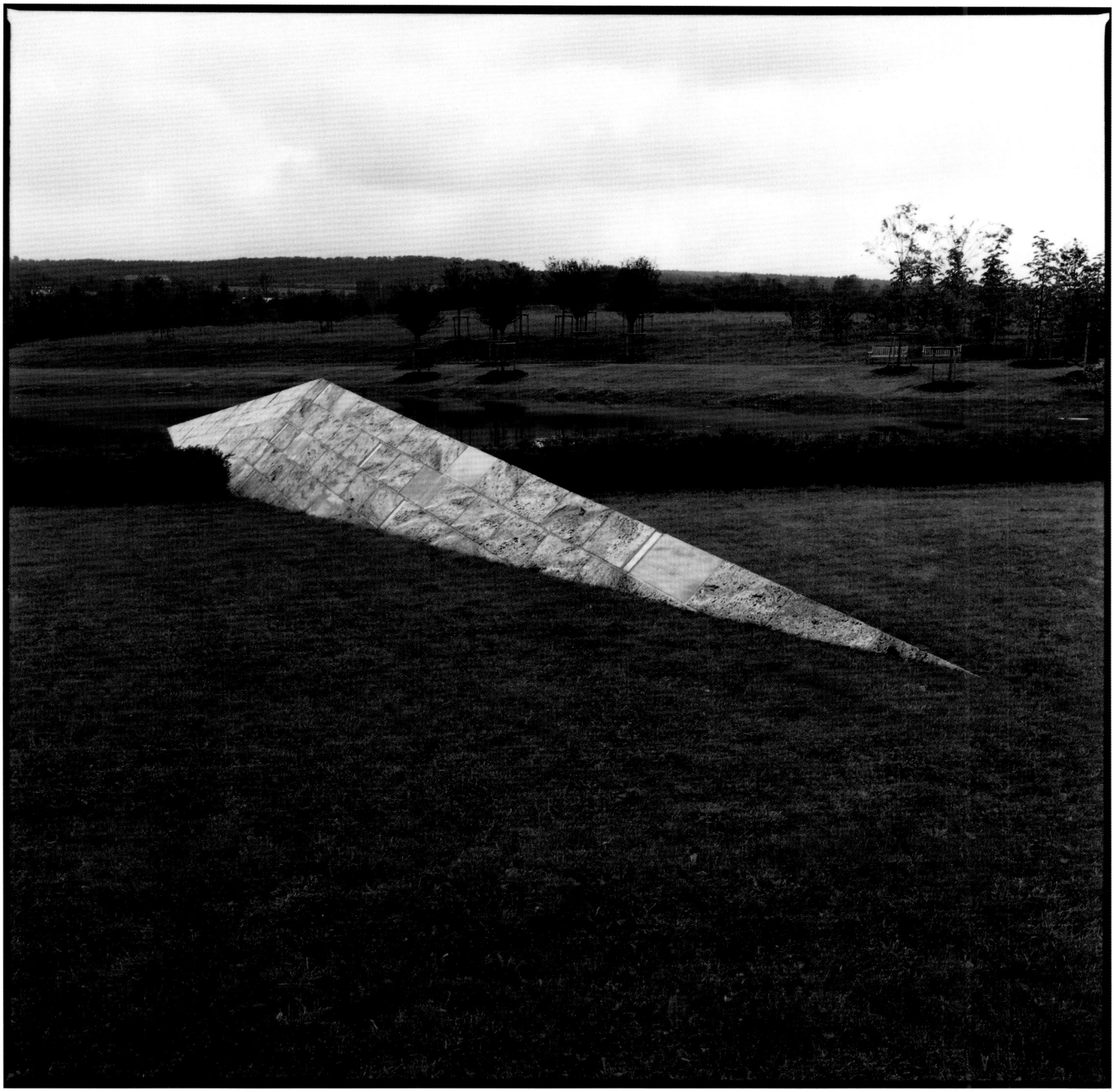

Tate Modern London

Die Tate Gallery hat zu ihrem bisherigen Haus an der Millbank nun neu die Tate Modern im sogenannten Armeleuteviertel an der Bankside in Southwark gefunden. Direkt an der Themse gelegen, gegenüber von St. Paul's Cathedral. Die Verbindung über den Fluß stellt eine neue Fußgängerbrücke, die Millennium-Brücke, von Sir Norman Foster her.

Die Tate ist ein gewaltiges «Kraftwerk der Kunst» für die Kunst, eine Turbinenhalle, die 1945 von Sir Gilbert Scott erbaut, schon lange nicht mehr in Gebrauch und bereits am Zerfallen war. Ein enormes Volumen, eine große Masse Backstein.

An der Vernissage war es Louise Bourgeois mit ihren riesigen, begehbaren Skulpturen, die in diesem Gebäude ihren eigenen Maßstab setzte.

Auf dieses gewaltige Volumen eine schlüssige Antwort für den Außenraum zu finden, war eine anspruchsvolle Herausforderung. Wie soll ein städtischer Raum an der Themse von so immenser Ausdehnung gestaltet werden, in einem Land mit ausgeprägter Tradition zum Landschaftsgarten?

Die formale Umsetzung zur Raumbildung – das Verdecken und Freigeben des Gebäudevolumens – ist auf der Themseseite mit den Birkenquadraten geschaffen. Die Birke signalisiert eine Anbindung an die Flußlandschaft. Die dichte Waldstruktur definiert den Raum, schafft unterschiedliche Räume und läßt immer wieder die Sicht auf die ehemalige Turbinenhalle zu. Vereinzelt stehen im großen städtischen Rasenfeld Birkensolitäre. Das Rasenfeld steht den Besuchern nach alter englischer Tradition zur Benutzung offen. Der Themseuferweg und das Rasenfeld mit Birkenhain stehen klar im Kontext zum städtischen Umfeld.

Der «Pleasure ground» – im traditionellen Sinne Vergnügungsplatz – ist der direkt am Haus gelegene innere Garten, der in den äußeren Waldpark überleitet. So ist hier für die Tate die Rasenfläche mit den Birkenhainen zwischen Museum und Stadt eine Neuinterpretation des Begriffes Pleasure ground.

Im Frühling blühen tausende weiße und gelbe Narzissen, die in Quadraten in das Rasenfeld eingelegt sind.

Im Winter sind es die Birkenstämme, die mit ihrem leuchtenden Weiß zwischen Bauvolumen und Besucher vermitteln

Tate Modern London

In addition to its existing Millbank site, the Tate Gallery now has a further location in the so-called Bankside poor-man's quarter in the borough of Southwark. The new gallery lies directly on the south bank, opposite St. Paul's Cathedral on the north bank. The link across the river is provided by a new footbridge, the Millennium Bridge, designed by Sir Norman Foster.

The Tate Modern is a colossal "powerhouse of art", for art, a turbine hall built by Sir Gilbert Scott in 1945, long since disused and already in the process of decay. An enormous volume, a vast mass of brickwork.

At the preview it was Louise Bourgeois who, with her giant, walk-in sculptures, defined scale in this building.

To find a convincing response to the outside space of this immense volume was something of a challenge. How to design an urban space by the Thames of such gigantic proportions, in a country with such a strong tradition of landscape gardening?

Formal realisation of spatial design – concealing and revealing the volume – is created by birch trees planted in squares on the side facing the Thames. The birch tree signals a link to the riverscape. The dense woodland growth defines the space, creates differing spaces and at intervals permits a view of the former Turbine Hall. Solitaire birch-trees stand scattered on the large expanse of lawn. In keeping with English tradition it can be used by visitors. The path along the Thames and the lawn with the groups of birches are clearly in the context to their urban surroundings.

The "pleasure ground" is directly adjacent to the inner garden by the building; the garden provides a link to the outer woodland park. For the Tate, the expanse of lawn with the grove of birches between the museum and the city is a new interpretation of the concept of the pleasure ground.

Thousands of white and yellow narcissi, set in the lawn in a grid pattern, flower in the spring.

In the winter, the shining white of the birch-tree trunks mediates between the building volume and visitors and gives the vast area of the former power station definition. A hedge of three different kinds of flowering shrubs bounds this expanse of

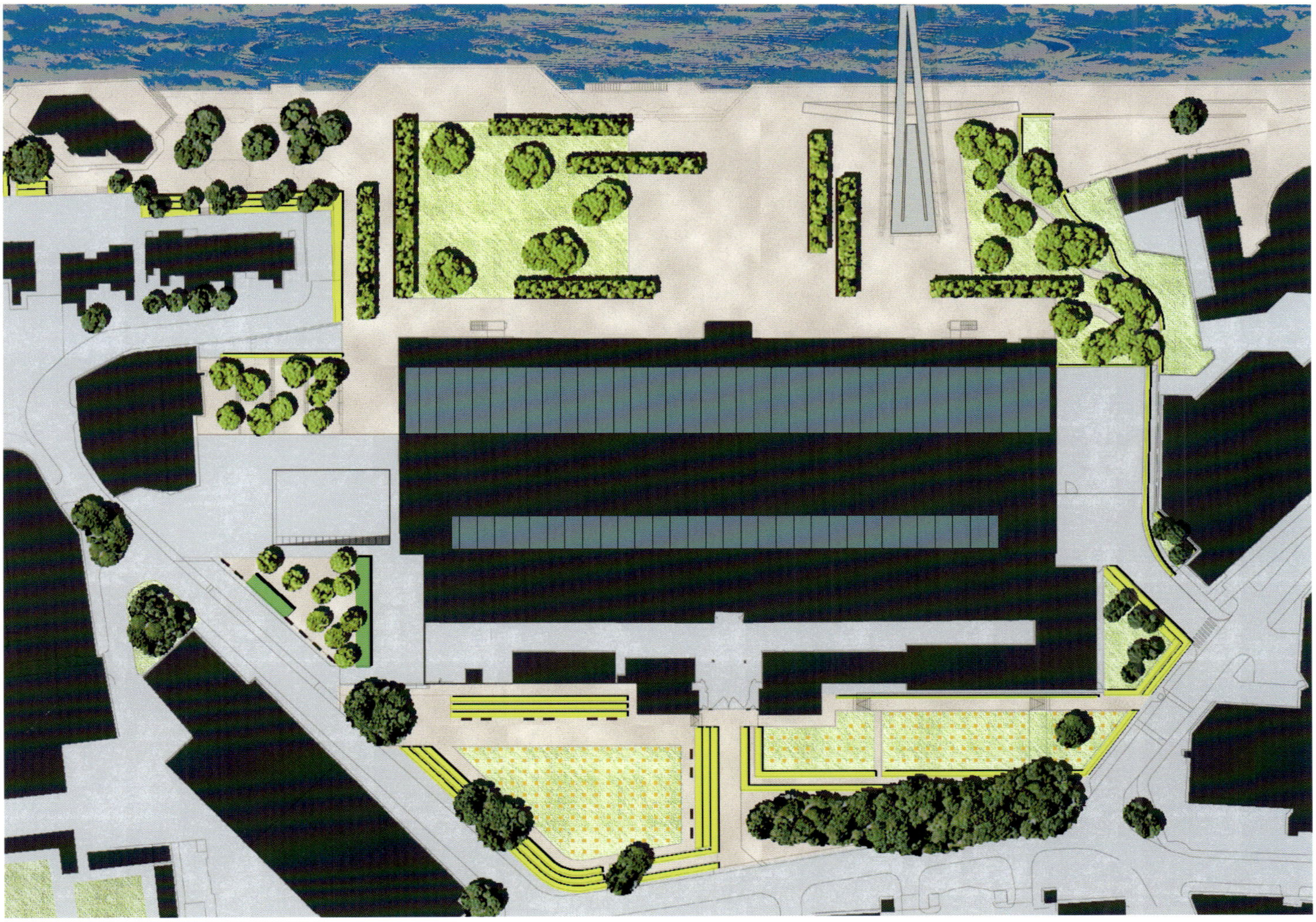

und die große Fläche der ehemaligen Power Station erfaßbar machen. Dreiteilige, verschieden blühende Hecken säumen dieses Rasenfeld, das auch hier ein städtisches ist, ein und nehmen Bezug auf den Ablauf der Jahreszeiten.

Der hortus conclusus, der in Form und Ausführung die Tradition der englischen Staudengärten fortschreibt, lehnt sich an die Rückseite des Gebäudes und ist ebenfalls durch Hecken unterschiedlichster Blühart eingefaßt.

Von Westen kommend, erreicht der Besucher den Haupteingang, der sich über die ganze Westfront ausbreitet. Unterschiedlichste Birkenarten definieren diesen gewaltigen Vorplatz. Loser und verfestigter Kies verweisen auf die unterschiedliche Nutzung des Platzes. Eine monumentale Rampe aus schwarz eingefärbtem Beton leitet den Ankommenden direkt in die Ausstellungsräume.

Mit der Tate Modern in Southwark bietet sich nun die Gelegenheit, die Sammlung zur Kunst des zwanzigsten Jahrhunderts aus ihren Lagern und dem bisherigen Dornröschenschlaf zu holen.

Erika Kienast

lawn that, here too, is urban in character and addresses the passage of the seasons.

The hortus conclusus which in form and execution continues the tradition of the English herbaceous garden adjoins the rear of the building and is also bordered by a hedge of different flowering shrubs.

Visitors approaching from the west arrive at the main entrance extending over the entire west front. This vast forecourt is defined by widely different kinds of birch trees. Loose and bonded gravel are a reference to the different uses of the forecourt. A monumental ramp of black-dyed concrete leads visitors directly into the exhibition areas.

The Tate Modern in Southwark has made it possible to take the collection of twentieth century art out of storage where it had slumbered for so long.

Erika Kienast

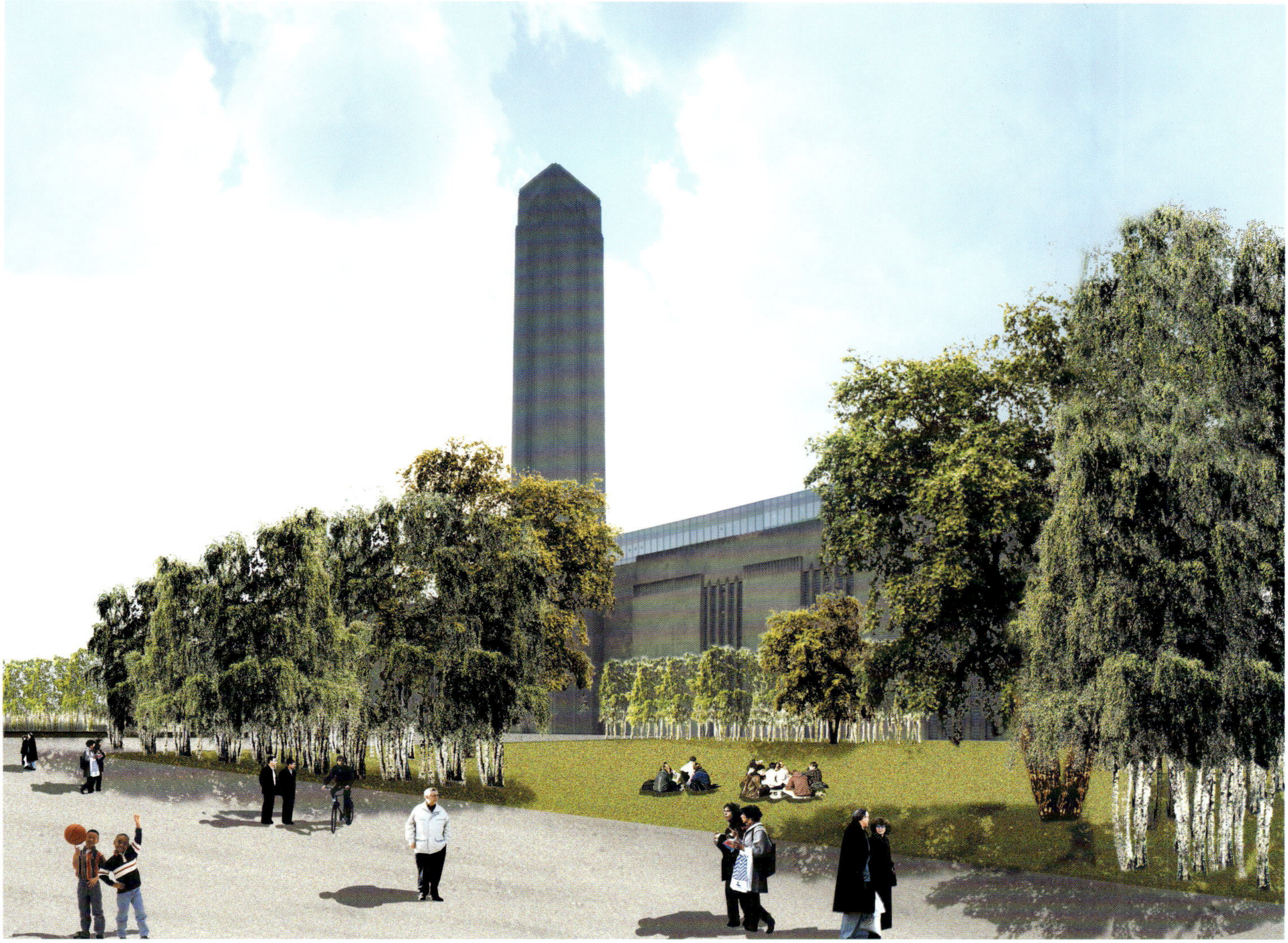

Zentral vor dem Nordeingang liegt ein offener Platz für Veranstaltungen, gefaßt durch einen Birkenhain.

An open plaza defined by groups of birches, intended as a venue for events, is located centrally in front of the north entrance to the Tate Modern.

Die Freiflächen des Zentrums für Kunst und Medientechnologie, Karlsruhe

In den Hallenbauten der ehemaligen Industriewerke Karlsruhe-Augsburg wurden die Städtische Galerie, die Hochschule für Gestaltung sowie das Zentrum für Kunst und Medientechnologie (ZKM) zu einer in Deutschland einzigartigen Sammlung zusammengefaßt.

Das äußere Erscheinungsbild der ehemaligen Munitionsfabriken, umgebaut von den Architekten Schweger und Partner aus Hamburg, blieb im denkmalpflegerischen Sinne gewahrt, wurde allerdings durch einen blauen Medienkubus vor dem Haupteingang ergänzt. Das ZKM präsentiert schwerpunktmäßig Kunst, die sich neuer Medientechnologien bedient: Videoinstallationen, Multimedia und Interaktion.

Städtebauliche Herausforderung war es, eine «Adresse» zu schaffen, da das ZKM von der stark befahrenen Brauerstraße aus aufgrund mehrerer neuer Gebäude in die zweite Reihe zu rücken drohte. Die Schwierigkeit der landschaftsarchitektonischen Aufgabe lag in der Behandlung des Tiefgaragendaches, das sich auf der gesamten Länge vor dem Hallenbau erstreckt und das lediglich um maximal sechzig Zentimeter überschüttet werden durfte. Trotz aller technischen Vorgaben sollte dabei eine vegetationsgeprägte Lösung gefunden werden, die sich in das Freiflächensystem der Stadt einfügt. Sicherheitsanforderungen der neugebauten Bundesanwaltschaft und unklare Planungsstände der benachbarten Baufelder (Großkino) verkomplizierten die Aufgabe.

Heute liegen acht Heckenschiffe mit lichten Baumhainen inmitten des sechshundert Meter langen Grünzugs. Impuls für dieses Motiv waren zwei bestehende, malerische Baumgruppen im Norden des Geländes. Durch die Rahmung mit niedrigen geschnittenen Hecken sowie einer Erhöhung des inneren Niveaus über Flachstahlkanten erfuhren die Baumgruppen eine Neuinterpretation: Der strenge städtebauliche Kontext wird durch das Thema der frei komponierten Elemente kontrastiert. Sie sind spielerisch und zugleich treffsicher gesetzt. Im Inneren der Heckenschiffe finden sich Ruheplätze, Bänke und Spielgeräte. Die Auswahl der Baumarten nimmt Rücksicht auf die Problematik des geringen Bodenaufbaus

The Grounds of the Center for Art and Media, Karlsruhe

The sheds of the former Karlsruhe-Augsburg industrial complex now house the Municipal Gallery, the School of Design and the Center for Art and Media – a collection which is unique in Germany.

The exterior of the former munitions factory, converted by the Hamburg architects Schweger und Partner, has been preserved as a historic monument and a blue media cube has been added in front of the main entrance. The focus of the Center for Art and Media is on art which uses new media technologies: video installations, multimedia and interaction.

From the point of view of urban design, the challenge was to create a "presence" as the centre was in danger of taking a back seat to a number of new buildings along the busy Brauerstrasse. The difficulty from the point of view of landscape architecture was how to respond to the roof of the underground garage, which extends in front of the former industrial building over its entire length and could only be covered up to a maximum of sixty centimetres. Despite all these technical restrictions, the envisaged solution was to be characterised by vegetation and was to fit in with the city's system of open space. Security requirements for the new building of the Federal public prosecution service and an unclear planning status of the neighbouring development (large cinema) made the task all the more difficult.

Today eight boat-shaped hedges enclosing scattered trees lie in the middle of the six-hundred-metre stretch of green. The idea for this motif was provided by two existing, picturesque groups of trees in the north of the site. Framing them with low, clipped hedges and raising the inner level by means of flat steel edges has given the groups of trees a new interpretation; the severity of the urban context is contrasted by the theme of the freely composed elements. They have been placed in a way which is playful but also unerring. Within the boat-shaped hedges there are places to relax, benches and playground equipment. The choice of trees reflects the problems associated with the elevation of the ground and the scale of the islands of hedge: black locust,

167

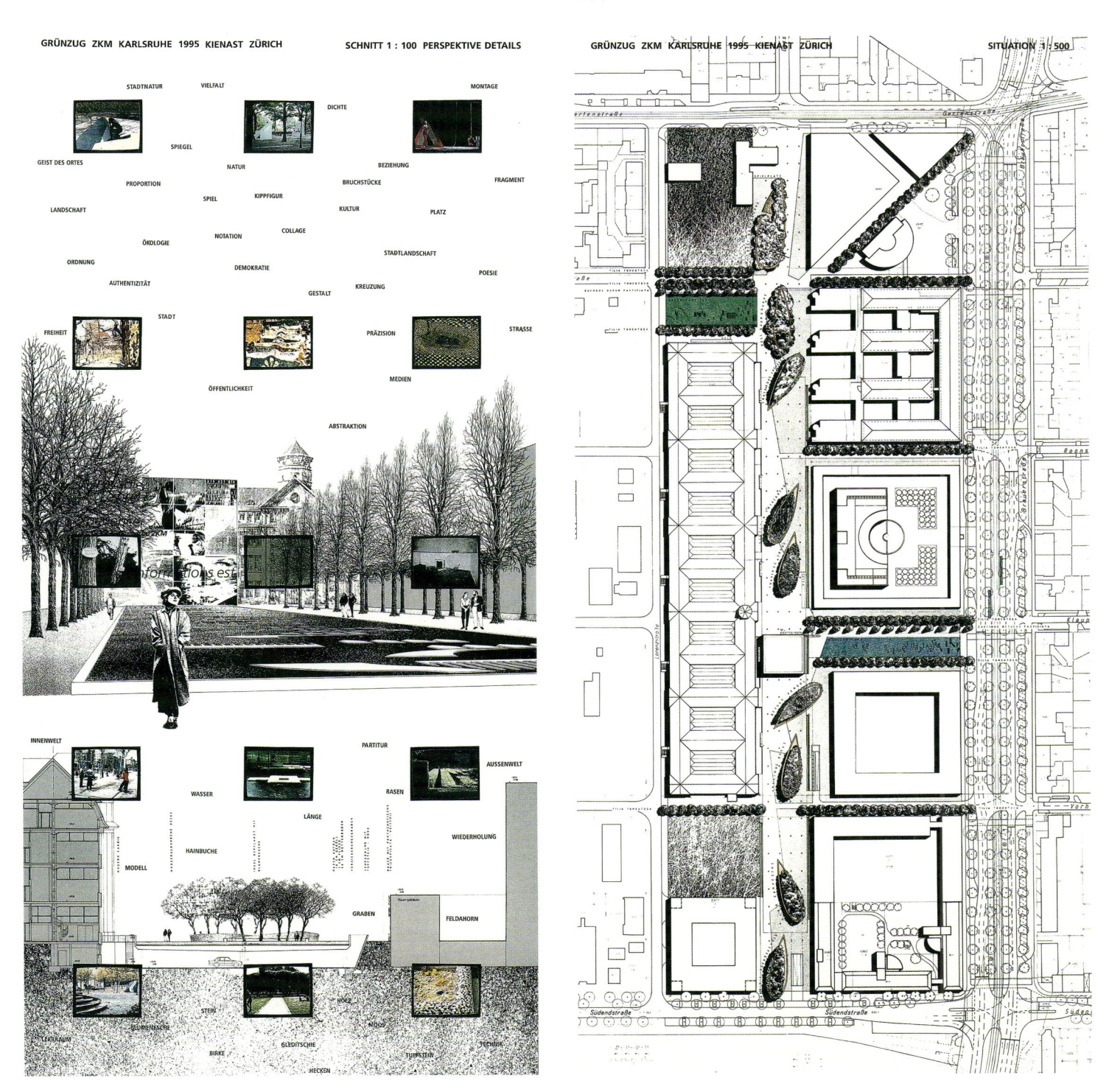

sowie die Maßstäblichkeit der Heckeninseln: Robinien, Feldahorn, Birnen, Schnurbaum. Die Hecken sind einheitlich mit Kornelkirsche gepflanzt. Die Baumhaine lösen sich aus dem städtischen Raum heraus und werden zu eigenständigen Objekten. Gleichzeitig definieren sie die Grenze zwischen Platz und Wiese.

Die Materialien sind prägnant und sinnfällig eingesetzt: rostender Corten-Flachstahl in Anlehnung an die Industriegeschichte des Ortes für die Aufhöhungen, Riffelstähle für Stufen und Rampen, grünliche Andeer-Platten im repräsentativen Eingangsbereich, Andeer-Kies und schlichte graulasierte Parkmöbel im Inneren der Heckenschiffe. Vor dem Medienkubus und in der Nachbarschaft des zukünftigen Großkinos übernimmt ein Holzdeck die Funktion eines unreglementierten Treffpunkts. Der Spielplatz unter den vorhandenen Kastanien ist mit grünen Holzschnitzeln ausgestreut, einfache Edelstahlgeräte erlauben ausgiebige Bewegungsspiele ohne jeden modischen Spielplatzkitsch.

Den fünfundvierzig Meter breite Hauptzugang von der Brauerstraße zum ZKM bildet eine Platzfläche, die durch eine zweireihige Allee begleitet wird. Darunter zieht sich auf der Nordseite eine neunzig Meter lange Parkbank entlang. In Verbindung mit der Leuchtinstallation von Prof. Jeffrey Shaw bildet sie einen markanten Auftakt, der das ZKM in Szene zu setzen vermag. Ein flaches Wasserbecken, das ursprünglich vor dem Medienkubus liegen sollte, kam nicht zur Ausführung. In ihm hätte sich das wechselhafte Spektakel der Medienfassade spiegeln können. Flache, aus Fußgängerperspektive nicht dechiffrierbare Steinskulpturen, die einer Partitur des avandgardistischen Komponisten György Ligeti entnommen waren, hätten einen Dialog zwischen dem Wasserspiegel und dem zitierten Tonfeld herstellen sollen.

Die begehbaren Oberflächen sind mit Kryorit befestigt, einer kunstharzgebundenen Splittdecke aus Rheinsand, der zu 20 % Andeer-Splitt beigemischt ist. Der Belag verunsichert beim Gehen: er hat das Aussehen einer fein gewalzten Splitdecke und die Haptik eines Sportplatzes. Auftritt und Gehgeräusch widersprechen vertrauten Erfahrungen in Freiräumen.

Die gesamte Fläche ist wasserdurchlässig ausgebildet und entwässert auf das Tiefgaragendach, von wo aus ein Sammler das Wasser zu Sickerschächten führt. Dieser Aufwand wurde

hedge maple, pear, Japanese pagode trees. The hedges are all of cornelian cherry. The groves of trees break out of the urban space and become independent objects. At the same time, they define the boundary between square and grass.

The materials have been used in a way which is distinctive and striking: rusting Corten flat steel reminiscent of the industrial history of the location for the elevated areas, fluted steel for the steps and ramps, greenish paving in the imposing entrance area, gravel and simple, grey-varnished park furniture in the interior of the boat-shaped areas bounded by hedges. A level made of wood in front of the media cube and in the vicinity of the planned large cinema assumes the role of an unconventional meeting place. The playground underneath the mature chestnut trees has a surface of green wood chippings, simple equipment of stainless steel provides opportunity for movement and play, while fashionable playground kitsch is noticeable by its absence.

The forty-five-metre wide main access to the centre from Brauerstrasse forms an area which is bounded by an avenue of double rows of trees. There is a ninety-metre long park bench on the north side. Together with the lighting installation by Prof. Jeffrey Shaw it forms a distinctive prelude, which provides a fitting setting for the center. A shallow pool, originally to be in front of the media cube, was not realised. It would have reflected the changeable spectacle of the media facade. Low stone sculptures, which cannot be deciphered from the viewpoint of the pedestrian and were inspired by a score by the avant-garde composer György Ligeti, were to have created a dialogue between the sheet of water and the sounds to which they refer.

The access areas are covered in kryorit, a synthetic resin-bound surface of chippings of Rhine sand to which 20 % Andeer stone chippings have been added. Walking on the surface is an unusual experience as it has the appearance of a finely rolled surface of stone chippings and the haptic qualities of a playing field. The sensation and sounds created by walking contradict familiar experiences in open space.

The entire area is permeable, water drains onto the roof of the underground garage, from where a collector channels the water to seepage drains. This was accepted in order to achieve a very tranquil design of the elevation of the ground

in Kauf genommen, um den Höhenverlauf der Fläche bei gering dimensioniertem Dachaufbau der Tiefgarage sehr ruhig zu gestalten. Außerdem ermöglicht er einen Wasseranstau zur Versorgung der Bäume, die sich dadurch auf der Tiefgaragendecke besser entfalten können.

An den Schnittpunkten der Belagsfugen finden sich schwarze Steinplatten.

Der ursprüngliche Gedanke war es, begehbare Spiegel in den Boden einzulassen, die die Besucher nach Stunden virtueller Erfahrungen im Inneren des ZKM auf sich selbst zurückwerfen sollten.

Freilandversuche mit Spiegeln im Boden führten aber zu dem Ergebnis, daß diese Elemente wegen der Gefahr des Ausrutschens und des Verkratzens den praktischen Anforderungen nicht gewachsen sind. Stattdessen entschied man sich für schwarzen, polierten schwedischen Granit, dessen Spiegelung der Ursprungsidee nahekam. Die Beleuchtung wird von Strahlern übernommen, die die Bäume nachts wie helle Segel erscheinen lassen. An den Geländern der Tiefgaragenschächte finden sich einfache, funktionale Leuchten.

Ein Phänomen überrascht nach dem Besuch des ZKM. Während die aufwendigen Installationen den Betrachter nach kurzer Zeit an den Rand der Wahrnehmungsfähigkeit bringen, vermag er sich im gestalteten Außenraum wieder zu sammeln. Verkehrslärm, Vogelgesang, Licht und Schatten, Geruch von Rasen und Stein, Wind und Regen machen den Ort zur vertrauten Umwelt.

Anstatt der Versuchung zu erliegen, auch im Außenraum mit aufwendigen, technischen Installationen zu arbeiten, wie sie sich im ZKM in allen Raffinessen präsentieren, bekannten sich Kienast Vogt und Partner dagegen zu prägnanten Lösungen, die dem Repertoire der Landschaftsarchitektur entstammen. Im Vertrauen auf die Vorstellungskraft des reflektierenden Betrachters liegt die sichere Haltung und große Qualität dieser Arbeit.

Thomas Göbel-Groß

given the low dimensions of the roof of the underground garage. It also makes it possible to collect water for the plants, which are, in consequence, able to develop better on the roof of the underground garage.

There are black paving stones at the intersecting points of the joints.

It was originally planned to insert mirrors into the surface; these would have enabled visitors emerging from the center after hours of exposure to virtual reality to relate to themsleves again.

However, experiments with mirrors let into the ground showed that they did not fulfil practical requirements on account of the risk presented by their polished surface and their tendency to scratch. Instead, it was decided to use black, polished Swedish granite, which has reflective qualities similar to those of the material originally envisaged. Illumination is provided by floodlights which at night give the trees the appearance of shining sails. Simple, functional lights are attached to the railings of the entrance to the underground garage.

Visitors leaving the center encounter a surprising phenomenon. While the elaborate installations inside soon take the beholder to the limits of his perceptive abilities, the design of the outside space gives him the possibility of collecting his thoughts. The noise of traffic, the song of birds, light and shadow, the smell of grass and stone, wind and rain all contribute to making the location a familiar environment.

Instead of succumbing to the temptation of using the same elaborate, technical installations for outside space as those presented so skilfully in the center, Kienast Vogt und Partner decided in favour of distinctive solutions drawing on the repertoire of landscape architecture. The certainty and high quality of this work depends on the powers of imagination of the reflective beholder.

Thomas Göbel-Groß

Heckenräume mit lichten Baumhainen
rhythmisieren den langgezogenen Stadtraum.

Hedges enclosing scattered trees
provide the elongated urban space with rhythm.

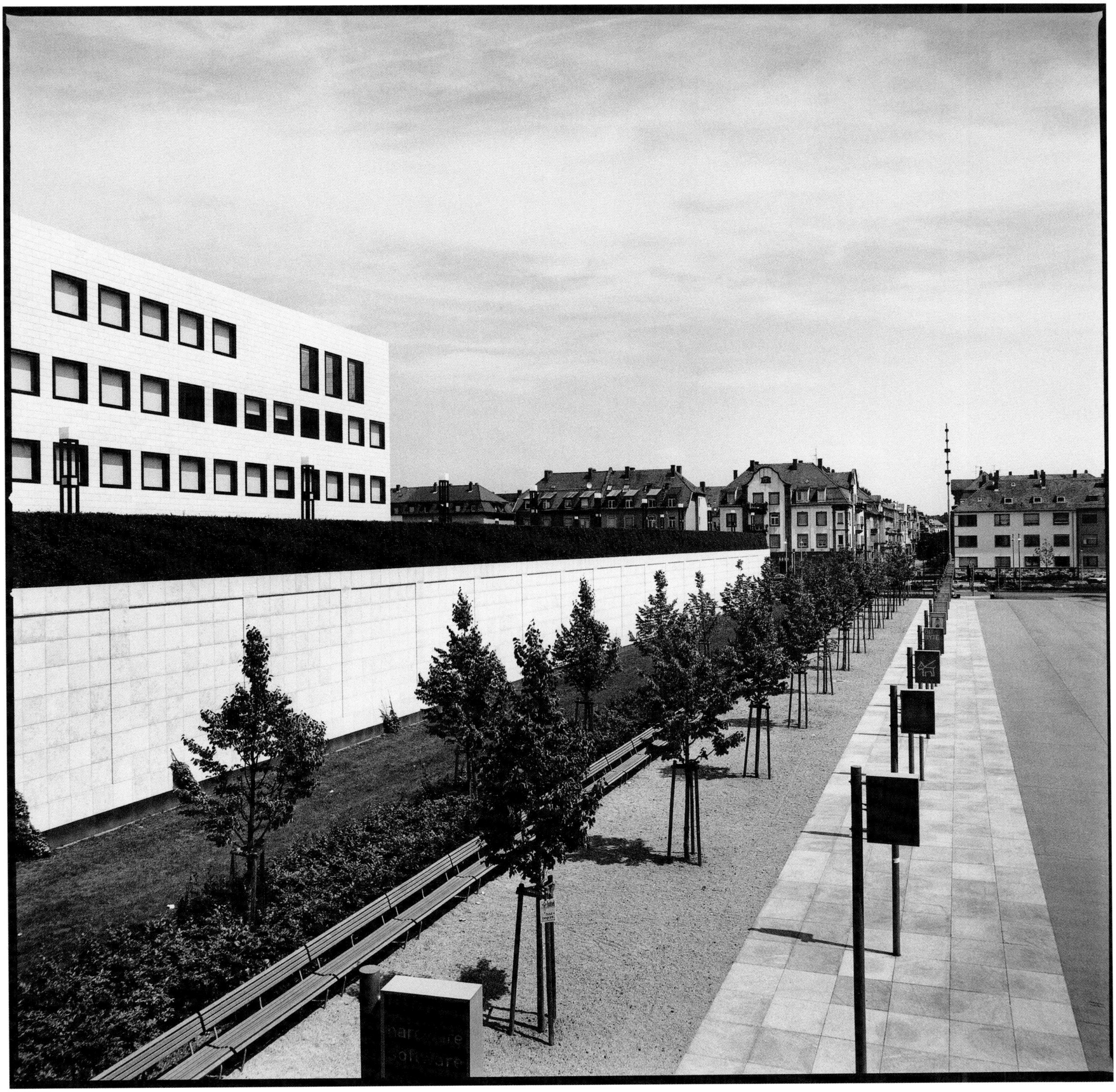

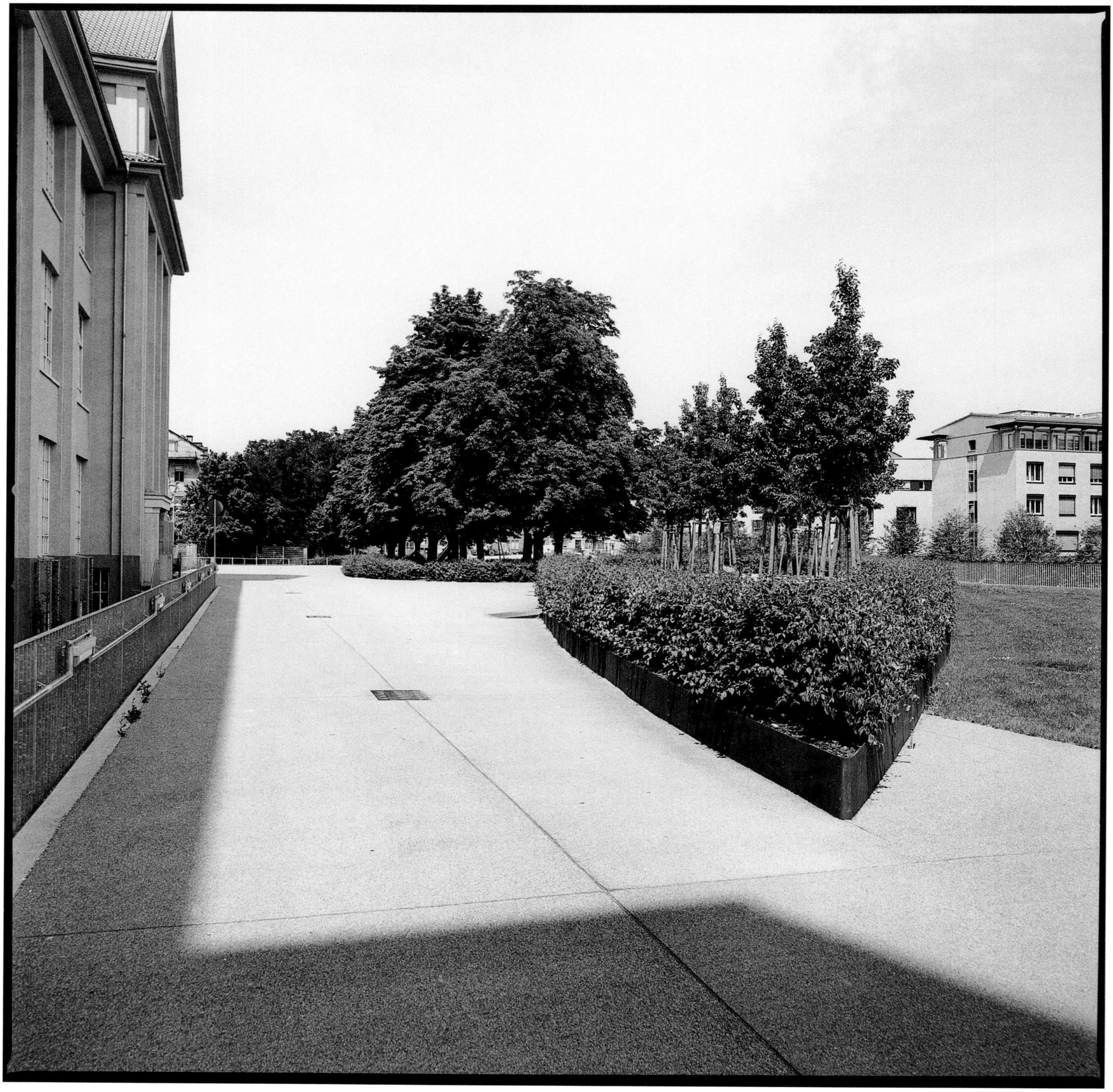

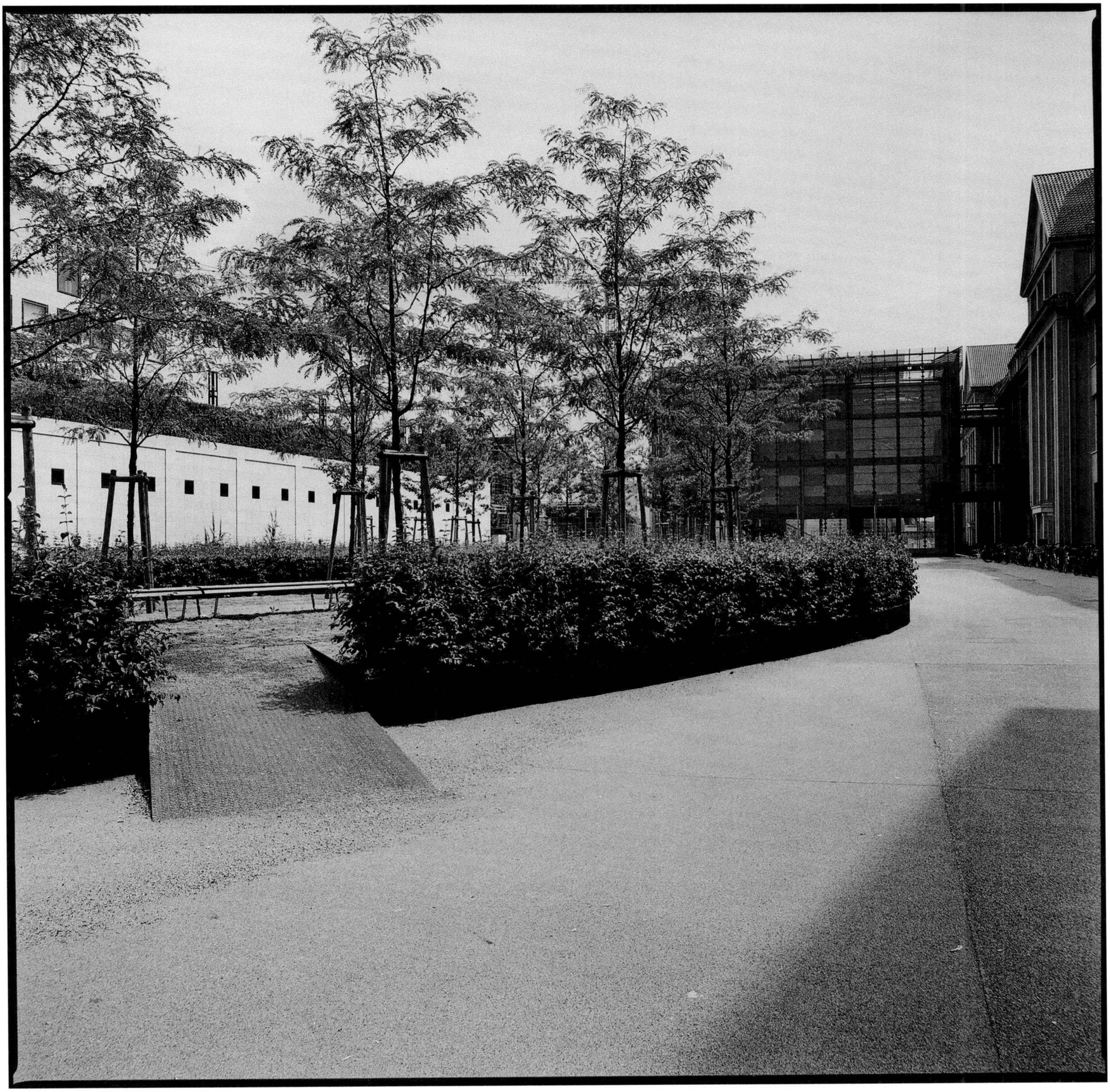

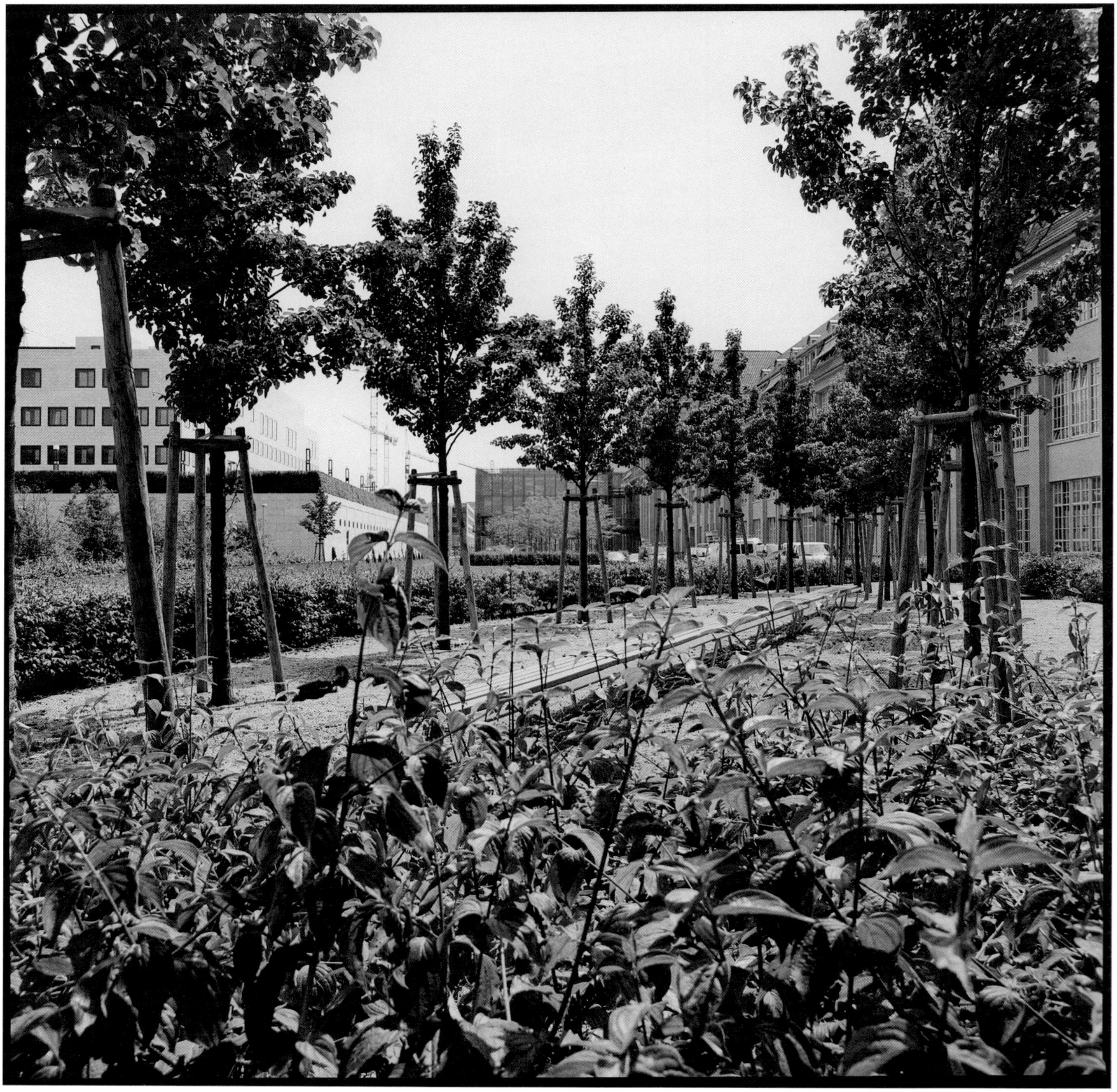

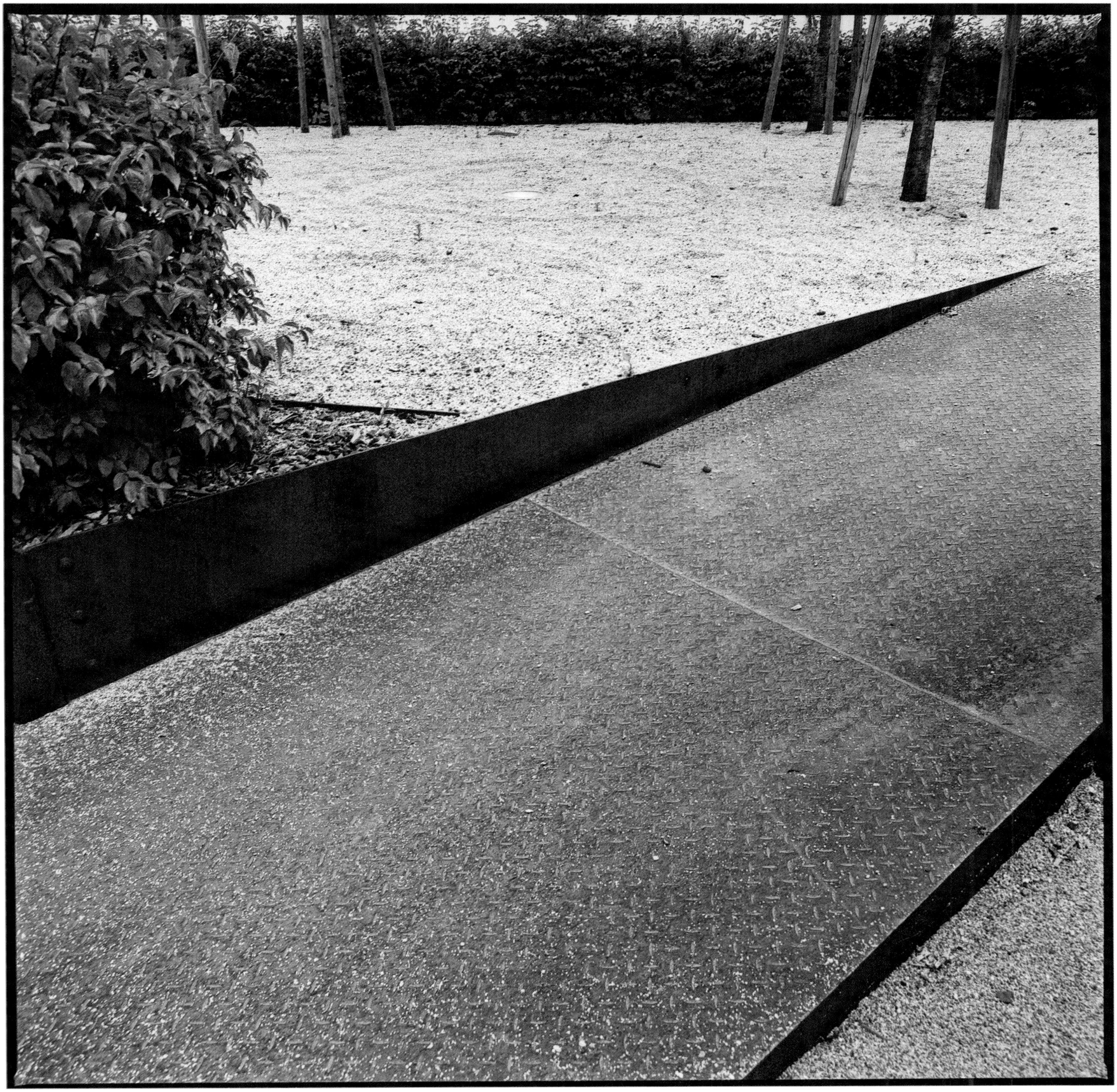

Stadtgarten am Neubau des Bundesarbeitsgerichts, Erfurt

Erfurt, in der Mitte des Deutschen Reiches gelegen, war Kreuzungspunkt alter Handelswege. Schon im 12. Jahrhundert war die Stadt an der Gera geistiger, kultureller und wirtschaftlicher Mittelpunkt des Landes Thüringen und wurde am Beginn des 16. Jahrhunderts zu einer Stätte der neuen Bewegung des Humanismus.

Bald nach der Deutschen Wiedervereinigung entschloß man sich, den Sitz des Bundesarbeitsgerichtes, bislang in Kassel, nach Erfurt zu verlegen.

Am Fuße der Barocken Festungsanlage der Stadt wurde daraufhin nach den Entwürfen der Berliner Architektin Gesine Weinmiller ein neues viergeschossiges Dienstgebäude inmitten einer ausgedehnten Grünanlage geschaffen. Im Zuge der Baumaßnahmen entsteht ein drei Hektar großer Stadtgarten, der als erster Teil der geplanten Parkanlagen am Petersberg realisiert wird.

Mit der ausgezeichneten Lage an der Westecke der Festungsanlage und der topografisch höchsten Erhebung im zukünftigen Grüngürtel rund um den Petersberg sind die Außenanlagen des Bundesarbeitsgerichtes von erheblicher Bedeutung für das innerstädtische Grünsystem. Die Grünanlage soll dem Typus des Stadtgartens entsprechen. Dieser wird durch seine begrenzte Dimension, seine Zuordnung zum Gebäude und durch eine städtisch geformte Natur charakterisiert. Er unterscheidet sich damit von einer landschaftlich-großräumigen Parkanlage und der ungestalteten, sich frei entwickelnden Natur.

Das Konzept des Stadtgartens orientiert sich an den Nutzungsansprüchen des Arbeitsgerichtes, den großräumigen Verflechtungen städtischer Freiräume sowie an der geschichtsträchtigen Lage. Schließlich nimmt der Stadtgarten wichtige Teile der ehemaligen Festungsanlage Petersberg im Sinne einer kritischen Rekonstruktion auf, die auf diese Weise zu selbstverständlichen Komponenten der neuzeitlichen Gartenanlage werden.

Auf der Grundlage historischer Pläne und dem Ergebnis archäologischer Grabungen werden Teile der Festungsanlage

Urban Garden for the New Building of the Federal Labour Court, Erfurt

Erfurt, located in the centre of the German Empire, lay on the crossing point of old trade routes. As early as the 12th century, the city on the Gera was the intellectual, cultural and commercial centre of the province of Thuringia; at the beginning of the 16th century became a home of the emerging Humanist movement.

Shortly after the reunification of Germany, it was decided to move the Federal Labour Court from Kassel to Erfurt.

At the foot of the Baroque fortifications of the city a new four-storey building based on designs by the Berlin architect Gesine Weinmiller has been built in the middle of an extensive green area. As part of this development a three-hectare urban garden is coming into being, the first part of the planned park at the Petersberg to be realised.

With their excellent location on the western corner of the fortifications and the highest elevation in the future green belt around the Petersberg, the grounds of the Federal Labour Court are already of considerable significance for the inner-city system of greenery. They are to be designed as an urban park, characterised by its limited dimensions, its relationship to a building and its urban nature. This distinguishes it from an extensive country park or areas where nature is not managed but left to develop freely.

The concept of the urban garden is based on the use requirements of the Labour Court, the large-scale interweaving of urban open space and the site rich in history. After all, the urban garden addresses important parts of the former Petersberg fortifications in the sense of a critical reconstruction, thereby making them integral components of the modern gardens.

With the help of historical maps and archaeological excavations, parts of the fortifications in the urban garden have been uncovered. The Gabriel bastion on the east side is to be reconstructed in its original size on the side facing the Federal Labour Court and to serve as an observation point from the Petersberg.

The site of the fortification and its walls are traced by a natural stone wall, without any attempt to reproduce their

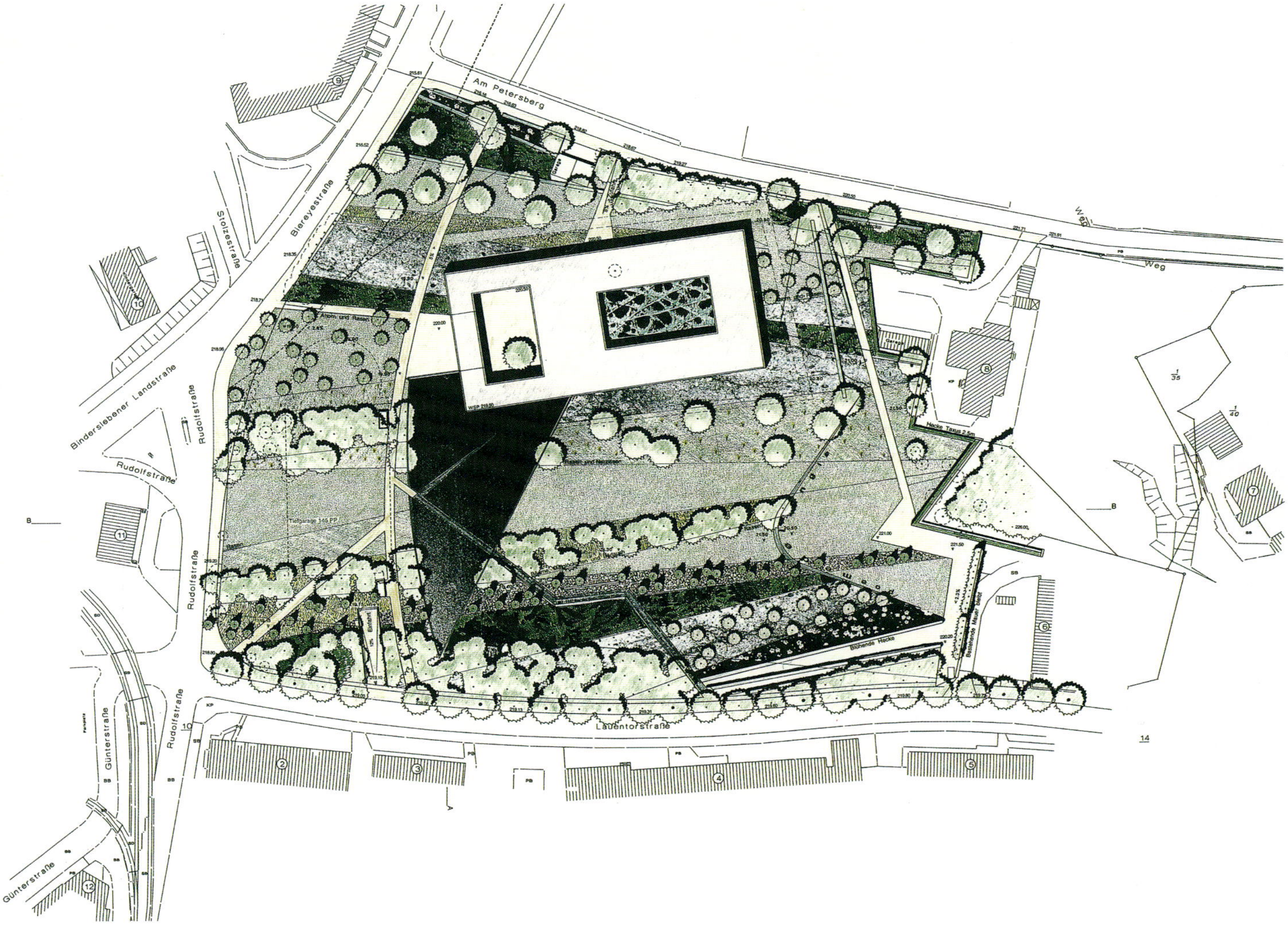
Am Petersberg
Biereyestraße
Stolzestraße
Binderslebener Landstraße
Rudolfstraße
Rudolfstraße
Rudolfstraße
Günterstraße
Günterstraße
Lauentorstraße
Weg
Weg
Blühende Hecke
14

im Stadtgarten wieder sichtbar. Die Bastion Gabriel auf der Ostseite wird auf der dem Grundstück des Bundesarbeitsgerichtes zugewandten Seite in einstiger Größe rekonstruiert und als Aussichtspunkt vom Petersberg her inszeniert.

Lünette 1 und Kontermauer werden mit Natursteinmauerwerk in ihrer Lage nachgezeichnet, ohne die frühere Höhenentwicklung nachzuahmen. Das «Hornwerk», das den südwestlichen Gartenteil durchquert und im Seerosenweiher langsam verschwindet, wird mit Natursteinplatten nachgebildet. Der achtzig Meter lange Seerosenteich zählt zu den attraktivsten Teilen der Gartenanlage. Das Verwaltungsgebäude steht mit einer Ecke direkt im See und spiegelt sich in der ruhigen Wasserfläche. Das Regenwasser der Dachflächen und das Quellwasser eines Brunnens, der beim Gebäudeeingang plaziert ist, speisen den maximal 1,20 Meter tiefen Teich.

«Sterilisque diu Palus aptaque remis vicinas urbes alit, et grave sentit aratrum – Da, wo ehemals Ruder die hohen Wellen teilten, da lockert jetzt der Pflug das Land.» Zwei Sitzbänke aus Schiefer, zwei Zeilen des römischen Dichters Horaz – einmal lateinisch, einmal auf deutsch – sind die künstlerische Antwort des eingeladenen schottischen Poeten Jan Hamilton Finlay auf den kulturhistorisch bedeutsamen Ort.

Das stimmungsvolle räumliche Gefüge des Stadtgartens wird durch einen lichten Baumbestand bestimmt, der in Längsstreifen gleiche Baum- und Straucharten aufweist. Der Blick auf die Bastion wird teilweise freigelegt, die Architektur bleibt durch einen transparenten «Baumschleier» sichtbar. Einheimische Baum- und Straucharten wie Eiche, Hainbuche, Ahorn, Linde wurden ebenso verwendet wie Pagodenhartriegel oder Schnurbaum. Stauden- und Farnbeete setzen blühende und frischgrüne Akzente. Schneeglöckchen, Narzissen und Bärlauch lassen die weiten Rasenflächen im Frühling erblühen und erfüllen die Luft mit Düften.

An ausgewählten Orten laden Parkbänke zum Verweilen ein. Eine Buchenhecke bildet die Abgrenzung des Stadtgartens entlang der Petersbergstraße und gegen Osten.

Auch im Eingangs- und Innenhof des repräsentativen Gebäudes kommt der Vegetation eine tragende Rolle zu. Um die Beziehung zwischen Innen und Außen zu unterstreichen, wird der Pflasterbelag aus Naturstein von den äußeren Wegen bis in den offenen Eingangshof hineingezogen. Vier Winter-

original height. The "Hornwerk" which passes through the south-west part of the garden and gradually disappears in the lily pond is reproduced in natural stone paving. The lily-pond, eighty metres long, is one of the most attractive parts of the gardens. One corner of the administrative building is directly in the lake and is reflected in the tranquil sheet of water. Rainwater from the roof areas and the spring water of a fountain placed at the entrance to the building feed the pond, which has a maximum depth of 1.20 metres.

"Sterilisque diu Palus apaque remis vicinas urbes alit, et grave sintit aratrum – Da, wo ehemals Ruder die hohen Wellen teilten, da lockert jetzt der Pflug das Land." (Where once oars divided the high waves is where a plough now tills the soil.) Two benches of slate, two lines written by the Roman poet Horaz – in Latin and in German – are the artistic reply by the Scottish poet Ian Hamilton Finlay, who was invited to make a contribution to this place of cultural and historical significance.

The interesting spatial structure of the urban garden is determined by sparsely planted trees, consisting of extended strips of trees or bushes of the same kind. The view of the bastion is partly unimpeded, its architecture remains visible through a transparent "veil of trees". Native trees and bushes such as oak, hornbeam, maple and lime were used as was pagoda dogwood. Herbaceous beds and beds of ferns provide

linden, im Quadrat gepflanzt, bilden einen markanten grünen Körper, dem die circa zehn Meter hohe Skulptur «Weltachse» von Jürgen Partenheimer gegenüber steht.

Aus dem Bibliotheksraum des Bundesarbeitsgerichtes blickt man hingegen in den Innenhof, bepflanzt mit einfachem und geschlitztblättrigem japanischen Ahorn. Im Sommer grün belaubt, im Herbst feuerrot gefärbt, stehen die Ahornbäume in reizvollem Kontrast zum Bodenbelag aus weißem Marmorkies.

flowering accents and fresh green. Snowdrops, narcissi and allium ursinum transform the wide expanses of grass into a field of flowers in spring and fill the air with their fragrance.

Park benches at selected places are an invitation to sit for a while. A hedge of beech forms the boundary of the urban garden along Petersbergstrasse and towards the east.

Vegetation also plays a central role in the entrance area and inner courtyard of the imposing building. In order to underline the relationship between inside and outside, the natu-

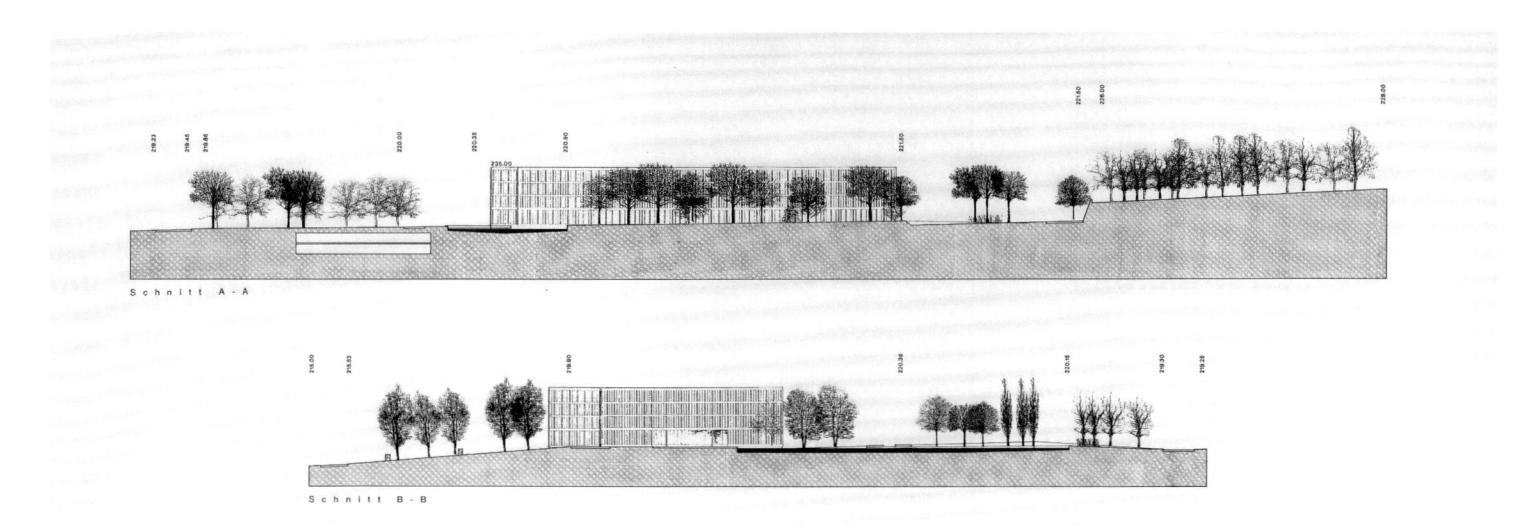

Architektur und Landschaftsarchitektur verbinden sich am neuen Bundesarbeitsgericht in Erfurt zu einem signifikanten Ensemble, das sich in das städtische, kulturhistorisch bedeutsame Gefüge am Petersberg integriert.

Dieter Kienast

ral paving stones of the outside paths are continued into the open entrance court. Four winter limes, planted in a square, form a striking green body, opposite to which lies an approximately ten-metre high sculpture entitled "Weltachse" (world axis) by Jürgen Partenheimer.

The view from the room forming the library of the Federal Labour Court is of the inner courtyard, planted with simple and spiky-leafed Japanese maple. With their green foliage in summer which turns fiery red in the autumn, the maple trees form an attractive contrast to the ground surface of white marble gravel.

Architecture and landscape architecture are combined in the new building of the Federal Labour Court in Erfurt to form an outstanding ensemble which is made an integral part of the urban, historical complex at the Petersberg.

Dieter Kienast

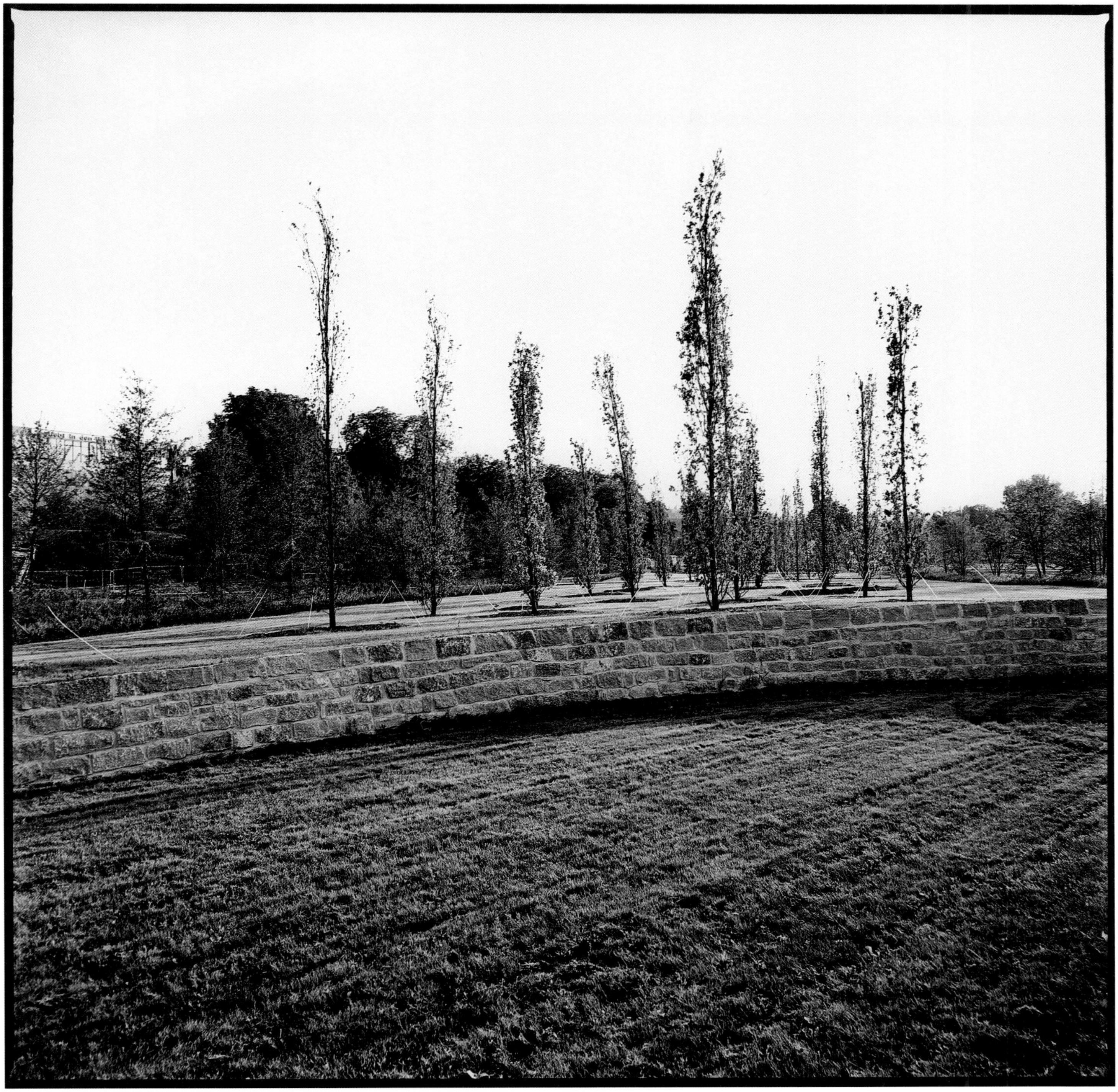

Von dem historischen Bauwerk – Bastion Gabriel – führen Sichtschneisen
in den Park und weiter in die dahinterliegende Stadt.

Vistas lead to the park and the city beyond from the historical building, the Gabriel Bastion.

Der kontemplative Innenhof ist mit farbenprächtigen Ahornen, die im Marmorkies stehen, bepflanzt.

The contemplative inner courtyard is planted with colourful maples standing in marble gravel.

Zwischen historischen Bauwerken und neuem Gebäude liegt der Seerosenteich als Bindeglied.

The lily-pond forms a linking element between the historical buildings and the new building.

Das historische «Hornwerk» ist als selbstverständlicher Teil
in das neue Parkkonzept integriert.

The historical "Hornwerk" has been integrated into the new park concept.

Internationale Gartenschau 2000 Steiermark, Graz

Schon ist mein Blick am Hügel, dem besonnten,
dem Wege, den ich kam, voran.
So faßt uns das, was wir nicht fassen konnten,
voller Erscheinung, aus der Ferne an.

Rainer Maria Rilke

International Garden Show 2000 Styria, Graz

Already my gaze is on the hill, the sunny one,
at the end of the path which I've only just begun.
So we are grasped, by that which we could not grasp,
at such great distance, so fully manifest.

Rainer Maria Rilke

Meine erste Begegnung mit der Vegetation der Steiermark hat nicht in lieblichen Gefilden, sondern beim Klettern, in Form eines stachligen Wacholderbusches in der Steilwand des Gesäuses, stattgefunden. Heute weiß ich, daß die Steiermark ein traditionelles und fruchtbares Ackerbau- und Gärtnerland ist.

Über kaum ein anderes Thema als über den Sinn und Unsinn von Gartenschauen ist in unserem Berufsstand, welcher nicht sehr «theorie-freundlich» ist, diskutiert worden. Eine Grundproblematik der meisten bekannten Gartenschauen ist, daß immer zuviel gewollt und letztendlich zu wenig eingehalten wird. Unser Hauptziel ist deshalb die Vermittlung eines nachhaltig sinnlichen Erlebnisses für alle Bevölkerungsschichten als Kontrasterfahrung zur zunehmend virtuellen Welt.

Das Konzept für die Internationale Gartenschau wurde unter zwei Grundsätzen entwickelt: Welches kann zu Beginn des neuen Jahrtausends die Message für eine Gartenschau sein und was ist unter den vorgegebenen Rahmenbedingungen, Örtlichkeit, Zeit, Finanzen, möglich? Thema des Entwurfes der Internationalen Gartenschau heißt «Gärten in der Landschaft»

Der Prototyp des Gartens

My first encounter with the vegetation of Styria was not in idyllic surroundings but during a climbing trip; my experience took the form of a thorny juniper bush growing on the steep face of the Gesäuse. I now know that Styria is an arable and garden region traditionally known for its fertility.

Hardly any other topic has provoked so much discussion in our profession – not exactly one that tends towards theory – than the point and pointlessness of garden shows. An underlying problem of most leading garden shows is always that what is planned ultimately falls well short of what is actually realised. For this reason, our priority is to achieve a sustainable experience for the senses for all sectors of the population as a contrast to an increasingly virtual world.

The concept for the International Garden Show was developed on the basis of two principles: What is the message of a garden show at the beginning of a new millennium and what is possible given the parameters of location, time, finances? The theme of the project for the International Garden Show is "gardens in the landscape", i.e. acceptance of the existing landscape

The prototype of the garden

und damit wird festgelegt, daß die vorhandene Landschaft mit allen Qualitäten und Nachteilen akzeptiert wird. Auf konzentriertem Raum werden vier thematisch unterschiedlich klar gefaßte Gärten gezeigt: Blumengarten, Berggarten, Fasanengarten, Ackergarten.

Das Planungsgebiet liegt vor den Toren von Graz und steht nicht mehr im städtebaulichen Kontext, sondern im «Schwarzl Freizeitzentrum». Dieses Freizeitzentrum verlangt nach einer Neukonzeption. In dieser Logik kann es nicht mehr darum gehen, die ganze Landschaft neu zu gestalten, sondern in konzentrierter Form das zentrale Thema «Gärten in der Landschaft» aufzunehmen.

Gärten in der Landschaft

Städtische Park- und Erholungsanlagen leben von der unmittelbaren Nachbarschaft von Wohnquartieren, Infrastruktureinrichtungen und Arbeitsstandorten. In diesem urbanen Geflecht wird alltägliche – gezielte oder auch beiläufige – Nutzung zur Selbstverständlichkeit. Anders unser Planungsgebiet, das, in der Peripherie von Graz gelegen, sich der alltäglichen Stadtnutzung entzieht und zum Ausflugsort nobilitiert. Ein Ort, der seiner spezifischen Ausgestaltung wegen aufgesucht wird. Das in der Ausschreibung erweiterte Freizeit- und Erholungsgelände ist nach unserer Auffassung mit dem vorgefundenen Bestand schon ausreichend gegeben, so daß eine nur flächenmäßige Vergrößerung kaum neue Besucher anziehen wird. Wir erachten deshalb die Gartenschau Steiermark als ein Instrument, das hervorragend geeignet ist, auch für die Nachnutzung attraktive Orte zu schaffen, für deren Besuch sich beispielsweise auch eine weitere Anfahrt lohnen wird. Das heißt: Der aus der Landschaft ausgegrenzte «Hortus conclusus» von höchster gartenkultureller Qualität führt in der gestalterischen Ausstrahlung – gepaart mit poetischer Kraft – zu einem unverwechselbaren sinnlichen Erleben.

Um dieses langfristig zu gewährleisten, ist eine intensive gärtnerische Haltung und ein begleitendes kulturelles Programm notwendig. Abschließbarkeit und Eintrittsgelder, auch

with all its qualities and drawbacks. Four clearly defined gardens with different themes are presented in a concentrated area: the Flower Garden, the Alpine Garden, the Pheasant Garden and the Field Garden.

Being outside the built-up area of Graz, the planning area does not have an urban context, but is located in the "Schwarzl Recreation Centre". The centre very much in need of redesign and, given this scenario, it is no longer a question of redesigning the entire landscape, but of addressing the central theme "gardens in the landscape" in a concentrated form.

Gardens in the landscape

Urban parks and recreation areas depend on their immediate vicinity to residential districts, infrastructure and places of work. Day-to-day – intended or accidental – use becomes a matter of course in this urban jumble. Our planning area, located on the periphery of Graz, is not a day-to-day urban place but a location to visit specially. A place that attracts visitors due to the specific nature of its design. The extensive leisure and recreational areas described in the competition brief are, in our view, already sufficiently in existence and, in consequence, enlargement of such areas is hardly likely to attract new visitors. For this reason, we see the Styria Garden Show as an instrument ideally suited to creating attractive places for subsequent further use, places that attract visitors from further afield. The result: design of a perfect "hortus conclusus" separated from the landscape and of superb quality – combined with poetic force – leads to an unmistakable experience for the senses.

What is needed to secure this on a long-term basis is intensive gardening and an accompanying cultural programme. Fencing in and admission charges, also for follow-up uses, are consequently a matter of necessity. Examples from England show that this is not only a means of financing upkeep, but that good marketing can create welcome synergies, added cultural value for the surrounding region, and even generate profits. Perhaps in future we will not only find the "Beautiful Gardens of Austria" in Vienna and Salzburg, but also in Graz.

in der Nachnutzung, werden somit zur Pflicht. Beispiele aus England zeigen, daß damit nicht nur der Unterhalt finanziert werden kann, sondern bei guter Vermarktung willkommene Synergien entstehen, kultureller Mehrwert für die weitere Region geschaffen und sogar Profit ermöglicht wird. Die zum Besuch einladenden «Schönen Gärten Österreichs» finden wir in Zukunft vielleicht nicht nur in Wien oder Salzburg sondern neu auch in Graz.

Das Konzept «Gärten in der Landschaft» beruht auf dem Prinzip, jedem Garten ein eigenes Thema zuzuordnen. Eine fünf Meter hohe Grenze definiert hierbei die Trennung zwischen den einzelnen Gärten. Die vier thematisch differenzierten Gärten sind aus der umliegenden Landschaft ausgegrenzt und stehen in klarem Kontrast zu dieser. Der «besondere Ort» kann in dieser Logik nicht aus dem Bestand weiterentwickelt, sondern muß vielmehr neu geschaffen werden. In den Zwischenbereichen werden attraktive Orte für Kinder geschaffen wie Spielplätze und ein Streichelzoo.

Die vier Gartenteile

Ackergarten

Wie alle vier thematischen Gartenbereiche wird auch der Ackergarten als eigenständiger Raum definiert. Der Ackergarten ist als Beispiel zur Thematik «nachwachsende Energie» durch einen fünf Meter breiten Streifen aus drei Meter hohem Chinaschilf räumlich gefaßt. Die Darstellung von unterschiedlichen landwirtschaftlichen Produkten und Produktionsmethoden folgt dem Muster eines seriellen Bildes von Richard Paul Lohse und stellt unter Beweis, daß Nützlichkeit mit Schönheit kompatibel ist.

Blumengarten

Der Blumengarten, ein begehbares Blumenbild, wird quadratisch gefaßt durch ein einfaches, fünf Meter hohes Baugerüst, das mit weißen Stoffbahnen überzogen ist, vergleichbar mit einem Bühnenvorhang. Ein traditionelles islamisches Teppichbild mit Gar-

The concept "gardens in the landscape" is based on the principle of giving each garden its own theme. A five-metre high boundary defines the division between the individual gardens. The four gardens on different themes are separate from and in contrast to the surrounding landscape. The "special place" cannot simply be evolved from what is already there, but has to be created anew. Children's attractions such as playgrounds and a petting zoo are to be created in the intervening areas.

The four variations on a garden

The Field Garden

As in all four garden themes, the Field Garden is also given its own spatial definition. The Field Garden is spatially conceived as an example of the theme of "renewable energy" by a five-metre-wide strip of three-metre-high Miscanthus sinensis giganteus. Presentation of different agricultural products and production techniques is based on the model of a serial picture by Richard Paul Lohse, documenting that usefulness and beauty are indeed compatible.

The Flower Garden

The Flower Garden, a composition of flowers accessible to visitors, is enclosed by a simple, quadrangular, five-metre-high construction covered with lengths of white fabric, reminiscent of stage curtains. The garden motif of a traditional Islamic carpet serves as a model for the spatial structure. For the flower show this framework is to be filled with over one million flowers and plants with blooms and fragrances according to season. Precise choreography of the sequence of plants and flower colours is necessary to achieve a coherent composition and not an arbitrary potpourri of colour. A new sound installation by Hans-Jürgen Schmölzer specially for the International Garden Show on the theme "Nature does not exist" is to be heard in the Flower Garden, giving it a new, acoustic dimension. An observation tower provides a view across the Field Garden and the Flower Garden.

tenmotiven diente der Raumstruktur als Vorlage. Für die gärtnerische Leistungsschau wird dieses Muster mit mehr als einer Million Blumen und Stauden gefüllt und je nach Saison zum Blühen und Duften kommen. Hier wird eine genaue Dramaturgie der Pflanzenabfolge und Blütenfarben notwendig, um ein stimmiges Pflanzenfeuerwerk und nicht ein beliebiges Farbpotpourri zu erreichen. Im Blumengarten wird eine eigens für die IGS komponierte Klanginstallation von Hans-Jürgen Schmölzer mit dem Thema «Die Natur gibt es nicht» zu hören sein, die dem Garten über die Akustik eine neue Dimension geben soll. Der Überblick über diese beiden Gartenteile, Acker- und Blumengarten, wird von einem Turm aus ermöglicht.

Berggarten

Der Berggarten zeigt eine stark skulptural überformte Erdtopographie. Die Abgrenzung erfolgt mit einem fünf Meter hohen, geometrisch ausgeformten Rasenwall. Hier wird die steilstmögliche Rasenböschung mittels geotextilen Hilfsmitteln gezeigt. Der Erdwall definiert den Gartenraum gegen Außen und Innen und hat gleichzeitig lärmdämmende Wirkung. Im Garteninnern erleben wir die plastische Kraft dieser zum Teil thematischen Bepflanzung einer geometrisch überformten Topographie. Die Schrägen sind thematisch und materiell unterschiedlich ausgeformt: Im Schotterfeld wachsen in den Zwischenräumen ausgewählte Gräser und Bergblumen, womit eine neue Form des tradierten Alpinums des 19. Jahrhunderts angestrebt wird. Vom höchsten Punkt aus geniessen wir die gelenkte Sicht auf das Landschaftslesebuch, auf die Berge und den angrenzenden See. Im Landschaftsbuch – das den Dialog zwischen Natur und Landschaft subtil weiterführt – lesen wir aus erhöhter Warte einen Text aus dem «Schilcher ABC» des steirischen Autors R. P. Gruber, welcher im Rasen mit Streckmetallplatten eingelassen ist:

«Die durchschnittlichen Gegenden der Welt sind formbare und daher bereits verformte und daher deformierte Gegenden. Die Weltgegend ist eine formende Gegend. Im eigentlichen Sinn ist die Weltgegend gar keine Gegend, weil eine Gegend passiven Charakter trägt: sie definiert sich als das Gegenüber des Men-

The Alpine Garden

The Alpine Garden has a strongly sculptural topography. Its perimeter is in the form of a five-metre-high, geometrically shaped embankment of grass. Its steepness is emphasised by geotextile fabrics. The embankment defines the garden space both outside and inside, and also serves to reduce noise. Within the garden we experience the graphic force of a geometrically shaped topography stocked with plants partially on specific themes. The slopes address a variety of themes and employ different materials: selected grasses and alpine flowers grow in the spaces in the gravel bed, a reference to the tradition of the alpinum of the 19th century. From the highest point, we enjoy the intended view of the landscape primer, of the mountains and the nearby lake. We read in the landscape primer – a subtle continuation of the dialogue between nature and landscape – a text taken from the "Schilcher ABC" by the Styrian author R.P. Gruber that has been set in the grass in pierced steel sheeting.

"The average areas of this world are malleable and therefore already distorted and deformed. The 'cultural area' is an area that forms. Actually, it is not an area at all, as an area has a passive character: it defines itself as the opposite of humans, as that which humans have distanced themselves from. In other words, area means opposition and, at the same time, it is transcended by distancing or superiority. In other words, insofar as the character of potentially being formed is always part of the concept of area, the notion of a cultural area which forms itself cannot actually exist."

The existing scattered trees in the pyramid-shaped windows in the northern section are largely retained. The existing spruce wood, enhanced by woodland plants, ferns, etc. dominates in the southern section. The new woodland pond is as an antipode to the popular bathing lake. An artificial topography is created in the existing clearings, intensifying the experience of spatial diversity. "Music chairs" are placed at selected locations, where standard works from the history of music can be heard. In addition to the impressions provided by vegetation, materials and topography, we hear music at six different places: Mozart, Philip

schen, als das, wovon sich der Mensch abgehoben hat. Gegend meint also Gegnerisches und gleichzeitig das Übersteigen des Gegenübers durch Abheben oder auch Überheben. Insofern, nämlich als im Begriff Gegend immer der Charakter eines möglichen Geformtwerdens eingeschlossen ist, kann es also so etwas wie eine Weltgegend, die ja selber formend ist, gar nicht geben.»

Im nördlichen Teil bleiben die vorhandenen Einzelbäume in den Pyramidenzwischenräumen weitgehend erhalten. Im südlichen Teil dominiert der bestehende Fichtenwald, der mit Waldstauden, Farnpflanzungen etc. angereichert wird. Darin eingeschnitten ist der neue Waldweiher, eine Antipode zum belebten Badesee. In vorhandenen Lichtungen wird hier eine künstliche Topographie erzeugt und somit die räumliche Erlebnisvielfalt verstärkt. An ausgewählten Stellen werden Musikstühle aufgestellt, in denen Standardwerke aus der Musikgeschichte zu hören sind. Neben den pflanzlichen, materiellen und topographischen Eindrücken hören wir an sechs ausgewählten Orten Musik: Mozart, Philip Glass oder Reich. Die thematisierte Musik an den verschiedenen Orten verstärkt das sinnliche Erleben des Gartens. Der Berg- und Fasanengarten bilden zusammen die langfristig zu erhaltenden Gärten.

Fasanengarten

Im nördlichen Teil bleiben die vorhandenen Einzelbäume weitgehend in den Wegen und Hecken erhalten. Der Fasanengarten wird durch die umfassende Lindenhecke begrenzt. Sein Inneres zeigt einen Lindenheckenmäander, der von West nach Ost schräg abfällt und in ein Labyrinth mündet. Der spannungsvolle Wechsel von räumlicher Enge und Weite, von different ausgestalteten Gartenräumen, wird auf den beiden Wegen unterschiedlich erlebt: dort befinden sich der Teich mit seinen Lotusblumen und der Kircheninsel, die Himmelstreppe neben der Erdrampe, die wilden, aber zugeschnittenen Topiarys, der Rosengarten, das große Rasenstück mit der Magnolienanhöhe. Im südlichen Teil liegen ein Irrgarten und ein Labyrinth. In der Mitte des Irrgartens bleibt eine alte Eiche erhalten. Im Zentrum des Labyrinthes finden wir nicht mehr Minotaurus: der Wande-

Glass and Reich. The theme of music at various locations heightens the experience of the garden. The Alpine Garden and the Pheasant Garden are the two gardens to be retained in the long term.

The Pheasant Garden

The existing solitaire trees in the northern section are largely retained in the path and hedge areas. The Pheasant Garden is enclosed by a hedge of limes. Its interior is traced by a meandering hedges of limes, descending from west to east and leading to a labyrinth. The interesting alternation of confinement and expanse, of differentiated garden spaces, is reflected along the two paths: the pool with its lotus plants and island of cherry trees, the "Sky Stairway" next to the earth ramp, the wild yet clipped topiaries, the rose garden, the large extent of grass with its elevated area of magnolias. The southern section contains a maze and a labyrinth. An old oak tree is retained at the central point of the maze. We no longer have to fear the Minotaur at the centre of the labyrinth; instead visitors are rewarded by a simple bench where they can take a rest. Again and again, we encounter hundreds of – uncaged – colourful pheasants.

On ecology and design

Special attention was paid to the ecological concept of the garden show with a view to disproving the frequent assumption that design and ecology are in themselves a contradiction in terms. Our aim was not to present ecological experimental areas, but to develop existing ecological approaches. In other words, the existing drainage ditches are largely retained and the meadow with its wide variety of species preserved. The fertiliser used in the flower garden is to be collected and purified. The system of paths is entirely in the form of a water-bound surface. As far as furniture is concerned, it by now goes without saying that no tropical wood is to be used. The existing trees and bushes are treated with care. A large part of the luxuriant hedges in the form of a clipped mixed hedge is to be stocked with different species of plants to achieve ecological diversity.

rer wird mit einer einfachen Bank zum Ausruhen belohnt. Im Fasanengarten begleiten uns immer wieder – frei umherlaufend – hundert farbenprächtige Fasane.

Zur Ökologie und Gestaltgebung

Besondere Aufmerksamkeit wurde der ökologischen Ausbildung des Gartenschaugeländes gewidmet, um die oft gehörte These zu widerlegen, daß Gestalt und Ökologie unvereinbare Antipoden darstellen. Dabei haben wir versucht, nicht ökologische Versuchsfelder darzustellen, sondern den vorhandenen Bestand an ökologischen Ansätzen weiterzuentwickeln. So bleiben die vorhandenen Entwässerungsgräben weitgehend erhalten und die jetzt teilweise artenreiche Wiese wird geschont. Im Blumengarten wird das anfallende Düngemittel gesammelt und gereinigt. Der Wegebau erfolgt ausschließlich durch eine wassergebundene Decke. Bei der Möblierung ist der Verzicht auf tropische Gehölze mittlerweile eine Selbstverständlichkeit. Die vorhandenen Bäume und Sträucher werden sorgsam behandelt. Ein Großteil der üppigen Hecken werden als geschnittene Mischhecke mit unterschiedlichen Pflanzenarten bestockt, um auch hier eine ökologische Vielfalt zu realisieren.

Musik in Gärten

Musik in Gärten ist ein uraltes Thema, das dem Garten eine sinnliche Dichte verleihen soll. Dafür wurde ein thematisch abgestimmter Kompositionsauftrag an Hans-Jörg Schmölzer in Auftrag gegeben. Die Gärten an der Internationalen Gartenschau stellen den Versuch dar, ein Stück rezente Gartenkultur in all ihrer Vielfalt aufleben zu lassen.

Dieter und Erika Kienast

Music in gardens

Music in gardens is an age-old theme designed to give the garden an added sensuous dimension. Hans-Jörg Schmölzer was commissioned to design an appropriate thematic composition. The gardens of the International Garden Show are an attempt to reflect part of modern garden culture in all its diversity.

Dieter and Erika Kienast

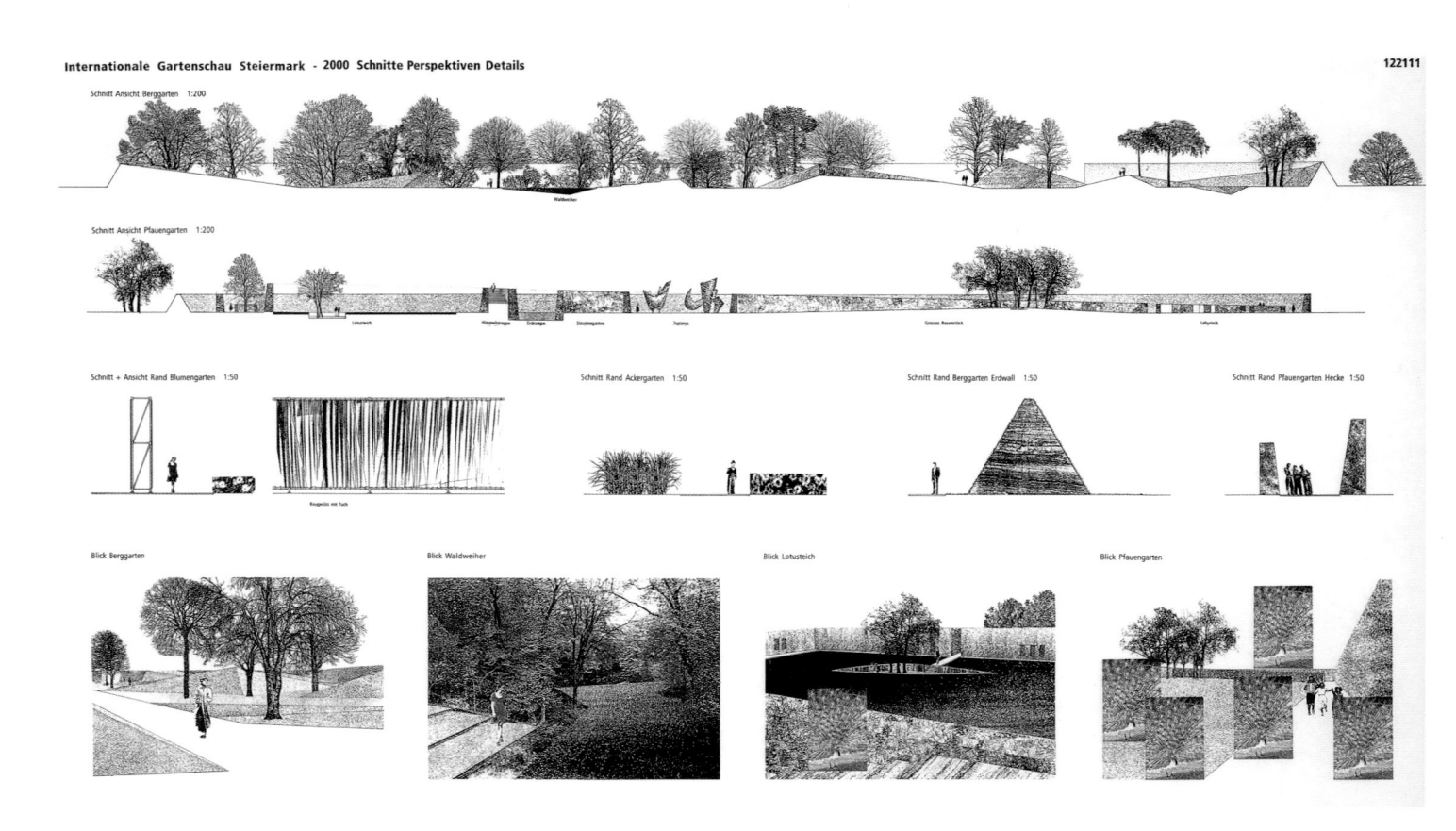

Internationale Gartenschau Steiermark - 2000 Schnitte Perspektiven Details

122111

Schnitt Ansicht Berggarten 1:200

Schnitt Ansicht Pfauengarten 1:200

Schnitt + Ansicht Rand Blumengarten 1:50

Schnitt Rand Ackergarten 1:50

Schnitt Rand Berggarten Erdwall 1:50

Schnitt Rand Pfauengarten Hecke 1:50

Blick Berggarten

Blick Waldweiher

Blick Lotusteich

Blick Pfauengarten

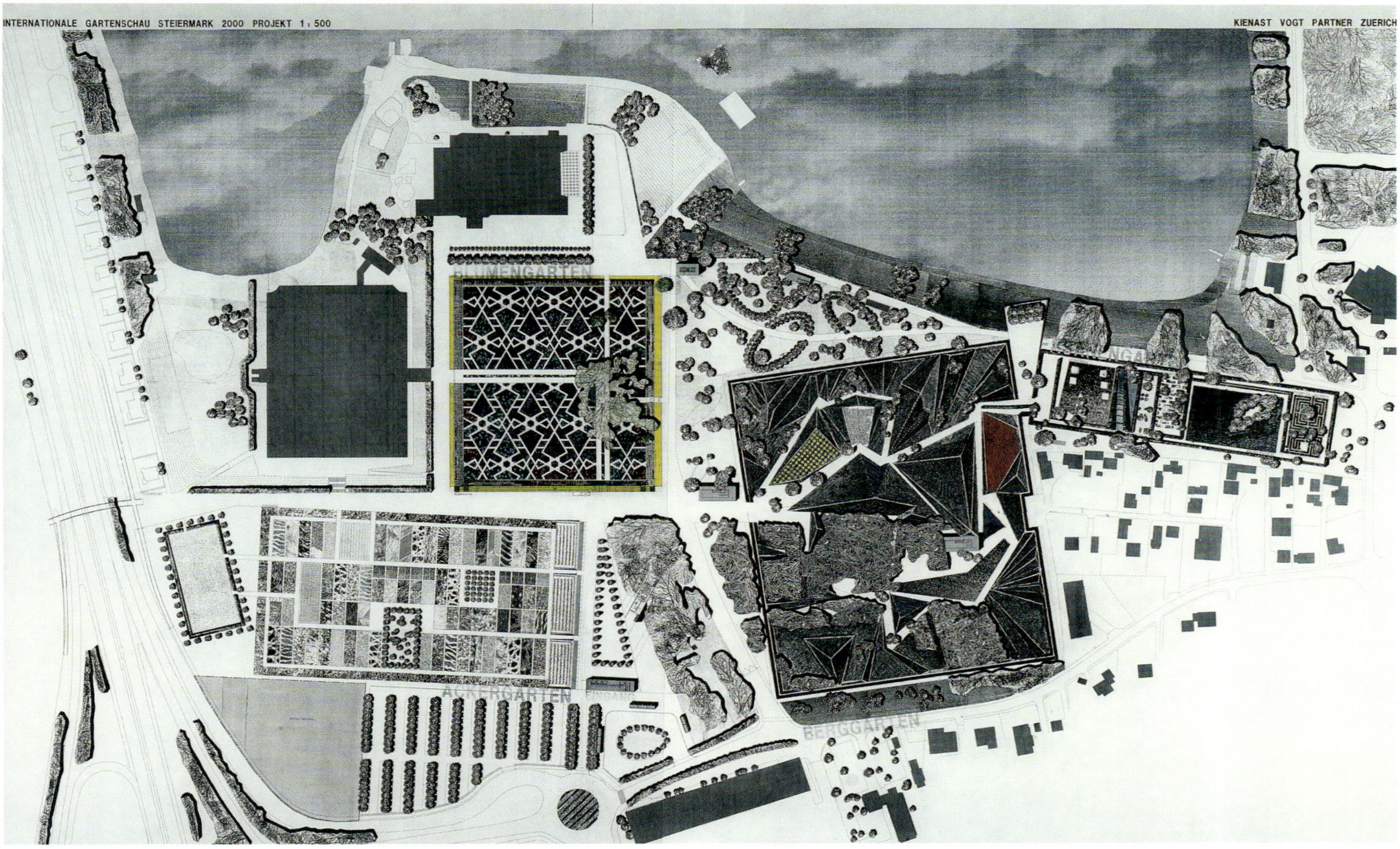
INTERNATIONALE GARTENSCHAU STEIERMARK 2000 PROJEKT 1 : 500
KIENAST VOGT PARTNER ZUERICH
BLUMENGARTEN
ACKERGARTEN
EINGANG
BERGGARTEN

Internationale Gartenscha Steiermark - 2000 Situation 1:500
122111
Blumengarten
Pfauengarten
Berggarten

Im Schotterfeld wachsen in den Zwischenräumen ausgewählte Gräser und Bergblumen. Hier wurde eine neue Form des tradierten Alpinums angestrebt.

Selected grasses and alpine flowers grow in the crevices in the gravel bed. This is intended as a new form of the traditional alpinum.

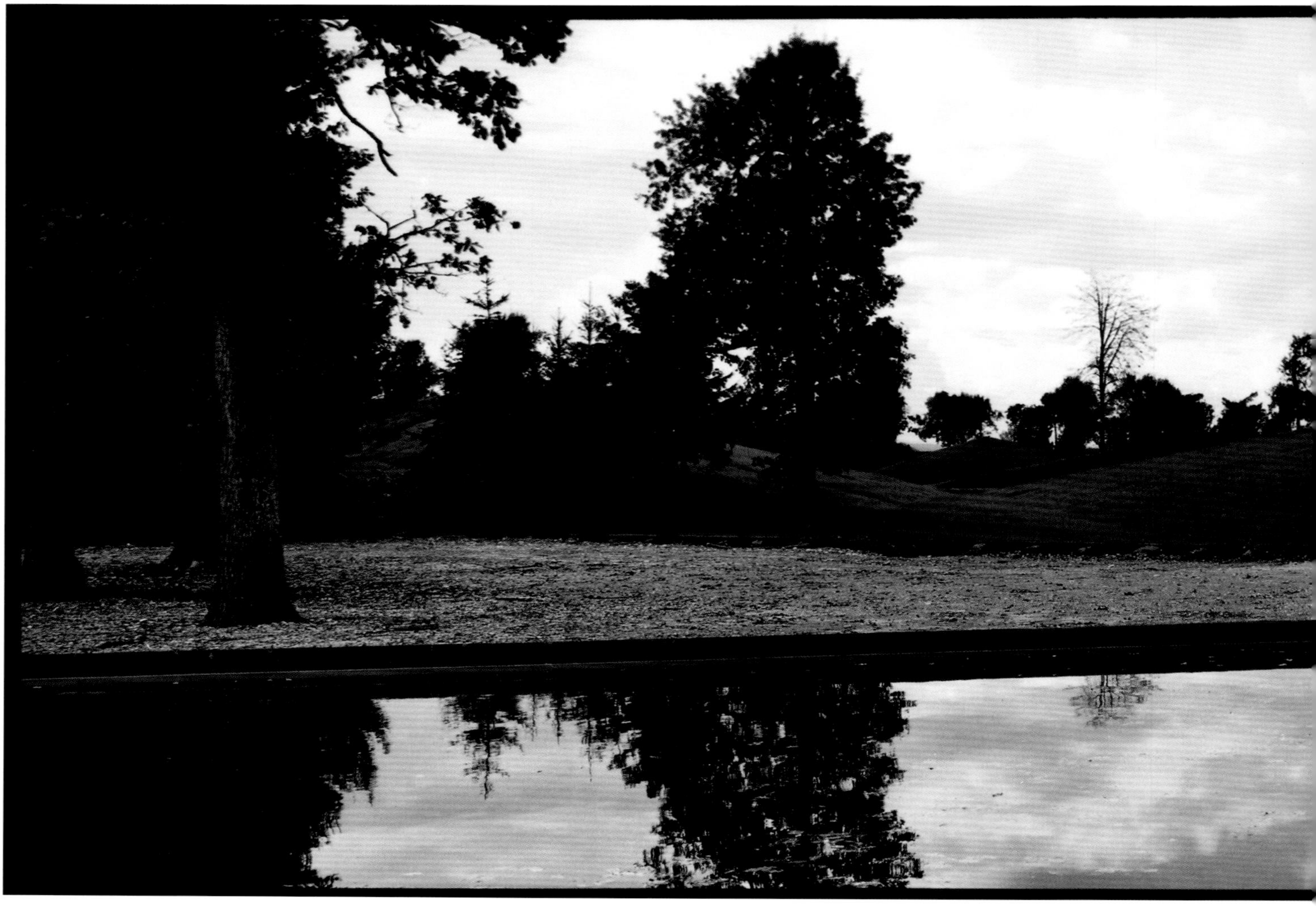

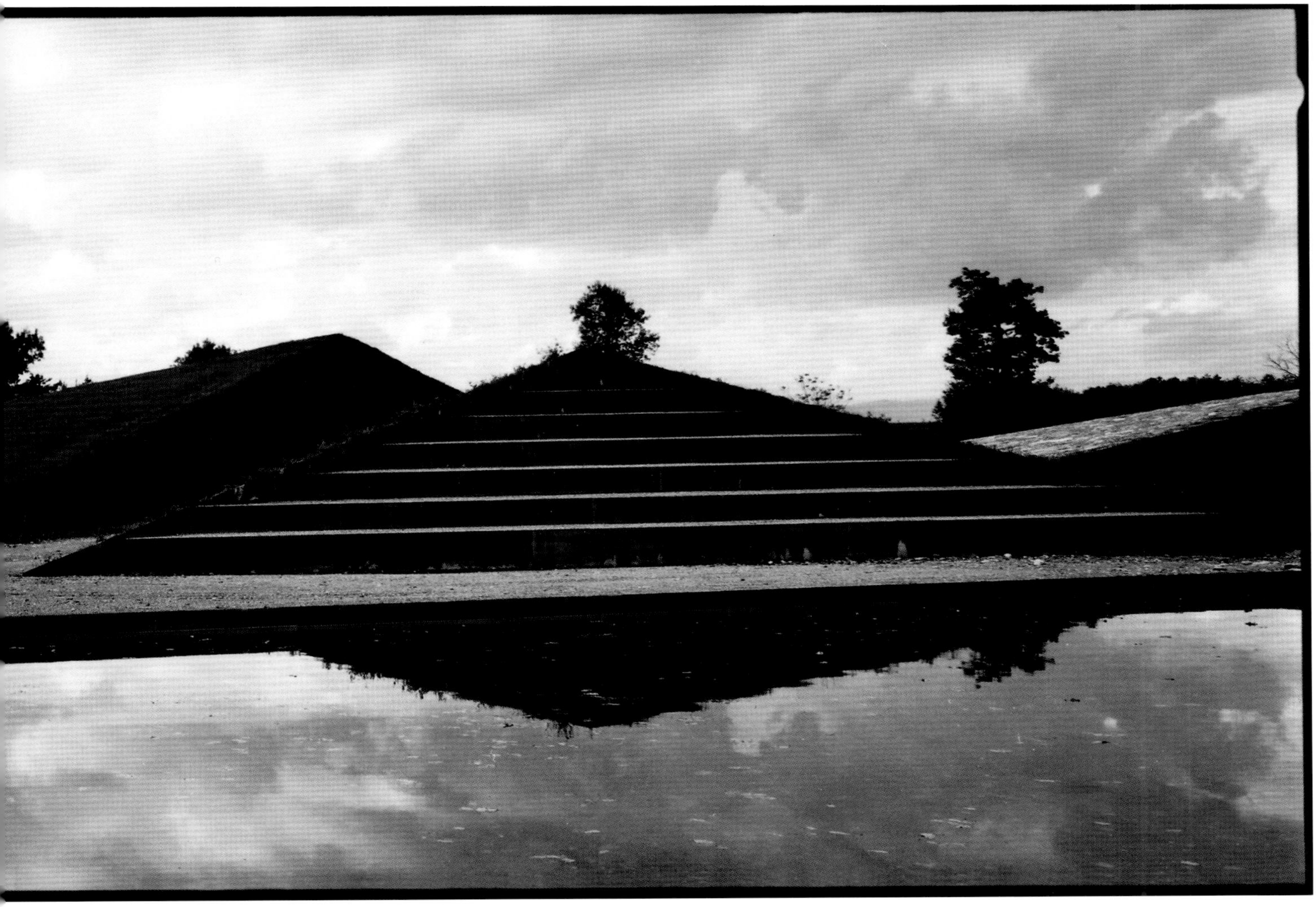

Im Garteninnern erleben wir die plastische Kraft dieser geometrisch überformten Topographie.

Within the garden we experience the graphic force of this geometrically shaped topography.

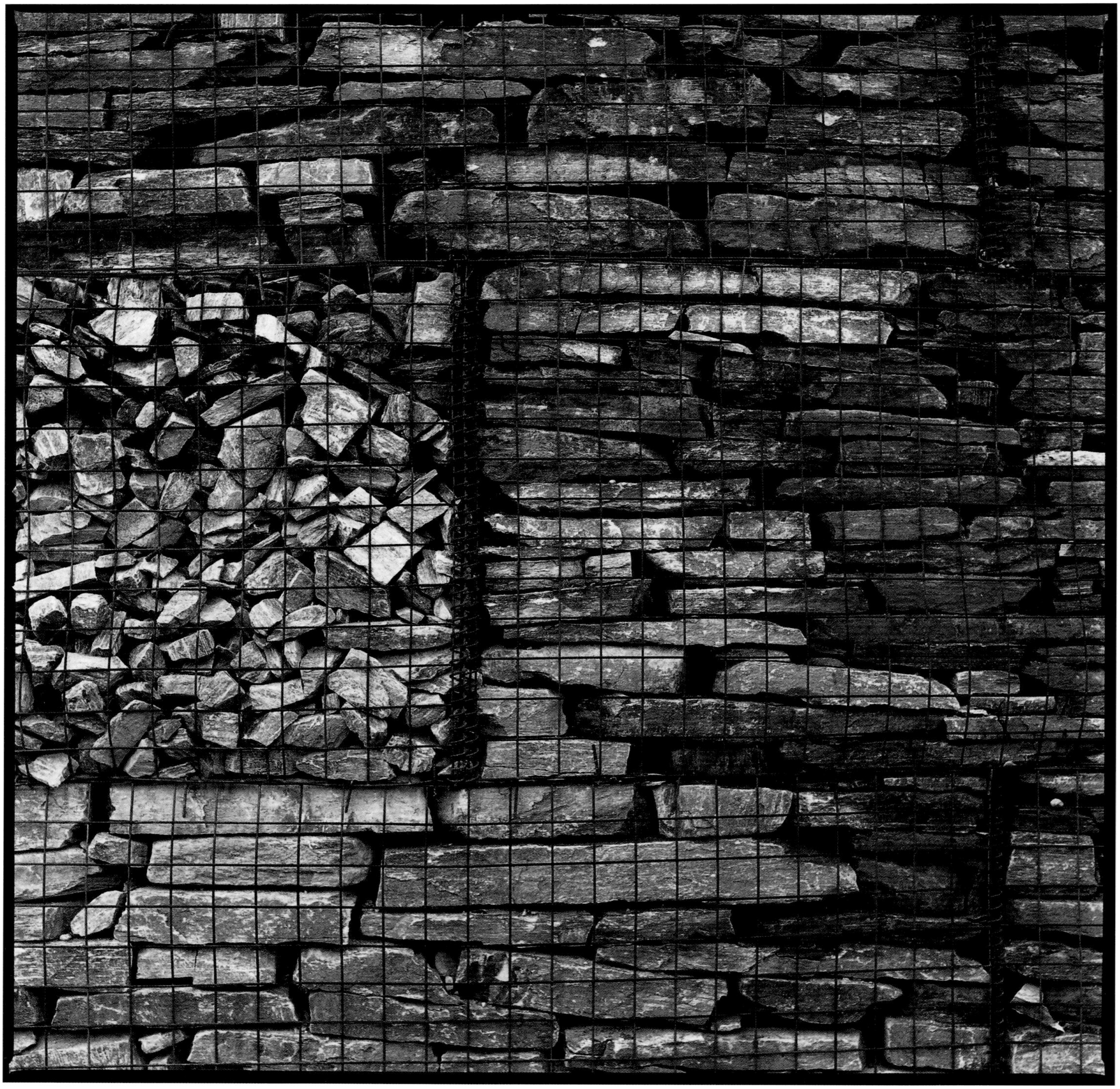

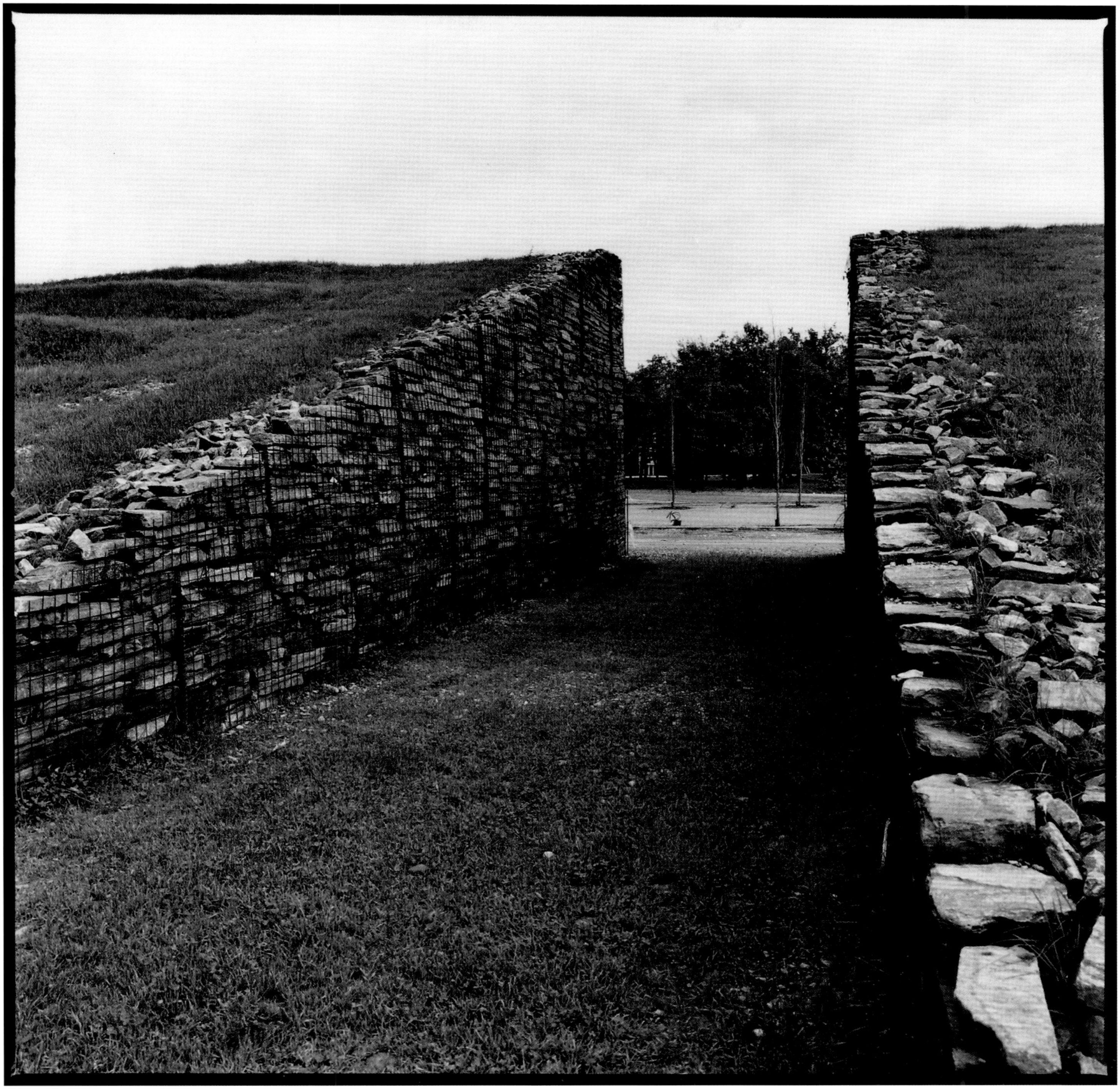

Innenhofgestaltung
Geschäftshaus der Swiss Re, Zürich

Wir betreten den Gartenhof durch den Restaurantausgang im Erdgeschoß und werden unterschiedliche Ansichten, eine Sammlung stimmungsvoller Bilder, entdecken. Mauern – drei Meter hoch – begrenzen den Gartenraum. Deren Oberkanten stellen eine horizontale Bezugsebene zum gewölbten Betonbelag her. Die Funktion der Mauern beschränkt sich nicht auf die Abgrenzung zum benachbarten Parkplatz: Sie erzeugen Raumtiefe und Transparenz und prägen darüber hinaus die Thematik des Hofes. So zum Beispiel verdeutlicht die Tuffsteinwand die Veränderbarkeit des Ortes. Sprühnebeldüsen befeuchten den Stein und die Luft. Mit der Zeit werden Moose und Flechten den ockerfarbenen Stein begrünen. Vor allem an heißen Sommertagen wird die Berieselung für angenehme Abkühlung sorgen.

    Vor den Mauern steht eine Gruppe von imposanten Katsurabäumen mit ihren charakteristischen herzförmigen Blättern, im Frühling bronzerot und im Herbst von gelber bis scharlachroter Farbe. Sie werden bis zu acht Meter hoch, bilden einen räumlichen Akzent und laden zum Verweilen im Schatten ein. Neben den Bäumen spiegelt das Wasserbecken ihre Kronen, den Himmel und die Fassade des transparenten Glasgebäudes. Der kreisrunde Wasserspiegel liegt wie eine Wasserwaage im schiefen Belag. Bestehende Betonaufbauten in der Tiefgaragendecke begründen die unterschiedlich stark gewölbte Hofoberfläche. Der gestreifte Betonbelag neigt sich zum Gebäude, was den räumlichen Bezug zwischen Haus und Garten unterstützt. Gestockte Querbalken auf den Betonbändern verringern je nach Standort deren Dominanz. Zwischen Betonstreifen kann Regenwasser versickern und an einigen Stellen blühen im Juni blaue Iris in den Sickerstreifen. Von der Dachterrasse aus betrachtet, erscheint der Hof als abstraktes Bild: die Mauern als Zickzacklinie, das schwarze kreisrunde Wasserbecken wie ein Edelstein, die Belagsstreifen mit den Querbalken vielleicht wie ein digitaler Code, die grünen Irislinien definieren ein geometrisch exaktes Feld, und die scheinbar zufällig eingestreuten Baumroste erinnern im Winter an die Blattform der Bäume.

Dieter Kienast

Courtyard Design:
Offices of the Swiss Re, Zurich

We enter the garden courtyard from the restaurant on the ground floor and discover different views, an array of idyllic images. The area is bounded by walls three metres high, their upper surfaces forming a horizontal reference to the vaulted concrete surface. The walls not only serve as a boundary to the adjacent parking area, they create depth and transparency and also set the theme of the courtyard. For example, the tuff wall underlines the changeability of the locus. Fine sprays of water moisten the stone and the air. In time, the ochre-coloured stone will be covered with moss and lichen. The spray of water provides a welcoming cooling on hot summer days.

    A group of imposing Katsura trees characterised by their heart-shaped leaves stands in front of the wall; their leaves are bronze-red in spring and yellow to scarlet in autumn. These trees, which grow up to eight metres high, form a spatial accent and are an invitation to enjoy their welcome shade. An adjacent pool reflects their crowns, the sky and the facade of the transparent glass building. The circular area of water lies in the sloping surface like a spirit level. The differences in the greatly curved surface of the courtyard are explained by existing concrete structures in the ceiling of the underground garage.

    The striped concrete surface is inclined towards the building and emphasises the spatial relationship between the house and the garden. Depending on their location, cross-beams on the concrete strips reduce dominance. Rainwater can seep between the strips of concrete and blue irises flower in June in some parts of the seepage area.

    Seen from the roof terrace, the court has the appearance of an abstract picture: the walls as a zigzag line, the black, circular pool like a jewel, the surface strips with the cross-beams – perhaps a digital code –, the green lines formed by the irises define a geometrically exact field and, in winter, the seemingly chance tree grills recall the shape of the trees' leaves.

Dieter Kienast

205

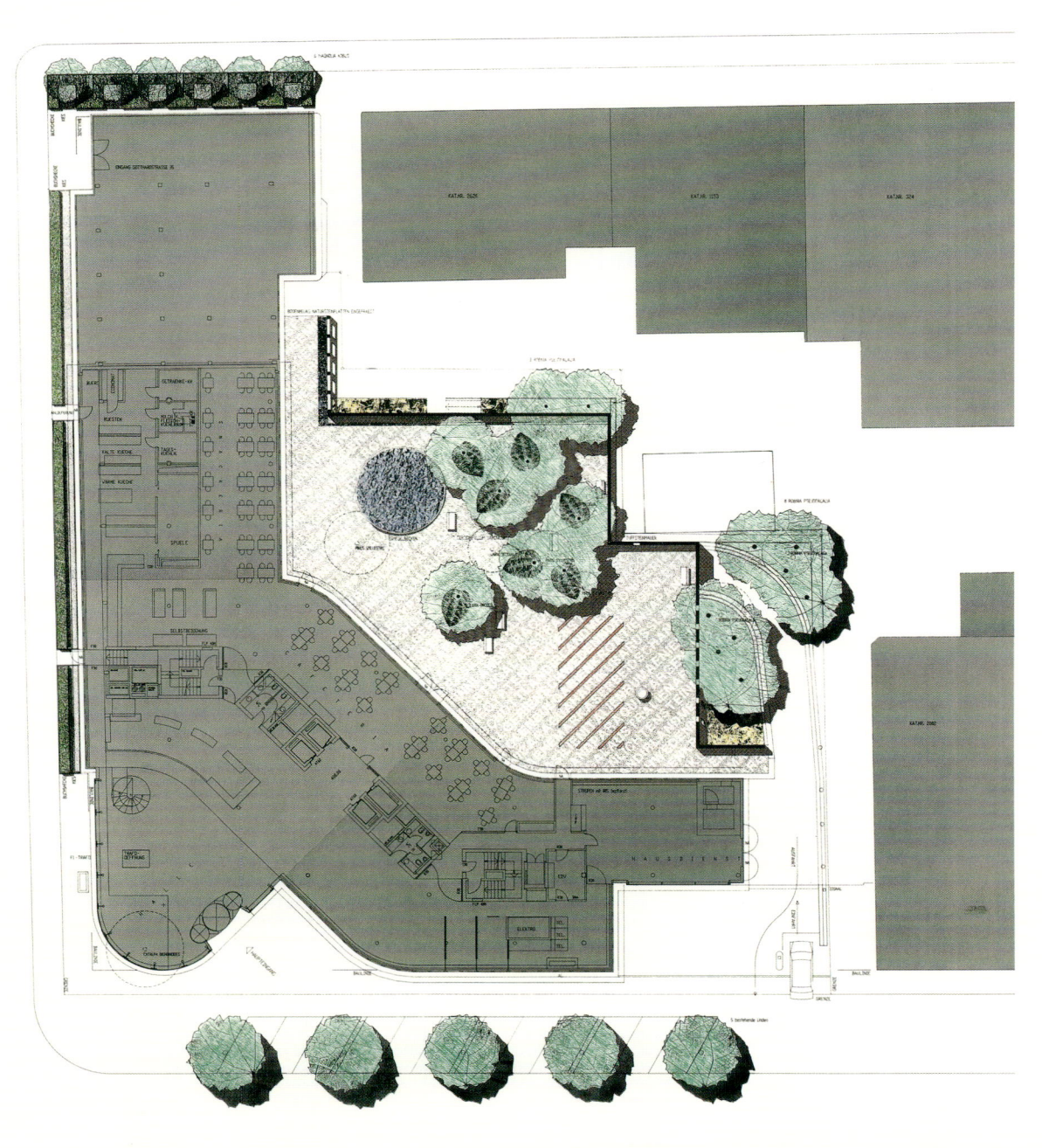

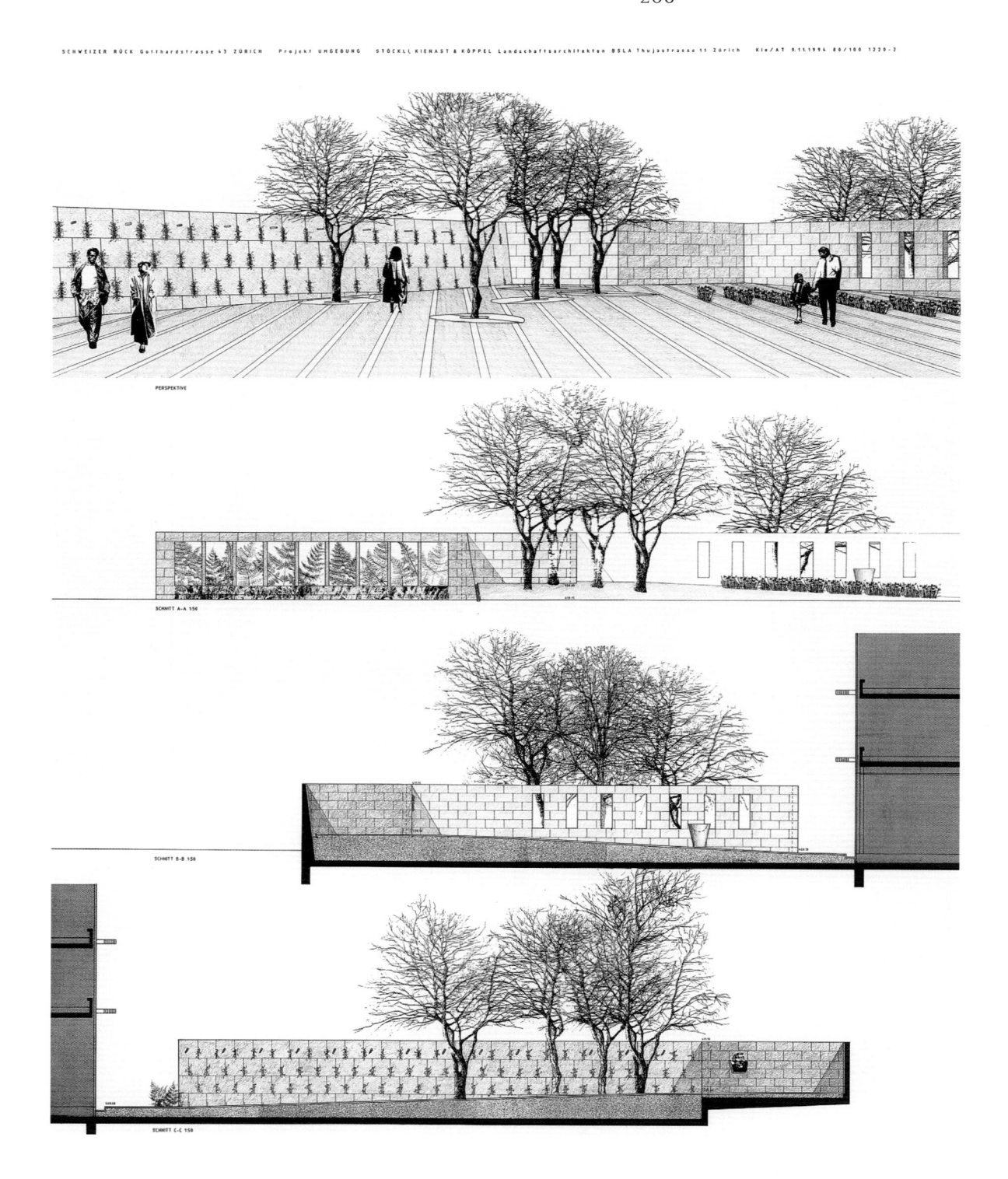

SCHWEIZER RÜCK Gotthardstrasse 43 ZÜRICH   Projekt UMGEBUNG   STÖCKLI, KIENAST & KOPPEL Landschaftsarchitekten BSLA Thujastrasse 11 Zürich   Kie/AT 9.11.1994 80/100 1220-2

PERSPEKTIVE

SCHNITT A-A 1:50

SCHNITT B-B 1:50

SCHNITT C-C 1:50

Riesige «Irisfenster» ermöglichen den Blick auf das Geschehen in der Nachbarschaft.

Giant "iris windows" afford a view of the surroundings.

Wie eine Wasserwaage liegt das schwarzschimmernde Wasserbecken im schiefen Belag.

The glittering black pool lies in the inclined surface like a spirit level.

Zu jeder Jahreszeit dominieren die Katsurabäume, deren Blattform sich im Baumrost wiederholt, den Hof.

The Katsura trees whose leaf form is repeated in the grilles of the trees dominate the court at all times of the year.

Die durchlaufenden Betonbänder sind durch Versickerungsstreifen und einen Strichcode gegliedert.

The continuous strips of concrete are structured by
seepage strips and a bar code.

Seminar- und Ausbildungszentrum Swiss Re, Rüschlikon

Gartenanlage Villa Bodmer

Das Gartenkonzept der Villa Bodmer stammt wahrscheinlich von den Architekten Richard von Sinner und Hans Beyeler. Einige Detailpläne des Gartenarchitekten Vivell lassen eine fachtechnische Begleitung vermuten.

Der Garten ist ein typisches Beispiel für einen großbürgerlichen Garten der damaligen Zeit. Die zwei wesentlichen Gartenkonzeptionen, der formale, architektonische «französische» und der landschaftliche, freie «englische» Typus, werden innerhalb eines Gartens vereint. Aus heutiger Sicht erscheint diese Gegenüberstellung des architektonischen Teils im Zentrum, des landschaftlichen Teils in den Randbereichen, als reizvoller Kontrast.

Mit Ausnahme des Wasserbeckens auf der Südseite und zwei Hochstammbäumen als räumlicher Abschluß auf der Ostseite ist der Garten in einem bemerkenswert originalen Zustand erhalten geblieben. Die baulichen und vegetativen Elemente, speziell das Buchsparterre, sind seit der Erstellung hervorragend instandgehalten und gepflegt worden.

Durch das Tor, gerahmt von Mauern, führt eine zweireihige Lindenallee auf einem steilen Weg seitlich zur Villa. Der Ausblick auf die angrenzende Landschaft ist anfänglich offen und wird auf dem Vorplatz durch Koniferen verdeckt. Die mittlerweile mächtigen immergrünen Bäume mit ihren unterschiedlichen Grüntönen bilden zusammen mit der Villa einen imposanten Gartenraum.

Die unmittelbar dem Gebäude vorgelagerte Terrasse war ursprünglich von zwei Hochstammbäumen gerahmt. Die heute vorhandenen Sträucher und die vor den Terrassenmauern gepflanzten Kleingehölze wirken deplaziert. Die zwei Buchsparterres mit den Rosen – und Sommerblumenpflanzungen – leiten geschickt auf den tiefer gelegenen Garten über. Die doppelreihige Baumallee, verstärkt durch die langgezogenen Wasserbecken, bilden einen stimmungsvollen Gartenraum. Die ursprüngliche Qualität, mit dem geschwungenen Wasserbecken flankiert von großen Orangeriepflanzen in Töpfen, kann anhand von Photos erahnt werden.

Training Centre of the Swiss Re, Rüschlikon

Grounds of the Villa Bodmer

The garden concept of the Villa Bodmer was probably devised by the architects Richard von Sinner and Hans Beyeler. A number of detailed plans by the garden architect Vivell indicate that he contributed his specialist knowledge to the design.

The garden is a typical example of an upper-middle class garden of the time. Two fundamental ideas of the garden, the formal, architectural "French" and the landscaped, free "English" type have been combined within one garden. From today's point of view, this juxtaposition of the architectural part in the centre, surrounded by the landscape part on the periphery, is a delightful contrast.

With the exception of the pool on the south side and two trees marking the eastern boundary, the garden has remarkably been preserved in its original state. Maintenance and care of the structural and vegetation elements, in particular the box parterre, have been excellent ever since they were first laid out.

The gate, framed by walls, opens onto an avenue of limes bordering a steep path leading to the villa from one side. The view of the surrounding landscape is initially unrestricted, only in the area of the forecourt is it obscured by conifers. What are by now stately evergreens in differing shades of green form imposing garden space juxtaposed with the villa.

The terrace immediately in front of the building was originally framed by two tall trees. The shrubs there today and the small trees in front of the walls of the terrace appear out of place. The two box parterres, planted with roses and other summer flowers, form a skilful transition to the garden at a lower level. The avenue of trees, emphasised by the long, narrow pool, provides garden space with atmosphere. The original quality, with the curved pool flanked by large potted orangery plants, can be seen from photos.

The western extension of the terrace and the box parterres is accentuated by densely planted conifers. The chapel, built in 1959, today forms the conclusion of this transverse

Die westliche Verlängerung der Terrasse und der Buchsparterres ist durch eine massive Koniferenpflanzung akzentuiert. Die 1959 erbaute Kapelle bildet heute den Abschluß dieser Querachse. Auf den Bauplänen wird ersichtlich, mit welcher Akribie sich die Projektverfasser mit der Geländemodulation und der Baumpflanzung dieses Parkbereichs befaßten. Die nachträglich erstellten Bauten verunklären die Gartenkonzeption.

Auf der Ostseite ist die ursprüngliche Gartenkonzeption nicht mehr nachvollziehbar. Der Ausblick auf den See ist durch gepflanzte oder spontan aufgekommene Bäume verstellt. Speziell erwähnenswert sind allerdings die zwei Dreiergruppen von Säulenpappeln, die ursprünglich den Ausblick rahmten.

Der geplante Neubau einer Parkgarage und von Seminarräumen sowie die neue Nutzung der Villa als Ausbildungszentrum bedingen konzeptionelle Aussagen zum Umgang mit dem Park. Dabei stehen Fragen zur Maßstäblichkeit, zur architektonischen Formulierung und der Erschließung sicher im Vordergrund. Die vorgesehenen baulichen Eingriffe in den Park bedeuten im vorliegenden Fall Rodungen und Terrainveränderungen, die mit hoher architektonischer Qualität ausgeführt werden.

Die Neugestaltung präzisiert die räumlichen und atmosphärischen Qualitäten der Anlage. Eine differenzierte Auswahl der Pflanzen schafft die verschiedenartigen Stimmungen in den unterschiedlichen Teilen des Parks. Aus Einzelbildern entsteht eine begehbare exakte Landschaft.

Dieter Kienast

axis. The building plans reveal the meticulousness with which the authors of the project approached modulation of the terrain and the planting of trees in this part of the park. The buildings which were added later on distort the underlying idea of the garden.

The original idea of the garden can no longer be seen on the east side. The view of the lake is obscured by trees which were either planted or grew there of their own accord. However, the two groups of three pyramid poplars which originally framed the view are worth mentioning.

Plans to build a new garage and two seminar rooms as well as the new use of the villa as a training centre call for conceptional statements on the approach to the park. Questions relating to scale, architectural expression and access will be of prime significance. The envisaged interventions in the park will consist of creating clearings and making changes to the terrain in a way which reveals high architectural quality.

This new design gives precision to the spatial qualities and atmosphere of the park. Selection of plants with different qualities creates different kinds of atmosphere in the individual sections of the park. An exact, accessible landscape is created from individual pictures.

Dieter Kienast

Schweizer Rück
AUFSICHT UMGEBUNG
Seminarzentrum und Gästehaus der Schweizer Rück in Rüschlikon

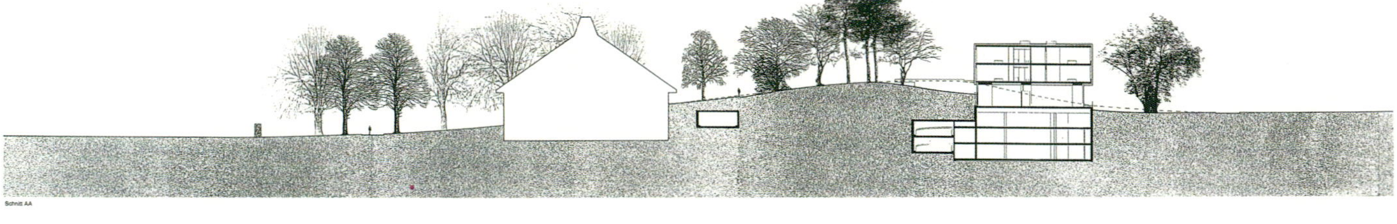

Schnitt AA

215

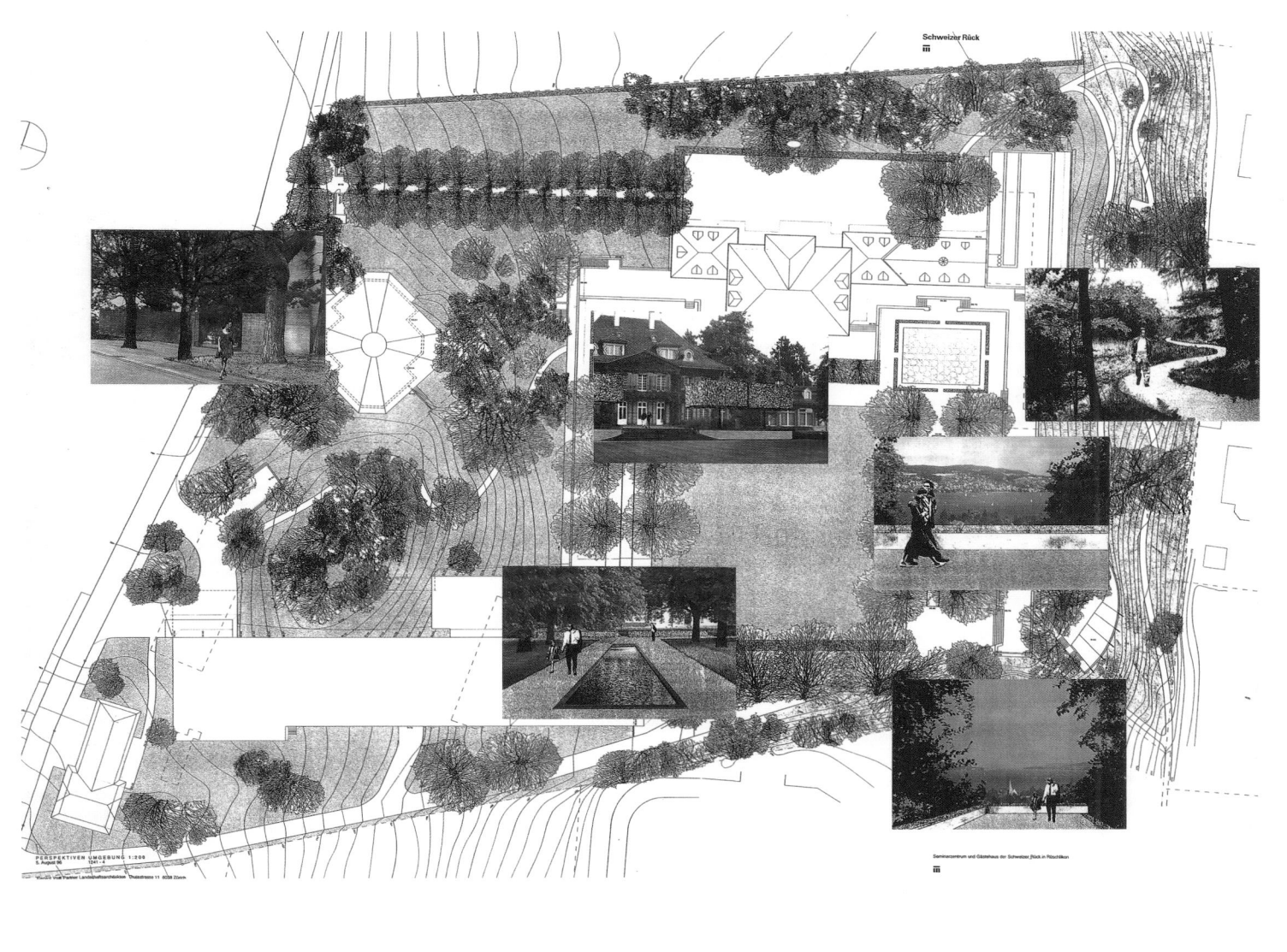

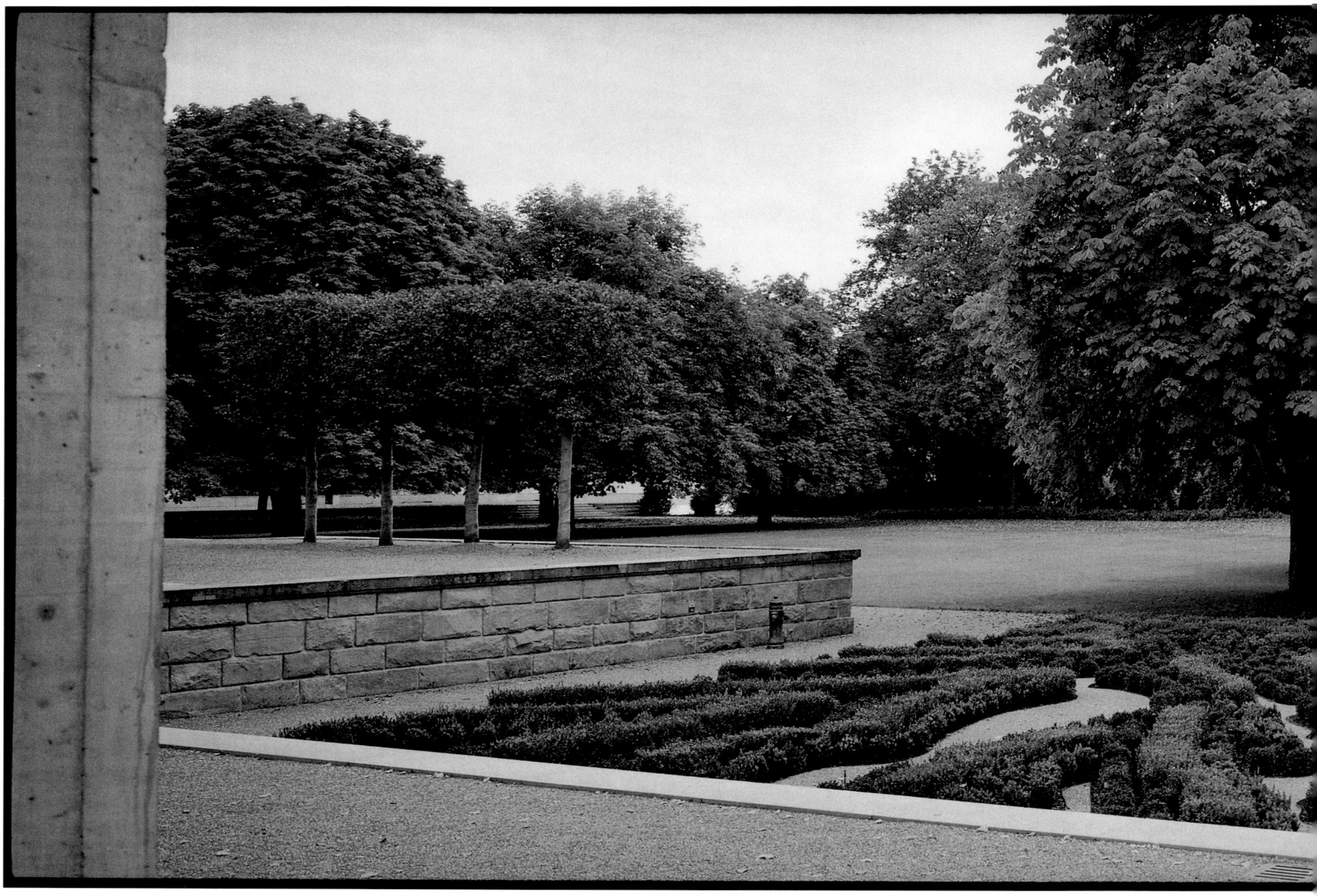

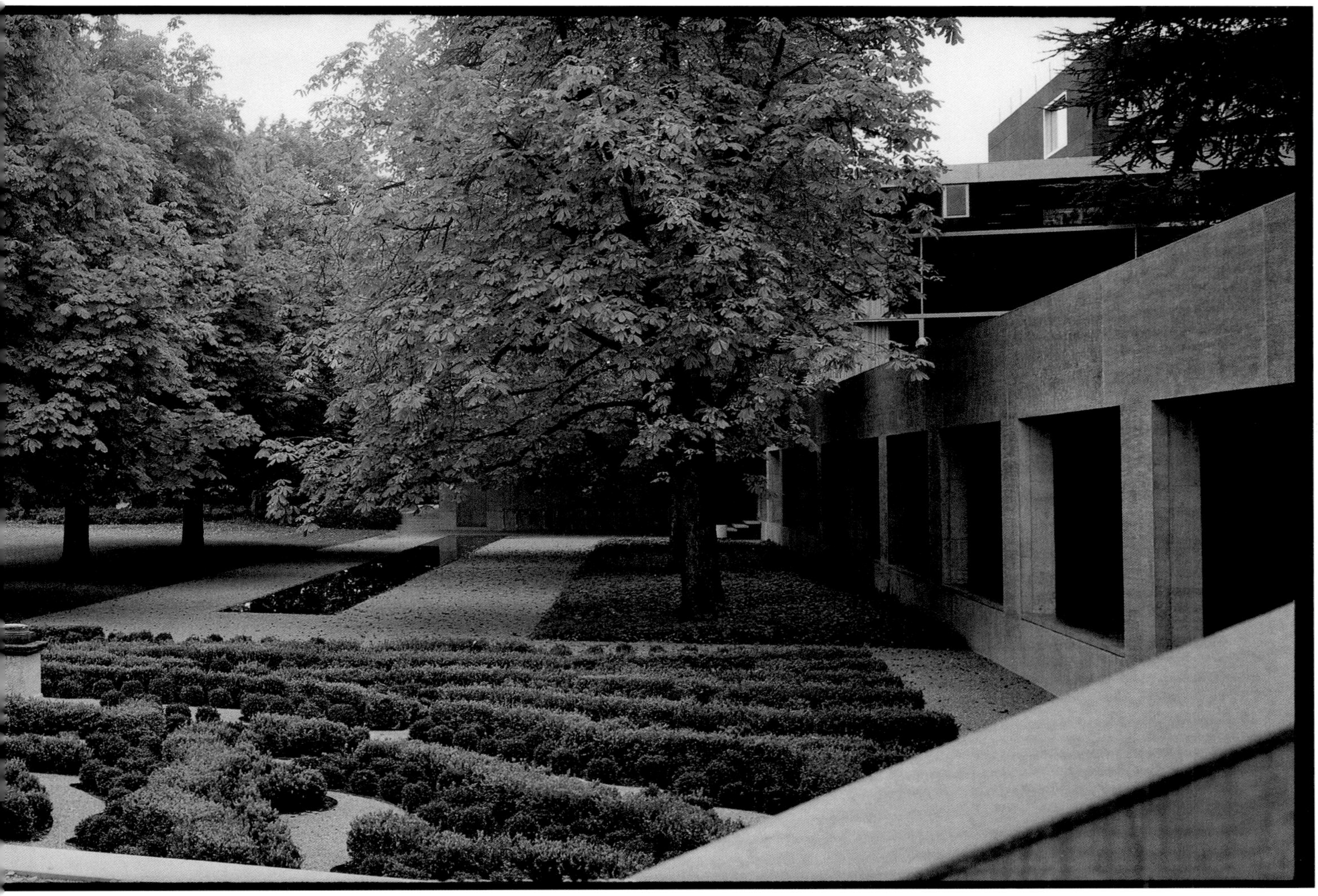

Die doppelreihige Baumallee, verstärkt durch die langgezogenen
Wasserbecken, bildet einen stimmungsvollen Gartenraum.

The avenue of trees, emphasised by the long, narrow pool,
provides garden space with atmosphere.

Umgebungsgestaltung Spar- und Landeskasse, Fürstenfeldbruck

«Natur und Kunst – Kunst und Natur» war das Thema des Außenraumwettbewerbes für das neue Verwaltungsgebäude der Sparkasse in Fürstenfeldbruck. Nun reden wir, wenn wir von unserer Arbeit sprechen, nicht von Gartenkunst, sondern etwas bescheidener von Gartenarchitektur und halten uns an den Philosophen Gadamer, der den Begriff «Kunst» nur da akzeptiert, wo keinerlei profane oder religiöse Zweckgebundenheit vorhanden ist. Anspruchsvoll sind wir jedoch in unserer inhaltlichen Arbeit. Hier streben wir eine radikale Außenraumkonzeption an, die auf der Grundlage des Ortes und seiner Geschichte entwickelt wird und die Aspekte Gestalt, Gebrauch und Ökologie spannungsvoll miteinander verknüpft. Mit Ökologie – der Lehre von den Beziehungen der Lebewesen zu ihrer Umwelt – werden häufig Bilder von Natürlichkeit verbunden: ökologisch sei die blumenreiche Magerwiese, der schilfbestandene See, die Feldhecke und im Garten das Feuchtbiotop, selbst wenn dieses mit einer nicht entsorgbaren PVC-Folie abgedichtet ist. Im Gegensatz dazu interessieren uns nicht die etwas ländlich stereotypen Bilder von Natur oder Ökologie, sondern ihre Wesenhaftigkeit. Wir propagieren eine städtische Natur, die ihre künstliche Gestaltgebung manifestiert und gleichzeitig einen wichtigen Beitrag zur Ökologie des Ortes leistet.

Auf der Straßenseite bilden die schlanken Säulenhainbuchen einen transparenten räumlichen Abschluß und lassen trotzdem den Blick auf den Gebäudekomplex frei. Die Besucherparkplätze sind in Heckenstreifen eingespannt, wobei die Hecken zweischichtig aufgebaut sind und geschnitten werden, vorne mit der blühenden Japanischen Zierquitte, hinten mit Buche. Am Boden entwickelt sich ein regelmäßig geschnittener Magerrasen, der trotzdem vielfältige Gräser und Blumen aufweist. Auf der Hinterseite des Gebäudes stehen die präzis gestalteten Höfe mit intensiver gärtnerischer Ausformung den naturnahen, wilden Vegetationsbereichen mit ausschließlich einheimischer Vegetation gegenüber. Die vier Höfe werden mit einem jeweils umlaufenden Wasserbecken akzentuiert. Diese sind teilweise bepflanzt und aus rostendem

Open Space Planning for the Spar- und Landeskasse, Fürstenfeldbruck

"Nature and art – art and nature" was the theme of the competition to plan the surrounding area of the new administrative building of the savings bank in Fürstenfeldbruck. However, when we refer to our work, we do not speak of garden art but, more modestly, of garden architecture and abide by the philosopher Gadamer, who only accepts the concept "art" where no profane or religious uses are associated with the work. However, as far as the contents of our work are concerned we have high standards. We endeavour to achieve a radical design of outside space, which is developed on the basis of the location and its history and creates fascinating links between the aspects of design, use and ecology. Ecology – the science of the relationship between living organisms and their environment – is often associated with images of naturalness: flower-filled poor meadows, lakes rich in reeds, field hedges and wetland in gardens are deemed to be ecological even if, in the case of the latter, they are sealed by a non-disposable sheet of PVC. In contrast, we are not interested in the somewhat rurally stereotype images of nature and ecology but in their sustainability. What we plead for is urban nature, which manifests itself in the artificiality of its design and, at the same time, makes a valuable contribution to the ecology of the location.

The slender hornbeam form a transparent spatial boundary on the street side, while providing an uninterrupted view of the building complex. The parking spaces for visitors are let into clipped strips of hedge, whereby the hedges are in two sections, in front blossoming ornamental Japanese quince and behind beech. A poor lawn is developing, which, despite being mown regularly, has numerous different kinds of grass and flowers. On the rear side of the building, the precisely designed courts with their pronounced garden designs are in contrast to the semi-natural areas of wild vegetation of purely native plants. The four courts are each accentuated by an encircling pool. These are planted in sections and set in steel which rusts, a material deliberately chosen for this property. Each court has a garden theme of its own.

Stahl gefertigt, einem bewußt wenig veredelten Material. Jeder Hof zeigt ein eigenständiges, gärtnerisches Thema.

Der Magnolienhof ist ruhig gehalten, der Erdschnitt aus einer Metallplatte trennt Magerwiese von kurz geschnittener, erhöhter Rasenfläche, auf der zwei Magnolien wachsen. Im Topiaryhof erkennen wir markant zugeschnittene Pflanzenfiguren aus Eiben und Linden. Der gärtnerische Kunstschnitt – Topiary genannt – ist bereits seit der Hochrenaissance bekannt und vor allem in den englischen Gärten tradiert. Die englischen Topiarys stellen häufig abstrahierte Tierfiguren dar – Pfau, Fasan, Hund, etc. Im Unterschied dazu sind unsere Figuren konkret, d.h. sie sind keine Abstraktion einer von Natur her bekannten Figur, einziges Kriterium ihrer Ausformung ist die skulpturale Wirkung. Im Hof der «blühenden Steine» wird das Thema des Pflanzenschnittes variiert. Hier werden Pflanzenfiguren in Steinform geschnitten, wobei solche Sträucher verwendet werden, die auch unter Schnitt ihre Blühfähigkeit bewahren, wie Rhododendren, Buchs, Japanische Zierquitte, Stechpalme, Hartriegel und Spiräe. Der Staudenhof zeigt schmale Staudenbeete, die in freier Anordnung mit differenzierten Blattformen und Blütenfarben die Geometrie der Fassade kontrastieren. Jedes Beet besteht aus einer Staudenart wie Lavendel, Aster, Geranium, Pfingstrose oder Salbei. Der zentrale Hof ist als Seerosenbecken ausgeformt. Vor dem Personalrestaurant kann auf der Terrasse auch draußen gegessen werden.

In Opposition zu den gärtnerisch thematisierten Höfen steht die naturnahe Gehölzentwicklung zur Grenze. Einheimische Sträucher und Bäume, wie Feldahorn, Spitzahorn, Hainbuche, Esche, Eiche, Kirsche, Hasel oder Schneeball rahmen das Grundstück, geben aber auch kontrollierte Durchblicke zum Sportplatz frei. Am Boden entwickelt sich in Übereinstimmung mit Nährstoff, Licht, Wasser und Nutzung eine Wildvegetation. Mit der intensiven Gestaltung der Außenanlagen haben wir versucht, ein eigenständiges Gegenüber zur Architektur zu schaffen, das diese nicht verleugnet oder sogar zudeckt, sondern stärker akzentuiert. Unsere Intentionen zielen auf einen stimmungsvollen, poetischen Beitrag zu einer Natur der Stadt, die gleichermaßen gestalterische Prägnanz und ökologische Wirkung berücksichtigt.

Dieter Kienast

The magnolia court is tranquil, a sheet of metal separates the poor meadow from the mown, elevated area of lawn upon which two magnolias grow. The topiary court contains yews and limes clipped to form striking plant shapes. The garden art of clipping – known as topiary – has been practised since the height of the Renaissance and has, in particular, been handed down in English gardens. English topiaries often consist of abstract animal figures – peacocks, pheasants, dogs, etc. In contrast, our figures are concrete, i.e. they are not an abstraction of a figure which occurs in nature; the only criterion of their design is their sculptural effect. The court of flowering stones is yet a further variation on the theme of clipping plants. Here plants are cut in the form of stones, whereby only plants are used which are still able to flower after having been clipped – rhododendron, box, ornamental Japanese quince, holly, dogwood and spirae. The herbaceous court has narrow herbaceous beds, which with their differing foliage and colours of flowers form a contrast to the geometry of the facade. Each bed is composed of a single type of herbaceous plant such as lavender, asters, geraniums, peonies, salvia. The central court is designed as a lily pond. The staff restaurant has a terrace where employees can eat during the summer months.

The garden designs of the courts are in contrast to the bushes and trees which have been allowed to grow naturally along the boundary. Native bushes and trees such as field maple, hornbeam, ash, oak, cherry, hazel and viburnum frame the property, while also permitting restricted views of the sports field. At ground level, wild vegetation is developing as permitted by nutrients, light, water and use. With our intensive design of outside space we have endeavoured to create an independent contrast to architecture which does not deny it, let alone cover it up, but provides it with greater accentuation. Our intention is to create an idyllic, poetic contribution to nature in the city, which takes both design qualities and ecological effects into consideration.

Dieter Kienast

Landschaft Gestalt und Oekologie

UMGEBUNG SPARKASSE FFB FELDBRUCK FEBRUAR 1997 1:200

Hof 5 Erdschnitt
- Wasserbecken als Umfassung mit naturnaher Wasserpflanzung
- Topografie mit Erdschnitt aus rostender Stahlplatte
- Zwei Magnolia soulangiana
- Magerrasen auf Kies und 'Normalrasen'

Hof 4 Topiarys
- Wasserbecken als Umfassung teilweise naturnahe Pflanzen
- Geschnittene Pflanzenfiguren 4-6 Meter hoch mit Buchs, Eibe, Linde, Buche
- Rasen Fahrspur Feuerwehr Schotterrasen

Hof 3 Seerosenbecken
- Umfassung der Wasserbecken mit Buxus 70 cm hoch
- Wasserbecken mit weissen Seerosen bepflanzt
- Terrasse mit Natursteinplatten
- Hauszugang Splittasphalt

Hof 2 Blühende Steine

- Wasserbecken als Umfassung ohne Pflanzen
- Pflanzen in Form grosser Steinblöcke geschnitten mit Azaleen bzw. Rhododendron, Chaenomeles, Cornus, Spirea, Buchs, Ilex, etc.(Schnitt jeweils nach Blüte)
- Rasenfläche Fahrspur Feuerwehr mit Schotterrasen

Hof 1 Tanzende Stauden

- Wasserbecken als Umfassung (siehe Detail) ohne Pflanzen
- Staudenbeete im Farbspektrum weiss-blau
- Rasenfläche Fahrspur Feuerwehr mit Schotterrasen

224

Blick von Brücke auf Wasserhof

Konzept

▨ Naturnahe Bereiche mit vielfältigen und differenzierten Pflanzengemeinschaften und Tierpopulationen. Extensive Pflege führt zu hoher Biodiversität, ausschliesslich einheimische Pflanzen.

▨ Höfe und Strassenraum als präzis gestaltete Aussenräume mit intensiver gärtnerischer Pflege. Einheimische und fremdländische Pflanzen mit auffälligen Blüten, Formen und Strukturen.

Schnitt Ansicht C-C Hof 5 Erdschnitt 1:100

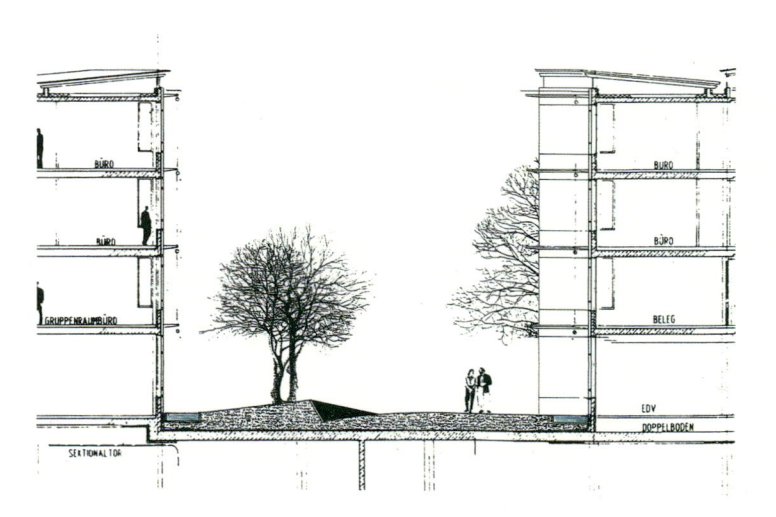

Schnitt Ansicht E-E Hof 4, Topiarys 1:100

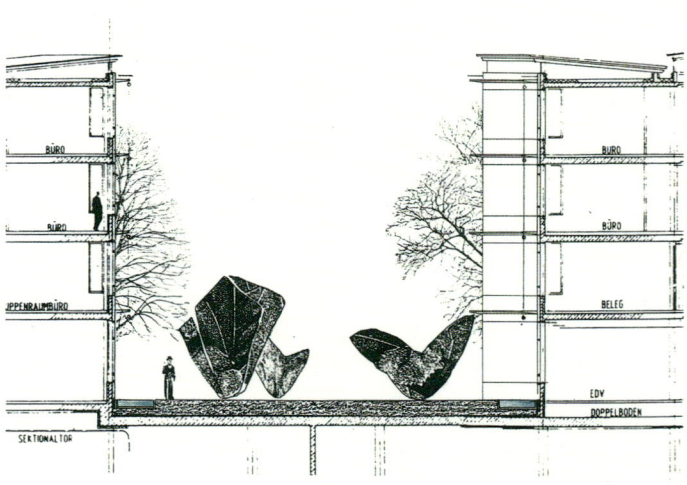

225

Blick Staudenhof 1

Schnitt A-A 1:10 Wasserkanal bepflanzt

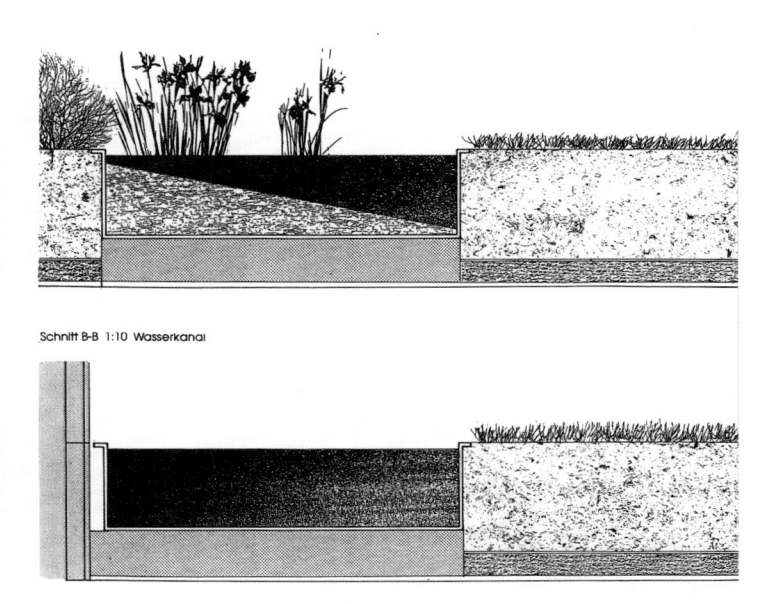

Schnitt B-B 1:10 Wasserkanal

Schnitt Ansicht D-D Hof 2 Blühende Steine 1:100

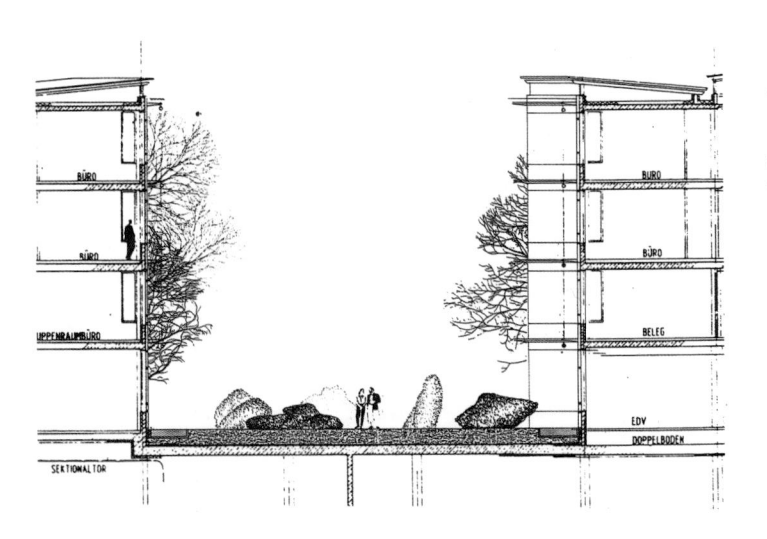

Schnitt Ansicht F-F Eingang - Strasse 1:100

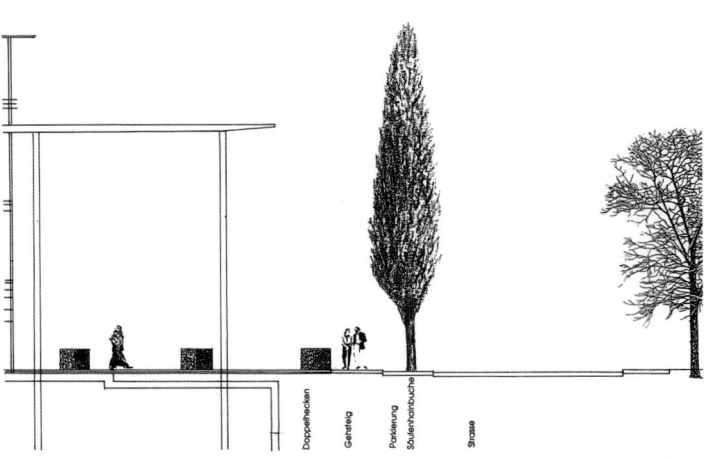

Das umlaufende Wasserbecken bildet
in allen vier Höfen einen virtuellen Raum.

The encircling pool forms virtual
space in all four courts.

Markant zugeschnittene Pflanzenfiguren aus Eiben und Linden prägen den Charakter des Topiaryhofes.

Distinctive plant shapes clipped from yew and lime give the topiary court its character.

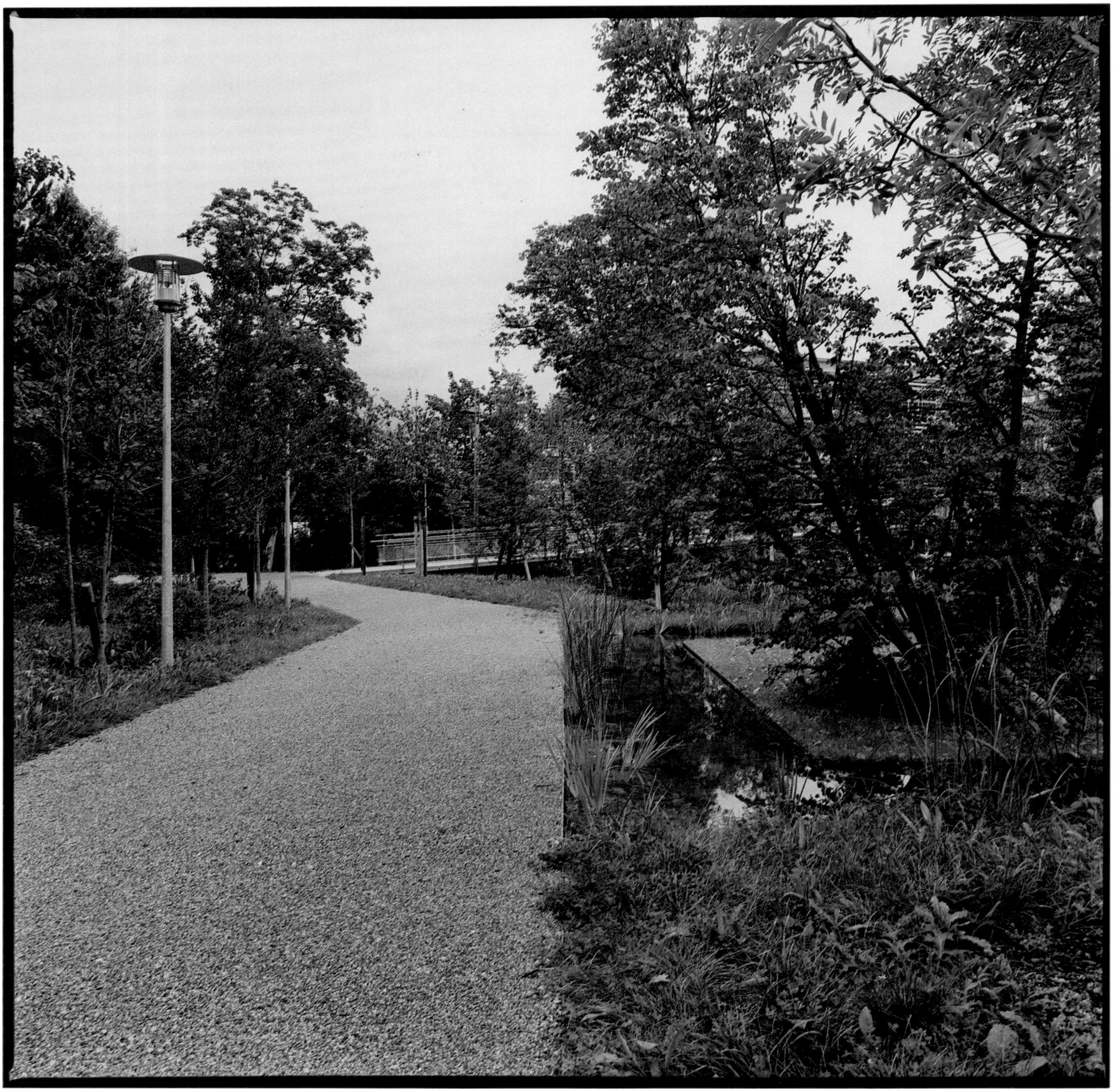

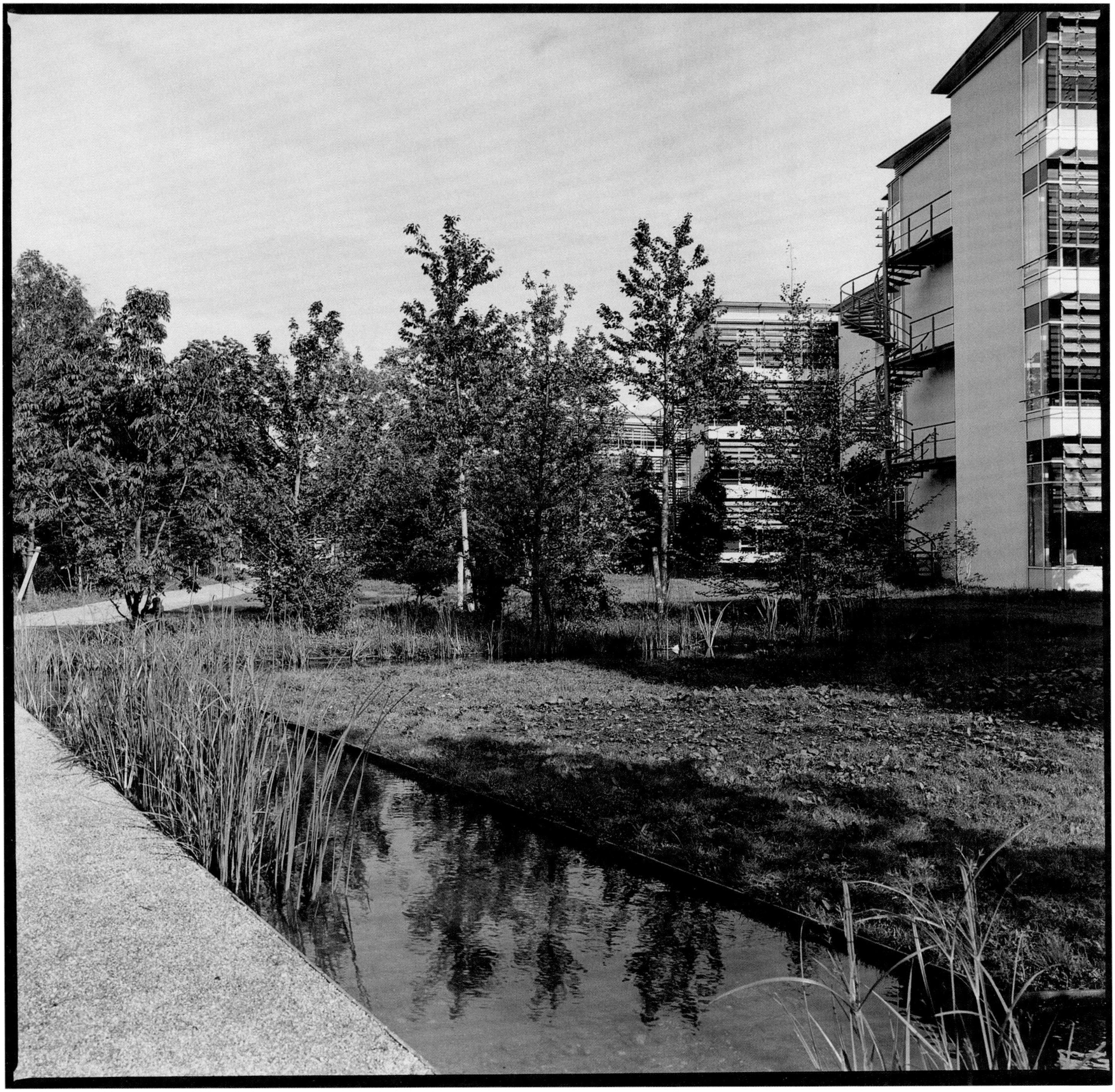

Stockalper Schloßgarten Brig

Nach der Überschwemmungskatastrophe im Herbst 1993 sind gewaltige Renovationen und Restaurationen der gesamten Altstadt zur Aufwertung des Stadtbildes erfolgt. Diese Maßnahmen erstreckten sich jedoch nur auf den Bereich der Weri, westlich des Schloßgartens. Von diesem urbanistischen Aufschwung wird nun auch der Garten des Stockalperschlosses profitieren. Die jetzige bescheidene Grünanlage gibt dem Schloß keinen adäquaten Rahmen, noch entspricht sie einer barocken Konzeption. Natürlich kann es heute nicht darum gehen, einen neobarocken Park zu erfinden, den es zu früheren Zeiten nicht einmal ansatzweise gegeben hat. Vielmehr wird eine neue Gartengestalt gesucht, die dem Schloß einen würdigen Rahmen zu geben vermag und für die Bevölkerung einen vielfältig nutzbaren Erholungsraum anbietet.

«Plätze und Gärten mach auf elegante Weise» – «Plateas et hortus fac elegantes»

Als 1666 der Rohbau zu seinem Schloß vollendet war, ließ Kaspar Jodok von Stockalper getreu dieser Vorstellungen seine Gartenanlagen zum Schloß erstellen.

Ausgangspunkt bei der Neukonzeption ist der vorhandene Bestand, insbesondere die Topographie sowie die bestehenden Mauern. Die immer wiederkehrenden Trinitätsvorstellungen des Jodok von Stockalper, die sich nicht nur im Schloß zeigen, sollen auch im Park entsprechend aufgenommen werden. Es sind dies: das Viridarium oder der Lustgarten vor dem Schloß, das Pomarium und der Wirtschaftsteil. Im Hinblick auf den etwas spröden Charme der Architektursprache des Schloßparks waren wir bestrebt, eine gartenarchitektonische Umsetzung für den Park zu finden, die über diese strukturellen Überlegungen hinausgeht.

Das Parterre

Vor der Hauptfassade liegt das mittig ausgerichtete Heckenparterre, wobei die Hauptachse nicht als barocke Achse ausgebildet ist. Auch im Schloß kann keine historische Entsprechung nachgewiesen werden. Die Hauptachse wird durch verschiedene Maßnahmen unterdrückt, um ihr so die allzu starke Dominanz

Stockalper Palace Gardens in Brig

Following the catastrophic flooding in the autumn of 1993, very extensive renovation and restoration of the entire old part of the town were carried out. However, these measures only covered the area of the Weri, to the west of the palace gardens. The grounds of the Stockalper Palace are now also to benefit from this urban renewal. The present modest park that is still baroque in style does not yet provide the palace with a fitting setting. Naturally, it is not today a matter of inventing a neo-baroque park that did not exist earlier in even rudimentary form. Instead, what is needed is a new garden design capable of giving the palace a fitting setting and providing residents and visitors with recreational space that can be used in a variety of ways.

"Create squares and gardens in a way that is elegant" – "Plateas et hortus fac elegantes"

When the shell of his new palace was completed in 1666, Kaspar Jodok von Stockalper had its grounds laid out in accordance with these notions.

The starting point of the new design was what was already in place, in particular the topography and the walls that are in place. Jodok von Stockalper's recurring conception of the trinity, not only present in the palace, is also to be reflected in the park: the viridarium (pleasance) in front of the palace, the pomarium and the vegetable garden. Bearing in mind the somewhat austere charm of the architectural language of the park, we have endeavoured to find an architectural solution for the park that goes beyond these structural considerations.

The parterre

The hedge parterre with its centre orientated alignment lies in front of the main façade, its principal axis not being baroque in form. Nor does the palace itself have any historical counterpart. A variety of means draw attention from the main axis in order to reduce its dominating effect. This is primarily achieved by the irregular hedge sections that converge conically. The hedge parterre consists of hedges of different breadths with flowering plants that are also still capable of flowering when they have been clipped. Narcissi grow on the lawn areas of the parterre.

STOCKALPER SCHLOSS

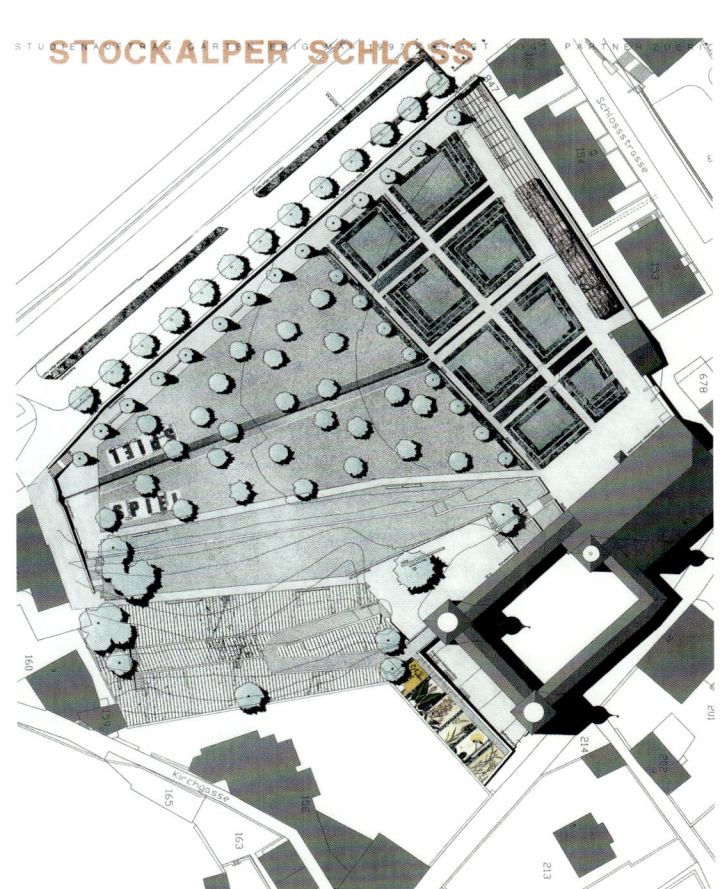

zu nehmen. Dies geschieht zunächst mit den unregelmäßig konisch zulaufenden Heckenkompartimenten. Das Heckenparterre zeigt unterschiedlich breite Hecken mit blühenden Pflanzenarten, die auch unter Schnitt ihre Blühfähigkeit bewahren. In den Parterrerasenflächen wachsen Narzissen. Die Wasserbecken sind mit Wasserdüsen ausgestattet. Zum Pomarium wird das Parterre südlich durch eine Hecke und mit Bänken abgeschlossen.

Das Pomarium

Das Pomarium wird mit einer Rampe von der Weri aus erschloßen und zeigt die einfache Ausbildung einer Obstwiese, in welcher einheimische Obstbäume angepflanzt werden. Drei differente neue Kinderspielplätze im Pomarium stellen ein attraktives Angebot für das Kinderspiel dar. Der bisher eingedolte Wuhrbach wird offengelegt und mittig durch das Pomarium geführt. Im Südhang bleiben die vorhandenen Trockenmauern erhalten, die ursprünglich von einem alten Weinberg stammen dürften. Der Weinberg wird wiederhergestellt und neu mit Walliser Reben angepflanzt.

Die Terrasse

Beim Eintritt vom Schloßhof her ist eine vergrößerte Terrasse für festliche Veranstaltungen vorgesehen.

Der Rosengarten

Das bereits begonnene Thema der kleinteiligen Blumenbeete in den vorhandenen Pflanzgärten über den westlich des Schlosses gelegenen Kellergewölben wird mit Stauden- und Rosenbeeten weitergeführt.

«Won't you come into the garden? I would like my roses to see you.» Sheridan

Ob der Park und das Schloß Stockalper mit den drei Granittürmen und den barocken Zwiebelhauben bald einmal zu den Postkartenklassikern der Schweiz gehören werden?

Dieter und Erika Kienast

The water pools have water jets. The south side of the parterre is separated from the pomarium by a hedge and benches.

The pomarium

The pomarium, accessible by a ramp leading from the Weri, is in the form of a "meadow" orchard planted with native fruit trees. Three different playgrounds in the pomarium provide various attractive forms of play for children. The cemented banks of the Wuhrbach are to be returned to their natural state so that the stream can flow through the pomarium. The present dry-stone walls on the southern slope, which were probably once part of a vineyard, are to be retained. The vineyard is to be restored and planted with vines native to Valais.

The terrace

An extensive terrace accessible from the palace courtyard is planned for festive occasions.

The rose garden

The theme of the small-scale flower beds already existing in the gardens above the vaulted cellars to the west of the palace is to be continued by means of beds of herbaceous plants and roses.

"Won't you come into the garden? I would like my roses to see you." Sheridan

Will the park and Stockalper Palace with its three granite towers and baroque onion domes soon be a feature of classic Swiss postcards?

Dieter and Erika Kienast

233

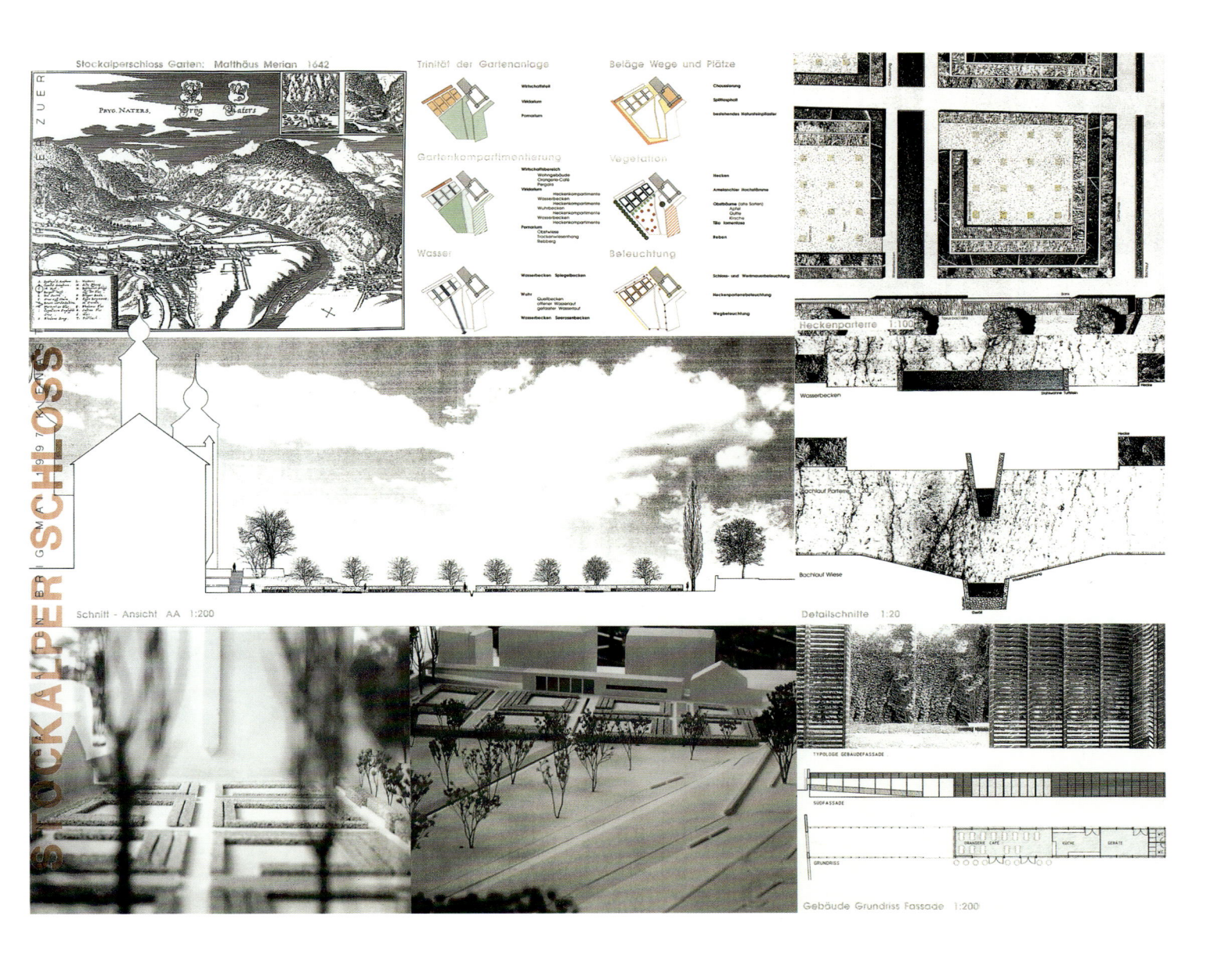

Der bisher eingedohlte Wuhrbach wird offengelegt und mittig durch das Pomarium geführt.

The cemented banks of the Wuhrbach are to be returned to their natural state so that the stream can flow through the pomarium.

Das Parterre wird durch ein Wasserbecken ergänzt.

A pool has been added to the parterre.

Neubau Madagaskarhalle, Zoo Zürich

Im Zoo Zürich soll mit Hightech-Hilfe ein mikroskopisch kleiner Ausschnitt des natürlichen madegassischen Regenwaldes mit seinen autochthonen Pflanzen und Tieren gezeigt werden.

«Jurassic Parc» von Steven Spielberg ist der erfolgreichste Film der Geschichte, in dem wir mit unserer Urnatur konfrontiert werden. Diese ist nicht bedroht, schutzbedürftig und durch die Errungenschaften der Technik drangsaliert, sondern überwältigend stark und vital und lehrt uns, die Furcht vor ihr wiederzuerkennen. Im gleichzeitigen Wissen, daß das filmische Feuerwerk nur dank höchster technischer Raffinesse denkbar ist, gründet offenbar der einmalige Erfolg des Filmes: die Sehnsucht nach urwüchsiger Natur einerseits und die trügerische Vorstellung von der Herrschaft und Lenkbarkeit der Natur durch die menschliche Kultur und Technik andererseits.

Ein naher Verwandter von Jurassic Parc dürfte der Zoo sein, scheinbar ein Relikt aus einer Zeit vor «Last Minute»-Reisen und spektakulären Fernsehtierserien aus aller Welt. Und doch verzeichnet nicht nur Jurassic Park, sondern auch der Zoo Besucherrekorde. Erzeugt vielleicht die im Film getötete Phantasie die Sehnsucht nach einer Teilauthentizität, nach einer geweckten Phantasie, wie sie der neu konzipierte Zoo vermitteln kann? Daß der Tiger sich nicht zwangsläufig in den Esso-Tank verwandelt, träge in der Sonne liegt, einen strengen Geruch ausdünstet oder das frische Fleisch zerbeißt? Und ist die Differenz vom Film- zum Zoobesuch nicht vergleichbar mit derjenigen zwischen Fernsehfußball und dem Erleben im ausverkauften Giuseppe-Meazza-Stadion?

Eines ist gewiß, der Zoo bewegt sich immer auf dem schmalen Grat von Realität und Imagination, von Sein und Schein. Mit der artgerechten Tierhaltung und entsprechender Gehegegestaltung wird der Zoobesuch zur Entdeckungsreise in künstlich hergestellte Naturausschnitte, in der die Erfahrung einer fremden Welt auch immer wieder an der Zoowirklichkeit bricht. In der neu geplanten Madagaskarhalle wird das Erlebnis einer exotischen Naturwelt perfektioniert. Die

New Madagascar Hall, Zurich Zoo

High-tech is to be used at Zurich zoo to present a minute part of the natural Madagascan rain forest and its autochthon plants and animals.

Steven Spielberg's "Jurassic Park", one of the most successful films ever, confronts us with primeval nature. This is not something which is under threat, in need of protection and oppressed by the achievements of technology, but is overwhelmingly powerful and vital and teaches us respect. The knowledge that this cinematic spectacle was only possible thanks to impressive special effects evidently explains the unique success of the film: the longing for untouched nature, on the one hand, and, on the other hand, the deceptive notion that human civilisation and technology can dominate and control nature.

The zoo would appear to be a close relation of Jurassic Park, seemingly a relic from a time before "last minute" holidays and spectacular TV series on animals from all over the world. And yet not only Jurassic Park but also zoos are experiencing record numbers of visitors. Has the fantasy killed in the film generated the longing for partial authenticity, for a living fantasy which can be imparted by the new zoo concept? That tigers do not automatically turn into Esso tanks, but laze in the sun, have a strong smell and tear raw flesh apart? And isn't the difference between watching a film and visiting a zoo not comparable with the one between watching a football match on television and experiencing it as one of a capacity crowd at the Giuseppe Meazza Stadium?

One thing is certain, the zoo is increasingly treading the fine line between reality and illusion. Keeping animals in a way which takes their needs into consideration and designing appropriate enclosures has turned a visit to the zoo into a journey of discovery through artificially created sections of nature in which the experience of a strange world always comes into conflict with the reality of the zoo. The planned new Madagascar Hall perfects the experience of an exotic natural world. The hall is conceived as a large enclosure in which visitors are both observers and actors, where no partitioning fences exist, and they can see, hear and smell exotic plants and animals in tempera-

237

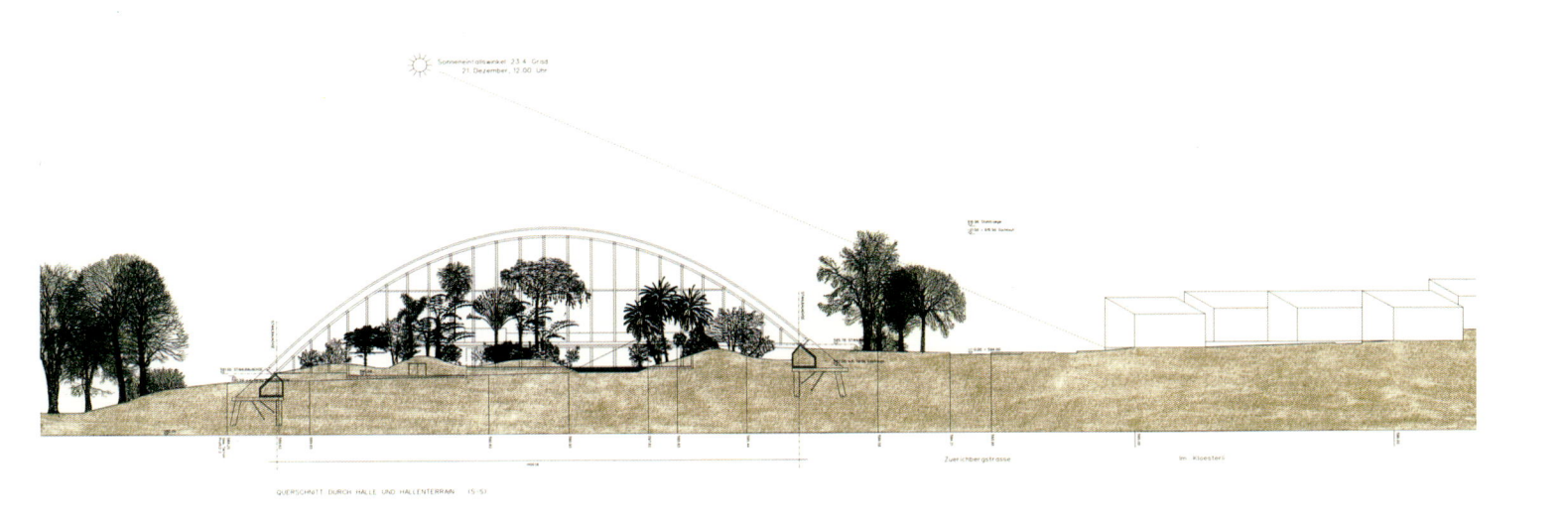

Halle wird zum Großgehege, in dem die Besucher gleichzeitig Betrachter und Akteure sind, in dem sie ohne Zaun bei dreißig Grad Wärme und fünfundneunzig prozentiger Luftfeuchtigkeit fremde Pflanzen und Tiere sehen, hören, riechen.

In der Madagaskarhalle soll das Ökosystem eines immer grünen Regenwaldes gezeigt werden, wie dieses auf der Masoala-Halbinsel auf Madagaskar vorgefunden wurde. Masoala ist das größte zusammenhängende Regenwaldgebiet von Madagaskar und ein Schwerpunktprojekt verschiedener internationaler Hilfsorganisationen. Ziel der Madagaskarhalle ist deshalb nicht nur die Darstellung eines spektakulären Umweltausschnittes, vielmehr soll durch intensive Zusammenarbeit mit den Organisationen vor Ort das Verständnis und die Kenntnis eines nachhaltigen Umganges mit dem Regenwald gefördert werden. Madagaskar wurde gewählt, weil durch die frühe erdgeschichtliche Trennung von Afrika hier eine große Zahl endemischer Pflanzen und Tiere beheimatet sind.

Die Halle ist im Ostteil der Zooerweiterung, im Bereich der derzeitigen Schießanlage plaziert. Die periphere Lage ist zwar aus städtebaulichen Überlegungen gewählt, macht aber auch aus zoogeographischen Gesichtspunkten – in Nachbarschaft zu Afrika – Sinn. Die Halle ist hundertzwanzig Meter lang, neunzig Meter breit und im Scheitel sechsundzwanzig Meter hoch, als Eisenbogenkonstruktion konzipiert und mit extrem lichtdurchläßigen, dreilagigen Kunststoffkissen überzogen. Mit höchster haustechnischer Raffinesse und neuesten Verfahren wird der gesamte Energie- und Wasseraufwand auf ein Minimum reduziert.

Das Grundprinzip des Dschungels, die mehrschichtige, üppige und unübersichtliche Pflanzenwelt wird durch die Gestaltung der Topografie, der Wasser- und Wegführung nachgezeichnet. Die Halle wird von der Nordseite betreten und über einen mäandrierenden Hauptweg auf der Osteite erschlossen, während die Westseite nur über schmale Pfade betretbar ist. Wegführung, Topografie und Vegetation sind so konzipiert, daß gegenseitige Einsicht und Besucheranhäufung vermieden werden. Die Topografie wechselt zwischen sumpfiger Ebene, sanften Hügeln und kleinen Tälern bis zu dramatischen Steilwänden aus rohem Beton, die aufgrund der hohen Luftfeuchtigkeit jedoch rasch von Algen, Moosen und höheren Pflanzen bewachsen werden. Direkt vor dem Restaurant auf der Süd-

tures of thirty degrees and ninety-five per cent humidity. The eco system of a rain forest which is always green is to be shown in the Madagascar Hall; this system exists on the Masoala Peninsula of Madagascar. Masoala is the largest area of continuous rain forest on Madagascar and a key project of various international aid organisations. For this reason, the aim of the Madagascar Hall is not just to present a spectacular part of the environment; rather intensive co-operation with organisations working in the field is intended to advance the understanding and knowledge of a sustainable approach to the rain forest. Madagascar was chosen as it was separated from Africa early in the earth's history and, in consequence, a large number of endemic plants and animals are indigenous to the island.

The hall lies in the eastern part of the extension to the zoo, in the vicinity of what is at present a shooting range. Although the peripheral location was chosen for urban design reasons, it also makes sense from the zoological and geographical points of view – neighbouring Africa. The hall is one hundred and twenty metres long, ninety metres wide and twenty-six metres high at its vertex, it is conceived as a structure of iron arches, covered by an extremely light-pervious, three-layer synthetic cushion. State-of-the-art technology is used to reduce energy and water consumption to a minimum.

The fundamental principle of the jungle, lush, chaotic levels of flora, is reproduced by the design of the topography, the layout of paths and water channels. Access to the hall is on the north side, a meandering main route leads to the east side, whereas access to the west side is only possible along narrow paths. Paths, topography and vegetation are designed in a way in which mutual observation and visitor bottlenecks can be avoided. The topography alternates between swampy plains, gentle hills and small valleys and dramatically steep faces of bare concrete, which will, owing to the high humidity, quickly become overgrown with algae, moss and higher plants. There is an elongated lake directly in front of the restaurant on the south-west side; the lemurs inhabit the islands in the lake. The lake spills into a small stream, which plunges as a waterfall into the central lake eight metres lower.
The most important and striking feature of the hall is its tropical vegetation, which serves as a habitat for a wide diversity of fauna – lemurs, birds, frogs, fish, reptiles such as chameleons,

westseite erstreckt sich ein langer See, auf dessen Inseln die Lemuren leben. Der Überlauf des Sees bildet einen Bach, der als Wasserfall in den acht Meter tiefer liegenden Zentralsee stürzt.

Wichtigster und auffälligster Bestandteil der Halle ist die tropische Vegetation als Lebensstätte für eine vielfältige Tierwelt. Es sind dies Lemuren, Vögel, Frösche, Reptilien wie Chamäleon, Schildkröten, Geckos und Fische. Für die Entwicklung der Vegetation ist der Bodenaufbau von größter Bedeutung. Um das Eindringen des kalkhaltigen Wassers zu verhindern, wird der Boden abgedichtet und drainiert. Das sechzig bis hundert Zentimeter starke Erdsubstrat muß auf Grund der Analysen vor Ort speziell gemischt und mit Mikroorganismen durchsetzt sein. Ziel der Vegetationsentwicklung ist die Bepflanzung mit weitgehend autochthonen, madegassischen Pflanzen, die sich dank der Hallenhöhe voll entfalten können. Dazu wurde in Antanandaheli eine kleine Baumschule aufgebaut, in der die Pflanzen ausgesät, aufgezogen und anschließend nach Zürich verschickt werden. Weil diese Pflanzen bei der Anlieferung relativ klein sein werden, ist eine Erstbepflanzung mit arten- und typengleichen Pflanzen aus Baumschulen in Größen bis zu zwölf Metern vorgesehen. In der Halle werden die madegassischen Pflanzen plenterartig eingesetzt und die Erstbepflanzung entfernt.

Im besten Fall können wir in zehn bis fünfzehn Jahren einen typischen, madegassischen Regenwald in der künstlichen, hochtechnisierten Hallenwelt erleben.

Dieter Kienast

turtles and geckos. The structure of the soil plays a vital role in the development of the vegetation. In order to prevent the seepage of hard water, the ground is to be sealed and drained. Analyses of the soil substrate, which is between sixty and one-hundred centimetres deep, show that it has to be specially mixed and micro-organisms introduced. With regard to the development of vegetation the aim is, as far as possible, to plant autochthone Madagascan plants which can, owing to the height of the hall, realise their full potential. For this purpose, a small nursery has been set up in Antanandaheli, where the plants are to be sown, nurtured and then sent to Zurich. As these plants will still be relatively small when they are delivered to the zoo, it is intended that initial planting will be in the form of nursery plants of the same species and type up to 12 metres in height. The Madagascan plants are to be introduced to the hall gradually and the initial plants removed.

If all goes well, we will be able to experience a typical, Madagascan rain forest in an artificial, high-tech zoo hall ten to fifteen years from now.

Dieter Kienast

ANSICHT X-X M. 1:100

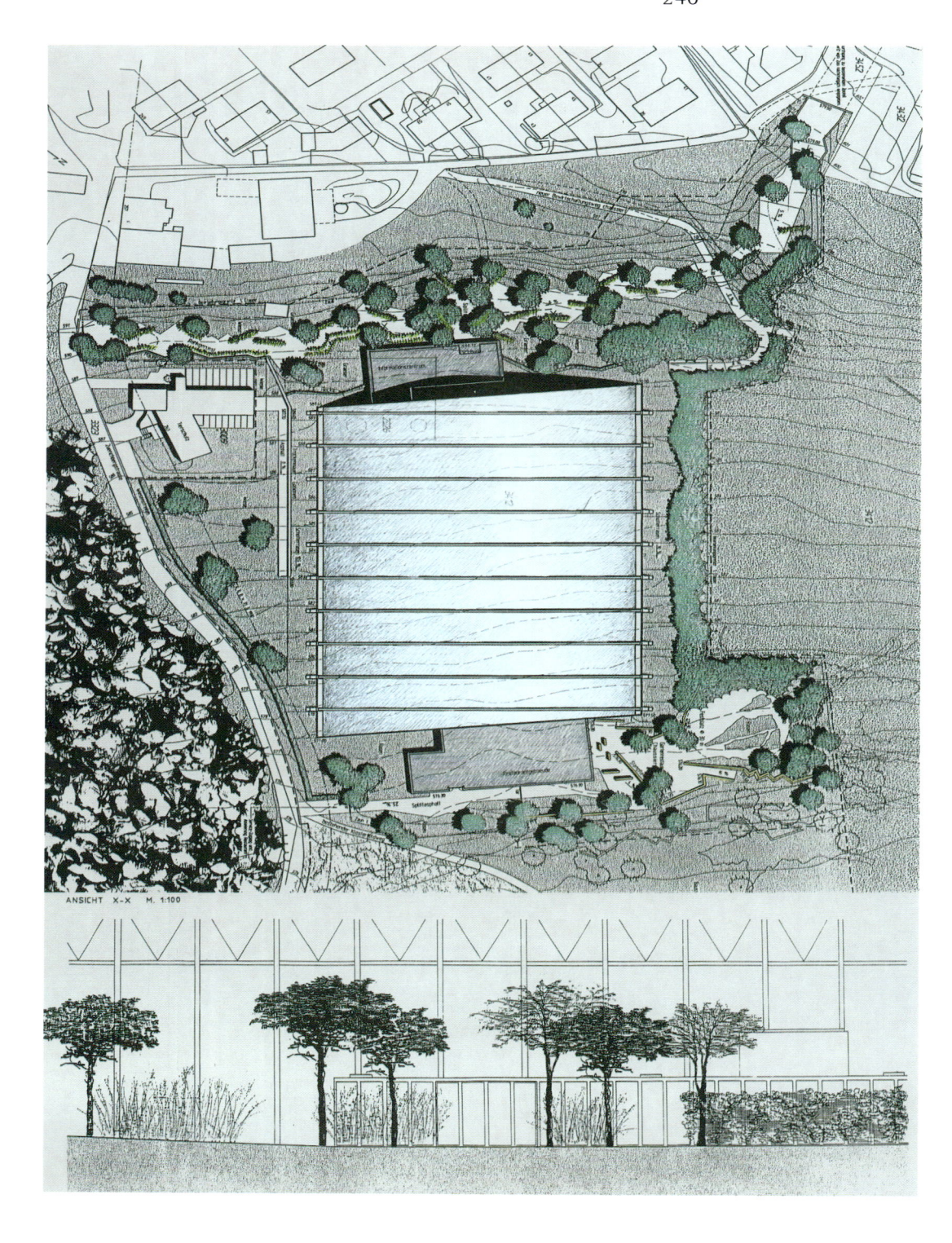

241

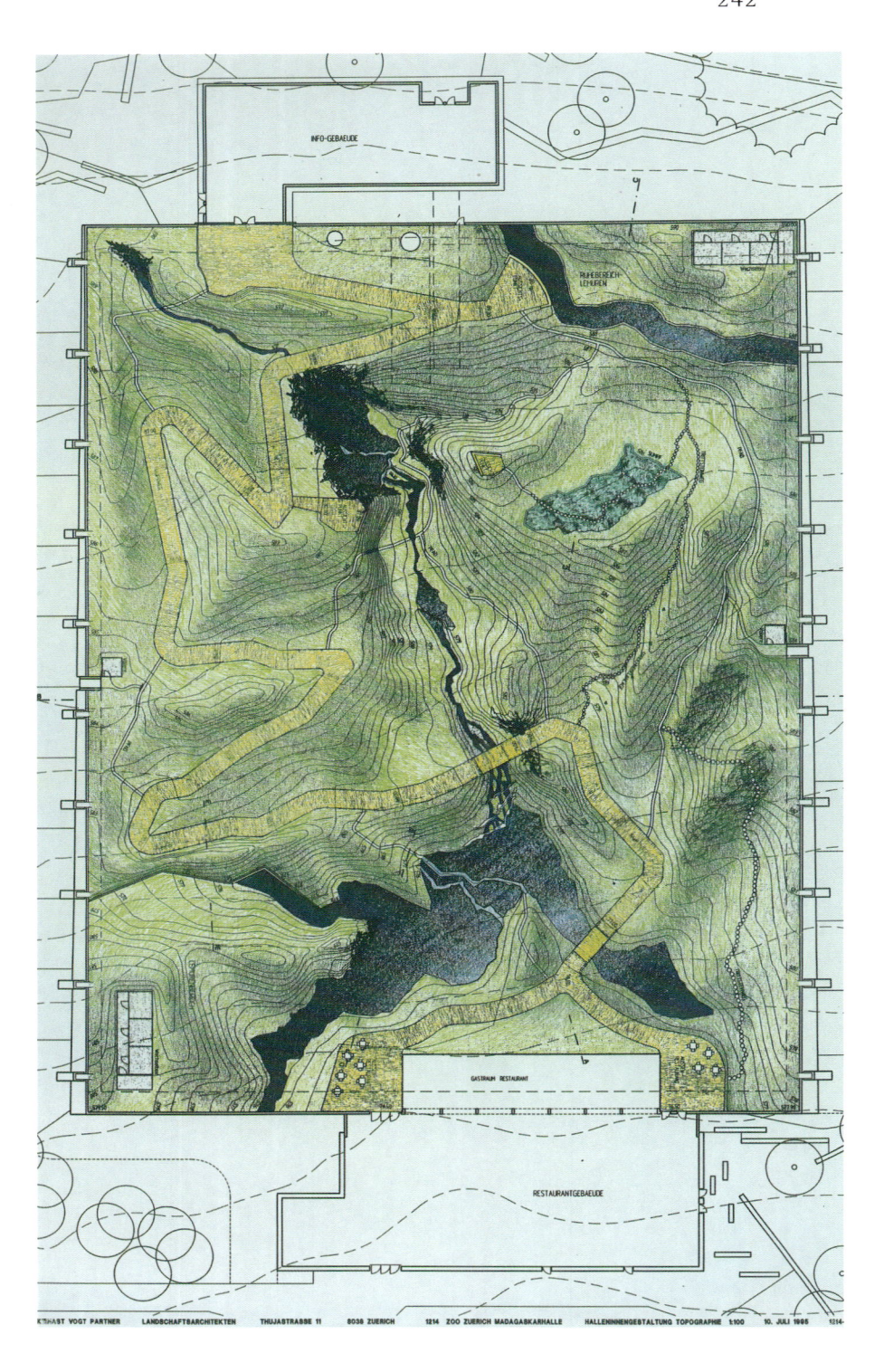

Topographie   Topography

Baumbestand Tree population

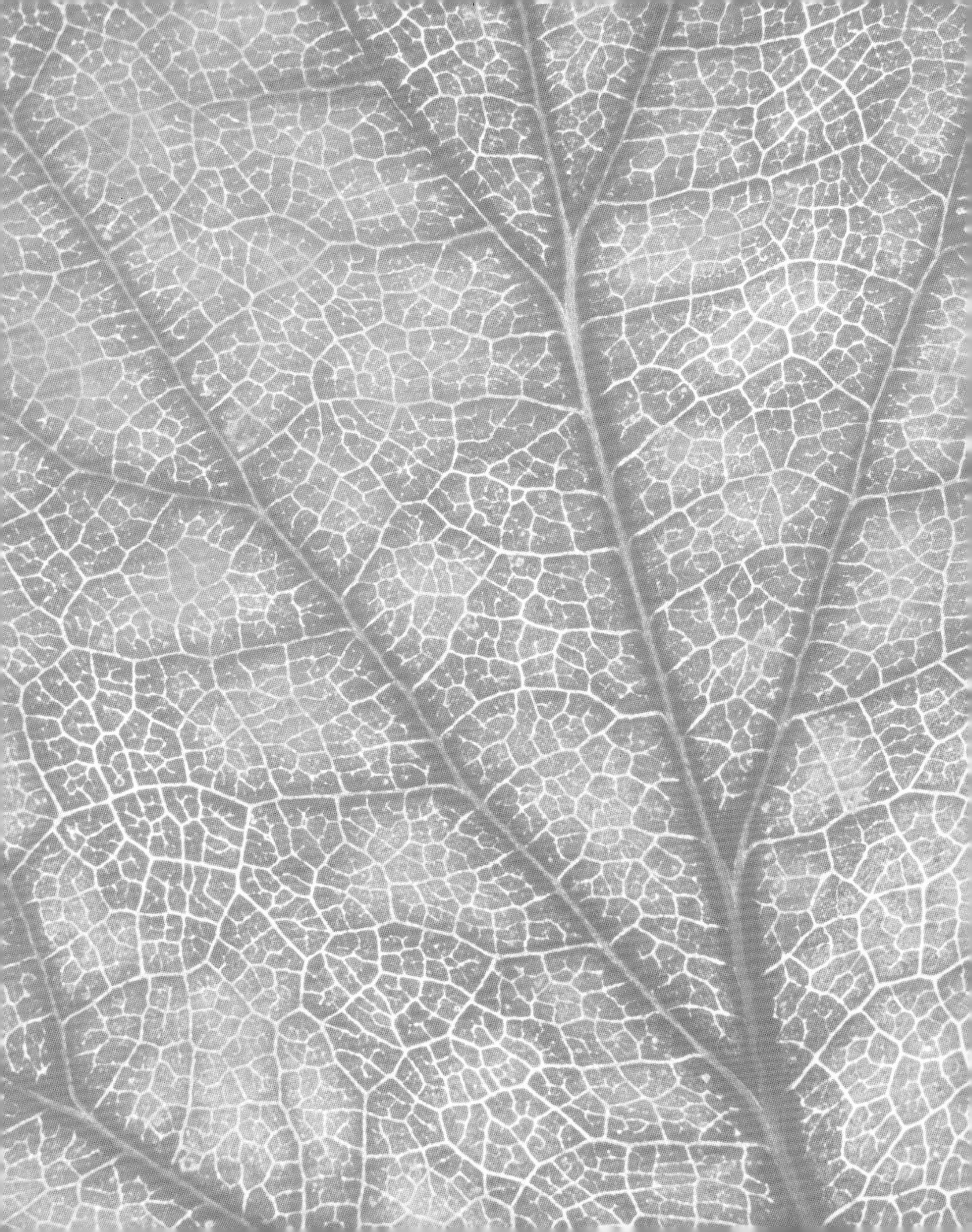

Zwischen Poesie und Geschwätzigkeit

«Das Hohelied von Gartenbau und Gartenkunst» und «Eine blühende Bilanz der Bundesgartenschauen» heißen die Titel der zwei maßgeblichen Bücher über die Gartenschauen in Deutschland, die Gustav Allinger 1963 und Helga Panten 1987 veröffentlicht haben. Ein hoher Anspruch wird formuliert, der inhaltlich – so zeigen die vielen Beispiele – kaum eingehalten werden kann.

Nun ist es natürlich ein leichtes, pauschal über die Gartenschauen herzufallen und sie bis ins Letzte zu verdammen. Denn, wer immer etwas tut, setzt sich der Kritik aus. So hat bereits in den siebziger Jahren eine fundamentale Kritik an den Gartenschauen eingesetzt – zum Beispiel Kassel und Frankfurt –, in der die Unsinnigkeit und Zwecklosigkeit solcher Veranstaltungen angeprangert wurde. Heute möchte ich neben der Kritik auch die Chancen und Möglichkeiten zur Diskussion stellen.

Die Geschichte der Gartenkunst zeigt uns, daß der Umgang mit dem Garten ein verläßlicher Zeiger für gesellschaftliche Zustände und Veränderungen ist, daß er aber auch das Verhältnis der jeweiligen Gesellschaft zur Natur reflektiert: von den Hängenden Gärten der Semiramis über mittelalterliche Klostergärten, absolutistische Prunkentfaltung, der Empfindsamkeit des 18. und 19. Jahrhunderts, den Gärten der Hunderttausend bis zu den ökologisch verbrämten Naturgärten des ausgehenden 20. Jahrhunderts.

Der Garten stellt die Gleichzeitigkeit von Natur und Kultur dar, er ist nicht reine Kultur, weil das Naturhafte notwendiger Bestandteil ist, wie er auch nicht reine Natur sein kann, weil der tätige Mensch sonst ausgeschlossen wäre und er damit sein Wesensmerkmal verloren hätte. Im Garten lernen wir, mit Natur umzugehen, ohne die in uns befindliche, schöpferische Kraft zu verleugnen. Damit wird er zum Modell und Testfall unseres Umganges mit der gesamten natürlichen und gebauten Umwelt. Denn – wir erhalten Natur langfristig nicht durch ihren Schutz, sondern durch die intensive Beschäftigung mit ihr. Der Schutz der Natur – so wäre in Klammern anzufügen – ist nichts anderes als das Eingeständnis unserer Unfähigkeit, mit Natur sorgsam umgehen zu können. Schutz ist in seinem Wesen reaktiv, ohne Hoffnung in zukünftige Entwicklungen.

Between Poetry and Garrulousness

«The Song of Songs of Horticulture and Garden Art» and «A thriving balance of National Horticultural Shows» are the titles of the two authoritative publications on horticultural shows in Germany, published by Gustav Allinger in 1963 and Helga Panten in 1987 respectively. An ambitious standard is postulated which – as the many examples show – can hardly be realised in practice.

Of course, there is nothing easier then to make sweeping condemnations of horticultural shows. After all, anyone who creates something runs the risk of criticism. Fundamental criticism of horticultural shows began as far back as the nineteen-seventies – Kassel and Frankfurt for example – and denounced the absurdity and pointlessness of such shows. I would like to discuss the opportunities presented by such shows in addition to looking at the points of criticism.

The history of garden art shows us that the way we approach the garden is a reliable indicator of the state of society and its changes, but that it also reflects the relationship of the society of the time to nature: from the Hanging Gardens of Semiramis via medieval cloister gardens, the display of magnificence in absolutist times, the sentimentality of the eighteenth and nineteenth centuries, to the gardens of the hundred thousands and the ecologically styled natural gardens at the end of the twentieth century.

The garden stands for the simultaneity of nature and culture, it is not entirely culture as the natural element is an indispensable part, nor can it be purely nature as the active human element would otherwise be superfluous and it would be lacking in what makes it a garden. We learn how to deal with nature in the garden without denying our own creative capacities. The garden becomes the model and test case of the way we approach the entire natural and built environment. After all – we cannot preserve nature in the long term by simply protecting it but by an intensive dialogue with it. Protection of nature – it could be put in brackets – is nothing more than admission of our inability to take care of it properly. Protection is by definition a reaction, lacking hope in future developments.

Gartenschauen als öffentliche Veranstaltungen stehen unzweifelhaft im jeweiligen gesellschaftlichen Kontext, sie sind ohne diesen nicht durchführbar – wie gerade die Entwicklung der letzten Jahre zeigt, wo geplante Gartenschauen verschoben oder abgesagt wurden. Es ist der Frage nachzugehen, welche Stellung sie innerhalb dieses Kontextes einnehmen: visionär oder reaktionär, am Rande oder eher in der flauen Mitte. Wenn wir davon ausgehen, daß Kritik zunehmend am Rand erfolgt, so ist die sich häufende Kritik an den Gartenschauen Indiz für ihre Randständigkeit. Und weil sich an deren Konzeption in den letzten zwanzig Jahren kaum etwas geändert hat, tippe ich auf die reaktionäre Randständigkeit. Anders als die träge Zustimmung erhält Kritik wach. Meine Vorstellung für kommende Gartenschauen ist deshalb nicht Kritiklosigkeit, sondern eine Vision neuer Gärten, die sich selbstbewußt auch der Kritik zu stellen vermag. Wir kämen damit auch wieder auf die dualen Charaktermerkmale der Gartenidylle und Utopie zurück. Der Garten als Ort der Geborgenheit, der Arbeit, der Schönheit, des Glücks und der Sinnlichkeit ist gleichzeitig verbunden mit der Utopie der Versöhnung mit der Natur, mit Heinrich von Kleists Vorstellung des von hinten wieder offenen Paradieses.

Zur Kritik

Gartenschauen werden von drei Grundanliegen bestimmt: Sie sind zunächst als Messe des grünen Berufszweiges zu begreifen, so wie es Bücher-, Computer- oder Möbelmessen gibt. Der Berufsstand zeigt seine Leistungsfähigkeit, er stellt die Breite seiner Tätigkeiten vor, demonstriert Neuheiten und verweist auf Altbewährtes. Das zweite Grundanliegen ist die städtebauliche Verbesserung unserer Städte. Erreicht werden soll dies durch Neuanlage von öffentlich zugänglichen Freiräumen: Plätze, Gärten und Parkanlagen. Das dritte Ziel ist ein halbjähriges Freilichtspektakel, ein festliches Unterhaltungsangebot für Jung und Alt, das damit gleichzeitig die PR für die Stadt sichert.

Diese Symbiose war solange erfolgreich, wie die drei Teile in einem ausgewogenen Verhältnis zueinander standen. Der Berufsstand der Gärtner war zufrieden, weil er ein preisgünstiges Forum zu seiner Selbstdarstellung fand, Landschaftsarchitekten bekamen Arbeit. Die Städte konnten Projekte realisieren, deren Finanzierung sie nicht alleine tragen mußten, durch die lange Medienpräsenz wurden Besucher von nah und fern in die Stadt gelockt.

Horticultural shows as public events undoubtedly take place in their respective social context and would not be possible without this – as in particular the development of the past few years has shown when planned horticultural shows were postponed or cancelled. It is necessary to address the question of their position in this context: visionary or reactionary, marginal or rather in the insipid mainstream. If we assume that criticism is increasingly taking place on the margins, the growing criticism of horticultural shows is an indication of their marginality. And as hardly any of their ideas has changed in the last twenty years, my sense is that they are marginal for reactionary reasons. Unlike sluggish consent, criticism keeps us awake. So my ideas for future horticultural shows are not shaped by an absence of criticism but by a vision of new gardens which have the confidence to face criticism. This would bring us back to the dual characteristics of garden idylls and utopia. The garden as a place of retreat, of work, of beauty, of joy and sensuousness, is at the same time linked with the utopia of reconciliation with nature, with Heinrich von Kleist's vision of Paradise unlocked.

On criticism

Horticultural shows are dominated by three fundamental considerations: They are first to be seen as fairs staged by the garden industry, just as the book trade and the computer and furniture industries hold fairs. The industry demonstrates its capabilities, shows the breadth of what it can achieve, present innovations and draws attention to what has been tried and tested. The second fundamental is to improve the urban quality of our cities. This is to be achieved by redesign of outside space accessible to the public: squares, gardens and parks. The third aspect is a six-month open-air spectacle, entertainment events designed to appeal to both young and old, while also being PR for the city in question. This symbiosis worked as long as there was a balance between the three parts. The horticultural industry was satisfied as these shows provided an inexpensive forum for self-presentation, landscape architects had commissions. Cities were able to realise projects which they did not have to finance alone, the extended media presence attracted visitors to the host city from both nearby and further afield.

Today's criticism is directed at the increasing imbalance between the three elements. Urban improvements which are long

Die heutige Kritik zielt auf das zunehmende Ungleichgewicht der drei Teile. Die besonders langfristig wirksamen städtebaulichen Verbesserungen haben zunehmend an Bedeutung verloren. Nachdem der Wiederaufbau nach dem Krieg längst abgeschlossen ist, ungenutzte Stadtbrachen nicht mehr zur Verfügung stehen, hat man begonnen, vorhandene Anlagen umzugestalten und lediglich marginale Bereiche neu hinzuzufügen. Den Gipfel an berufsständischem und städtebaulich/freiraumplanerischem Unvermögen hat man zweifelsohne in Dortmund erreicht, wo kein Quadratmeter Land hinzugewonnen wurde und die ansprechende Patina eines gereiften Parks durch eine gärtnerische Frischzellenkur entfernt wurde. Es ist evident, daß Gartenschauen zunehmend zur Berufsmesse und Stadtwerbung degradiert werden und damit die notwendig langfristige Wirkung ausbleibt. Auch Stuttgart macht keine Ausnahme, wenn es stimmt, daß hier erstmals die Aufwendungen für die halbjährige Schau mit 130 Millionen Mark zu Buche schlagen, während die langfristigen Investitionen nur 100 Millionen Mark betragen. Mit Recht fragen sich Zuschußgeber und Steuerzahler – nicht nur in Stuttgart –, was und warum hier ein Ereignis dermaßen großzügig alimentiert werden soll. Eine zweite Kritik meinerseits, die jeder fachlichen Fundierung entbehrt: Ich glaube, wir haben verlernt, Feste zu feiern – fröhliche, überbordend üppige, nicht endende, farbige, heiße, feuchte, zusammenführende.

Es erscheint wahrscheinlich, daß der städtebauliche Handlungsbedarf vor allem in den Städten der neuen Bundesländer auch in nächster Zeit gegeben ist. Dies macht unsere Diskussion um so wichtiger, müßte es doch möglich sein, in diesen Ländern zumindest nicht die alten Fehler zu wiederholen und nur noch neue Fehler zu begehen. Gefragt werden muß weiter nach der Kompatibilität von freiraumplanerischen und städtebaulichen Interventionen und dem Messecharakter. Bisher wurden meist integrierte Lösungen gewählt, in der zum Beispiel Vergleichsschauen der Pflanzen, Grabstellengestaltung, Stände für Kleingartenzubehör, Naturschutzberatung in die Parkgestaltung einbezogen wurden. Das Ergebnis ist meist katastrophal ausgefallen, weil damit Prämissen vorgegeben waren, die inhaltlich und gestalterisch gar nicht mehr zu bewältigen sind. Größe und Farbkombination von Wechselpflanzungen richten sich nicht nach verträglichem Maß, sondern nach der Zahl der Aussteller

term in their effect have increasingly become less important. Now that reconstruction following World War II has long since been completed and urban wastelands are no longer available, the trend has turned to redesigning existing sites and just adding marginal areas. The height of inability on the part of the profession and urban and open space planners was undoubtedly reached in Dortmund, where not one single square metre of land was gained and the attractive patina of a mature park was removed by gardening live-cell treatment. It is evident that horticultural shows are increasingly being degraded to the status of a trade fair and promotion of the host city with the result that the necessary long-term effect is lost. Stuttgart is no exception here, either, if it is true that the six-month show cost DM 130 million, while long-term investments only accounted for DM 100 million. Subsidisers and taxpayers – not only in Stuttgart – are right to ask why such generous support was given to this event. A second piece of criticism levelled by me, which is not based on any objective criteria: I believe we no longer know how to celebrate properly – parties that are exuberant, extravagant, never-ending, colourful, hot, convivial, uniting.

It seems probable that the need to take action in an urban context will in particular continue to exist in towns and cities in former East Germany. This makes our discussion all the more important as it should after all be possible at least not to repeat the old mistakes there, but only make new ones. The question of the compatibility of interventions in terms of planning of open space and urban design on the one hand and trade fair character on the other needs to be addressed further. So far, only integrated solutions have been chosen in which, for example, comparative shows of plants, design of burial plots, stands for accessories for small gardens, advice on protection of nature were included in park design. The result was a disaster in most cases as the given premises could not be realised either in terms of content or design. The extent and colour combination of plantings according to season are no longer based on an acceptable combination, but on the number of exhibitors and the varieties they grow. The same garden themes are repeatedly presented like a payer wheel, whether they are appropriate or not is evidently irrelevant. It is my firm conviction that this compulsive combination is no more than a culmination of disadvantages, in which incompatibilities are combined – just as if we were to acquire a

und deren Züchtungen. Einer Gebetsmühle ähnlich werden immer gleiche Gartenthemen dargestellt, ob sie hineinpassen oder nicht, spielt offenbar keine Rolle. Ich bin der festen Überzeugung, daß diese zwanghafte Kombination nur eine Kumulation von Nachteilen darstellt, in der Unvereinbares zusammengeführt wird, was nicht zusammenpaßt – etwa so, wie wenn wir eine Skulptur erwerben, die gleichzeitig als Wegweiser dienen soll. Die abgesagte Berliner Buga 1995 hatte hier einen vielversprechenden Versuch gestartet, der die Trennung von einem stark konzentrierten Messeteil und der Entwicklung innerstädtischer Freiräume beinhaltete.

Diese Loslösung der Messe bietet eine große Chance, maßgeschneiderte, innovative Konzepte zu entwickeln, wie es bei anderen Fachmessen in jüngster Zeit zu beobachten ist. Anstelle der braven Aneinanderreihung von gleichartigen Pflanzen, begrenzt in Zeit und Raum, ein gärtnerisches, bunt schillerndes Feuerwerk, das nicht nur Fachleute, sondern auch Laien ansprechen könnte. Lernen von Las Vegas empfiehlt Venturi den Architekten. Lernen von Eurodisneyland empfehle ich an dieser Stelle. Es ist ein durchaus lohnendes Unterfangen, sich einmal näher mit dieser Konzeption professioneller Ausstellungsmacher zu befassen.

Nach diesen grundsätzlichen Überlegungen wollen wir uns etwas detaillierter auf die Gartenschauen einlassen. Im Titel heißt es: Zwischen Poesie und Geschwätzigkeit. Ich meine, die meisten zurückliegenden Gartenschauen hatten ihren Schwerpunkt eindeutig auf der Seite der Geschwätzigkeit, ein fortdauernder Schwall optischer und teilweise auch akustischer Reize. Ich möchte meine inhaltliche Kritik auf sechs Punkte beschränken.

1. Die permanente Belehrung

Auf Schritt und Tritt begegnen wir Tafeln, die uns aufklären und belehren. Über die Artenzusammensetzung der Blumenwiese, die Ursprünge des Labyrinthes, des Käferbesatzes an der Blumenesche, die Bedeutung des Klimas im Hinblick auf die Oechslegrade der Weintrauben oder die Ernährungsgewohnheiten der Bewohner der Partnerstadt in Indonesien. Die Allgegenwärtigkeit der Tafeln verleitet uns dazu, zuerst zu lesen und dann zu sehen. Umgekehrt wird, was nicht angeschrieben ist, überhaupt nicht zur Kenntnis genommen.

sculpture which is also intended to serve as a signpost. The 1995 Berlin Horticultural Show, which was cancelled, launched a promising attempt here, namely separation of a compact trade fair section and the development of urban outside space.

Making the trade fair a separate part provides a perfect opportunity to develop tailor-made, innovative concepts – a trend which could be observed at other recent trade fairs. Instead of stringing together similar plants for a limited time and in limited space, a colourful and shimmering display which would not only appeal to experts but also to laymen, Venturi recommends architects that they learn from Las Vegas. And, at this point, I recommend that a lesson be drawn from Euro Disneyland. There is nothing wrong with taking a closer look at this idea created by those whose profession is to design exhibitions.

Following on from these fundamental considerations, we now want to take a closer look at horticultural shows. This essay is entitled "Between Poetry and Garrulousness". It is my opinion that most garden shows of past years clearly had their focus on the side of garrulousness, a continuous flood of optical and in some cases also acoustic stimuli. I intend to confine my criticism to six points.

1. The permanent lecturing

Wherever we turn, we encounter signboards explaining things and lecturing us. About the combination of the species in the flower meadow, the origins of the labyrinth, the stock of beetles on the flowering ash, the significance of the climate with regard to the measure of alcohol content in grapes, or the eating habits of the inhabitants of the town in Indonesia with which the host city is twinned. The omnipresence of the signboards encourages us to read first and then to look. And vice versa, what is not written about is not noticed at all.

A particularly "successful" example of this was the Garden of Sounds at the 1993 Stuttgart Horticultural Show. I lay there in a deck chair for a while and watched the visitors to the garden. Although the music was clearly audible, most of them went up to the signboard and read they could hear music there, and then joined us as they meditatively hummed the melody of "A little night music".

Should the purpose of a horticultural show be to stimulate the senses of its visitors, hundreds of signboards are an ideal

Ein besonders gelungener Einfall stellt in diesem Sinne der Klanggarten auf der IGA Stuttgart 1993 dar. Dort habe ich mich eine Zeitlang auf einen Liegestuhl gelegt und die Besucher beobachtet. Obwohl die Musik vernehmlich erklingt, gehen die meisten zur Tafel, lesen, daß hier Musik zu hören ist, und gesellen sich dann zu uns, um verklärt «Die kleine Nachtmusik» nachzusummen.

Falls es ein Ziel einer Gartenschau ist, die Sinne der Besucher anzuregen, könnte dieses nicht besser verhindert werden, als es mit den Hunderten von Tafeln geschieht.

Neben der schulmeisterlichen Volksbelehrung steht wohl auch noch die Angst, daß sich die Besucher langweilen. Vicino Orsini zeigt uns in seinem heiligen Wald von Bomarzo das Gegenbeispiel – unbegrenzte Möglichkeiten, wie des Gartenbesuchers Intellekt und Sinnempfindungen aufs höchste beansprucht werden.

2. Die Negation des besonderen Ortes

Wir blättern nochmals zurück im Buch der Gartenkunst und sehen uns die zwei Grundtypen an, den barocken Garten und den Englischen Landschaftsgarten. Ein primäres Kennzeichen des Barockgartens ist sein Bezug auf sich selbst. Die Gesamtgestalt wird unabhängig vom Ort geschaffen, ja es ist gerade Ziel, im Garten die Gegenwelt zur Umgebung zu inszenieren. Die Reglementierung der Konzeption wie deren Einzelteile wird festgeschrieben, entsprechende Publikationen und Lehrbücher sorgen für eine weite, gleichartige Ausbreitung. Demgegenüber intendiert der Englische Landschaftsgarten, den Geist des Ortes aufzunehmen und diesen weiterzuentwickeln. Der Englische Landschaftsgarten fügt sich nicht nur in die Landschaft ein, vielmehr lebt er wesentlich von dieser.

Wenn wir die Gartenschauen ansehen, werden Gemeinsamkeiten zu den beiden Grundtypen deutlich. Inhaltlich erkennen wir die Nähe zum barocken Garten. Unabhängig vom Ort werden eine immer gleiche Konzeption und deren Einzelelemente dargestellt, wobei die Frage offen bleibt, ob dies aufgrund von Festlegungen der Gartenschauinitiatoren oder der Einfallslosigkeit der Landschaftsarchitekten zustande kommt. Auf der formalen Ebene – und nur da – wird scheinbar dem Prinzip des Englischen Landschaftsgartens gehuldigt. Und so schlängelt sich der Weg elegant um Hügel und Seen, die zuerst noch auf-

way to prevent this. In addition to this sermonising, a further aspect is probably the fear that visitors are bored. Vicino Orsini shows the opposite example in his "Holy Forest of Bomarzo" – unlimited possibilities of addressing the intellect and senses of the garden visitor.

2. The negation of the special place

Let us leaf back through the book of garden art and take a look at the two basic types, the Baroque garden and the English landscape garden. A primary feature of the Baroque garden is its reference to itself. The overall design is independent of the place, indeed the very aim is to stage a garden which is a counterworld to its surroundings. The underlying idea and its individual parts are prescribed, corresponding publications and textbooks ensure that it is perpetuated homogeneously. In contrast, the intention of the English landscape is to capture the spirit of the place and develop it further. The English landscape garden not only blends into the landscape, indeed it essentially depends on it.

When we look at horticultural shows, the things they have in common with the two basic types become apparent. In terms of content, we see the influence of the Baroque garden. The same scheme with its individual component parts is always used, whereby it is a moot point whether this is due to specifications set out by the initiators of horticultural shows or lack of imagination on the part of landscape architects. The principle of the English landscape garden is apparently embraced at the formal level – and only there. For example, paths meander elegantly around hills and lakes which first had to be thrown up or dug out, small gardens are integrated that had first been cleared and recreated in all splendour, or Baroque parterres created where the pleasure ground had once stood. The result is the absurdity of a reaction to something already there, but that first has to be created. Andy Warhol's creed of postmodernism – anything goes – is fundamentally misunderstood, the gardens have become senseless, degraded to arbitrary playing around with forms or banal fulfilment of a purpose.

3. The decline of meaning

The journal entitled "Daidalos" devoted one of its issues to "Gardens with Meaning"[1]. It is no coincidence that nearly all the

---

1 Daidalos no 46, Gütersloh (Germany) 1992

geschüttet oder ausgehoben werden müssen, werden Kleingärten integriert, die vorher abgeräumt und in strahlender Schönheit neu errichtet werden, oder Barockparterres gebaut, wo vorher der Pleasureground gewesen ist. So entsteht eine Absurdität, nämlich die Reaktion auf etwas Vorhandenes, das zuerst noch geschaffen werden muß. Andy Warhols Credo der Postmoderne – anything goes – wird grundlegend mißverstanden, die Gartenanlagen sind sinnlos geworden, verkommen zur beliebigen Formenspielerei oder banalen Zweckerfüllung.

3. Der Bedeutungsverschleiß

Die Zeitschrift «Daidalos» widmete eine Ausgabe den «Bedeutsamen Gärten»[1]. Nicht von ungefähr kommt, daß darin fast ausschließlich alte Gärten zur Darstellung gelangen. Zweierlei läßt sich daraus folgern: Zum einen sind Gärten nicht nur in unseren Fachkreisen wichtig geworden, zum anderen gibt es offenbar keine neuen bedeutsamen Gärten. In zunehmendem Maße wird Bedeutung mißbraucht oder in Frage gestellt. Ein unbelastetes Beispiel zur Erläuterung. Am Zürichsee hat man beim Bau die Schiffsanlegestellen mit italienischen Pappeln bepflanzt. Von weit her konnte man dank der Pappeln die Anlegestelle erkennen. Der Bedeutungsverschleiß ist eingetreten, als man unzählige weitere Pappeln am Seeufer gepflanzt und so das Signalhafte der Pappeln aufgehoben hat. In Städten, Parkanlagen und Gartenschauen erleben wir beispielhaft Bedeutungsverschleiß: wenn etwa auf trockensten Kiesterrassen scheinbar natürliche Seggenrieder inszeniert werden, wenn Neu für Alt ausgegeben wird, wenn der begradigte Bach mäandrierend neugestaltet wird, obwohl das dünne Rinnsal die Fließform Lügen straft, wenn in der flachen Niederterrasse natürlich erscheinende Hügel wachsen, wenn Schweizer Alpen nach Bayern auswandern oder wenn große Achsen an der Toilettentür des Gemeindehauses enden.

4. Die Plünderung der Gartenkunstgeschichte

Während es lange Zeit als besonders fortschrittlich galt, Gartengeschichte zu negieren, beobachten wir heute – sehr zeitgemäß – ein zunehmendes Interesse an der Vergangenheit. Leider wird der daraus erwachsende Erkenntnisfortschritt nicht dazu benutzt, um aus der Analyse vergangener Konzeptionen adäquate Folgerungen zur Gestaltung neuer Gärten zu gewinnen. Viel-

gardens portrayed are old. Two conclusions can be drawn from this: One is that gardens have become important not just among us experts, the other is that apparently there are no new gardens with meaning. Meaning is increasingly being misused or called into question. A neutral example serves to illustrate this. Italian poplars were planted when the moorings on Lake Zurich were built. The poplars made it easy to locate the moorings from further away. The decline in meaning set in when countless further poplars were planted on the shore of the lake and the signal effect of the poplars was lost. We see examples of decline in meaning in towns and cities, parks, and horticultural shows: when seemingly natural reeds are bedded on bone-dry gravel terraces, when new pretends to be old, when the steam that has been straightened is redesigned so that it meanders, despite the fact that such a paltry rivulet belies water flowing in this form, when seemingly natural hills protrude from a flat terrace, when Swiss Alps migrate to Bavaria, or when major axes end at the WC door of the community hall.

4. The looting of the history of garden art

While negating garden history was seen to particularly progressive for a long period of time, we observe today the modern trend of increasing interest in the past. Unfortunately, the ensuing progress in realisation is not used to make an analysis to draw adequate conclusions for the design of new gardens. Instead, the history of the garden is treated like a collection of props to be looted and exploited without scruples. The discovery of the garden as a place to be protected as a monument – actually a praiseworthy development – then turns out to be a double-edged sword. On the one hand, fabric worth protecting is ascertained with scientific accuracy and its future ensured. On the other hand – and contrary to the calls made by all authoritative garden publications – the number of garden reconstructions, of creative garden preservation and, most frequently, of historicising gardens is on the increase. Recourse to what is old or seems old falls on particularly fertile ground in a time of extensive social change and uncertainty, while what is new and modern seems, at the least, to be problematic and suspect. If horticultural shows prominently display new-old cottage gardens, cloister, Art Nouveau, Baroque, or Chinese gardens, this awakens fatal desires to imitate them on the part of future home

---

1 Daidalos Nr. 46, Gütersloh 1992

mehr wird die Gartengeschichte als Fundus aufgefaßt, den man hemmungslos plündern und ausschlachten kann. Die an sich lobenswerte Entdeckung des Gartens als Denkmalschutzobjekt erweist sich dabei als zweischneidiges Schwert. Einerseits wird mit wissenschaftlicher Genauigkeit schützenswerte Substanz festgestellt und deren Zukunft gesichert. Andererseits häufen sich – entgegen den Forderungen aller fachlich fundierten Publikationen – die Zahl von Gartenrekonstruktionen, von schöpferischer Gartendenkmalpflege und am häufigsten die Anlage von historisierenden Gärten. In einer Zeit weitgreifender gesellschaftlicher Unsicherheit und Veränderung fällt der Rückgriff auf das Alte oder Altscheinende auf besonders fruchtbaren Boden, während das Neue, Moderne zumindest problematisch und verdächtig ist. Wenn an Gartenschauen an prominenter Stelle neu-alte Bauern-, Kloster-, Jugendstil-, Barock- oder chinesische Gärten gezeigt werden, weckt dies bei zukünftigen Bauherren und -frauen fatale Nachahmungsgelüste. Die wahllose Plünderung und Inszenierung von Gartengeschichte fördert so keine Kenntnis.

5. Ökologie als Heilmittel

Nach anfänglichem Zögern hat der Berufsstand der Landschaftsarchitekten sein ökologisches Gewissen entdeckt. Waren Anlagen eines Le Roy oder Schwarz in den sechziger und siebziger Jahren noch revolutionär und subversiv, so sind die einstigen Revolutionäre längst rechts und links überholt worden. Ökologische Erkenntnisse fließen schon fast selbstverständlich in Bestandsanalyse und Neukonzeption ein. So wurden auch für die IGA in Stuttgart eine sorgfältige, wissenschaftlich fundierte Bestandsaufnahme erarbeitet, Pflanzen kartiert, Käfer, Heuschrecken und Vögel gezählt und das Klima untersucht. Doch wie so häufig droht die Gefahr, daß wir von einem Extrem ins andere fallen. Plötzlich ist alles Vorhandene schätzenswert. Der Naturschutz in der Stadt hat vergessen, daß da noch Menschen wohnen.

Vorhandene oder neu geschaffene Naturbilder werden mit Stacheldraht abgezäunt. Ein Signal: ab hier wird die Natur empfindlich. Der Schutz als ultima ratio, als Allheilmittel gegen eine immer böser werdende Welt, zeigt gelegentlich groteske Züge. Zum Expo-Wettbewerb in Hannover wurden mehrere hundert Seiten umfassende Untersuchungen abgegeben, die zum be-

owners. Indiscriminate looting and staging of garden history does not lead to any realisations.

5. Ecology as a remedy

Landscape architects have, following their initial hesitation, discovered their ecological conscience. While the designs of architects such as Le Roy or Schwarz may have still been revolutionary and subversive in the nineteen-sixties or nineteen-seventies, the revolutionaries of that time have long since been overtaken on both the left and the right. Insights into the world of ecology are included in analyses of what is there and to be redesigned more or less as a matter of course. For example, careful, scientifically based stocktaking was carried out for the Stuttgart Horticultural Show, plants were card-indexed, beetles, locusts, and birds counted, and the climate analysed. Yet, as is so often the case, the danger is that we move from one end of the scale to the other. Everything already there is suddenly estimable. Protection of nature in the city has forgotten that this is still a place where people live.

Existing or newly created images of nature are fenced off by barbed wire. The message conveyed is that this is the point were nature becomes sensitive. Protection as the ultima ratio, as the panacea against a world growing increasingly evil, occasionally displays itself in grotesque contours. Several hundred pages of detailed studies submitted for the Hanover Expo competition came to the remarkable conclusion that a field hedge approximately 50 metres long in an agricultural area approximately six kilometres in length had to be protected at all costs. And in Weil am Rhein, the site of a regional horticultural show, a gravel pit embankment – located directly next to detached houses – was declared to be sacrosanct even though gravel was still being excavated. Nature conservationists and landscape architects tell the baffled observer that this could become a valuable nesting area for kingfishers at some point. What seems necessary is understanding that ecological aspirations are neither a goal nor a panacea, rather they are just one of the aspects of our work as planners.

6. The "monarchs of the glen" of garden architecture

First things first, I do not mean the garden gnomes who at least have a diminutive garden house as a shelter at the horticultural

merkenswerten Schluß kommen, daß in dem etwa sechs Kilometer langen Ackerbaugebiet eine 50 Meter lange Feldhecke unbedingt zu schützen sei. Und in Weil am Rhein, Standort einer Landesgartenschau, wurde eine – direkt an Einfamilienhausparzellen angrenzende – Kiesgrubenwand als unantastbar erklärt, obwohl mit dem Bagger immer noch Kies abgebaut wird. Naturschützer und Landschaftsarchitekt erklären dem verdutzten Beobachter, daß dies einmal ein wertvolles Nistgebiet für den Eisvogel werden könnte. Eine Erkenntnis erscheint notwendig: Ökologische Forderungen sind weder Ziel noch Allheilmittel, vielmehr sind sie eine von mehreren Grundlagen unserer planerischen Arbeit.

6. Die röhrenden Hirsche der Gartenarchitektur

Um es vorwegzunehmen, ich meine damit nicht die Gartenzwerge, denen auf der IGA wenigstens ein Kleingartenhäuschen als Unterschlupf dient und sie so in ihrer Puppenstube noch besser als im Freien unsere ungeteilte Zuwendung bekommen. Denn Kitsch in seiner reinen Form ist in kindlicher Unvoreingenommenheit wundervoll genießbar wie die verbotene Zigarette in der Primarschule. Und Jeff Koons lehrt uns, wie wir die scheinbare Inkarnation des schlechten Geschmacks mittlerweile bereits in renommiertesten Kunstausstellungen bewundern sollen. Meine röhrenden Hirsche sind leise, aber geschwätzig und bewegen sich in der heiklen Zwischenzone von gestalterischem Populismus, modernistischem Formengeplänkel, falsch verstandenen Ordnungsprinzipien und unverdaulichem Materialpotpourri. Sie sind windschlüpfrig und beweglich wie ein Aal, sie ecken nirgends an, weil jede Ecke und Kante fehlt. Sie sind ungeschlacht und roh, ohne dies zu thematisieren, und zeugen allzu oft vom Unvermögen des Berufsstandes, handwerklich saubere Konstruktionen zu erarbeiten. Zurückzuführen sind diese Ergebnisse auf fehlende gestalterische Auseinandersetzung, die offenbar weder in der Ausbildung noch im Büroalltag hinreichend trainiert wird. Ein berufsständisches Defizit, das uns letztlich die Zusammenarbeit mit guten Architekten erschwert oder gar unmöglich macht.

Ausblick

Als Zusammenfassung und Ausblick auf zukünftige Gartenschauen zwölf Gedanken:

show, making them more a subject of our undivided attention in their "doll's house" than outside. In other words, kitsch in its purest form can be enjoyed perfectly through the eyes of a child just as can the prohibited cigarette smoked clandestinely at primary school. And Jeff Koons teaches us we are now to applaud the seeming incarnation of bad taste in art exhibitions of the finest. My "monarchs" are not loud, but they have plenty to say and operate in the tricky territory between design populism, modernist shop-talk squabbling about form, falsely understood principles of order, and an indigestible potpourri of materials. They are streamlined and as slippery as an eel, they never offend as they are lacking in anything that could produce such a reaction. They are monstrous and crude without addressing this as a theme and all too often bear witness to the inability of the profession to produce designs that had been properly thought out in terms of craftsmanship. These results are attributable to a lack of dialogue with design – a skill which is evidently not adequately learnt during training or in day-to-day practice. This is a shortcoming which ultimately makes it very difficult if not impossible to work with good architects.

Outlook

I would like to put forward twelve ideas as a summary and outlook for horticultural shows of the future:

1. Given the fact that national and regional horticultural shows exist as a recognised instrument, horticultural shows should continue to be held in the future. However, their prerequisite is redefinition of the aims and contents of horticultural shows.

2. Horticultural shows should only take place when it is proved that there is substantial need for action in terms of planning of urban and outside space. Evaluation of the need for action should be made by a body which is as independent as possible. No redesign of existing areas should be permitted.

3. The trade fair part of the horticultural show is to be clearly separate from the new park and garden areas. It should be as compact as possible in terms of space. It must be equally interesting and entertaining for both laymen and professionals. Reconversion measures are to be concentrated primarily on this section.

1. Nachdem es das anerkannte Instrumentarium der Bundes- und Landesgartenschauen gibt, soll es Gartenschauen auch in Zukunft geben. Voraussetzung ist die Neuformulierung von Zielen und Inhalten der Gartenschauen.

2. Gartenschauen dürfen nur da stattfinden, wo ein gewichtiger städtebaulich-freiraumplanerischer Handlungsbedarf nachgewiesen werden kann. Die Prüfung des Handlungsbedarfes erfolgt durch ein möglichst unabhängiges Gremium. Die Umgestaltung bereits vorhandener Anlagen ist ausgeschlossen.

3. Der Messeteil der Gartenschau ist klar von den neuen Parkanlagen zu trennen. Er soll flächenmäßig möglichst kompakt konzipiert werden. Er muß für Laien und Fachleute gleichermaßen interessant und unterhaltend sein. Rückbaumaßnahmen haben sich im wesentlichen auf diesen Bereich zu konzentrieren.

4. Für die Neugestaltung innerstädtischer Freiräume gibt es inhaltlich keine festgelegten Vorgaben. Damit kann gezielt auf die besonderen örtlichen Verhältnisse eingegangen und originäre Beiträge zur Entwicklung von neuen Plätzen, Gärten und Parkanlagen geschaffen werden.

5. Die Konzeption der Gartenschauen soll weiterhin über Wettbewerbe entschieden werden. Geprüft werden muß, ob die Planung für den Messeteil und den Parkanlagenteil nicht sinnvollerweise über getrennte Wettbewerbe entschieden werden soll.

6. Stuttgart 1993 hat den letzten Beweis der Unsinnigkeit von Internationalen Gartenschauen mit sogenannten Nationengärten erbracht. Internationale Beiträge für einzelne Teilbereiche wären allenfalls über die Zuladung von ausländischen Wettbewerbsteilnehmern zu erreichen, wie das zum Beispiel bei der IBA Emscher Park mit Erfolg gepflegt wird.

7. Die Einbindung der neuen Parkanlagen in die Alltagswelt der Bewohner ist entscheidend für deren Akzeptanz. Die Mitsprache der Anwohner ist zu Beginn bei der inhaltlichen Festlegung notwendig und nicht bei deren späteren Umsetzung.

4. There are no hard and fast rules for redesigning outside space in inner-city areas. In consequence, it is possible to address specific local conditions and make original contributions to the development of new squares, gardens and parks,

5. The underlying idea of horticultural shows should continue to be decided via competition. Consideration should be given to the question as to whether it would not make sense to decide planning of the trade fair section and the garden and park section in separate competitions.

6. The 1993 Stuttgart Horticultural Show provided the ultimate proof of the absurdity of international horticultural shows with so-called national gardens. International contributions to individual parts can at best be achieved by inviting entries from foreign competitors, as was, for example, successfully practised at the Emscher Park International Building Exhibition.

7. Incorporation of the new park areas as part of the day-to-day life of local residents is essential for their acceptance. Residents need to be consulted on definition of contents from the very beginning and not just at the later stage of implementation.

8. It goes without saying that it is essential that attention is paid to ecological needs in the context of developing urban open space, in particular attention to building and maintenance work which is sparing in its use of resources. This is not to be understood as a demand for natural space only, after all design and ecology are not mutually exclusive.

9. Horticultural shows must fulfil stringent demands of design quality and recent garden culture. The yardstick is to be an idea which is coherent in terms of both content and formal aspects.

10. National horticultural shows need to become far less expensive to hold. This must be achieved in all areas of organisation, implementation, construction and future maintenance. This is not only something which makes financial sense in times of empty coffers, but also from the ecological point of view.

8. Die Berücksichtigung ökologischer Erfordernisse ist selbstverständlicher Teil bei der Entwicklung städtischer Freiräume, insbesondere die Berücksichtigung ressourcenschonender Bau- und Unterhaltsarbeiten. Dies beinhaltet nicht die alleinige Forderung nach naturbelassenen Freiräumen, denn Gestalt und Ökologie schließen sich nicht aus.

9. Gartenschauen müssen höchsten Ansprüchen an Gestaltqualität, an rezenter Gartenkultur genügen. Diese bemißt sich an der schlüssigen inhaltlichen und formalen Konzeption.

10. Bundesgartenschauen müssen wesentlich billiger werden. Erreicht werden muß dies in allen Bereichen der Organisation, der Durchführung, dem Bau und zukünftigen Unterhalt. Das ist nicht nur eine ökonomische Notwendigkeit in Zeiten leerer Kassen, sondern auch eine ökologische.

11. Die Neuschaffung von öffentlichen Plätzen, Gärten und Parkanlagen muß zukünftig auch ohne Gartenschauen möglich werden.

12. Jenseits der Geschwätzigkeit wünsche ich mir alltägliche, intellektuelle, sinnliche, stimmungsvolle, grüne und farbige, große und kleine, helle und dunkle, offene und geschlossene, geordnete und wilde Gärten voller Poesie.

Dieter Kienast

11. It must in future be possible to create new squares, gardens and parks without a horticultural show.

12. And leaving garrulousness aside, my wish is for ordinary, intellectual, sensuous, green and colourful, great and small, light and dark, open and secluded, well-ordered and wild gardens filled with poetry.

Dieter Kienast

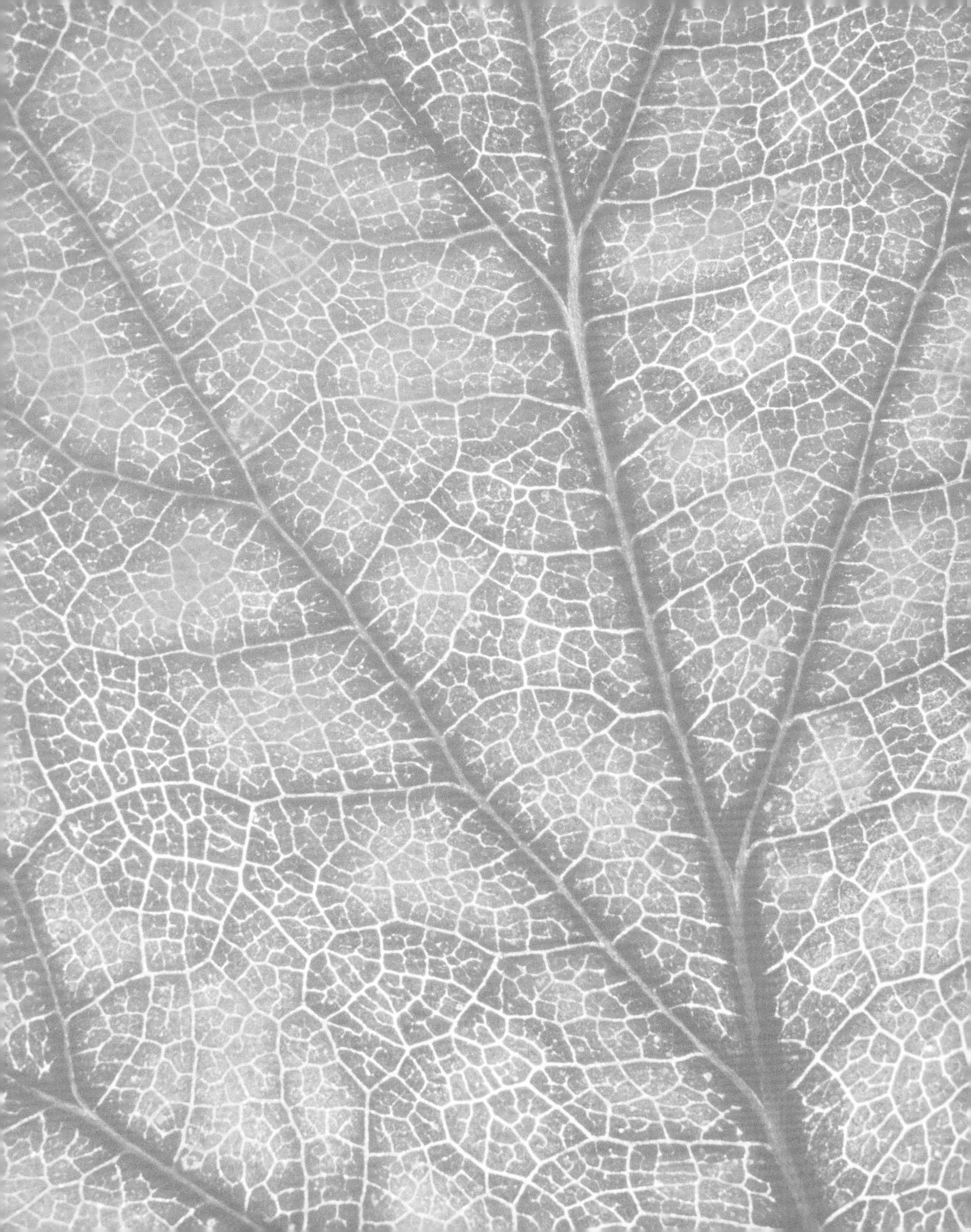

Dornröschen am Mechtenberg

Die Geschichte der Landschaft am und um den Mechtenberg wird von intensivster Bodennutzung bestimmt. Zum Besonderen wird das Gebiet einerseits durch den Mechtenberg – eine der wenigen natürlichen topographischen Erhebungen in dieser Gegend – und andererseits durch die Ideen unterschiedlichster Planer, die im Sommer 1992 anläßlich des Mechtenberg-Seminares zusammen kamen. Zur ortsüblichen Nutzung durch die Landwirtschaft sind der unterirdische Bergbau und die oberirdischen Deponien hinzugekommen, die wiederum – soweit möglich – ackerbaulich genutzt werden. Der Boden ist abgesackt, die Deponien sind mehr oder weniger stark durch Giftstoffe belastet. Dank seiner Steilhänge ist der oberste Teil des Mechtenberges von der landwirtschaftlichen Nutzung ausgenommen. Bismarckturm und Extensivvegetation prädestinieren diesen Bereich zum beliebten Naherholungsgbiet.

Das Prinzip «Dornröschen» will in dieser allgegenwärtigen Vorstellung von Nützlichkeit der Landschaft ein gegenteiliges Zeichen setzen. Anstelle von Zweckbestimmtheit tritt Sinnerfülltheit, anstelle von Hektik tritt Ruhe, anstelle des Säen-Ernten-Rhythmus das langsame, ungestörte Wachsen der Natur. Begrenzte Landflächen werden jeglicher Bewirtschaftung entzogen.

«Dornröschen» wurde durch die vergiftete Spindel in einen jahrzehntelangen Schlaf versetzt und von einem Prinzen wachgeküßt. Ebenso gewährt das Prinzip «Dornröschen» der Natur im abgegrenzten Bereich Ungestörtheit für die nächsten Jahrzehnte.

Die Mechtenbergkuppe ist Ausgangspunkt der analytischen und konzeptionellen Überlegungen und steht für das Prinzip «Dornröschen». Beim Bau des Bismarckdenkmals wurde ein geometrischer Bereich mit Weißdornhecken eingefaßt und gegen die Landwirtschaftsflächen abgegrenzt. In diesem Quadrat hat sich die Vegetation neunzig Jahre lang zu einem Wald entwickelt, in dem das Bismarckdenkmal langsam «versunken» ist. Brombeeren haben im Laufe der Zeit die Weißdornhecken überwachsen und lassen nur einige wenige Eingänge in der Waldkuppel frei.

Sleeping Beauty at Mechtenberg

The history of the countryside on and around the Mechtenberg hill has been shaped by intensive land utilisation. What gives the place its special character is, on the one hand, Mechtenberg itself – one of the few natural topographical elevations – and, on the other hand, the ideas created by planners of very different persuasions in the summer of 1992 during the Mechtenberg Seminar. The agricultural use typical of the area was augmented by underground mining and above-ground dumps, which, in turn, are – as far as possible – used for agricultural purposes. The soil has subsided, the dumps are contamiated with toxic waste to a greater or lesser degree. The upper part of the Mechtenberg hill is too steep to be used for agricultural purposes. The Bismarck Tower and extensive vegetation have predestined this area as a popular recreational place.

The "Sleeping Beauty" principle aims to set a contrary example to the prevelant notion of the usefulness of the countryside. Usefulness is replaced by meaning, hustle and bustle by tranquility, the rhythm of sowing and harvesting by the slow, undisturbed growth of nature. Limited areas are deprived of any form of agricultural use.

"Sleeping Beauty" pricked her finger on a poisoned spinning wheel and slept for 100 years until she was kissed awake by a prince. The "Sleeping Beauty" principle is intended to give nature in the defined area "peace and quiet" in the decades to come.

The Mechtenberg dome forms the point of departure of analytical and conceptional considerations and stands for the "Sleeping Beauty" principle. When the Bismarck Monument was built, a geometrical area was enclosed by a hedge of whitethorn and separated from the agricultural areas. The vegetation in this square has developed into a wood in the course of the last ninety years and, in turn, the Bismarck Monument has gradually "sunk". Over time, the whitethorn hedges have become overgrown with blackberries, with the result that only very few paths leading to the hilltop dome.

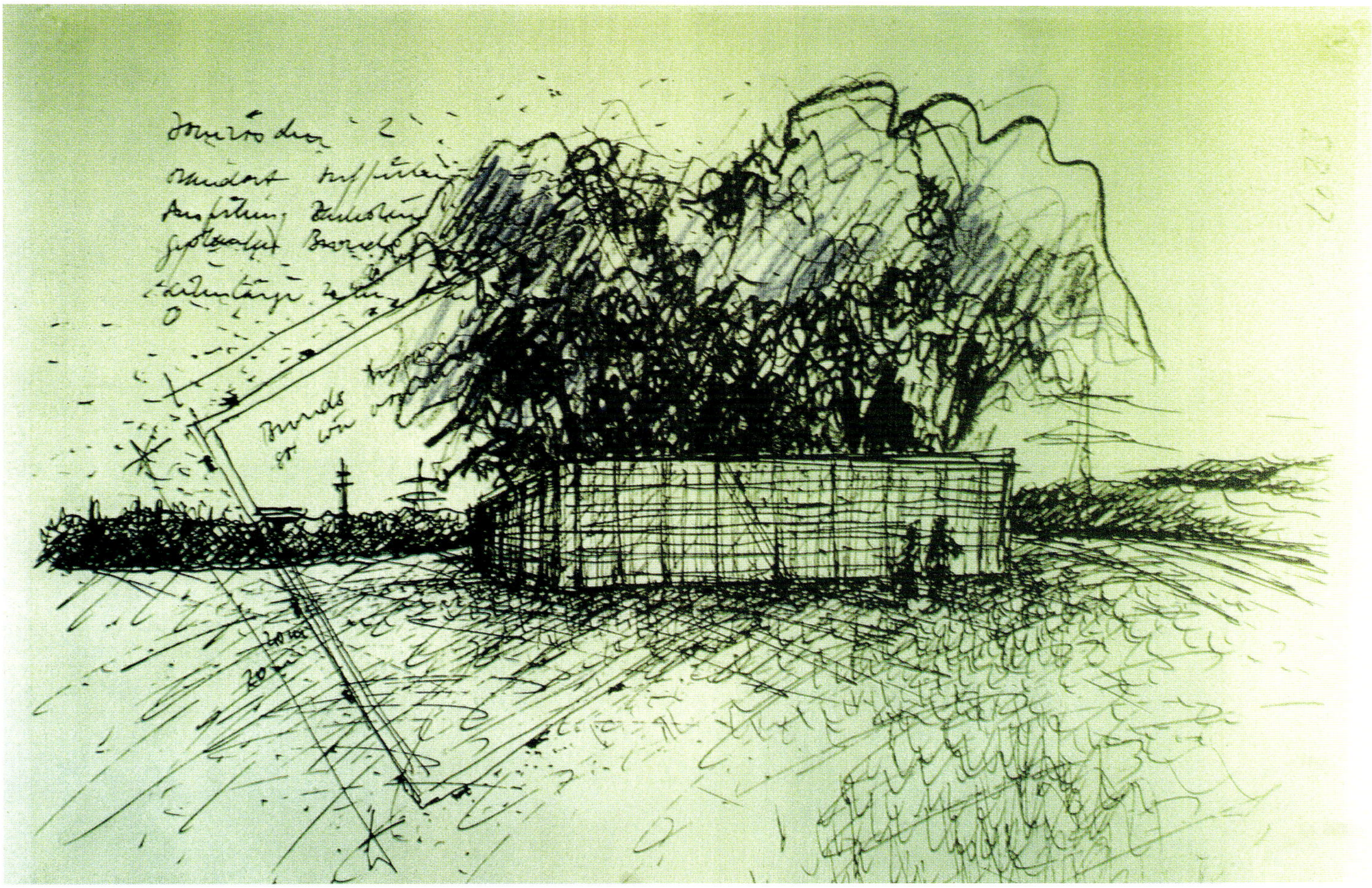

Dornröschengarten

Im Bereich des Planungsgebietes Mechtenberg werden acht Dornröschengärten an ausgezeichneten Orten angelegt. Die Bedeutung und Wirkung der Dornröschengärten ist vielschichtig. Zunächst wird der Ort seiner utilitären Nutzung entzogen. Durch den Menschen nicht mehr betreubar, entwickelt sich in Übereinstimmung mit dem Standort eine vielfältige Vegetation, die wiederum zum Habitat für unterschiedlichste Tierpopulationen wird. Für den Spaziergänger werden die Dornröschengärten wegen ihrer speziellen Ausformung zum Topos, zu unverwechselbaren Landmarken, aber auch zum Bedeutungsträger unseres veränderten Umganges mit Landschaft und Natur. Durch die Serie der im ganzen Gebiet verteilten Gärten wird der Zusammenhang des vielfältig fraktionierten Geländes mit seinem natürlichen und sinnstiftenden Zentrum Mechtenberg manifest.

Die Ausformung der Dornröschengärten variiert das Konzept der Mechtenbergkuppe. Ausgehend von einem Quadrat mit 15 Metern Seitenlänge wird ein Baumstammraster von 2,5 Metern vorgesehen. Das Zentrum ist und bleibt ein vom Menschen unberührbarer Ort. Der Rand des Baumstammquadrates wird durch eine dichte, zweischichtige Rosen- bzw. Fliederhecke gebildet. Zu jedem Baumstamm wird ein junger Baum (Weißdorn, Feldahorn und Eiche) gepflanzt. Im Lauf der Jahre wird die Vegetationsschicht zum Waldstück heranwachsen; die den jungen Baumbestand schützenden Baumstämme werden verfaulen, die Rosen-Fliederhecken werden locker und lassen die Entdeckung des «inneren» Dornröschengartens zu.

Mechtenbergkuppe

Wegen der Steilheit der westlichen und südlichen Hänge wurde die landwirtschaftliche Nutzung aufgegeben. Die Sukzession der Vegetation führt zum Wald, etwa die Hälfte der Flächen sind bereits mit Sträuchern und Bäumen bestockt. Aus landschaftsgestalterischer und ökologischer Sicht erscheint es zwingend, daß die charakteristisch bewaldete Hügelkuppe mit dem «eingeschlossenen» Bismarckdenkmal nicht in eine unmittelbar anschließende Hangbewaldung übergeht.

Deshalb sollen die noch vorhandenen Wiesen gemäht bzw. von Gehölzen freigehalten werden, so daß der Bestockungsanteil im bisherigen Umfang bestehen bleibt. Die Hügelkuppe soll

Sleeping Beauty Garden

Eight "Sleeping Beauty Gardens" are to be created at selected places within the Mechtenberg planning area. The meaning and effect of the "Sleeping Beauty Gardens" are complex. As a first step, the place is to be deprived of its utlitarian use. Escaping human care, a diversity of vegetation is developing in harmony with the location – vegetation which will become the habitat of a wide range of animal populations. People taking walks will appreciate the "Sleeping Beauty Gardens" on account of their design to form a topos, unmistakable landmarks, as well as their testimony to our changed approach to landscape and nature. The series of the gardens distributed throughout the area manifests the cohesion of the widely fractionated area with its natural and formative centre of Mechtenberg.

The form of the "Sleeping Beauty Gardens" is a variation on the theme of the Mechtenberg hilltop. A 2.5-metre by 2.5-metre grid of tree trunks is envisaged on the basis of a square 15 metres by 15 metres. The centre is and shall remain to be a place to which people have no access. The edge of the square of tree trunks is formed by a dense, double hedge of rose bushes and lilacs. A young tree (whitethorn, maple, oak) is to be planted adjacent to every tree trunk. The vegetation will grow to become a piece of woodland over the years: the tree trunks protecting the fledgling tree population will rot, the hedge of roses and lilacs will become intertwined, permitting discovery of the inner "Sleeping Beauty Garden".

Mechtenberg hilltop

Agricultural use was abandoned on account of the steepness of the west and south slopes. The succession of vegetation has resulted in a wood; approximately one half of the area is already populated with bushes and trees. From the point of view of landscape design and for ecological considerations, it would seem to make sense that the typically wooded hilltop with the "enclosed" Bismarck Monument does not simply become part of a directly adjacent wooded slope.

It is for this reason that the meadows still in existence are to be mown and kept free of undergrowth, to enable the existing stocks to remain to their present extent. Careful means should be chosen to give the hilltop spatial definition so that the original intention of a clearly defined highest point can be experienced.

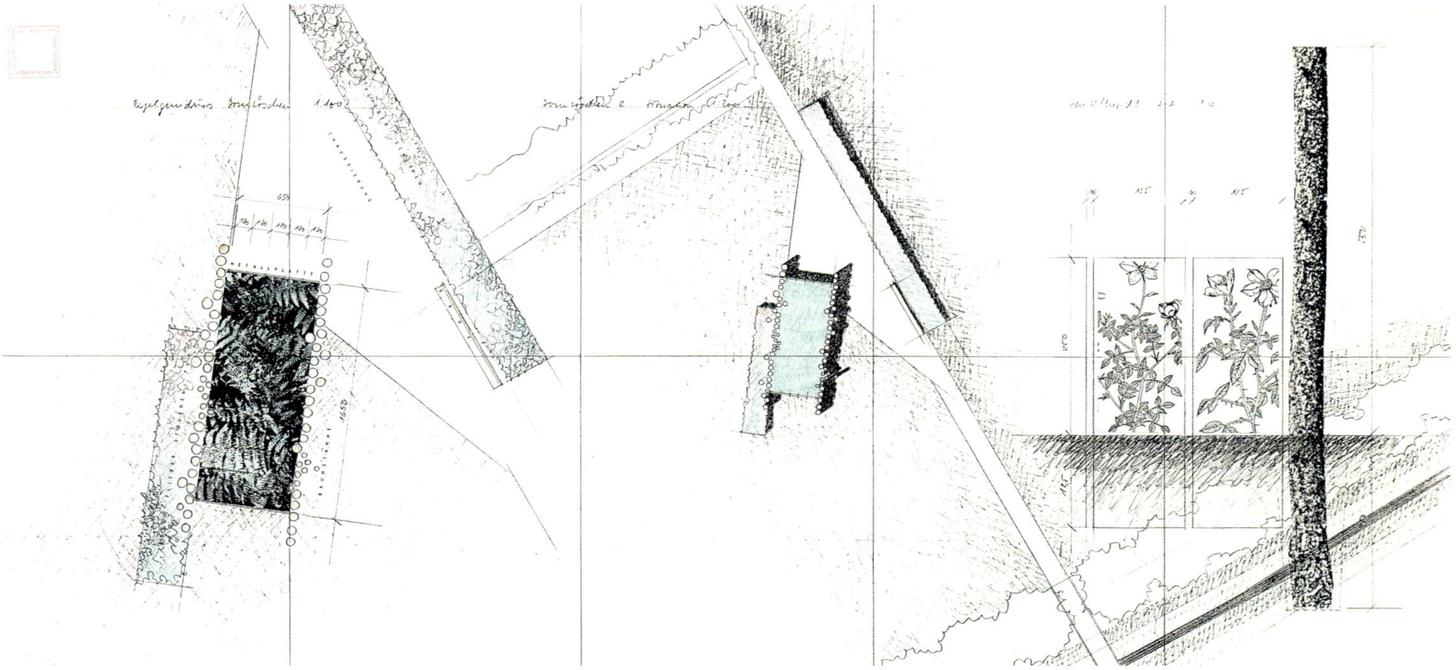

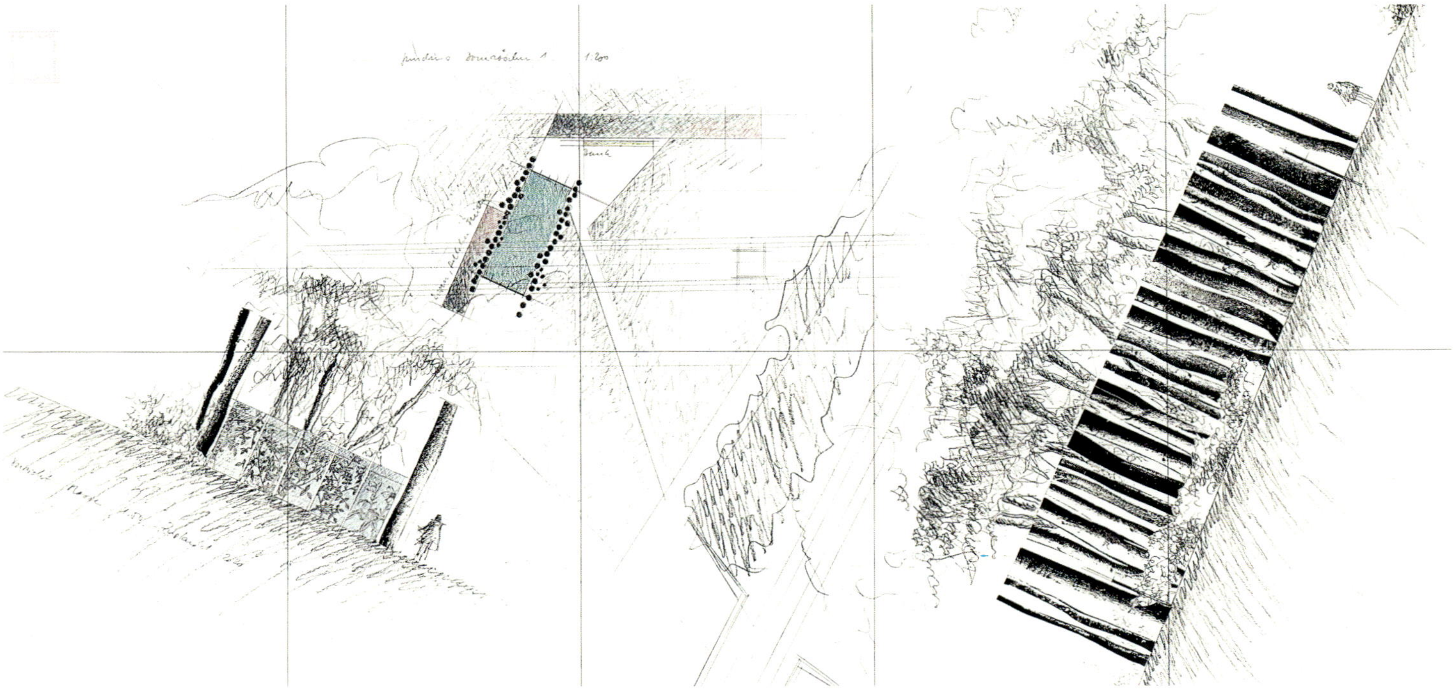

mit behutsamen Mitteln präzisiert werden, damit die ursprüngliche Intention eines klar definierten Höhepunktes in der Landschaft erlebbar bleibt. Der Waldrand wird durch Weißdorn und Rosen verstärkt, großflächig sich ausbreitendes Brombeergebüsch wird reduziert. Dem Bismarckdenkmal werden Rankstangen vorangestellt, die mit Clematis, Lonicera und Rosen bewachsen sind. Der perspektivische Blick auf das martialische Denkmal wird somit überlagert von leicht gekippten Stangen. Ein zusätzliches Angebot zur zunehmenden Naherholungsnutzung des Mechtenberges bieten Bänke im inneren und Landschaftsliegestühle im äußeren Bereich der Kuppe.

Dieter Kienast

The woodland edge is given greater definition by whitethorn and roses; proliferate blackberry bushes are to be cut back. Trellises overgrown with clematis, lonicera and roses are to be placed in front of the Bismarck Monument. In other words, slighty inclined trellises obscure the view of the military monument. Among Mechtenberg's other attractions as an increasingly significant recreational area are benches in the inner part and reclining chairs in the outer part of the hilltop.

Dieter Kienast

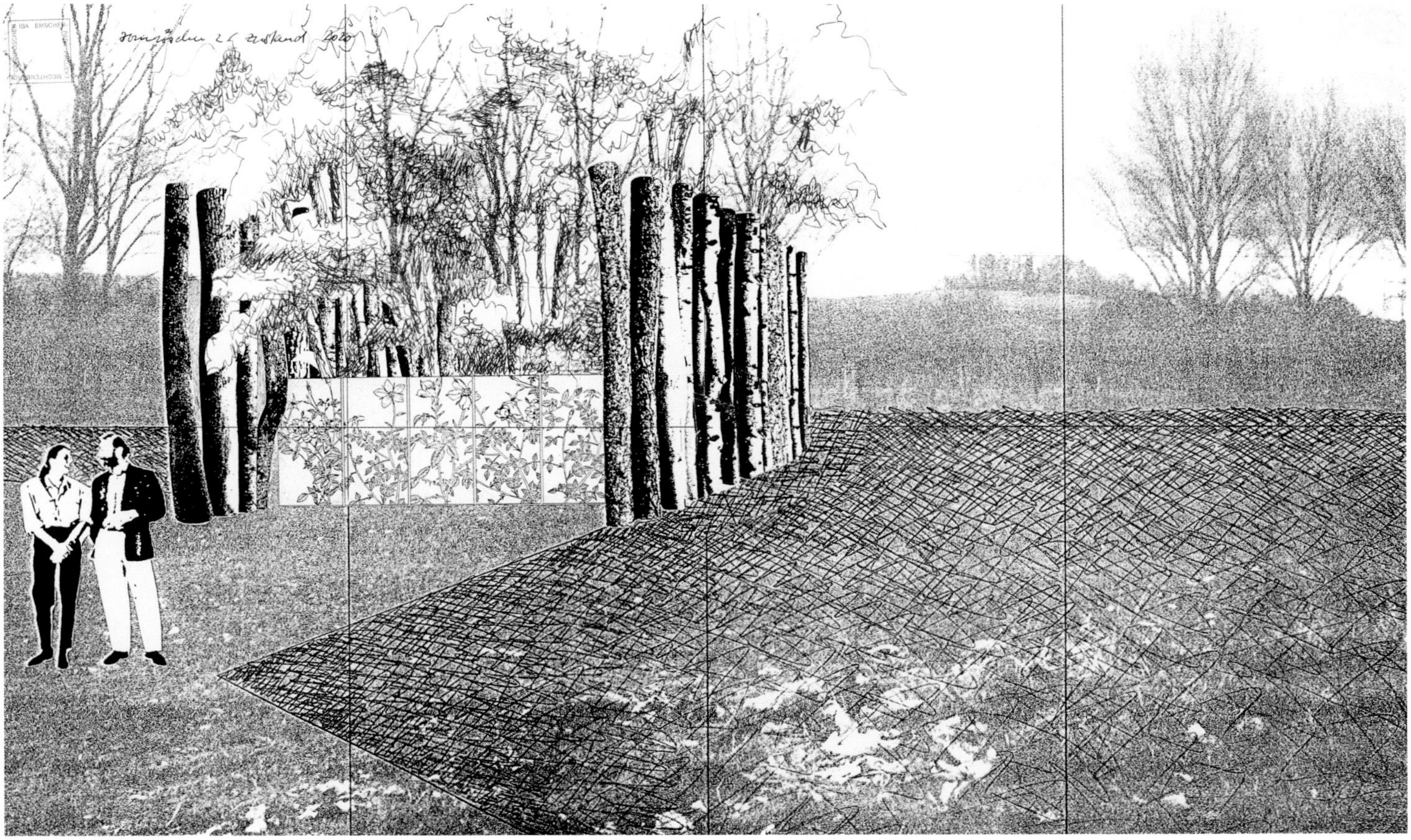

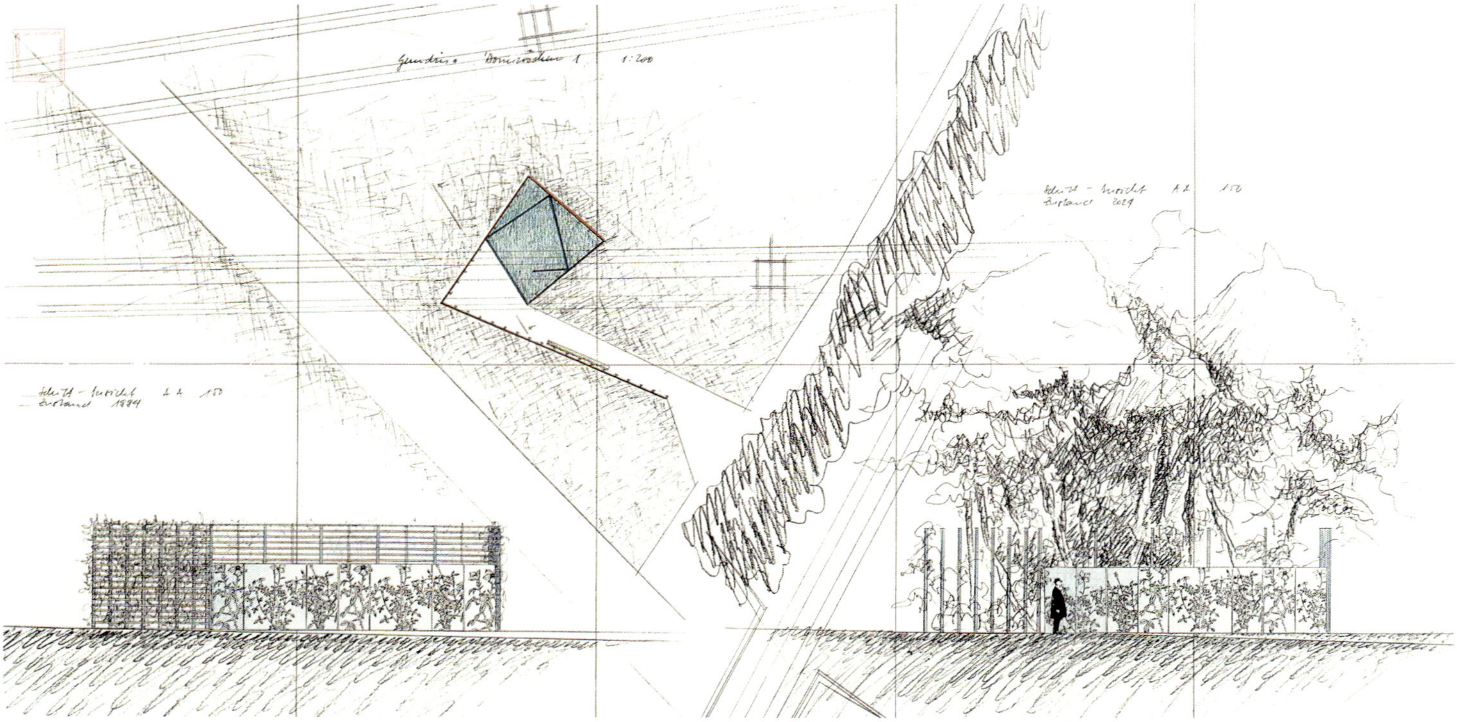

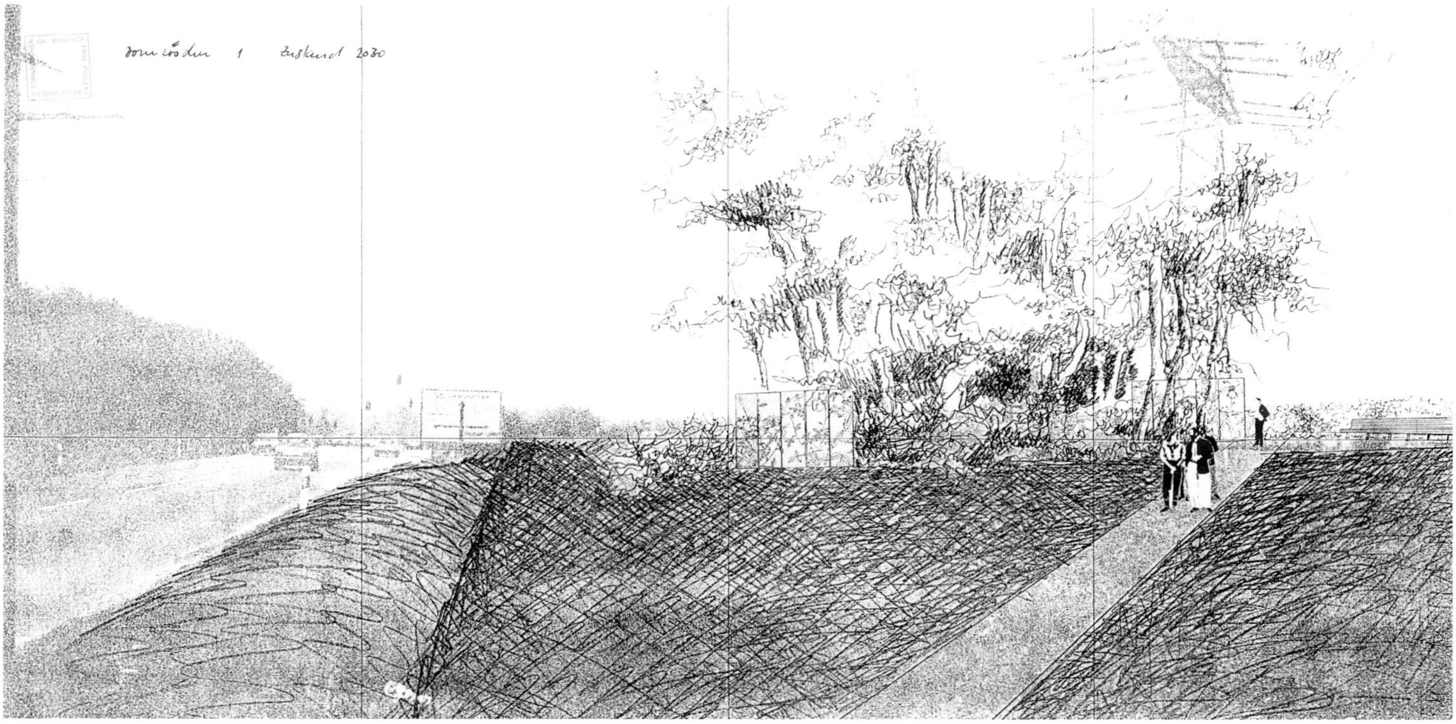

Straße der Nationen, Chemnitz

«Hommage an John Cage»

Das vorgegebene städtebauliche Konzept akzeptiert auf sympathische Weise bestehende Bauten und strebt durch Verdichtung ein kompaktes, aber differenziertes Stadtgefüge an. Der Straßenraum bekommt dadurch eine verstärkte Bedeutung als Raumkontinuum, Orientierungs- und Ordnungssystem. Unser Gestaltungskonzept der Außenräume zeigt eine nahe Verwandtschaft zum städtebaulichen Gesamtentwurf: Nicht tabula rasa mit der – mittlerweile ungeliebten – Vergangenheit, sondern gelassenes Aufnehmen und Weiterentwickeln vorhandener Situationen und Elemente. Unser Augenschein hat ergeben, daß die vielgeschmähte sozialistische Architektur gerade auch in Chemnitz teilweise von beachtlicher Qualität ist. In diesem Sinne verstehen wir unsere Interventionen im Außenraum nicht als Camouflage architektonischer Mißstände, sondern als präzise Ergänzung oder Gegenüberstellung.

Der etwas pathetische Name «Straße der Nationen» soll nicht nur zur Erinnerung an die Opfer des Krieges stehen, sondern auch als rezentes Programm für einen offenen Umgang mit Menschen aller Nationen verstanden werden. Der umgestaltete Straßenzug soll zum städtebaulichen Rückgrat der Innenstadt werden, das Zusammenhängende betonen, das Verbindende stärken. Neben dem Straßenraum als Ganzem stellen dies in unserem Projekt die Säuleneichenallee und die speziell ausformulierte Straßenbahntrasse sicher. Diese Kontinuität wird durch episodisch angedockte Außenräume auf der Straßenwestseite rhythmisiert. Je nach Lage, Zustand, Gebrauch und Größe sind sie markant unterschiedlich ausgebildet, wobei jedem Raum ein eigenes Thema zugeschrieben wird, wie: Altstadtplatz, Stadthallengarten, Kulturplatz, Park, etc.

Obwohl das Straßenprofil differiert, betrachten wir den Abschnitt Rathaus bis Wilhelm-Külz-Platz als Einheit mit sekundär in Erscheinung tretenden Variationen. Die der Säuleneichenallee gegenüberliegende Straßenseite ist mit einer abschnittweisen, ein-, beziehungsweise zweireihigen Lindenallee definiert. Mit dieser Ungleichseitigkeit des Straßenraumes reagieren wir auf die jeweils unterschiedlichen An-

Strasse der Nationen, Chemnitz

"Homage to John Cage"

The present urban concept accepts existing buildings in a pleasing manner and by densification seeks to achieve a compact, yet differentiated urban structure. This gives street space greater importance as continuum of space, a system providing order and orientation. Our design concept of the public space reveals a close relationship to the overall urban design: not tabula rasa, a complete break with the – by now – unloved past, but uncomplicated inclusion and further development of existing situations and elements. Our inspection of the site showed us that in Chemnitz too the widely rejected architecture of the GDR is in some cases of impressive quality. And so we see our intervention not as camouflage of architectural failures but as precise complements or a contrast.

The somewhat melodramatic name "Strasse der Nationen" (Street of the Nations) is not only intended to bring to mind the victims of war, but also to be understood as a new programme for an open-minded approach to people of all nations. The redesigned stretch of the street is intended to become the backbone of the urban structure of the city centre, to emphasise relationships, strengthen linking elements. Apart from the street space as a whole, this is achieved in our project by the avenue of oak trees and the special layout of the route of the tram line. This continuity is given rhythm by areas of outside space added on the west side of the street. Depending on the location, condition, use and size they are laid out in distinctive different ways, whereby each has its own theme, for example square of the old town, garden of the city hall, place of culture, park, etc.

Although the profile of the street differs, we see the section from the Town Hall to Wilhelm-Külz-Platz as a unit with variations which are secondary, The side of the street facing the avenue of oak trees is defined by an avenue in sections of single and double rows of lime trees. By giving street space a layout which is not equilateral, we have responded to the differing adjoining areas and give the street a unique image. At present, street space is divided through the middle by the tram line. The location of the lines is not only to be retained for practical and

schlußbereiche und geben der Straße ein unverwechselbares Profil. Der bisherige Straßenraum wird mittig durch die Straßenbahntrasse geteilt. Die Trasselage wird nicht nur aus funktionalen und ökonomischen Gründen beibehalten. Vielmehr wird somit auch ein räumlich markantes Profil erreicht.

Von besonderer Bedeutung ist der Gleiskörper der Straßenbahn. Wir haben festgestellt, daß die Straßenbahn je nach Art des Gleiskörpers (Schotter, Asphalt, Rasen etc.) unterschiedliche Fahrgeräusche erzeugt. Davon ausgehend wollen wir aus der Gleisanlage ein visuelles und akustisches Ereignis schaffen. Durch unterschiedliche Materialien und Verlegearten wird eine spannungsvolle, über einen Kilometer lange Bildkomposition geschaffen, die auch akustisch different beim Überfahren wahrgenommen wird. Je nach Material und Geschwindigkeit erzeugt die Straßenbahn unterschiedliche Töne, eine neue, leise Alltagsmusik der Stadt. «Hommage à John Cage» nennen wir den Gleiskörper und verweisen damit auf den bedeutenden Künstler und Komponisten, der sich eingehend mit experimenteller Musik, aber auch mit der Verbindung unterschiedlicher Kunstgattungen auseinandergesetzt hat.

Raumbildung und Wegführung des bestehenden Schillerplatzes sind nach dessen Zweiteilung unverständlich geworden. Deshalb wird ein räumlich klar gefaßter Park vorgeschlagen, dessen wichtigste Nutzung nicht mehr der Durchgang, sondern der Aufenthalt geworden ist. In den Randlagen sind wassergebundene Decken als breite Wege und Plätze ausgebildet. Verschiedene Spielbereiche für unterschiedliche Altersstufen, Sitzplätze und der bestehende Baumbestand gewährleisten vielfältige Nutzungsmöglichkeiten und bilden einen stimmungsvollen Ort. Die zentrale Rasenfläche wird von langen und flachen Wasserbecken unterteilt, die eine durchgehende Wasserführung aufweisen.

Bevor die Straße der Nationen zur reinen Wohnstraße mutiert, bildet der neu gestaltete Wilhelm-Külz-Platz einen prägnanten Abschluß. Der rechteckige Platz wird durch ein orthogonales Felsenraster präzisiert, das mit dem bestehenden Baumbestand kontrastiert. Achtundachzig Nationen schicken einen – für ihr Land typischen – Felsen nach Chemnitz. Die Felsen sind gleichzeitig Skulptur und Programm einer vielfältigen, aber gemeinsamen Welt.

Dieter Kienast

economic reasons, it also provides a distinctive spatial image.

The bed of the tracks of the tram is of special importance. We found out that moving trams make different noises depending on the type of bed (ballast, asphalt, grass etc.). Taking this observation as our point of departure, we want to use the mundane tracks to create a visual and acoustic experience. By means of different materials and ways of laying them, an interesting picture composition over one kilometre in length is to be created and will produce different sounds as trams travel over it. Depending on the materials and speed, the trams create different sounds, new, soft everyday music of the city. We call the tracks "Homage to John Cage", a reference to this important artist and composer, who studied experimental music in detail as well as the links between different genres of art.

The spatial structure and means of access on the existing Schillerplatz made no sense after it was divided into two parts. For this reason, a park with a clear spatial definition is proposed; this park is not to serve as a thoroughfare but as a place to spend time. Water-bound surfaces are laid out as wide paths and areas on the periphery. A variety of play areas for different age groups, places to sit and the existing tree population ensure that the square can be used in a number of ways and give it its atmosphere. The central lawn is divided up by elongated, shallow pools which form a continuous system of water.

At the point where Strasse der Nation becomes a purely residential street, the redesigned Wilhelm-Külz-Platz forms a distinctive transition. The quadrangular square is given precision by an orthogonal pattern of boulders, forming a contrast to the existing tree population. Eighty-eight countries are to send a piece of rock which is typical of their country to Chemnitz. The boulders are both sculpture and agenda for a world which is both diverse and needs to find common ground.

Dieter Kienast

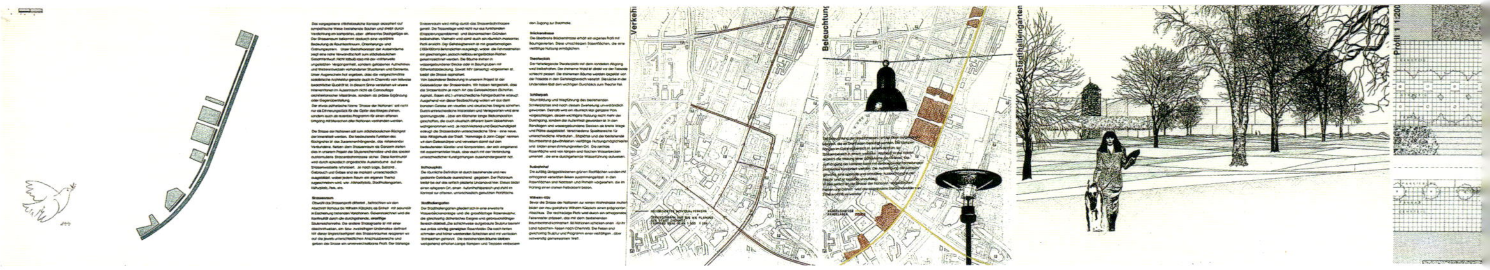

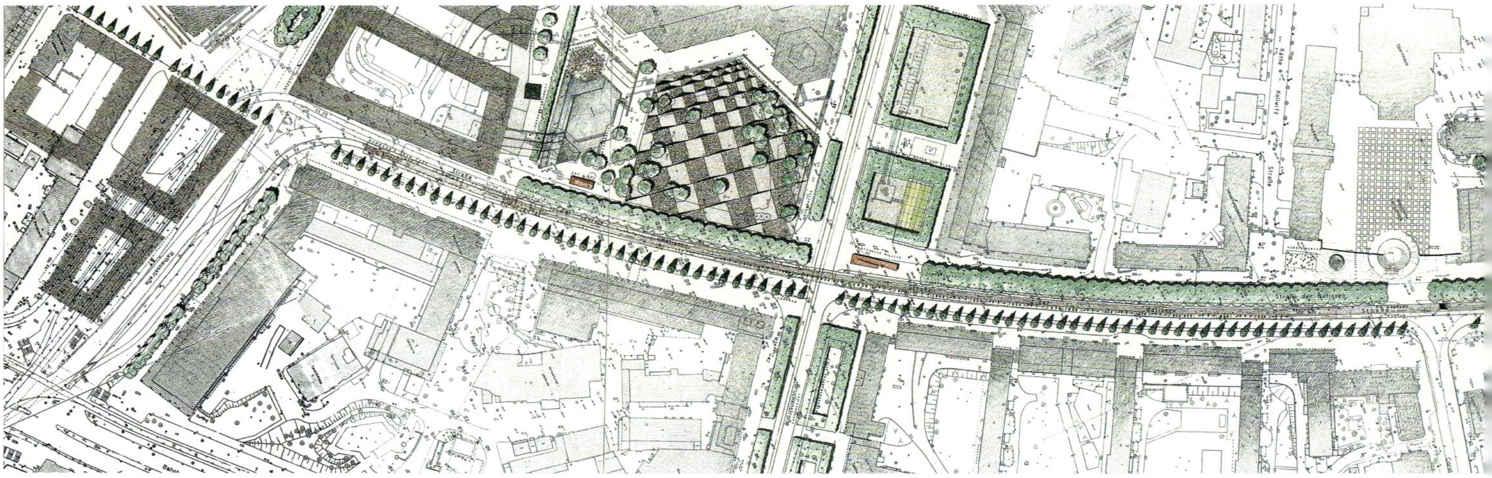

269

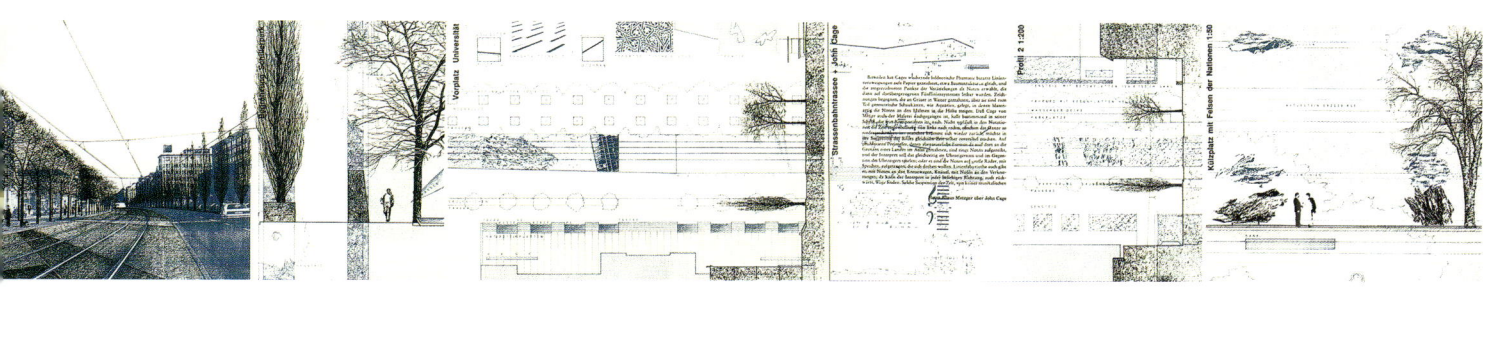

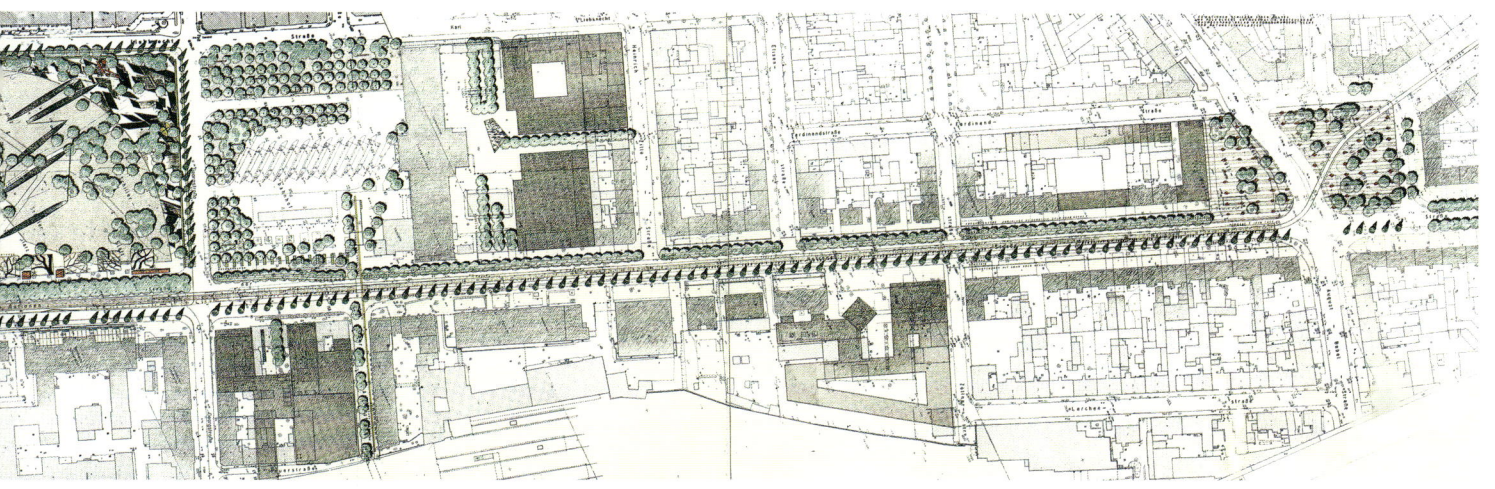

Conrad Gessner Park Zürich Oerlikon

Naturwandel
Ein Paradoxon selbstverständlich, denn Natur steht gleichsam für das Immerwährende, das einzig Beständige, das Ewige. Gewandelt hat sich nicht die Natur, sondern unsere Rezeption von Natur. Dies besonders stark im städtischen Territorium, weil hier Veränderungen umfassend und rasch erfolgen und alltäglich direkt wahrgenommen werden. Es ist eine wesentliche Aufgabe der Disziplin Landschaftsarchitektur, in diesem rasanten Wechsel zeitadäquate Bilder und Vorstellungen zur Gestalt der Stadt und damit auch zur Natur der Stadt zu entwickeln. Diese müssen über die quantitative Verteidigung des Bestandes, über die Implantate ländlicher Natur und über die ökologische Heilserwartung einer ruderalisierten «Rückeroberung» hinausgehen. In der hektischen städtebaulichen Entwicklung steht die Natur der Stadt, der Außenraum für die Langsamkeit. Langsamkeit meint das Pflanzenwachstum, aber auch den Gebrauch, die Materialbeständigkeit und zielt auf die verfeinerte, sinnliche Wahrnehmung der Stadt.

Stadtpark
Das städtebauliche Entwicklungsleitbild Zürich Nord zeigt eine Neuordnung des Gebietes, in der neben den Baufeldern vier öffentliche Parkanlagen ausgewiesen sind. Die nachfolgenden Pläne und der Text stellen unseren Beitrag zum Studienauftrag dar, den das Gartenbau- und Landwirtschaftsamt 1996 für den ersten Park, den «Oerliker Park», ausgelobt hatte.

Ort und Geschichte
Die Geschichte des Ortes wird durch den landschaftlichen und städtebaulichen Wechsel geprägt, der im wesentlichen durch die sozialen und wirtschaftlichen Verhältnisse determiniert ist. Ehemals weit vor den Toren gelegen, bestimmte die Senke des Binzmühlebaches das Aussehen der ursprünglichen Waldlandschaft. Die Zunahme der Bevölkerung bewirkte die landschaftliche Nutzung auch dieser wenig geeigneten Böden. Im 19. und 20. Jahrhundert erfolgte die Industrialisierung der Stadterweiterung Zürichs. Dabei wurde das ländlich geprägte Naturbild

Conrad Gessner Park in Zurich-Oerlikon

Nature in flux
Needless to say a paradox, as nature, so to speak, stands for what is always there, what is constant, everlasting. It is not nature that has changed but our approach to nature. This is particularly perceptible in urban areas as changes taking place there are comprehensive and rapid, and experienced directly on a daily basis. It is one of the essential tasks of the discipline of landscape architecture to develop adequate images and concepts for modern urban design and, hence, for nature in the city in these times of rapid change. Ideas must go beyond defending existing stocks just on account of their sheer quantity, beyond implants in country style and beyond ecology-based expectation of a ruderal-style "reconquest". Given the hectic pace of urban development, nature in the city and outside space stand for gradualness. Gradualness refers to growth of plants, as well as to use, durability of materials and is intended to achieve a more subtle, sensuous perception of the city.

Urban park
The master plan for the urban development in the north of Zurich restructures the area; in addition to the development areas, four public parks are planned. The following plans and text are our contribution to the study commissioned in 1996 by the parks and agriculture department for the first park, the "Oerliker Park".

The place and its history
The history of the place has been shaped by alternating country and urban use that was essentially determined by social and economic factors. Once well outside the city gates, the vale of the Binz millstream characterised the appearance of the original woodland. Increases in population led to agricultural use of this land actually unsuited for the purpose. Industrialisation of the extended Zurich urban area took place in the course of the 19th and 20th centuries. In consequence, countryside nature gave way to a highly fragmented patchwork of urban vegetation determined by human beings. With alternating industrial use and

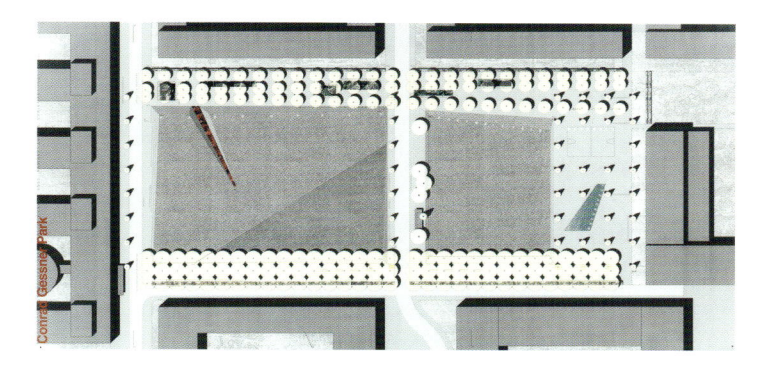

anticipated building development this has become short-lived and transitory. The post-industrial re-structuring of Zurich Oerlikon is intended to preserve the urban character of the Oerlikon park space on a long-term basis.

Nature

Just as nature has changed in our planning area over the course of time, the relationship of human beings to manifestations of nature has also changed. Until well after medieval times, nature was not so much seen as an important basis of life but more as a threat to which the rural population was exposed in everyday life. Fear of nature only faded with increasing awareness of its character.

In the 16th century, Zurich became known throughout Europe for the works of the scholar Conrad Gessner (1516-1565), who, in addition to writing in the fields of history, philology and medicine, also carried out outstanding studies as a naturalist. He was the first scientist to determine the sex organs of plants as the basis of a comprehensive plant systematology and recorded his findings in drawings in his "Catalogus planatarum". He carried out studies on the distribution of plants at different altitudes and also founded a botanical garden. His "Historia animalium" was to be the essential foundation of scientific zoology, depicting and describing some 3,500 mammals, amphibians, reptiles, aquatic animals, and birds. In other words, Gessner laid the foundation of modern natural science and the conception – revolutionary at the time – that nature was not an enemy but the basis for life. Today, nature – or rather its surrogate – is under threat and therefore seen as a luxury. Alienation from nature in our high-technology world has led to yearning for an authentic experience of nature. However, in an urban context, this can only mean propagating nature in a form that also includes aspects of urban life. We understand the redesigning of Oerliker Park as the latest sediment in a story dating back centuries, as a deposit that continues the transformation of nature and its appreciation. To put it another way, not a melancholic reflection on past, more natural forms of life, but rather a process of

durch ein stark fraktioniertes Fleckenmuster anthropogen bestimmter Stadtvegetation abgelöst. Diese ist im Wechsel von industrieller Nutzung und Bauerwartung kurzlebig und transitorisch geworden. Die postindustrielle Neustrukturierung von Zürich Oerlikon sichert jetzt langfristig den Erhalt des städtisch geprägten Oerliker Parkraumes.

Natur

So wie sich die Natur in unserem Planungsgebiet im Verlaufe der Zeit verändert hat, hat sich auch das Verhältnis der Menschen zur äußeren Natur verändert. Bis weit über das Mittelalter hinaus bedeutet Natur weniger Lebensgrundlage als vielmehr Bedrohung im Lebensalltag der Landbevölkerung. Die Angst vor der Natur verliert sich erst mit der zunehmenden Kenntnis ihrer Wesensart.

Zürich wird im 16. Jahrhundert europaweit durch die Arbeiten des Universalgelehrten Conrad Gessner (1516–1565) bekannt, der neben Geschichte, Sprache und Medizin seine hervorragenden Studien als Naturforscher gefertigt hat. Als erster Wissenschaftler bestimmt er die Geschlechtsorgane der Pflanzen zur Grundlage einer umfassenden Pflanzensystematik und hält diese in seinem «Catalogus plantarum» zeichnerisch fest. Er betreibt Studien über die Pflanzenverbreitung in verschiedenen Höhenlagen und gründet zudem einen botanischen Garten. Seine «Historia animalium» wird zur eigentlichen Grundlage der wissenschaftlichen Zoologie, indem er 3500 Säugetiere, Amphibien, Reptilien, Wassertiere und Vögel darstellt und beschreibt. Gessner bereitet somit die Grundlage zur modernen Naturwissenschaft und zur damals revolutionären Auffassung, daß Natur nicht als Feindbild, sondern als Lebensgrundlage zu begreifen ist. Heute ist Natur – oder besser ihre Ersatzformen – bedroht und damit gleichzeitig kostbar geworden. Mit der Entfremdung von Natur in unserer hochtechnisierten Welt wächst die Sehnsucht nach authentischer Naturerfahrung. Im städtischen Territorium kann dies nur heißen, eine Natur der Stadt zu propagieren, die urbanes Leben mit einschließt. Wir verstehen die Neugestaltung des Oerliker Parkes als die jüngste Sedimentation einer Jahrhunderte alten Geschichte, die den Wandel ihrer Natur und

heightening our awareness of the particular cultural and natural history of the place.

The park

The park is defined by a three-row population of trees to the north and the south and by common hornbeam to the west and the east. The central section of the park is defined by topographically differentiated areas of grass. They are surrounded by broad areas of gravel in the shape of a horseshoe. The road dissects the park and also marks an ecological difference between its two halves. Owing to the presence of hazardous waste, the western section is to be sealed with a layer of asphalt one metre below the surface, whereas the eastern section has normal soil structure. Areas of trees and grass make up the underlying simple structure of the park. The three rows of trees to the north consist entirely of Tilia cordata "Greenspire". The rows, which are not perfectly aligned with each other, permit different perspectives and stand for order and its slight deviations. In contrast, the tree area to the south consists of a strictly orthogonal grid of different species of trees. 93 different deciduous trees make up a grove which constitutes a new form of the 20th-century aboretum. The topographically irregular area of grass in the left section of the park provides open space. The embankments have different forms. Untreated sheets of steel are envisaged for the north and south sides, whereby the curved form on the north side is likely to be of particular interest to inline skaters. The lateral embankments are conceived as steps or wide terraces for sitting. The clearly defined incision serves as a link between the promenade and the area of grass. This incision takes up and adresses the basis of all growth – the soil. Resembling scientific display cases, the photographs of all past and present soil types that existed or exist here are made visible by the area of glass let into the ground. The broad south and north promenades are framed by hedges; their species being chosen to correlate to the tree areas. A uniform hedge of limes is envisaged for the north, a mixed hedge for the south. We understand the "islands" that have been marked as a metaphor for subsequent development

deren Wertschätzung fortschreibt. Kein melancholischer Blick also auf vergangene, naturnahere Lebensformen, wohl aber das Bewußtsein schärfen für die besondere Kultur- und Naturgeschichte des Ortes.

Park

Der Park wird durch dreireihige Baumkörper im Norden und Süden und Säulenhainbuchen im Westen und Osten zusammengefaßt. Der zentrale Parkteil ist durch topographisch differenzierte Rasenfelder bestimmt. Diese werden durch breite Kiesflächen U-förmig umschlossen. Die Straße bildet die mittige Zäsur, die zugleich auch eine ökologische Differenz der zwei Parkteile markiert. Der westliche Teil wird aufgrund vorhandener Altlasten einen Meter unterhalb der Oberfläche mit einer Asphaltschicht versiegelt, während der östliche Teil einen normalen Bodenaufbau aufweist. Baum- und Rasenfelder bilden die einfache Grundstruktur des Parkes. Die nördlichen drei Baumreihen sind einheitlich mit Tilia cordata «Greenspire» bepflanzt. Die leicht gegeneinander verschobenen Reihen zeigen wechselnde Perspektiven und thematisieren Ordnung und deren leichte Abweichung. Im Gegensatz dazu zeigt das südliche Baumfeld einen strengen, orthogonalen Baumraster, in dem jeder Baum eine andere Art aufweist. 93 verschiedene Laubbaumarten bilden einen Hain, der auch gleichzeitig eine neue Form des Aboretums des 20. Jahrhunderts darstellt. Im linken Parkteil bildet das topographisch geknickte Rasenfeld freien Raum. Die Böschungen sind differenziert ausgebildet. Nord- und südseitig sind unbehandelte Stahlplatten vorgesehen, wobei die Bogenform auf der Nordseite besonders die Inlineskater interessieren dürfte. Die Seitenböschungen sind als Treppen oder Sitzstufen konzipiert. Der markante Einschnitt dient der Verbindung der Promenade mit dem Rasenfeld. Er thematisiert und verweist gleichzeitig auf die Grundlage allen Wachstums – den Boden. Wissenschaftlichen Schaukästen gleich werden die Photographien aller hier vorgekommenen und vorhandenen Böden durch das Bodenglas sichtbar gemacht. Die breiten Promenaden im Süden und Norden werden randseitig mit Hecken gefaßt, wobei deren Arten-

in collaboration with different interest groups. Playgrounds for small children, places to sit and rest, equipment for games and sports are examples of what could be realised.

The central section of the right-hand section of the park is defined by the existing, sunken football pitch. We understand ecology as also being an economical use of elements. The grass pitch is framed by gravel areas of differing widths. The eastern part is bounded by European hornbeam which has been planted orthogonally and provides spatial transparency. As an analogy to the incision in the left-hand section of the park, the area of glass let into the ground display photographs of once native species of plants and vegetation units. Together with the plants that are now in place, the compendium serves as a comprehensive guide to the nature of the place. The water space is ambivalent – it can be perceived as either a decorative pool or one intended for paddling – and is a contemplative reference to the surrogate of the original marshland.

Homage

As part of the development of the northern part of Zurich, the city of Zurich paid tribute to commendable artists and politicians in the way it named new streets, squares, alleys and parks. For this reason, rather than the unimaginative name of "Oerliker Park", we propose that the park be named after a person with connections to Zurich who was well-known beyond the borders of Switzerland, namely after the naturalist Conrad Gessner. The public garden or park should not only to bear his name, but also be a reference to his lifetime work – a homage to Gessner – as well as a modern discourse on a changed approach to nature.

Dieter Kienast

wahl mit den Baumfeldern korreliert. Im Norden ist eine einheitliche Lindenhecke, im Süden eine verschiedenartige Mischhecke vorgesehen. Die eingezeichneten «Inseln» verstehen wir als Metapher eines späteren, in Zusammenarbeit mit verschiedenen Interessengruppen zu realisierenden Ausbaus. Kleinkinderspielplätze, Ruheplätze, Spiel- und Sportgeräte seien als Beispiele einer konkreten Umsetzung genannt.

Im rechten Parkteil bestimmt der tiefliegende, vorhandene Fußballplatz die Mitte. Ökologie verstehen wir auch als ökonomischen Einsatz der Elemente. Das Rasenspielfeld wird umrahmt von unterschiedlich breiten Kiesplätzen. Der Ostteil wird durch orthogonal gepflanzte Säulenhainbuchen räumlich transparent abgeschlossen. In Analogie zum Erdschnitt im linken Parkteil zeigen die im Boden eingelassenen Schaukästen Photographien am Ort heimisch gewesener Pflanzenarten und Vegetationseinheiten. Zusammen mit den real existierenden Pflanzen erschließt sich das Kompendium der umfassenden Ortsnatur. Das Wasserfeld wird ambivalent als Zier- oder Planschbecken wahrgenommen und verweist bei nachdenklicher Betrachtung auf das Surrogat des ursprünglich vorhandenen Feuchtgebietes.

Hommage

Die Stadt Zürich hat im Rahmen der Gebietsentwicklung von Zürich Nord bei der Benennung der neu entstandenen Straßen, Plätze, Gassen und Parkanlagen verdienstvolle Persönlichkeiten aus Kunst und Politik geehrt. Wir schlagen deshalb vor, anstelle des einfachen Namen «Oerliker Park» uns eines Zürcher Namens zu erinnern, der hinsichtlich der Erforschung von Natur weit über die Landesgrenzen bekannt geworden ist, dem des Naturforschers Conrad Gessner. Der öffentliche Garten oder Park erinnert nicht nur an den Namen, sondern zeigt auch die inhaltliche Verbindung zu seinem Lebenswerk – eine Homage an Gessner – mehr aber noch eine rezente Auseinandersetzung mit sich gewandelter Rezeption von Natur.

Dieter Kienast

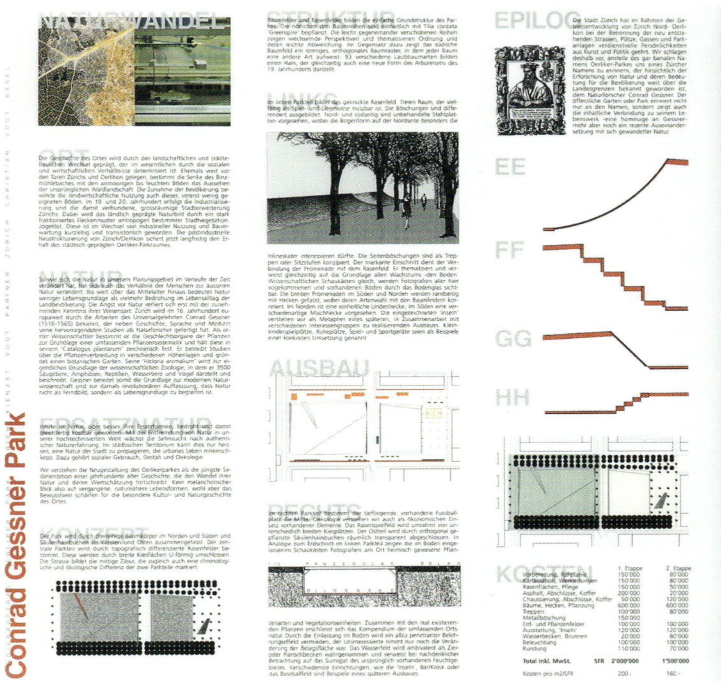

Conrad Gessner Park

ERNST · VOGT · PARTNER ZÜRICH · KÖNIZ/BERN · BASEL

NATURWANDEL

Die Geschichte des Ortes wird auch durch die landschaftlichen und städtebaulichen Wechsel geprägt, der im wesentlichen durch die sozialen und wirtschaftlichen Verhältnisse determiniert ist. Ehemals war der Raum zwischen den Toren Zürichs und Oerlikon gelegen, bestimmt von der Senke des Bruchmühlebachs und den anmoorigen bis feuchten Böden das Aussehen der ursprünglichen Waldlandschaft. Die Zunahme der Bevölkerung bewirkte die landwirtschaftliche Nutzung auch dieser, vorerst wenig ergiebigen Böden. Im 19. und 20. Jahrhundert erfolgte die Industrialisierung und die damit verbundene, grossräumige Stadtentwicklung Zürichs. Dabei wird das ländlich geprägte Naturbild durch ein stark funktionelles Fleckenmuster anthropogen bestimmter Stadtvegetation abgelöst. Diese ist ein Wechsel mit industrieller Nutzung und Bauerwartung ausdrückt und transitorisch geworden. Die postindustrielle Neustrukturierung von Zürich/Oerlikon sichert jetzt langfristig den Erhalt des städtisch geprägten Oerlikon-Parkraumes.

NATUR

Sowie sich die Natur in unserem Planungsgebiet im Verlaufe der Zeit verändert hat, hat sich auch das Verhältnis der Menschen zur äusseren Natur verändert. Je weit der das Mittelalter hinaus bedeutet Natur weniger Lebensgrundlage als vielmehr Bedrohung im Lebensalltag der Landbevölkerung. Die Angst vor Natur verliert sich erst mit der zunehmenden Kenntnis. Peter Wiesemann Zürich wird im 16. Jahrhundert mit Conrad Gessner (1516-1565) bekannt, der neben Geschichte, Sprache und Medizin seine hervorragenden Studien als Naturforscher gefertigt hat. Als einer der Wissenschaftler bestimmt sich die Geschichtsgruppe der Pflanzen zur Grundlage einer umfassenden Pflanzensystematik und hält diese in seinem "Catalogus plantarum" zeichnerisch fest. Er betreibt Studien über die Pflanzenverteilung in verschiedenen Höhenlagen und gründet einen botanischen Garten. Sein "Historia animalium" wird zu einer Grundlage der wissenschaftlichen Zoologie, in dem er 3500 Säugetiere, Amphibien, Reptilien, Wassertiere und Vögel darstellt und beschreibt. Gessner bereitet somit die Grundlage zu modernen Naturwissenschaft und zur damals revolutionären Auffassung, dass Natur nicht als Feindbild, sondern als Lebensgrundlage zu begreifen ist.

ERSATZNATUR

Natur ist keine, oder besser, ihre Existenzform bedroht sind in unserer hochtechnisierten Welt. Im Willen der Sehnsucht nach authentischer Naturerfahrung. Im städtischen Territorium kann dies nur horizont, eine Natur die Stadt zu propagieren, die urbanes Leben mitvorstellt. Dazu gehört sozialer Gebrauch, Gestalt und Ökologie.

Wir verstehen die Neugestaltung des Oerlikonparks als die jüngste Segmentierung einer jahrhundertelangen Geschichte, die den Wandel einer Natur und deren Wechselklang fortschreibt. Eine melancholische Blick auf vergangene naturnähere Lebensformen, wohl aber das Bewusstsein schärfen für die besondere Kultur- und Naturgeschichte des Ortes.

KONZEPT

Der Park wird durch Bewährte Baumkörper im Norden und Süden und in der Parklandschaft des Wiesenlandes Otto zusammengefasst. Der extrale Park wird durch topographisch differenzierte Rasenfelder. Die Strasse bildet die mittige Zäsur, die zugleich auch eine chronologische und ökologische Differenz markiert.

STRUKTUR

Baumfelder und Rasenfelder bilden die erodierte Grundstruktur des Parkes. Die nördlichen Baumfelder aus Feldahorn mit Tilia cordata "Greenspire" bepflanzt. Die licht gegeneinander verschobenen Reihen zeigen wechselseitige Perspektiven und thematisieren Ordnung und deren kurze Abweichung, im Gegensatz dazu zeigt das südliche Baumfeld im strengen, orthogonalen Baumraster, in dem jeder Baumart eine andere Art aufweist. 93 verschiedene Laubbäume bilden einen Hain, der gleichsam auch eine neue Form des Arboretums des 19. Jahrhunderts darstellt.

LINKS

Im linken Parkteil bildet das gestreckte Rasenfeld freien Raum, der vielfältig als Spiel- und Liegewiese nutzbar ist. Die Böschungen sind differenziert ausgebildet: Nord- und Südseite wird unterschiedliche Sitzplätzen vorgesehen, wobei die Bogenform auf der Nordseite besonders die Inlineskater interessieren dürfte. Die Seitenböschungen sind als Treppen oder Sitzstufen konzipiert. Der markante Einschnitt dient der Verbindung der Promenade mit dem Rasenfeld. Im Bowlerlust wird gleichwertig auf die Grundlage allen Wachstums »den Boden«. Wissenschaftlichen Schaukasten gleich, werden Fotografien aller hier vorkommenden und vorhandenen Böden durch des Bodenfeld sichtbar. Die breiten Promenaden im Süden und Norden werden randseitig mit Hecken gefasst, deren Artenwahl mit dem Baumfeld korrespondiert. In Norden ist eine einheitliche Lindenhecke, im Süden eine verschiedenartige Mischhecke umgesetzen. Die eingewachsenen "Inseln" verstehen wir als Sonderplätze, in Zusammenarbeit mit verschiedenen Interessengruppen zu realisierenden Ausbauten. Kleinkinderspielplätze, Rutschbäume, Spiel- und Sportgeräte seien als Beispiele einer konkreten Umsetzung genannt.

AUSBAU

Zertenten und Vegetationseinheiten. Zusammen mit der real existierenden Pflanzen erschliesst sich das Kompendium der umfassenden Ortsnatur. Durch die Einbeziehung im Boden wird ein allzu penetranter Belichtungseffekt vermieden. Der Deckel wird durch orthogonal gepflanzte Säulenhanbüchen räumlich neuerschlossen. In Analogie zum Einschnitt im linken Parkteil zeigen die im Boden eingelassenen Schaukasten Fotografien aller im Perimeter gewesene Pflanzenarten und Vegetationseinheiten.

EPILOG

Die Stadt Zürich hat im Rahmen der Gebietsentwicklung von Zürich-Nord-Oerlikon an der Benennung der neu entstehenden Strassen, Plätze, Gassen und Parkanlagen verdienstvolle Persönlichkeiten aus Kunst und Politik gefragt. Wir schlagen deshalb vor, anstelle des gar banalen Namens "Oerlikon-Park" uns einen Zürcher Namens zu erinnern, der hinsichtlich der Bedeutung für die Bevölkerung und über der Landesgrenzen bekannt geworden ist, des Naturforschers Conrad Gessner. Der öffentliche Garten oder Park erinnert nicht nur an den Namen, sondern zeigt auch die gestaltete Verbindung zu seinem Lebenswerk. »eine Hommage an Gessner sowie auch eine recente Auseinandersetzung mit sich wandelnder Natur.

KOSTEN

	1. Etappe	2. Etappe
Vorbereitung, Baustelle	150'000	80'000
Kleinarchitektur, Werkleitungen	150'000	80'000
Rasenflächen, Pflege	150'000	90'000
Asphalt, Abschlüsse, Koffer	200'000	20'000
Chaussierung, Abschlüsse, Koffer	50'000	120'000
Bäume, Hecken, Pflanzung	600'000	600'000
Treppen	150'000	80'000
Metallbelag	150'000	
Erd- und Pflanzenbelger	100'000	100'000
Ausstattung, "Inseln"	150'000	120'000
Wasserbecken, Brunnen	20'000	80'000
Beleuchtung	100'000	100'000
Rundung	110'000	70'000
Total inkl. MwSt. SFR	**2'000'000**	**1'500'000**
Kosten pro m2/SFR	200.-	160.-

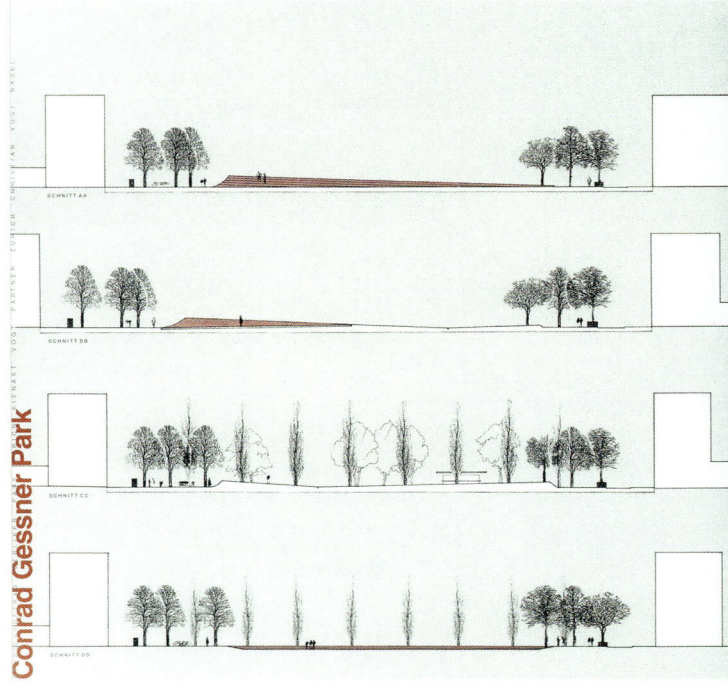

Töölönlahtipark Helsinki

Das Planungsgebiet ist von der Konfrontation landschaftlicher und städtischer Strukturen geprägt. Außergewöhnlich ist dabei, daß es sich nicht, wie üblich, in der Peripherie, sondern im Zentrum der Stadt befindet. Im Kontrast zwischen Gebautem und Natürlichem wird die jeweilige Eigenart in verstärktem Maße wahrgenommen. Die städtische Struktur wird durch Blockrandbebauung, markante Einzelgebäude und Geleiseanlage geprägt. Die landschaftliche Struktur zeigt ein hügeliges Gelände mit dem eingeschlossenen Töölönlathisee. Diese natürlichen Gegebenheiten sind stark anthropogen überformt und bilden eine Parklandschaft mit reizvollem Wechselspiel zwischen gestalteten und natürlichen Teilen. Die Gestaltung folgt dabei der Grundkonzeption des Englischen Landschaftsparks, in dem der «genius of place» entdeckt und weiterentwickelt wird. Lediglich im Bereich des «Botanical garden» und «Winter garden» werden architektonisch gestaltete Gartenteile sichtbar.

Das Konzept ist aus der Ortsgeschichte entwickelt und stellt eine rezente Stadtlandschaft dar. Im Westen, Süden und Osten wird der neue Park klar durch Bauten gefaßt. In Ergänzung zu vorhandenen und in Bau befindlichen Gebäuden sind weitere öffentliche Geschäfts- und Bürogebäude geplant. Die städtebauliche Fassung wird durch das durchgehende Kanalsystem verstärkt, das einerseits ein attraktives Vorgelände zu den Bauten darstellt, andererseits den neuen Parkteil zur Insel werden läßt. Der Park wird durch die Ebene und die skulptural geformte Topographie bestimmt.

Mit der neu geschaffenen Topographie werden gezielte Ein-, Aus- und Durchblicke, aber auch Verhüllungen erreicht. Während die umliegenden Hügel natürliche Ausprägung zeigen, sind die Parkhügel streng geometrisiert. Der 8 Meter hohe Birkenhügel hat wie seine «natürlichen» Nachbarn eine Felsenkuppe ohne Baumbestand. Der Blick ist somit introvertiert und fällt auf den runden Waldspiegel, in dessen glattpolierten Granitplatten sich die Bäume und der Himmel spiegeln. Zur Ostseite bilden langgezogene Erdpyramiden einen räumlichen Abschluß. Die Flanken sind unterschiedlich ausformuliert: Die Hügelostseite ist mit Bäumen akzentuiert, während die Westseite

Töölönlahti Park in Helsinki

The planning area is characterised as a place where town and country structures meet. The unusual thing about it is that this does not occur on the edge of a town where we would normally expect it, but in the centre. In the contrast between the manmade and the natural, the special characteristics of each are very noticeable. The town structure is characterised by perimeter block development, by prominent individual buildings and by a railway line. The country section consists of a hilly area surrounding the Töölönlahti lake. This natural environment has been greatly altered by man and forms an area of parkland with the designed and natural elements interacting to create an attractive whole. The design follows the basic concept of an English landscape garden, where the "genius of place" is revealed and developed. Architecturally designed gardens are only to be found in the area of the botanical garden and the winter garden.

The concept was developed from the history of the location, and represents a living townscape. To the west, the south and the east, the new park's boundary is clearly defined by buildings. In addition to the existing buildings and those under construction, further public, commercial and office buildings are planned. The surrounding urban development is intensified by the canal system which passes through it, on the one hand providing an attractive foreground for the buildings, and, on the other hand, making the new section of park into a large island. The park's appearance is determined by the plateau, the sculptured topography.

The newly created topography will result in well-placed views into, across and from the park, but will also hide some features. Whilst the surrounding hills have a natural shape, the park's hills are strictly geometric in design. The 8-metre high birch hill has, like its "natural" neighbours, a treeless rocky top. This directs the eye back in towards the round "wood mirror", whose highly polished granite slabs reflect the trees and the sky. On the eastern side, the area is bounded by elongated pyramids of earth. The margins differ from one another; the eastern sides of the hills are accentuated with trees, whereas the west side is partly covered with flat grassy terraces. The main approach is

teilweise mit flachen Rasenstufen versehen ist. Den markanten Auftakt bildet die südliche Felspyramide, auf der sich spiralförmig ein Vegetationsband mit rockflowers zur Spitze windet. Unter der Eiche geniessen wir einen erhabenen Blick auf Stadt, Park und Landschaft.

Die Wasserkanäle sind unterschiedlich breit ausgebildet. Der Hauptkanal ist nahe an die Finlandia herangerückt, im Wasser spiegeln sich die markanten Gebäude und die davor in weitem Abstand gepflanzten Pappeln. Das Seeufer wird im Parkteil neu gefaßt, die bestehenden Inseln werden mit Ausnahme der Rousseauinsel integriert. Die Wasserkante des Parkes kann bei genauerer Betrachtung als landschaftsarchitektonische Transformation der Finlandia-Umrisse gelesen werden.

Mit der Baumpflanzung wird nicht nur Raumbildung erreicht, vielmehr zielt sie auf eine eigenständige Stimmung und Atmosphäre der verschiedenen Park- und Stadtteile. Populus italica wird auf der Nord- und Westseite des Seeufers an markanten Stellen und entlang des Hauptkanals gepflanzt. Tilia vulgaris sind als Alleebäume entlang der Straßen vorgesehen. Die Hügelostseite ist mit gemischtem Baumbestand aus Pinus sylvestris, Fraxinus excelsior, Acer platanoides, Quercus robur, Sorbus aucuparia, Populus tremula, etc. bepflanzt. Die Ulmeninseln sind räumlich mit Hecken gefaßt.

Die Erschließung des Parkes erfolgt über ein einfaches, großmaschiges Wegnetz, womit einmal mehr die Differenz zu den angrenzenden Parkanlagen mit den kleinteiligen Erschließungen manifest wird. Um den See ist ein Rundwanderweg vorgesehen. Die Erschließung und Anbindung an die Stadt erfolgt mittels einfacher Brücken. Auf die Parkierungsanlage über den Geleisen wird aus landschaftsarchitektonischer Sicht bewußt verzichtet. Die Geleiseanlage ist ein erhaltenswertes kulturhistorisches Zeugnis, das keiner Überdeckung oder Verschönerung bedarf.

Mit der Neugestaltung des Töölönlathiparks wird den vorhandenen Parkanlagen das jüngste Mitglied einer «Parkfamilie» beigestellt, das erkennbar gleichen Ursprungs ist, und dennoch Jugend und Eigenständigkeit zeigt. Er ist Solitär und gleichzeitig Teil des verbindenden Ganzen, mit seinem Hang zur Geometrie zeigt er die Liebe zur Stadt. Er wird zum Ort des vielfältigen Gebrauchs, in Gemeinschaft oder Zweisamkeit.

Dieter Kienast

formed by the southern rocky pyramid, up which there winds a spiral strip of vegetation with alpine flowers, leading up to the summit. From beneath the oak tree we have a wonderful view down over the town, park and countryside.

The canals are of varying widths. The main canal passes close by the Finlandia building; the water reflects the prominent buildings and the widely separated poplars in front of them. The bank of the lake will be given new surroundings in the park section. With the exception of the Rousseau Island, the existing islands will be integrated. The water's edge in the park can, on closer inspection, be seen as the transformation into landscape features of the outlines of the Finlandia building.

As well as creating an impression of space, the planting of trees is intended to give a distinctive mood and atmosphere to the various sections of the park and the town. Populus italica is being planted in prominent positions on the northern and western sides of the lake shore, and along the main canal. Tilia vulgaris are planned along the roads to form avenues. The eastern sides of the hills are planted with a mixture of Pinus sylvestris, Fraxinus excelsior, Acer platanoides, Quercus robur, Sorbus aucuparia, Populus tremula, etc. The "elm islands" are bordered by hedges.

Access to the park is via a simple, wide network of paths, which serves to emphasise the distinction between this and the neighbouring park facilities with their segmented access routes. A walkway is planned to go around the lake. Access and links to the town are via simple bridges. It has been decided, for landscaping reasons, not to create a parking area over the railway. The railway line is a piece of cultural history which is worth preserving and does not need to be covered up or improved.

The redesigning of the Töölönlathi park will place alongside the existing park facilities the newest member of a "park family", which can be seen as having the same origins, whilst showing its youth and individuality. This park is a unique gem and, at the same time, part of the whole area to which it is linked; its geometric tendencies show its attachment to the town. It will be a many-faceted place to be enjoyed by large crowds, small groups and couples alike.

Dieter Kienast

Starting position

The planning area is characterised as a place where town and country features meet. the unusual thing about it is that this does not occur on the edge of a town where we would normally expect it, but in the centre. In the contrast between the man-made and the natural, the special characteristics of each are very noticeable. The town structure is characterised by the "Gründerzeit" development, by prominent individual buildings and by a railway line. The country section consists of a hilly area surrounding the Töölönlahti-lahte. This natural environment has been greatly altered by man, and appears as an area of parkland with the designed and natural elements interacting to form an attractive whole. The design follows the basic concept of an English landscape garden, where the "genius of place" is revealed and developed. The visitor is led via a close-knit network of paths to varying views of parkland and countryside. Architectonically designed gardens are only to be found in the area of the botanical garden and the winter garden.

Concept

The concept developed out of the history of the location, and represents a living townscape. This shows the relationship between the existing park facilities and parts of the town, and at the same time emphasises their individuality. To the west, the south and the east, the new park's boundary will be clearly defined by buildings. In addition to the current buildings and those under construction, further public, commercial and office buildings are planned. The surrounding urban development is intensified by the canal system which passes through it, on the one hand providing an attractive foreground for the buildings, and on the other hand making the new section of park into a large island. The water's edge in the park can, on closer inspection, be seen as the transformation into landscape features of the outlines of the Finlandia building. The park's appearance is determined by the plateau, the sculptured topography, and effective use of space for tree planting.

Topography

The newly created topography will result in well-placed views into and from the park, but will also become tourist attractions. Whilst the surrounding hills have a natural shape, the park's hills are strictly geometric in design. The 8 metre high birch hill, like its "natural" neighbours, has a treeless rocky top. This directs the eye back in towards the round "wood" microcosm. The highly polished granite slabs reflect the trees and the sky. On the eastern side the area is bounded by elongated pyramids of earth. The margins differ from one another; the eastern sides of the hills are accentuated with trees, whereas the west side is part-covered with flat grassy terraces. The main approach is formed by the southern rocky pyramid, up which there winds a spiral strip of vegetation with alpine flowers, leading up to the 12 metre high summit. From beneath the oak tree we have a wonderful view down over the town, park and countryside.

Water

The canals are of varying widths. The main canal goes close to the Finlandia building, the waters reflecting the prominent buildings and the widely separated plateau in front of them. The back of the lake will be given new surroundings in the park section. With the exception of the Rousseau Island, the existing islands will be integrated.

Vegetation

As well as creating an impression of space, the planting of trees is intended to give a distinctive mood and atmosphere to the various sections of the park and the town. Populus italica is being planted in prominent positions on the lake shore (northern and western sides), and along the main canal. Tilia vulgaris are planted along the roads to form avenues. The eastern sides of the hills are planted with a mixture of Pinus sylvestris, Fraxinus excelsior, Acer platanoides, Quercus robur, Sorbus aucuparia, Populus tremula, etc. The "etto islands" are bordered by hedges.

Access

Access to the park is via a simple, wide network of paths, which serves to emphasise the distinction between this and the neighbouring park facilities with their segmented access routes. A walkway is planned right around the lake. Access and links to the town are simple and direct. It has been decided, for landscaping reasons, to create a parking area over the railway line. The railway line is a piece of cultural history which is worth preserving, and which does not need to be built up or improved.

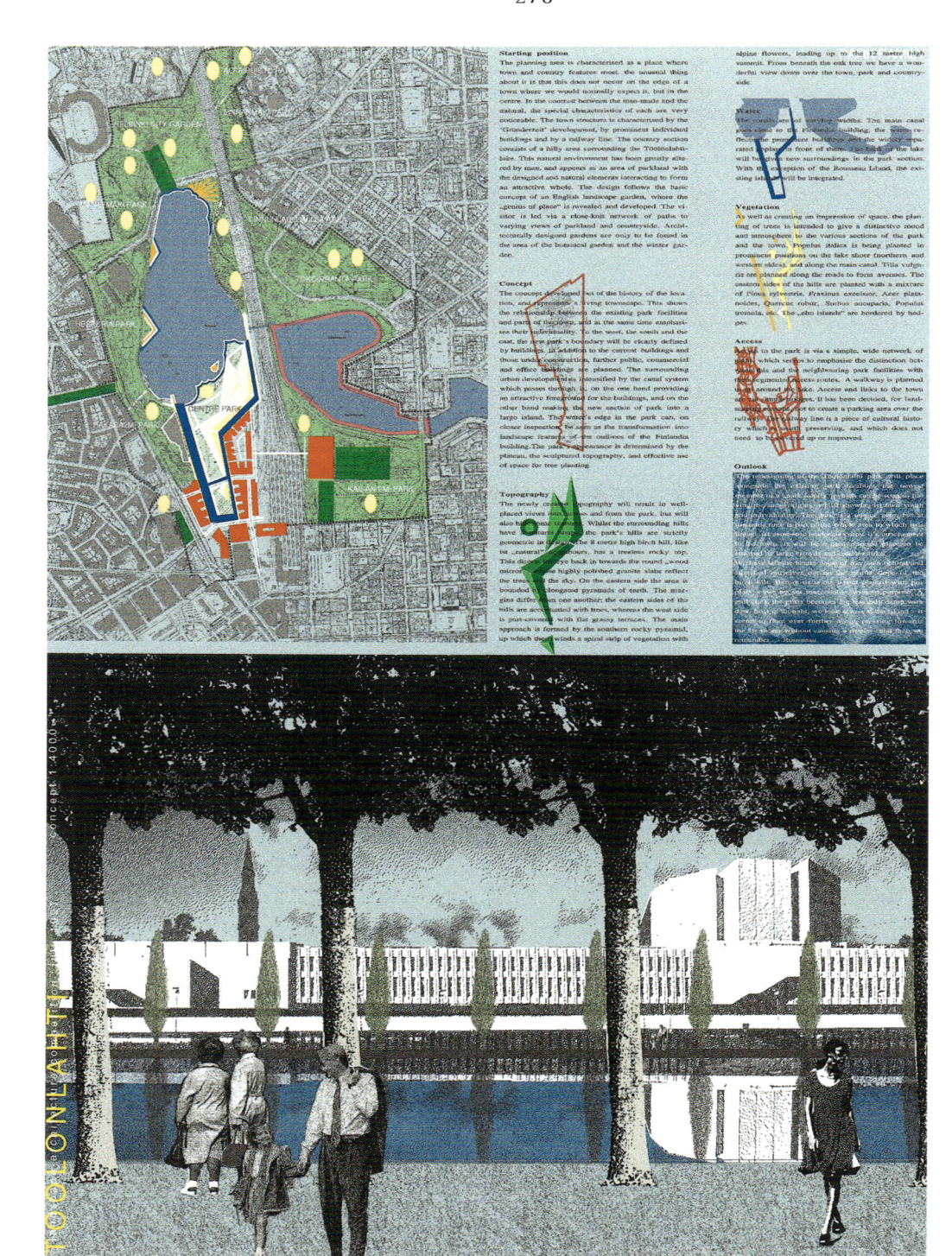

Outlook

The reshape of the Töölönlahti park will place alongside the existing park facilities the newest element in a park family which can be seen as illustrating the whole history of parks in Helsinki and worldwide. The park is a living story-book situated at prominent locations within a conurbation in its history, it will be an important milestone on the way to a new round of development. Instead of a closed and fixed form, the new park grows in an open-ended way and is open to all kinds of new interpretations. "Nature never deceives us; it is we who deceive ourselves. Look above, look around, and never forget what you have in front of you — a stream and the stream will always go on saying the same thing." — Rousseau

TÖÖLÖNLAHTI

PARK FAMILY

TÖÖLÖNLAHTI

PARK FAMILY

PARK FAMILY

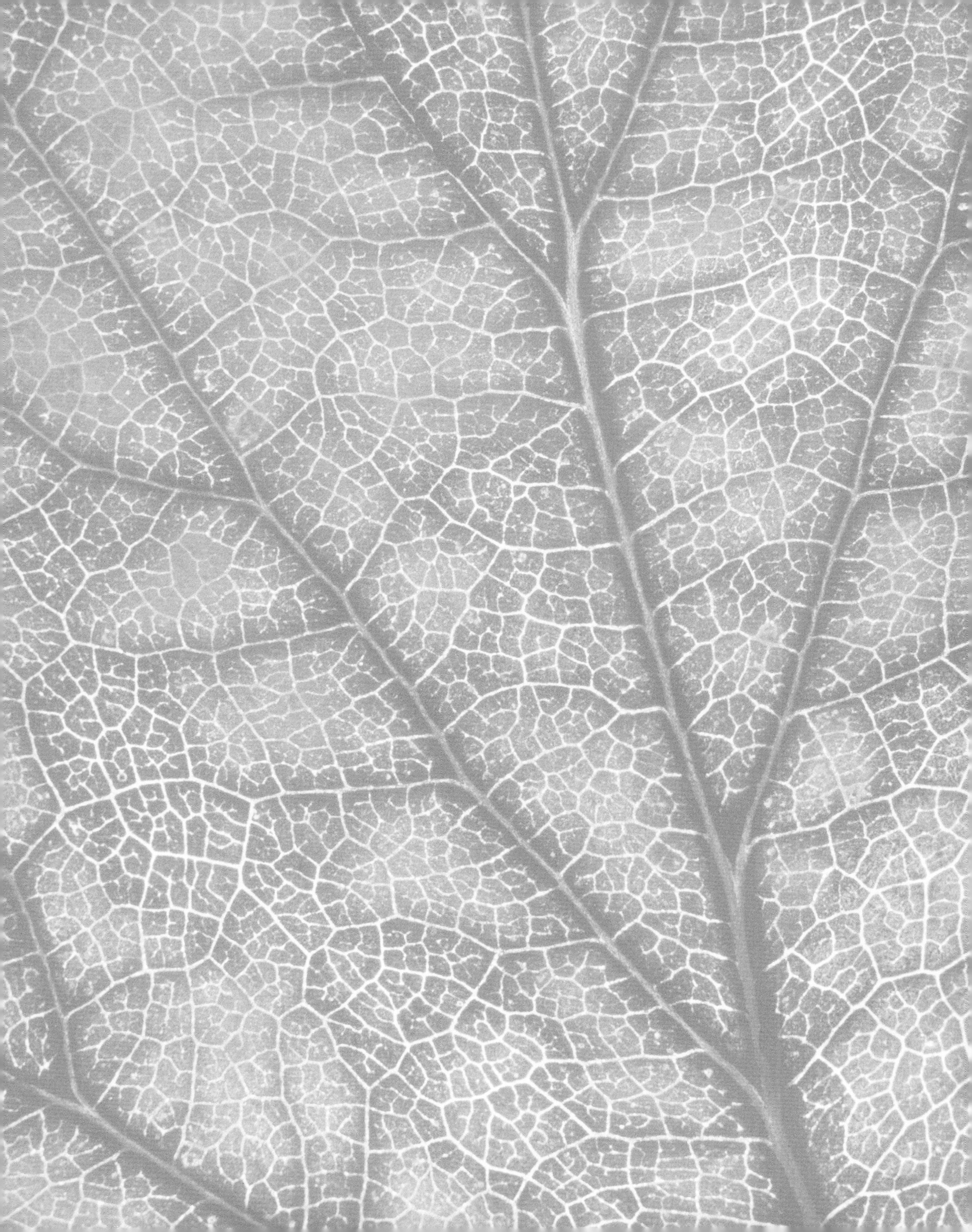

Fährtenlese

Wirkungen des protagonistischen Schaffens von Dieter Kienast

Die Gegenwart könne ihre bedeutenden und charakteristischen Leistungen in der Regel nicht beurteilen, weil ihr einerseits die zeitliche Distanz fehle, um das Geschaffene kritisch zu reflektieren und weil sie zudem nicht wisse, was nachfolgt. Das wird zumindest in Fachkreisen der Landschaftsarchitektur- und Gartenkunstgeschichte immer wieder betont und zum Anlaß genommen, jahrzehntelang mit Orientierungsversuchen zu warten, bis sich die Sedimente der Geschichte endlich abgesetzt haben. Vielleicht ist seit dem Winter 1998 tatsächlich noch nicht genügend Zeit vergangen, um zu einer bleibenden Einschätzung darüber zu gelangen, wie sich das Denken, Entwerfen und Lehren von Dieter Kienast, sein landschaftsarchitekto-

Dieter Kienast, 1996

Scanning Tracks

Effects of the principal creative work of Dieter Kienast

The present is not, as a rule, able to judge its significant and characteristic achievements as, on the one hand, it does not have the necessary temporal distance to reflect critically on what has been created and, on the other hand, does not know what will follow. At least, this is what is repeatedly pointed out by experts on the history of landscape architecture and garden art and used as grounds to postpone orientation attempts for decades until the sediments of history have finally settled. Perhaps the time that has elapsed since the winter of 1998 has indeed not been enough to make a lasting appraisal of the effects that the thinking, designs and teaching of Dieter Kienast, as well as his creative work in the field of landscape architecture have had on landscape architecture design and its perception. However, the continuing international interest in his work and the numerous publications by and on Dieter Kienast would indicate that his creative ideas for the development of landscape architecture have on no account been restricted to Switzerland since the end of the 20th century. A first attempt to trace the effects of the principal creative work of Dieter Kienast reveals closely interlinked signs at least as numerous as the propositions he himself puts forward. Many of the signs are still very fresh and easy to read, some are yet to be discovered, and others already covered over threatened by complete obliteration if the time span becomes too great.

The most enduring and direct contributions made by Dieter Kienast were undoubtedly those which benefited students, assistants, and staff when he taught at the University of Applied Sciences Rapperswil, the University of Karlsruhe, and the Swiss Federal Institute of Technology Zurich. However, it was only at Rapperswil, the single technical school of landscape architecture in German-speaking Switzerland that he trained young landscape architects between 1980 and 1991. In his capacity of professor for garden architecture, Dieter Kienast taught – in close association with colleagues from neighbouring disciplines – numerous self-assured landscape architects, who today are

Zulauf Seippel und Schweingruber: Museumspark Kalkriese

Vogt Landschaftsarchitekten: Esplanade der Allianz Arena in München / Esplanade of the Allianz Arena in Munich

nisches Schaffen, auf die Gestaltung und Wahrnehmung von Landschaftsarchitektur ausgewirkt hat. Immerhin zeichnet sich aber angesichts des anhaltenden internationalen Interesses an der Arbeit und den vielfältigen Publikationen von und über Dieter Kienast ab, daß dessen Impulse für die Entwicklung der Landschaftsarchitektur seit dem Ende des 20. Jahrhunderts keineswegs nur auf die Schweiz beschränkt waren. Eine erste Suche nach Auswirkungen des protagonistischen Schaffens von Dieter Kienast offenbart eng miteinander vernetzte Fährten, deren Zahl den von ihm selbst vorgetragenen Thesen nicht nachsteht. Manche Fährten sind noch ganz frisch und gut lesbar, einige noch unentdeckt und andere bereits verwischt, bedroht völlig zu verschwinden, wenn die zeitliche Distanz zu groß würde.

Die nachhaltigsten und direktesten Impulse hat Dieter Kienast zweifellos als Lehrender am Interkantonalen Technikum in Rapperswil, an der Universität Karlsruhe und an der ETH Zürich bei StudentInnen, AssistentInnen und MitarbeiterInnen hinterlassen. Doch nur in Rapperswil, der einzigen Hochschule für Landschaftsarchitektur in der Deutschschweiz, bildete er zwischen 1980 und 1991 junge Landschaftsarchitekten aus. Als Professor für Gartenarchitektur unterrichtete Kienast in enger Zusammenarbeit mit KollegInnen der Nachbardisziplinen eine ganze Reihe selbstbewußter LandschaftsarchitektInnen, die heute zu den Erfolgreichsten ihres Faches zählen. Ihre Arbeit

among the most successful in their profession. Their work in the last few years has given Swiss landscape architecture a reputation which goes well beyond the country's borders. The Spreebogen Park in Berlin, the Kalkriese Museumspark near Osnabrück, and the esplanade of the Allianz Arena in Munich are ample evidence of this. Interdisciplinary teaching that Dieter Kienast provided at Rapperswil in association with artists, botanists, and architects was an entirely promising approach that he had come into contact with during his own studies in the nineteen-seventies at the Kassel Comprehensive University.

Many of the young Rapperswil graduates oriented themselves in the projects of the Stöckli, Kienast & Koeppel office at the beginning of their professional career: for example, Lukas Schweingruber, who today is a partner in the eminent Baden-based Zulauf Seippel and Schweingruber landscape architecture office. "Kienast's designs were something like a measuring stick for me from the very beginning."[1] Others – not only students, but also colleagues, members of staff, and project partners – associated both pressure as well as motivation with the charismatic person of Dieter Kienast. "In one way, Dieter Kienast was a massive burden, and evidently not only for me. His presence was very overpowering for many of us," says Swiss landscape architect Rainer Zulauf, reflecting on his relationship to his former mentor: "At the same time, the desire for liberation provided a

1 Schweingruber, Lukas in: Wirz Heinz (ed.): Arkadia. Zulauf Seippel Schweingruber, Baden, Luzern 2004

prägte in den letzten Jahren jenes Image, welches die Schweizer Landschaftsarchitektur nicht nur im eigenen Land bekannt machte. Der Spreebogen Park in Berlin, der Museumspark Kalkriese bei Osnabrück oder die Esplanade der Allianz Arena in München zeugen davon. Die interdisziplinäre Lehre, die Kienast in Zusammenarbeit mit bildenden Künstlern, Botanikern und Architekten in Rapperswil gestaltete, hatte er bereits im eigenen Studium in den 70er Jahren an der Gesamthochschule in Kassel als erfolgversprechend kennen gelernt.

An den Projekten des Büros Stöckli, Kienast & Koeppel orientierten sich viele junge Rapperswiler Studienabsolventen zu Beginn ihrer Laufbahn, so etwa Lukas Schweingruber, heute Partner im renommierten Landschaftsarchitekturbüro Zulauf Seippel und Schweingruber in Baden: «Kienasts Anlagen waren am Anfang fast eine Art Gradmesser für mich.»[1] Andere hingegen – nicht nur Studenten, sondern auch Weggefährten, Mitarbeiter und Projektpartner – verbanden mit der charismatischen Figur Dieter Kienast sowohl Druck als auch Ansporn gleichermaßen. Aus beiden Haltungen erwuchs die Stärkung eigenständiger Positionen. «Für mich war Dieter Kienast einerseits eine gewaltige Last, aber offenbar nicht nur für mich. Seine Präsenz war für viele sehr erdrückend», charakterisiert der Schweizer Landschaftsarchitekt Rainer Zulauf rückblickend das Verhältnis zu seinem ehemaligen Mentor. «Gleichzeitig erwuchs aus dem Drang nach Befreiung eine gewaltige Beflügelung, und seine Art des Umgangs mit der Kraft, die er erlangt hatte, erlebte ich sehr positiv. Eine Zeit lang lud Kienast eine Gruppe interessierter Studenten und junger Landschaftsarchitekten zu regelmäßigen Gesprächsrunden über Gartenarchitektur ein. Dabei versuchte er uns immer von dem zu befreien, was er selbst machte und bemühte sich, seine Präsenz wieder auf ein erträgliches Maß zu reduzieren. Im Rahmen des von ihm entfachten Diskurses gelang es einem allmählich, sich wieder zu befreien.»[2]

Charakteristische formale, inhaltliche oder manchmal auch nur plangraphische Ähnlichkeiten zwischen verschiedenen Projekten junger Schweizer Landschaftsarchitekturbüros und Arbeiten von Stöckli, Kienast & Koeppel aus den 80er und frühen 90er Jahren waren anfangs daher kaum zufällig. Vor allem die sensible, zugleich stringente Kombination von architektonischen und landschaftlich-gärtnerischen Elementen sowie die durchdachte Integration konstruktiv-konkreter Kunst in die

Zulauf Seippel und Schweingruber: Friedhof Küttigen / cemetery Küttigen

great source of inspiration, and his way of dealing with the strength he had achieved was something I found very positive. There was a period when Kienast invited a group of students who were interested and young landscape architects to regular discussion rounds on garden architecture. And he always tried to free us from what he did himself and return his presence to what was endurable. It was the discourse he initiated that gradually gave us the ability to find freedom again."[2]

Given this background, it is hardly surprising that initially there were typical formal, content and sometimes planning similarities between the various projects of young Swiss landscape architecture offices and the work of Stöckli, Kienast & Koeppel from the nineteen-eighties and the early nineteen-nineties. What particularly springs to mind is the combination of architectonic, landscape and gardening elements which is as sensitive as it is stringent, and the well-thought-out integration of constructive-concrete art into landscape architecture. The collaboration between artists and landscape architects, collaboration to which Dieter Kienast always attached special importance, has been further developed by some of his younger colleagues in recent years and in exceptional cases has even achieved recognition in art museums of international repute. The exhibition entitled "The mediated motion" by the Danish artist Olafur Eliasson in collaboration with landscape architect Günther Vogt at the

---

1 Schweingruber, Lukas in: Wirz Heinz (Hg.): Arkadia. Zulauf Seippel Schweingruber, Baden, Luzern 2004
2 ebda.

2 ibid.

Olafur Eliasson – Installationsansicht im Kunsthaus Bregenz 2001
Olafur Eliasson – installation view at the Kunsthaus Bregenz 2001

Olafur Eliasson – Installationsansicht im Kunsthaus Bregenz 2001
Olafur Eliasson – installation view at the Kunsthaus Bregenz 2001

Landschaftsarchitektur fallen dabei ins Auge. Die Zusammenarbeit zwischen bildenden Künstlern und Landschaftsarchitekten, auf die Kienast immer besonderen Wert legte, ist von manchem seiner jüngeren Kollegen in den vergangenen Jahren weiterentwickelt worden und hat in bemerkenswerten Fällen sogar den Sprung in international renommierte Kunstmuseen geschafft: Die Ausstellung «The mediated motion» vom dänischen Künstler Olafur Eliasson in Zusammenarbeit mit dem Landschaftsarchitekt Günther Vogt im Kunsthaus Bregenz 2001 wurde nicht zuletzt wegen ihrer geglückten Symbiose mit der Museumsarchitektur von Peter Zumthor zu einem herausragenden Ereignis zwischen Kunst, Landschaftsarchitektur und Architektur.[3]

Spontane Vegetationsdynamik in der urbanen Außenraumgestaltung, ebenfalls von Dieter Kienast thematisiert, hat sich mittlerweile zu einem der zentralen Themen der aktuellen Landschaftsarchitektur entwickelt und wurde, wie beispielsweise in den neuen Parks in Zürich-Oerlikon, in eindrucksvollen Dimensionen verwirklicht. Mancher jedoch, der Kienasts Konzentration auf das Minimalistische als zu dogmatisch empfand, bekennt sich heute wieder entspannt zu viel üppigerer Farb-, Form- und Gestaltungsvielfalt, ohne befürchten zu müssen, sich «gestalterischer Geschwätzigkeit» schuldig zu machen, und so sind die Diskussionen über «less aesthetics, more ethics»[4] erneut erwacht.

Kunsthaus Bregenz in 2001 was an outstanding presentation of art, landscape architecture and architecture ultimately due to its successful symbiosis with the museum architecture of Peter Zumthor.[3] The dynamism of spontaneous vegetation in the design of outside urban space, an aspect which was also a concern of Dieter Kienast, has by now become one of the central themes of contemporary landscape architecture and has been realised in impressive dimensions, as, for example, in the new parks in Zurich-Oerlikon. However, many of those who felt Kienast's insistence on minimalism was too dogmatic are today again happy to prescribe to a far greater diversity of colours, forms and designs, without having to fear being guilty of garrulousness in design, – and, in consequence, there has been a revival of the discussion on "less aesthetics, more ethics"[4].

Beginning in the early nineteen-eighties, Dieter Kienast and his team cultivated the dialogue between architectonic severity and naturalness with a consistency and skill virtually unrivalled by any other Swiss architect. His inspiration was not only derived from his interest in the fine arts, in particular in American Minimal Art, and also in radical works dating from the nineteen-fifties and sixties, particularly those of the Zurich garden architects Ernst Cramer and Fred Eicher. "The things which were relevant in the early eighties are not the same as those which are relevant in 1995, but, despite this, the works of Ernst

---

3 vgl. Kunsthaus Bregenz (Hg.): The mediated motion. Olafur Eliasson in Zusammenarbeit mit Günther Vogt Landschaftsarchitekt, Bregenz 2001
4 Motto der 7. Internationalen Architekturbiennale in Venedig 2000

3 cf. Kunsthaus Bregenz (ed.): The mediated motion. Olafur Eliasson in Zusammenarbeit mit Günther Vogt Landschaftsarchitekt, Bregenz 2001
4 Motto of the 7th International Architecture Biennial in Venice in 2000

Zulauf Seippel und Schweingruber: Oerlikerpark in Zürich / Park in Zurich-Oerlikon

Zulauf Seippel und Schweingruber: Oerlikerpark in Zürich / Park in Zurich-Oerlikon

Den Dialog zwischen architektonischer Strenge und natürlicher Lebendigkeit kultivierte seit den frühen 80er Jahren kaum ein anderer Schweizer Landschaftsarchitekt so konsequent und gekonnt wie Dieter Kienast und sein Team. Die Inspiration dazu schöpfte er nicht nur aus der Beschäftigung mit der bildenden Kunst, vor allem mit der amerikanischen Minimal Art, sondern auch aus den radikalen Werken der 50er und 60er Jahre, darunter bevorzugt jene der Zürcher Gartenarchitekten Ernst Cramer und Fred Eicher. «Anfang der 80er Jahre waren zwar andere Dinge aktuell als 1995, aber die Arbeiten von Ernst Cramer begeistern mich noch heute und die wohltuende Einfachheit im Schaffen von Fred Eicher habe ich in kaum einer anderen Arbeit je wieder gefunden. [...] Einige der Arbeiten von Fred Eicher halte ich noch heute für das Beste, was in den letzten zwanzig bis dreißig Jahren entstanden ist.»[5] Die Querbezüge zu solch kraftvollen, klar konzipierten Projekten wie dem Friedhof Eichbühl in Zürich-Altstetten aus den frühen 60er Jahren von Fred Eicher oder zum minimalistisch-abstrakten «Garten des Poeten» von Ernst Cramer vom Ende der 50er Jahre lassen sich in vielen von Kienasts besten Projekten wie dem Friedhof Fürstenwald in Chur, dem Brühlpark in Wettingen oder dem Berggarten in Graz wieder erkennen. Dieses Interesse an der Gartenkunst- und Architekturgeschichte sowie den vielfältigen Bezügen zwischen Vergangenheit, Gegenwart und Zukunft vermittelte er auch sei-

Cramer still inspire me today. As for the agreeable simplicity of the work of Fred Eicher, this is a quality which I have virtually never encountered in any other work. [...] I still today consider some Eicher's works to be the best to have come out of the last twenty to thirty years."[5] The cross-references to powerful, clearly designed projects such as Eichbühl Cemetery in Zürich-Altstetten, dating from the early nineteen-sixties, by Fred Eicher, or to the minimalist-abstract "Poet's Garden" by Ernst Cramer, dating from the late nineteen-fifties, are reflected in many of Dieter Kienast's best projects such as Fürstenwald Cemetery in Chur, Brühlpark in Wettingen, and Berggarten in Graz. He passed this interest in the history of garden art and architecture as well as in the varied relations between the past, present, and future on to his students during the nineteen-eighties. "When I studied under Dieter Kienast, I learnt that there is a history of garden architecture with data, facts, figures, images and societal background to which I can make deliberate reference in creating or rejecting images," explains Rainer Zulauf. "It was only then that I realised that I was dealing with subject matter and material that one had to fully understand either to work with it consciously or distance oneself from it."[6]

The "Archiv für Schweizer Gartenarchitektur und Landschaftsplanung"[7] (Swiss Archives for Garden Architecture and Landscape Planning) was established at Rapperswil in 1982, as it

5 Kienast, Dieter in: Weilacher, Udo: Zwischen Landschaftsarchitektur und Land Art, Basel, Berlin, Boston 1996, S.142

5 Kienast, Dieter in: Weilacher, Udo: Between Landscape Architecture and Land Art, Basel, Berlin, Boston 1996, p.142
6 Zulauf, Rainer in: Wirz Heinz (ed.): Arkadia. Zulauf Seippel Schweingruber, Baden, Luzern 2004

nen Studenten in den 80er Jahren. «Im Studium bei Dieter Kienast lernte ich, daß es eine Geschichte der Gartenarchitektur mit Daten, Fakten, Zahlen, Bildern und gesellschaftlichen Hintergründen gibt, auf die ich mich bewußt bei der Produktion oder der Ablehnung von Bildern beziehen kann», erläutert Rainer Zulauf. «Erst jetzt merke ich, daß es sich dabei um Werkstoff, um Materie, um Material handelte, das man beherrschen mußte, um damit zu arbeiten oder um sich bewußt davon zu distanzieren.»[6]

1982 – gewissermaßen im Gleichklang mit dem neu aufkeimenden Geschichtsbewußtsein in der Landschaftsarchitektur – wurde in Rapperswil das «Archiv für Schweizer Gartenarchitektur und Landschaftsplanung»[7] eingerichtet, welches sich seither der Erforschung der eidgenössischen Gartenkunstgeschichte widmet. Der erste Nachlaß, der im Rahmen einer Dissertation an der ETH Zürich, mit Unterstützung des Archivs und anfangs betreut von Dieter Kienast in Rapperswil, erforscht wurde, war nicht zufällig der von Ernst Cramer.[8] Weitere Forschungsarbeiten und Publikationen über die Geschichte der Schweizer Gartenausstellungen, über Gustav Ammann, Willi Neukom und andere prägende Persönlichkeiten der Schweizer Landschaftsarchitektur werden in Zukunft die jüngere Geschichte der Schweizer Landschaftsarchitektur verständlicher machen. Nicht zuletzt durch eine vorbildliche Dokumentation seiner eigenen Projekte in Fotos, Plänen und Texten hat Dieter Kienast, maßgeblich unterstützt durch seine Frau Erika Kienast-Lüder, dazu beigetragen, daß das Interesse an der jüngsten Geschichte der Landschaftsarchitektur nicht so rasch versiegen wird.

Seit und gerade in den frühen 80er Jahren, als die rein ökologisch motivierte, Natur imitierende Gartengestaltung ihren Höhepunkt erreicht hatte und zu einem «Naturdiktat»[9] zu erstarren drohte, wirkten Kienasts architektonisch konzipierte Projekte für die junge Generation der Schweizer Landschaftsarchitekten wie ein lange ersehnter Befreiungsschlag, der neue gestalterische Spielräume eröffnete. Angespornt durch die internationale Trendwende zu mehr Ästhetik in der Landschaftsarchitektur und beschleunigt durch Kienasts Einfluß setzte sich in der Schweiz im Laufe der 90er Jahre der architektonisch gestaltete Außenraum allmählich sowohl gegen das postmoderne Design – als auch gegen das Naturdiktat im Garten durch. Die aufsehenerregenden internationalen Wettbewerbserfolge der Büros Stöckli, Kienast & Koeppel bis 1994

were in accord with the renascent awareness of the history of landscape architecture. Since its inception the focus of the archives centre has been on research into the history of Swiss garden art. The first estate to be researched was the subject of a thesis at the Swiss Federal Institute of Technology Zurich, carried out with the help of the archives and initially supervised by Dieter Kienast, and, by no coincidence, was that of Ernst Cramer.[8] Further research work and publications on the history of Swiss horticultural exhibitions, on Gustav Ammann, Willi Neukom, and other leading Swiss landscape architects will help to make the recent history of Swiss landscape architecture more comprehensible in future. Dieter Kienast, with the substantial support of his wife, Mrs. Erika Kienast-Lüder, has made a major contribution, in particular by his exemplary documentation of his own projects in the form of photographs, plans and texts, ensuring that interest in the recent history of landscape architecture will fade quickly.

Since the early nineteen-eighties and particularly then, when garden design sought to imitate nature on purely ecological grounds reached its peak and threatened to freeze into a "dictate of nature"[9], the projects of Dieter Kienast based on architectonic principles have had the effect of long-sought-after liberation for the young generation of Swiss landscape architects, a liberation which opened up new design aspects. With the incentive of the new international trend to more aesthetics in landscape architecture and helped by Dieter Kienast's influence, outside space designed using architectonic principles gradually asserted itself in Switzerland in the nineteen-nineties against both the post-modernist design dictate as well as against the dictate of nature in the garden. The sensational international competition successes of the Stöckli, Kienast & Koeppel office as it existed until 1994 and of Kienast Vogt Partner as of 1995 made substantial contributions to an increase in thinking beyond the borders of Switzerland as to what a new balance between architecture and landscape, design and ecology might look like. This change, increased collaboration with the field of architecture and the fines arts, as well as heightened awareness of the urban development dimension of the concept of landscape increasingly returned the focus of many architects to landscape architecture. "I can imagine we have reached a point where dealing with nature and the incorporation of landscape into urbanisation has become unavoidable," said Jacques Herzog, the

---

6 Zulauf, Rainer in: Wirz Heinz (Hg.): Arkadia. Zulauf Seippel Schweingruber, Baden, Luzern 2004
7 heute: Archiv für Schweizer Landschaftsarchitektur
8 vgl. Weilacher, Udo: Visionäre Gärten. Die modernen Landschaften von Ernst Cramer, Basel, Berlin, Boston 2001
9 vgl. Kienast, Dieter: «Vom Gestaltungsdiktat zum Naturdiktat – oder: Gärten gegen Menschen?», in: Landschaft + Stadt, Heft 3/1981, S. 120–128

7 now: Archiv für Schweizer Landschaftsarchitektur
8 cf. Weilacher, Udo: Visionary Gardens. The modern landscapes of Ernst Cramer, Basel, Berlin, Boston 2001
9 cf. Kienast, Dieter: "Vom Gestaltungsdiktat zum Naturdiktat – oder: Gärten gegen Menschen?", in: Landschaft + Stadt, 3/1981, pp. 120–128

Nachbau der Pyramiden aus dem «Garten des Poeten» von Ernst Cramer an der Universität Hannover 2003 / Reconstruction of the pyramids from the "Poet's Garden" by Ernst Cramer at the University of Hanover

Videodokumentation des Pyramidenbaus an der Universität Hannover / Video documentation of the pyramids' construction at the University of Hanover

sowie Kienast Vogt Partner ab 1995 trugen einen nicht geringen Teil dazu bei, daß man auch außerhalb der Schweiz verstärkt darüber nachdachte, wie die neue Balance zwischen Architektur und Landschaft, Gestaltung und Ökologie aussehen könnte. Dieser Wandel, die verstärkte Zusammenarbeit mit der Architektur und der bildenden Kunst sowie ein geschärftes Bewußtsein für die städtebauliche Dimension des Landschaftsbegriffes rückten die Landschaftsarchitektur für viele Architekten wieder stärker in den Mittelpunkt ihres Interesses: «Ich kann mir vorstellen, daß wir einen Punkt erreicht haben, wo der Umgang mit Natur und das Einbeziehen von Landschaft in die Urbanisation unumgänglich geworden sind. Jeder Eingriff durch Architektur bedingt immer auch eine Arbeit mit der Natur», erkannte der Basler Architekt und regelmäßige Projektpartner von Kienast Vogt Partner Jacques Herzog. Er prophezeite: «Es wird eine explosionsartige Zunahme von Landschafts- und Gartenarchitektur geben.»[10]

Die Gründung einer eigenen Professur für Landschaftsarchitektur an der renommierten Architekturabteilung der ETH Zürich unter der Leitung von Dieter Kienast zählt zu den nachhaltigsten Erfolgen seines protagonistischen Schaffens im Dialog zwischen Architektur und Landschaftsarchitektur. Wichtige Fährten, die Dieter Kienast bei der Gründung der Professur 1997

Basel-based architect and regular project partner of Kienast Vogt Partner and he stated that any intervention went hand in hand with working with nature. He forecast: "There will be a phenomenal increase in landscape and garden architecture."[10]

Establishment of a chair for landscape architecture under Dieter Kienast at the distinguished department of architecture at the Swiss Federal Institute of Technology Zurich can be seen as one of the most lasting successes of his work in the dialogue between architecture and landscape architecture. Important signs provided by Dieter Kienast when the chair was established in 1997 will be pursued further under the leadership of Professor Christophe Girot in the fields of teaching and research. Central topics include, in particular, appraisal of the history of the development of Swiss garden architecture in the 20th century and research into the digital medium of video as a largely unexplored instrument of perception and design in landscape architecture. The expectation Dieter Kienast had of this medium was that it would not only generate an abstract experience of space as do plans, drawings, and computer animation, but would also convey the way that the garden, city, and landscape come together in a dynamic way to create rich, living complexes of inside and outside space. The first results of this experiment, substantially influenced by the creativity of the video-film maker and architect

---

10 Herzog, Jacques in: ARCH+ 142, Juli 1998, S. 34
11 Auch am Institut für Grünplanung und Gartenarchitektur der Universität Hannover widmet man sich seit 2003 diesem Thema.
12 vgl. Kienast, Dieter: «Die spontane Vegetation der Stadt Kassel in Abhängigkeit von bau- und stadtstrukturellen Quartierstypen», in: Urbs et Regio 10/1978

10 Herzog, Jacques in: ARCH+ 142, July 1998, p. 34
11 This topic has been examined at the Institut für Grünplanung und Gartenarchitektur at the University of Hanover since 2003
12 cf. Kienast, Dieter: "Die spontane Vegetation der Stadt Kassel in Abhängigkeit von bau- und stadtstrukturellen Quartierstypen", in: Urbs et Regio 10/1978
13 cf. Grosse-Bächle, Lucia: Eine Pflanze ist kein Stein. Strategien der Gestaltung mit der Dynamik von Pflanzen. Thesis at the Faculty of Landscape Architecture and Environmental Planning at the University of Hanover 2003

legte, werden zukünftig unter der Federführung von Professor Christophe Girot in Lehre und Forschung weiter verfolgt. Zu den zentralen Themen zählen vor allem die Aufarbeitung der Entwicklungsgeschichte der Schweizer Gartenarchitektur des 20. Jahrhunderts und die Erkundung des digitalen Mediums Video als überwiegend unerforschtes Wahrnehmungs- und Entwurfsinstrument in der Landschaftsarchitektur.

Kienast erhoffte sich von diesem Medium, daß es nicht nur wie Pläne, Zeichnungen und Computeranimationen ein abstrahiertes Raumerlebnis generieren, sondern darüber hinaus vermitteln würde, wie sich Garten, Stadt und Landschaft dynamisch zu reichhaltigen, lebendigen Außen- und Innenraumkomplexen zusammenfügen. Die ersten Ergebnisse dieses Experimentes, maßgeblich geprägt vom kreativen Geist des Videoschaffenden und Architekten Marc Schwarz, beflügelten schon Dieter Kienasts eigene Phantasie. Die Entwicklungen auf diesem Gebiet sind indes noch lange nicht abgeschlossen und führen zur Hinterfragung der traditionell statischen Leitbilder der Landschaftsarchitektur – nicht nur an der ETH Zürich.[11]

Schon als junger Forscher war Dieter Kienast der Frage nach dem bewußten Umgang mit dynamischen Prozessen und mit spontaner Vegetationsentwicklung in der Stadt auf der Spur.[12] Was als Dissertation in Kassel Ende der 70er Jahre begann, mündete etwa 15 Jahre später in die Entwicklung von urbanen Landschaftsarchitekturprojekten, die in aktuellen Forschungsarbeiten, jüngst erst an der Universität Hannover,[13] exemplarisch untersucht und als richtungweisend für den Umgang mit Natur in der Stadt hervorgehoben werden. Noch 1981 plädierte Kienast unter der Überschrift «Vom Gestaltungsdiktat zum Naturdiktat – oder: Gärten gegen Menschen?»[14], basierend auf den Theorien des Basler Soziologen Lucius Burckhardt, dafür, die populären Naturbilder kritisch zu hinterfragen, vor allem aber den Menschen aus dem naturnahen Garten nicht zu verbannen. Ökologie galt in seinen Augen nicht mehr als Allheilmittel und die Natur nicht mehr als alleinige Gestalterin[15], aber die Erkenntnisse und Erfahrungen aus dem bewußten Umgang mit den ökologischen Grundlagen waren trotzdem keineswegs außer Acht zu lassen, gerade im städtischen Raum. Genau dieses Vermögen zur Verbindung vermeintlich divergierender Positionen zwischen Erhaltung und Gestaltung, Prozeßorientierung und Formbewußtsein ist es, was den Arbeiten von Dieter Kienast

Marc Schwarz, gave concrete expression to what Dieter Kienast had already imagined. Developments in this area are, however, far from being complete and have led to questioning of the traditional static models provided by landscape architecture – not only at the Swiss Federal Institute of Technology Zurich.[11]

While still a young researcher, Dieter Kienast investigated the question of a conscious approach to dynamic processes and spontaneous development of urban vegetation.[12] What began as a thesis at Kassel in the late nineteen-seventies led fifteen years later to the development of urban landscape architecture projects which have been highlighted in latest research work, only just recently at the University of Hanover,[13] as outstanding examples pointing the way ahead for the approach to nature in the city. As far back as 1981, Dieter Kienast pleaded for a critical questioning of the folksy images of nature, without, however, banning people from the natural garden in an essay entitled "From the Dictate of Design to the Dictate of Nature – or: Gardens versus People?"[14], based on the theories put forward by Basel-based sociologist Lucius Burckhardt. It was his view that ecology was no longer a cure-all and nature no longer the sole designer[15], but that the realisations and experience derived from the conscious approach to the principles of ecology were, nonetheless, by no means to be ignored, in particular in urban space. It is particularly this ability to combine seemingly divergent positions between preservation and design, orientation towards processes and awareness of form which guarantees the work of Dieter Kienast a central place in present international discourse. "Despite this valuing of process over design – which retrieves the profession's devotion to ecological process during the 1960s and '70s – some landscape designers have continued to operate with equal facility in both modes. One of those was the Swiss landscape architect Dieter Kienast, whose work embraced a full range of concerns from the small to the large, from the fixed to the mutable, and from the natural to the constructed," wrote garden art expert Marc Treib in "Landscape Architecture" 2003.[16]

Kienast Vogt Partner gave illustrative demonstration to an innovative integration of spontaneous growth processes in urban space coupled with the skilful consideration of ecological concerns – in this case rainwater management – in two of its smallest inner-city landscape architecture projects, namely design of the small courtyard and confined area of outside space

---

13 vgl. Grosse-Bächle, Lucia: Eine Pflanze ist kein Stein. Strategien der Gestaltung mit der Dynamik von Pflanzen. Dissertation am Fachbereich Landschaftsarchitektur und Umweltentwicklung der Universität Hannover, Hannover 2003

14 Kienast, Dieter: «Vom Gestaltungsdiktat zum Naturdiktat – oder: Gärten gegen Menschen?», in: Landschaft + Stadt, Heft 3/1981, S. 120–128

15 vgl. Kienast, Dieter: «Sehnsucht nach dem Paradies», in: Hochparterre, Heft 7/1990, S.49, in diesem Band S. 84–91

14 Kienast, Dieter: "Vom Gestaltungsdiktat zum Naturdiktat – oder: Gärten gegen Menschen?", in: Landschaft + Stadt, 3/1981, p. 120–128

15 cf. Kienast, Dieter: "Sehnsucht nach dem Paradies", in: Hochparterre 7/1990, p. 49, in this volume pp. 84–91

16 Treib, Marc: "The Hedge and the Void. The landscapes of Dieter Kienast and an overview over his career», in: Landscape Architecture volume 93, January 2003

Rohe Tuffsteinwand im Projekt Swiss Re in Zürich / Raw tuff wall as part of the project of the Swiss Re in Zurch

Überwucherte Tuffwand im Projekt Basler und Partner / Overgrown tuff wall as part of the Basler und Partner project

im heutigen internationalen Diskurs besondere Aufmerksamkeit sichert. «Despite this valuing of process over design – which retrieves the profession's devotion to ecological process during the 1960s and '70s – some landscape designers have continued to operate with equal facility in both modes. One of those was the Swiss landscape architect Dieter Kienast, whose work embraced a full range of concerns from the small to the large, from the fixed to the mutable, and from the natural to the constructed», schrieb der amerikanische Gartenkunstexperte Marc Treib in «Landscape Architecture» 2003.[16]

In zwei ihrer kleinsten innerstädtischen Landschaftsarchitekturprojekte, der Gestaltung der engen Hof- und Außenräume für die Ingenieurfirma Basler & Partner sowie der Innenhofgestaltung am Geschäftshaus der Swiss Re in Zürich, demonstrierten Kienast Vogt Partner anschaulich eine innovative Integration spontaner Wachstumsprozesse in den städtischen Raum und zugleich die gekonnte Berücksichtigung ökologischer Belange, in diesem Fall des Regenwassermanagements. Augenfälligste Elemente beider Projekte sind senkrechte Wände aus Kalktuff, die wie Installationen zeitgenössischer Minimal-Künstler wirken. Kontinuierlich befeuchtet, verbessern sie nicht nur das örtliche Stadtklima, sondern es entwickelt sich seit Jahren auf den porösen Wandflächen durch spontanen Bewuchs ein lebendiges, wandelbares Feuchtbiotop, das in seiner ästhetischen Erschei-

at the Basler & Partner engineering firm, as well as the design of the interior courtyard of the office building of the Swiss Re in Zurich. The most conspicuous elements of both projects are vertical walls of limestone tuff, which seem like installations by contemporary Minimalist artists. Being permanently moist, they not only improve the local urban climate, but over the years spontaneous vegetation has led to a living, changeable wet biotope on the porous wall areas – a biotope which has nothing to do with the clichéd notions of ecological gardens either in terms of is aesthetic manifestation or precision of structure. And it is precisely this that stimulates reflection on one's own conception of nature, the image of nature in one's own mind's eye. Current approaches to research evaluate these projects as pointing the way ahead for a more consistent approach to designing vibrant inner-city areas of spontaneous vegetation without constantly only resorting to the repeated static ideal images from the repertoire of classic garden art. The principles of process and openness are the key concepts in current discussion on the future of landscape architecture in a society which no longer knows processes, but is consumer-orientated. This is why even in discourse on an entirely different sense of aesthetics, which understands itself as being specifically ecological, notice is taken of the work of Dieter Kienast and its integrating synthetic force is acknowledged.[17]

16 Treib, Marc: «The Hedge and the Void. The landscapes of Dieter Kienast and an overview over his career», in: Landscape Architecture, Vol. 93, Januar 2003

17 cf. Prigann, Hermann; Strewlow Heike (ed.): Aesthetics of Ecology, Basel, Berlin, Boston 2004
18 Tischer, Stefan: "Minimalismus als Irrweg", in: Topos 33/2000, p. 68–72
19 cf. Enzensberger, Hans Magnus: "Reminiszenzen an den Überfluß" in: Der Spiegel 51/1996, p. 117

nung und präzisen Konstruktion nichts mit den Klischeevorstellungen von ökologischen Gärten zu tun hat. Gerade dadurch wird aber das Nachdenken über das eigene Naturverständnis, über das eigene Bild von Natur im Kopf anregt. Aktuelle Forschungsarbeiten sehen in diesen Projekten richtungweisende Ansätze, wie in Zukunft konsequenter mit innerstädtischen, lebendigen Spontanvegetationsflächen gestalterisch umgegangen werden kann, ohne sich immer nur auf die stets wiederkehrenden statischen Idealbilder aus dem Fundus der klassischen Gartenkunst zu beziehen. Prozessualität und Offenheit sind die Schlüsselbegriffe in aktuellen Diskussionen um die Zukunft der Landschaftsarchitektur in einer prozeßentwöhnten, konsumorientierten Gesellschaft. Kienasts Arbeiten werden deshalb selbst im Diskurs über eine ganz anders geartete, sich selbst als spezifisch ökologisch verstehende Ästhetik wahrgenommen und in ihrer lagerübergreifenden synthetischen Kraft anerkannt.[17]

Dieter Kienasts Plädoyer für den Garten als letzten Luxus unserer Tage folgen die meisten Landschaftsarchitekten bis heute völlig ohne Widerspruch und verbreiten diese Auffassung weiter. Doch sein damit verbundenes Bekenntnis zu einer eigenen Art von reichhaltigem Minimalismus, insbesondere seine explizite Bezugnahme auf die amerikanische Minimal Art wurden immer wieder kontrovers diskutiert und gelegentlich aus Angst vor asketischer Freudlosigkeit mit Verweis auf die vorgeblich traditionell stark im Dekorativen liegenden Wurzeln der Gartenarchitektur als Irrweg[18] abgetan. Kienast, dem asketische Freudlosigkeit völlig fern lag, bezog sich hingegen auf jenen «Luxus der Zukunft», den der von ihm so geschätzte zeitkritische Lyriker und Essayist Hans Magnus Enzensberger so definierte: «Der Luxus der Zukunft verabschiedet sich vom Überflüssigen und strebt nach dem Notwendigen, von dem zu befürchten ist, daß es nur noch den wenigsten zu Gebote stehen wird.»[19] Zu den zukünftigen Luxusgütern zählt Enzensberger elementare Lebensvoraussetzungen, darunter die frei verfügbare Zeit, die bewußt selbstbestimmte Aufmerksamkeit, der Raum für freie Bewegung, die Ruhe, die intakte Umwelt und die Sicherheit. Das heutige Gesellschaftssystem zehrt massiv an diesen begehrten Ressourcen und gibt werbewirksam vor, dieses im Interesse individueller Freiheit zu tun. «Minimalismus und Verzicht könnten sich als ebenso selten, aufwendig und begehrt erweisen wie einst die ostentative Verschwendung»[20], so Enzensbergers Einschätzung.

Dieter Kienast's plea for the garden as the last place of luxury in our times is one which until today most landscape architects have followed without contradiction and propagated. Yet, his associated belief in an independent form of varied Minimalism, in particular his explicit references to American Minimal Art have frequently been the subject of controversial discussion and occasionally, for fear of ascetic cheerlessness, dismissed as a mistake by invoking the strongly decorative roots of garden architecture.[18] Kienast, who had no interest whatsoever in ascetic cheerlessness, instead spoke of the "luxury of the future", which the lyricist and essayist Hans Magnus Enzensberger, whose criticism of the present time he greatly admired defined as: "The luxury of the future takes its leave of the superfluous and aspires to the necessary, of which is it to be feared that this will only be at the disposal of the few."[19] Enzensberger numbers fundamental prerequisites for living among the luxuries of the future, as including spare time, consciously self-determined focus of attention, space for freedom of movement, tranquillity, the intact environment, and security. Today's society is greatly sapping these much sought-after resources and manages to convey the message it is doing this in the interest of individual freedom. In Enzensberger's view, "Minimalism and abstention could prove to be just as rare, extravagant and desirable as was once ostentatious wastefulness."[20] It was in this sense that Dieter Kienast pleaded against garrulousness in design and for creation of viable, freely available outside space, which should stand out by the strength of its capability for enrichment.[21] The discussion on the garden as the ultimate luxury of our time has admittedly not only been in progress since Dieter Kienast's "Sehnsucht nach dem Paradies"[22] (Longing for Paradise), but he provided some decisive contributions, which still have not been sufficiently debated and, again and again, play a central role in discussion on the future of landscape architecture.

Dieter Kienast always deplored the serious absence of theory in landscape architecture, "as it's not possible to carry out an important aspect of landscape design on an emotional level."[23] He, however, did not see himself as a theorist, let alone as the creator of pioneering theories in today's landscape architecture. In addition to the French landscape architect Bernard Lassus, whose theory-backed work he held in very high regard, Dieter Kienast was, as Stefanie Krebs stated in her thesis, "one of the few land-

---

17 vgl. Prigann, Hermann; Strewlow Heike (Hg.): Ökologische Ästhetik, Basel, Berlin, Boston 2004
18 Tischer, Stefan: «Minimalismus als Irrweg», in: Topos 33/2000, S. 68–72
19 vgl. Enzensberger, Hans Magnus: «Reminiszenzen an den Überfluß» in: Der Spiegel 51/1996, S. 117
20 ebda., S. 118

20 ibid. p. 118
21 cf. Kienast, Dieter in: Weilacher, Udo: Between Landscape Architecture and Land Art, Basel, Berlin, Boston 1996, p. 150
22 Kienast, Dieter: "Sehnsucht nach dem Paradies" in: Hochparterre 7/1990, pp. 46–50; in this volume pp. 84–91
23 Kienast, Dieter in: Weilacher, Udo: Between Landscape Architecture and Land Art, Basel, Berlin, Boston 1996, p. 143

In diesem Sinne plädierte Kienast gegen gestalterische Geschwätzigkeit und für die Schaffung tragfähiger, frei verfügbarer Außenräume, die durch ihre Anreicherungsfähigkeit ausgezeichnet sein sollten.[21] Die Diskussion um den Garten als letzten Luxus unserer Tage wird zwar nicht erst seit Dieter Kienasts «Sehnsucht nach dem Paradies»[22] geführt, aber er hat einige entscheidende Impulse geliefert, die noch lange nicht ausreichend erörtert sind und in den Debatten um die Zukunft der Landschaftsarchitektur immer wieder eine zentrale Rolle spielen.

Dieter Kienast bemängelte stets das gravierende Theoriedefizit in der Landschaftsarchitektur, «denn ein wichtiger Teil der Landschaftsarchitektur kann nicht von der emotionalen Seite aus bestritten werden.»[23] Er selbst sah sich aber nicht als Theoretiker oder gar als Schöpfer richtungweisender Theorien der aktuellen Landschaftsarchitektur. Neben dem französischen Landschaftsarchitekten Bernard Lassus, dessen theoretisch angereicherte Arbeiten er außerordentlich schätzte, zählte Dieter Kienast, wie Stefanie Krebs in ihrer Dissertation feststellt, «zu den wenigen Landschaftsarchitekten, die sich über die Beschreibung ihrer eigenen Projekte hinaus auf einer verallgemeinernden theoretischen Ebene zur Landschaftsarchitektur äußern.»[24] Insbesondere Kienasts Bekenntnisse zum offenen Umgang mit Brüchen im vermeintlich geschlossenen Weltbild und sein Faible für das Heterogene in einer Landschaftsarchitektur «zwischen Arkadien und Restfläche»[25] werfen nicht nur anregende Fragen nach seinen eigenen theoretischen Bezugspunkten auf, sondern bieten vor allem lohnende Ansatzpunkte für Erkundungen aktueller Theorien der Landschaftsarchitektur, denn, so Kienast: «Es ist nun mal eine Tatsache, daß unsere aktuelle gesellschaftliche, politische und religiöse Situation in der Schwebe ist, und dagegen können wir sehr wenig tun.»[26] An diesem Befund hat sich in den vergangenen Jahren prinzipiell nichts geändert, im Gegenteil: Am Beginn des 21. Jahrhunderts sehen sich alle umweltgestaltenden Disziplinen mit neuen, äußerst dynamischen Entwicklungstendenzen konfrontiert, die das Bild der Landschaft und der Stadt sowie die Naturwahrnehmung des Menschen und die Vorstellungen von Lebenswelt viel gravierender und zugleich subtiler verändern als das im vergangenen Jahrhundert vorherzusehen war.

Aktuelle Debatten um die Nachhaltigkeit von Städten, die Urbanisierung der Kulturlandschaft, die zunehmende Privatisie-

Berggarten an der IGA Graz 2000 / Alpine garden at the Graz International Garden Show, 2000

scape architects to discuss landscape architecture at a generalising, theoretical level as well as describing his own projects."[24] In particular, Dieter Kienast's belief in an approach to discontinuity in a supposedly self-contained conception of the world and his penchant for heterogeneity in a landscape architecture "between Arcadia and leftovers"[25] not only pose interesting questions as to his own theoretical points of reference, but, above all, provide worthwhile points of departure for exploring current theories in landscape architecture, as, according to Kienast, "It is quite simply a fact that our present social, political and religious situation is hanging in the balance, and there is very little we can do about it."[26] There have been no fundamental changes to these conclusions in the past few years. On the contrary: At the beginning of the 21st century all disciplines concerned with designing and shaping the environment see themselves confronted with new, exceptionally dynamic development trends changing the image of the landscape and the city as well as our perception of nature and ideas of environment far more radically and, at the same time, more subtly than could have been envisaged in the last century.

Current debate on the sustainability of cities, urbanisation of cultivated land, increasing privatisation and the ensuing disappearance of public space, urban decline and urban perforation, worsening economic and ecological crises as well as dwindling confidence in the effectiveness of human attempts to

---

21 vgl. Kienast, Dieter in: Weilacher, Udo: Zwischen Landschaftsarchitektur und Land Art. Basel, Berlin, Boston 1996, S. 150

22 Kienast, Dieter: «Sehnsucht nach dem Paradies» in: Hochparterre 7/1990, S. 46–50; in diesem Band S. 84–91.

23 Kienast, Dieter in: Weilacher, Udo: Zwischen Landschaftsarchitektur und Land Art, Basel Berlin Boston 1996, S.142

24 Krebs, Stefanie: Zur Lesbarkeit zeitgenössischer Landschaftsarchitektur. Verbindungen zur Philosophie der Dekonstruktion. Dissertation am Fachbereich Landschaftsarchitektur und Umweltentwicklung der Universität Hannover, Hannover 2001, S. 90

24 Krebs, Stefanie: Zur Lesbarkeit zeitgenössischer Landschaftsarchitektur. Verbindungen zur Philosophie der Dekonstruktion. Thesis at the Faculty of Landscape Architecture and Environmental Planning at the University of Hanover, Hanover 2001, p. 90

25 Kienast, Dieter: Zwischen Arkadien und Restfläche, Luzern 1992

26 Kienast, Dieter: "10 Thesen zur Landschaftsarchitektur" (1998), in: Professur für Landschxaftsarchitektur ETH Zürich (ed.): Dieter Kienast – Die Poetik des Gartens. Über Ordnung und Chaos in der Landschaftsarchitektur, Basel, Berlin, Boston 2002

rung und das dadurch verursachte Verschwinden des öffentlichen Raums, Stadtrückbau und Stadtperforation, sowie die Zuspitzung ökonomischer und ökologischer Krisen als auch das schwindende Vertrauen in die Wirksamkeit menschlicher Korrekturversuche in einem komplex vernetzten, heterogenen Umweltsystem werfen die schwierige Frage auf, ob Dieter Kienasts Positionen, seine «10 Thesen zur Landschaftsarchitektur»[27] ihre Halbwertszeit womöglich schon überschritten haben. Für jene seiner Thesen, die sich deutlich spürbar an traditionellen, tendenziell statischen und zuweilen romantischen Stadt- und Landschaftsvorstellungen des 20. Jahrhunderts orientierten, mag diese Gefahr bestehen. Einem anderen Teil seiner Thesen, die sich auf die Modernität des Dauerhaften, die Rückkehr zur Einfachheit, die Ordnung in der Vielfalt oder die Beschränkung auf das Wesentliche beziehen, darf man angesichts ihres zyklisch, nicht erst seit Ende des 20. Jahrhunderts immer wiederkehrenden Auftretens in der europäischen Kulturgeschichte getrost eine gewisse Zeitlosigkeit attestieren. Jene Positionen aber, mit denen sich Kienast zur Unschärfe, zur Hybridität, zum Fragmentarischen, zum Transparenten, zum Unfertigen, zum Prozeßhaften und scheinbar Chaotischen bekannte, sind nicht nur in anbetracht des anhaltenden gesellschaftlichen Schwebezustandes von verblüffender Aktualität. «Je länger dieser Schwebezustand anhält, desto mehr neigen wir dazu, uns an bestimmte Prinzipien oder Leitbilder zu klammern», resümierte Kienast und bekannte: «Ich finde diesen Schwebezustand aber besonders spannend, weil er die Möglichkeit bietet, sich unbeschwert zu bewegen und Dinge auszuprobieren.»[28]

Udo Weilacher

Dieter Kienast auf Spurensuche in Indien 1997 / Dieter Kienast tracing trails in India, 1997

make corrections in a complexly interlinked, heterogeneous environmental system pose the difficult question as to whether Dieter Kienast's positions, his "10 propositions on landscape architecture"[27] have perhaps already passed their half life. This may be true of those of his propositions that are clearly orientated towards 20th century conceptions of city and landscape, traditional, tending to be static and sometimes romantic. However, there is no reason not to accord a certain timelessness to other of his propositions relating to the modernity of the enduring, the return to simplicity, order in diversity, or restriction to the essential, as their occurrence in European cultural history has been cyclical and is not only a phenomenon which has just existed since the end of the 20th century. But the positions in which Kienast declared his support for indistinctness, for the hybrid, for the fragmentary, for the transparent, for the unfinished, for what is ongoing, and for the seemingly chaotic are of surprising present relevance not only in view of the continuing state of flux in society. "The longer this precarious situation continues, the greater our tendency to cling to particular principles or role-models," concluded Dieter Kienast and continued: "I find this state of flux particularly exciting as it offers the possibility of moving unencumbered and experimenting."[28]

Udo Weilacher

25 Kienast, Dieter: Zwischen Arkadien und Restfläche, Luzern 1992
26 Kienast, Dieter: «10 Thesen zur Landschaftsarchitektur» (1998), in: Professur für Landschaftsarchitektur ETH Zürich (Hg.): Dieter Kienast – Die Poetik des Gartens. Über Ordnung und Chaos in der Landschaftsarchitektur, Basel, Berlin, Boston 2002
27 ebda.
28 Kienast, Dieter in: Weilacher, Udo: Zwischen Landschaftsarchitektur und Land Art, Basel, Berlin, Boston 1996, S.146

27 ibid.
28 Kienast, Dieter in: Weilacher, Udo: Between Landscape Architecture and Land Art, Basel, Berlin, Boston 1996, p.146

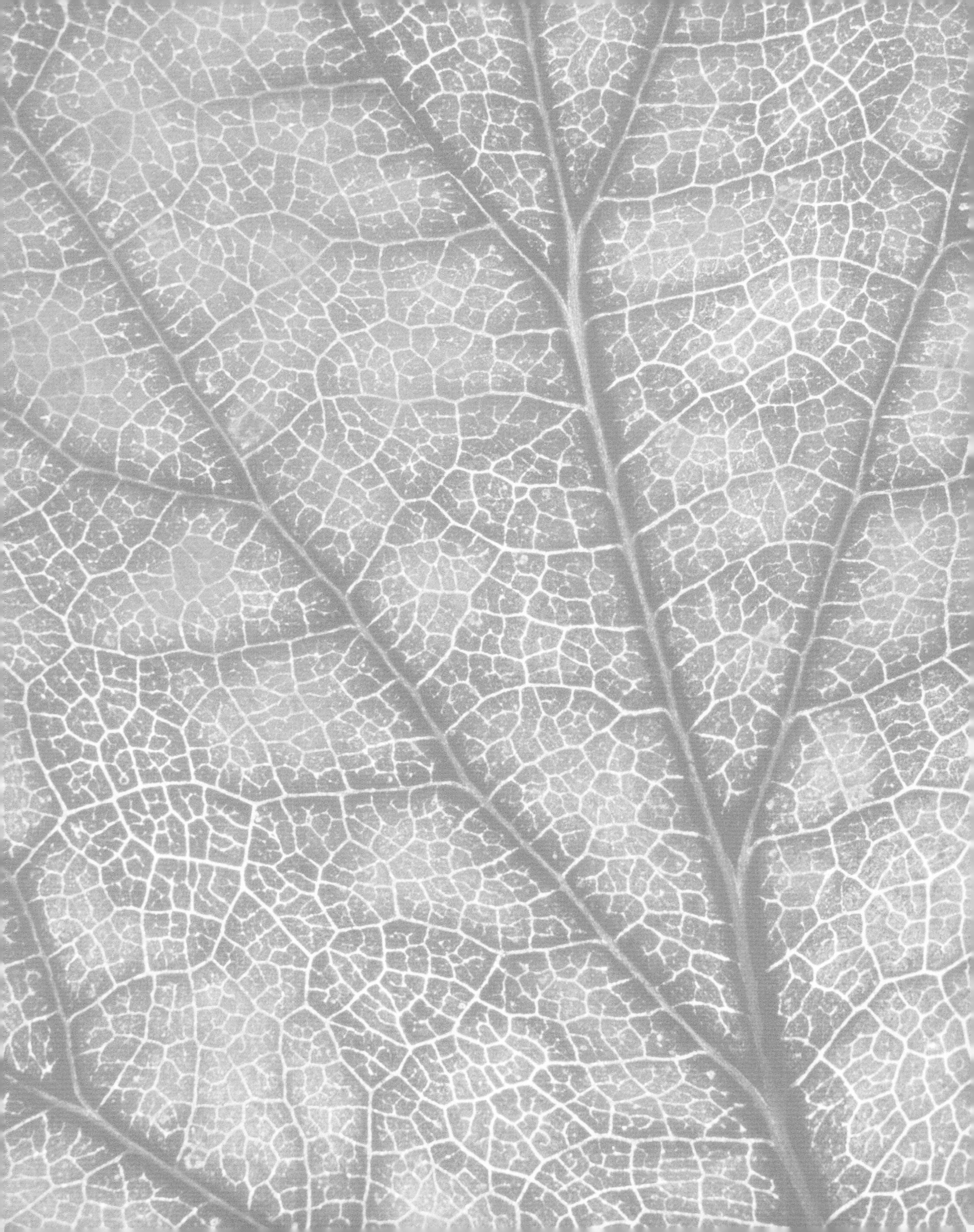

Projektdaten / Project Data

Stöckli, Kienast & Koeppel, Landschaftsarchitekten 1979–1994
Kienast Vogt Partner, Landschaftsarchitekten 1995–1999

Garten K-L.
(Eintritt in den autobiographischen Garten /
Entering the Autobiographical Garden)
Ausführung: seit 1980 in Bearbeitung /
since 1980 in progress
Größe: ca. 1000 m²

Garten M.
(Vielfalt und Dichte / Variety and Density)
Architekt Um- und Ausbau: Marbach und Rüegg,
Zürich
Ausführung: 1988–1989
Größe: 1600 m²

Garten E.
(Wo ist Arkadien? / Where is Arcadia?)
Ausführung: 1. Phase 1989, 2. Phase 1994
Größe: ca. 3500 m²

Garten N.
(Grenzen und Zäune / Borders and Fences)
Ausführung: 1994
Größe: 2000 m²

Garten in Ulm
(Lob der Zweideutigkeit / In Praise of Ambiguity)
Architekt Um- und Neubau: Karljosef Schattner,
Eichstätt, Wilhelm + Maria Huber, Kempten
Größe: 2400 m²

Garten K.
(Zwischen Tradition und Innovation /
Between Tradition and Innovation)
Architekt Umbau, Renovation: Romero & Schäfle,
Zürich
Ausführung: 1994–1995
Größe: 400 m²

Schloßgarten in Yverdon
(Neue Gärten zum alten Schloß /
New Gardens for the Old Castle)
Ausführung: 1994–1998
Größe: 13 000 m²

Stadtpark Wettingen
Bauherr: Gemeinde Wettingen
Mitarbeiter: Paul Bauer und W. Vetsch
Wettbewerb: 1. Preis / 1981
Ausführung: 1982–1983
Größe: 11 300 m²

**Gartenanlagen der Psychiatrischen Klinik
Waldhaus, Chur**
Loestrasse 220, 7000 Chur
Bauherr: Hochbauamt des Kantons Graubünden
Architekten: F. Censi + F. Chiaverio, Grono
(Neubauten)
R. E. Vogel, Chur (Altbauten)
Ausführung: 1990–1996
Größe: 26 600 m²

Friedhof Fürstenwald Chur
Bauherr: Stadtgemeinde Chur
Architekten: U. Zinsli + F. Eberhard, Chur
Wettbewerb: 1. Preis / 1992
Ausführung: 1993–1996
Größe: 20 000 m²

**Verwaltungsgebäude Swisscom,
Worblaufen Bern**
Alte Tiefenaustrasse 6, 3048 Worblaufen
Bauherr: Swisscom AG
Architekt: Indermühle, Bern
Künstlerin: Jenny Holzer
Wettbewerb: 1. Preis / 1993
Ausführung: 1993–1998
Größe: ca. 7000 m²

Expo 2000 und Messegelände Hannover
Bauherr: Expo 2000 Hannover + Deutsche Messe
AG + Messe GmbH Hannover
Architekten: Thomas Herzog, München;
Prof. Ackermann, Prof. Albert Speer, Frankfurt;
Arnaboldi Cavaldini, Lugano
Künstler: Fischli Weiss, Zürich
Masterplan: 1992
Ausführung: 1995–2000
Größe: ca. 450 000 m²

Kurpark Bad Münder
Bauherr: Stadt Bad Münder
Wettbewerb: 1. Preis / 1994
Ausführung: 1994–1997
Größe: ca. 28 000 m²

Tate Modern London
Bauherr: Tate Gallery London
Architekten: Herzog & de Meuron, Basel
Ausführung: 1995–2000
Größe: 20 000 m²

Bauherr – client | Architekt – architect | Um- und Ausbau – conversion and interior design | Um- und Neubau – conversion and new building
Umbau, Renovation – conversion, renovation | Künstler – artist | Mitarbeit – collaboration | Wettbewerb – competition | Ausführung – realisation | Größe – area

Die Freiflächen des Zentrums für Kunst und
Medientechnologie, Karlsruhe
Brauerstraße, D-76124 Karlsruhe
Bauherr: LEG Landesentwicklungsgesellschaft
Baden-Württemberg mbH, Treuhänderin der Stadt
Karlsruhe für die Neuordnung des IWKA-Gelände
Architekt: P. Schweger, Hamburg / Karlsruhe
Wettbewerb: 1. Preis / 1995
Ausführung: 1995–1997
Größe: ca. 21 000 m^2

Stadtgarten am Neubau des Bundesarbeits-
gerichts, Erfurt
Rudolfstraße 47, D-99013 Erfurt
Bauherr: Staatsbauamt Erfurt
Architektin: Gesine Weinmiller, Berlin
Künstler: Jan Hamilton Finlay, Jürgen Partenheimer
Wettbewerb: 1. Preis / 1995
Ausführung: 1996–1999
Größe: 7 833 m^2

Internationale Gartenschau 2000
Steiermark, Graz
Bauherr: Internationale Gartenschau 2000 Graz
Architekt: ARGE Eisenköck / Zinganel, Graz
Wettbewerb: 1. Preis / 1996
Ausführung: 1997–2000
Größe: 121 ha

Innenhofgestaltung Geschäftshaus
der Swiss Re, Zürich
Gotthardstrasse 43 / 45, 8002 Zürich
Bauherr: Swiss Re Zürich
Architekt: Stücheli, Zürich
Ausführung: 1997
Größe: 1800 m^2

Seminar- und Ausbildungszentrum Swiss Re,
Rüschlikon
Gheistrasse 31-39, 8803 Rüschlikon
Bauherr: Swiss Re Zürich
Architekten: M. Meili + M. Peter, Zürich
Künstler: Sol LeWitt
Ausführung: 1997–2000
Größe: 28 000 m^2

Umgebungsgestaltung Spar- und Landeskasse,
Fürstenfeldbruck
Oskar-von-Miller-Straße 4,
D-82256 Fürstenfeldbruck
Wettbewerb: 1. Preis / 1997
Bauherr: Spar- und Landeskasse Fürstenfeldbruck
Architekten: Stammberger Wild, München
Ausführung: 1997
Größe: 11 500 m^2

Stockalper Schloßgarten Brig
Bauherr: Schweizerische Stiftung für
das Stockalperschloß Brig
Architekten: M. Burkhalter und Ch. Sumi, Zürich
Wettbewerb: 1. Preis / 1996
Ausführung: 1998–2001
Größe: 13 000 m^2

Neubau Madagaskarhalle, Zoo Zürich
Bauherr: Zoo Zürich
Architekten: Ch. Gautschi, B. Storrer, Zürich
In Planung: seit 1994
Größe: 40 000 m^2

Parklandschaft Mechtenberg
Gelsenkirchen (D)
Wettbewerb: diverse Studien 1990–1993
Ausführung: nicht realisiert

Straße der Nationen, Chemnitz
Projekt «Hommage an John Cage»
Bauherr: Stadt Chemnitz
Wettbewerb: 1994, nicht prämiert

Conrad Gessner Park Zürich Oerlikon
Bauherr: Stadt Zürich, Garten- und
Landwirtschaftsamt
Künstler: Christian Vogt, Fotograf, Basel
Wettbewerb: 2. Preis / 1996

Töölönlahtipark Helsinki
Bauherr: City of Helsinki Planning Department
Wettbewerb: nicht prämiert / 1997

Bibliographie / Bibliography

1976
Kienast, Dieter / Roelly, Thom: «Standortökologische Untersuchungen in Stadtquartieren – insbesondere zur Vegetation – unter dem Aspekt der freiraumplanerischen Verwertbarkeit», in: Schriftenreihe der GHK Kassel, Reihe 3(2) 1976

1977
Kienast, Dieter: «Die Ruderalvegetation der Stadt Kassel – Beiträge zur Vegetationskunde Nordhessens», in: Tüxen, R. / Dierschke, H. (ed.): 50 Jahre Floristisch-soziologische Arbeitsgemeinschaft (1927–1977), Göttingen 1977

1978
Kienast, Dieter: «Pflanzengesellschaften des alten Fabrikgeländes Henschel in Kassel», in: Philippia III/5 1978; p. 408–422
Kienast, Dieter: «Assoziationskomplexe (Sigmeten) und ihre praktische Anwendung», in: Tüxen, R. (ed.): Berichte der Internationalen Symposien der Internationalen Vereinigung für Vegetationskunde, Vaduz 1978; p. 329–362
Kienast, Dieter: «Die spontane Vegetation der Stadt Kassel in Abhängigkeit von bau- und stadtstrukturellen Quartierstypen», in: Urbs et Regio 10/1978

1979
Kienast, Dieter: «Bemerkungen zum wohnungsnahen Freiraum», in: Anthos 4/1979; p. 2–9
Kienast, Dieter: «Wohngrün zu Mehrfamilienhäusern in Wollishofen/Zürich» in: Anthos, 4/1979; p. 10–13
Hülbusch, Karl Heinrich / Bäuerle, Heidbert / Hesse, Frank / Kienast, Dieter: «Freiraum- und landschaftsplanerische Analyse des Stadtgebietes von Schleswig», in: Urbs et Regio 11/1979
Kienast, Dieter: «Vom naturnahen Garten oder von der Nutzbarkeit der Vegetation», in: Der Gartenbau 25/1979; p. 1117–1122

1980
Kienast, Dieter: «Grün im Quartier», in: Weiss, M. / Lanz, P. (ed.): Handbuch für Quartierverbesserer, Zurich 1980
Kienast, Dieter: «Botanischer Garten Südteil. Naturnahe Biotope», in: Anthos 1/1980; p. 56–65
Kienast, Dieter: Sigma-Gesellschaften der Stadt Kassel. Phytocoenologia Festband Tüxen, Stuttgart, Braunschweig 7/1980
Kienast, Dieter: «Der Beitrag des Gartens zur Verbesserung der Wohnumwelt», in: SIA/FGA-Bulletin 2/1980

1981
Kienast, Dieter: «Vom Gestaltungsdiktat zum Naturdiktat – oder: Gärten gegen Menschen?», in: Landschaft + Stadt 3/1981; p. 120–128
Kienast, Dieter: no title («Ein Spiel ist der Weg der Kinder zur Erkenntnis,...»), in: Öffentliche Baumappe der Ostschweiz, Goldach 1980/81; p. 30–34

1982
Kienast, Dieter: «Zum Ausbau und Unterhalt des Botanischen Gartens Basel», in: Brüglinger Mosaik 5/1982, no. 25; p. 15–23
Kienast, Dieter / Stöckli, Peter Paul: «Grünplanung Aarau. Ein Versuch, Freiraumplanung zu betreiben», in: Anthos 3/1982; p. 29–38.

1984
Kienast, Dieter: «Ideenwettbewerb Kurpark Bad Zurzach AG», in: Anthos 1/1984

1985
Kienast, Dieter: «Kein Platz für Zürich», in: Anthos 1/1985; p. 33–36
Kienast, Dieter: «Der landschaftsarchitektonische Beitrag im interdisziplinären Planerteam», in: SIA-Dokumentation 87/1985 (Quelle unsicher).

1986
Kienast, Dieter: «Bemerkungen zum Wettbewerb Kasernenareal Zürich – gesehen aus landschaftsarchitektonischer Sicht», in: Anthos 3/1986; p. 42–45
Kienast, Dieter: «Kultur oder Natur?», in: Aktuelles Bauen + Planen 3/1986
Kienast, Dieter: «Ohne Leitbild», in: Garten + Landschaft 11/1986; p. 34–38

1989
Kienast, Dieter: «Zur Bedeutung von Freiräumen», in: Das Kommunal Magazin, 1989; p. 1–7
Kienast, Dieter: «Interiorscaping oder Begrünungslust im Innenraum», in: Anthos 1/1989; p. 28–31
Kienast, Dieter: «Die Gestalt des öffentlichen Raumes», in: SWB Innerschweiz (ed.) Stadt-Stadtraum-Raumqualität, Luzern, 1989

1990
Kienast, Dieter: «Die Sehnsucht nach dem Paradies», in: Hochparterre 7/1990; p. 46–50
Kienast, Dieter: «Über den Umgang mit Friedhof», in: Anthos 4/1990; p. 10–14
Kienast, Dieter: «Ökologie gegen Gestalt? – oder Natürlichkeit und Künstlichkeit als Programm», in: SRL Schriftenreihe 25/1990; p. 102–107
Kienast, Dieter / Loidl, Hans / Haag, Holger; Interview with Robert Schäfer and K.H. Ludwig «Leidenschaft läßt sich nicht lehren», in: Garten + Landschaft 2/1990; p. 43–48

1991
Kienast, Dieter: «Von der Notwendigkeit künstlerischer Innovation und ihrem Verhältnis zum Massengeschmack in der Landschaftsarchitektur», in: Choreographie des öffentlichen Raumes, Vortragsreihe Nov. 1991, Fachgebiet Bauplanung TU-Berlin, 1994
Koenigs, Tom (ed.): Vision offener Grünräume, Frankfurt am Main 1991

1992

Kienast, Dieter: «Bemerkungen zur Natur der Stadt / Zwischen Arkadien und Restfläche», in: Gründerzeit – Grün der Zeit, öGLA/IFLA (ed.), Wien 1992

Kienast, Dieter: «Ein neuer Park in Berlin», in: Anthos 2/1992; p. 86–89

Kienast, Dieter: «Vom Kirchhof zum Erholungsraum», in: Der Gartenbau 3/1992; p. 86–89

Kienast, Dieter: «Die Poesie der Stadtlandschaft», in: Garten + Landschaft 3/1992; p. 9–13

Kienast, Dieter: «Remarques sur la nature de la ville», in: Faces 24/1992; p. 14–17

Kienast, Dieter: «Aussenräume der Ecole Cantonale de langue francaise, Bern», in: Topos 1/1992; p. 76–77

Kienast, Dieter: «Zwischen Arkadien und Restfläche», Architekturgalerie Luzern, 1992

1993

Kienast, Dieter / Vogt, Günther: «Die Form, de Inhalt und die Zeit», in: Topos 2/1993; p. 6–17

Kienast, Dieter: «Zwischen Stadtkante und Schloß», in: Garten + Landschaft 12/1993; p. 26–28

Kienast, Dieter: «Die Natur der Sache – Stadtlandschaften», in: Koenigs, Tom (ed.): Stadt-Parks, Frankfurt am Main, 1993, p. 10–21

Bartetzko, Dieter: «Die Natur der Großstädter – Frankfurts künftiger neu-alter Günthersburgpark», in: StadtBauwelt 12/march 1993; p. 594–597

1994

Kienast, Dieter: «Begrünungslust im Innenraum», in: Der Gartenbau 16/1994; p. 34–35

Kienast, Dieter: «Zur Dichte der Stadt», in: Topos 7/1994; p. 103–109

Kienast, Dieter: «Zwischen Poesie und Geschwätzigkeit», in: Garten + Landschaft 1/1994; p. 13–17

Radziewsky, Elke von: «Der Künstler ist immer der Gärtner», in: Architektur & Wohnen 3/1994; p. 58–68

1995

Kienast, Dieter: «Der Garten als geistige Landschaft», in: Topos 11/1995; p. 68–79

Kienast, Dieter: «Stadtlandschaft», in: ZOLLtexte 2/1995, Wien; p. 43–46

Kienast, Dieter: «Safari – oder wo ist Madagaskar»', in: Topos 13/1995; p. 63–72

Kienast, Dieter: «Un decalogo – a Set of Rules», in: Lotus 87/1995; p. 63–81

Bund Schweizer Architekten (BSLA) Regionalgruppe Zürich (ed.): «Gute Gärten», Zürich 1995; p. 31, 32, 37

Tremp, Andreas: «Wege sind wie Löcher», in: Der Architekt 2/1995; p. 103–105

1996

Kienast, Dieter: «La nuova città paesaggio – The New City Landscape», in: Lotus 90, 1996; p. 116–117

Kienast, Dieter; Interview mit Udo Weilacher: «Die Kultivierung der Brüche», in: Weilacher, Udo: Zwischen Landschaftsarchitektur und Land Art, Basel, Berlin, Boston 1999, 2. Auflage; p. 137–156

König, Kathrin: «Ein Garten für zwei Botaniker», in: Anthos 4/1996; p. 4–7

Marquart, Christian: «Das Wallmeisterhaus», in: Bauwelt 16/1996; p. 953–957

1997

Kienast, Dieter: Kienast Gärten – Gardens, Basel, Boston, Berlin 1997

Kienast, Dieter; Interview with Robert Schäfer: «Funktion, Form und Aussage», in: Topos 18/1997; p. 6–12

Kienast, Dieter: «Retorno a las raicep. Jardin en St. Gallen y entorno del Inselspital en Berna», in: Arquitectura Viva 53, march/april 1997; p. 50–53

Kienast, Dieter: «Madagaskar in Zürich», in: Anthos 4/1997; p. 31–85

Kienast, Dieter: «Stadt und Natur. Gartenkultur im Spiegel der Gesellschaft», in: Archithese 4/1997; p. 4–11

Danzer, Robert / Oberrauner, Helmut: «Wettbewerb: Internationale Gartenschau – Steiermark 2000», in: Architekturjournal Wettbewerb 159/160, march/april 1997; p. 76–85

Valda, Andreas: «Mit Gärten gegen die Grünen», in: Tagesanzeiger 23.12.1997; p. 49

Wormbs, Brigitte: «Satz und Gegensatz», in: Basler Zeitung no. 14, 5.4.1997; p. 12–13

1998

Kienast, Dieter: «Stadt und Natur – Gartenkultur im Spiegel der Gesellschaft», in: Passagen/Passages, no. 24/spring 1998; p. 33ff. Schweizer Kulturstiftung Pro Helvetia.

Kienast, Dieter: «Naturwandel», in: Anthos 1/1998; p. 10–15

Kienast, Dieter: «Die Natur der Stadt», in: Verlag Hochparterre (ed.): Kulturlandschaft Stadt. Architektur Städtebau Denkmalschutz. Texte für Ursula Koch, Stadträtin von Zürich von April 1986 bis März 1998, Zurich 1998; p. 66–74

Kappeler, Susanne: «Gärten als Kunstwerke – Neue Arbeiten des Landschaftsarchitekten Dieter Kienast», in: NZZ, 31.01.1998

Kappeler, Susanne: «Gartenkunst im Dialog mit der Architektur. Landschaftsarchitekt Dieter Kienast gestorben», in: Neue Zürcher Zeitung, 28.12.1998; p. 35

Rüegg, Arthur: «Mit Natur Architektur gebaut», in: Tages-Anzeiger, 30.12.1998; p. 50

1999

Kienast, Dieter: «Zehn Thesen zur Landschaftsarchitektur», in: disp 138, 1999, p. 4–6

Kienast, Dieter: «10 Thesen zur Landschaftsarchitektur», in: Der Gartenbau 13/1999; p. 6–9

Aberle, Waltraud: «Landschaft der Gärten beim Swisscom-Neubau», in: Der Gartenbau 15/1999; p. 6–9

Detzelhofer, Anna: «Zauber der Gärten. Die IGS 2000 in Graz in der Steiermark», in: LA Landschaftsarchitektur 12/1999; p. 26–28

Diedrich, Lisa: «Dieter Kienast 1945-1998», in: Bauwelt 4/1999; p. 150

gta, ETH Zürich: «Dieter Kienast. Lob der Sinnlichkeit», Zurich 1999

Henningsen, Jens: «Stadtteilpark und Wuhlegrünzug», in: Landschaftsarchitekten BDLA Deutschland 1/1999; p. 25.

Huber, Silvia: «Umgebungsgestaltung Sparkasse D – Fürstenfeldbruck. Mosaikartige Eingriffe», in: Architektur & Technik 4/1999; p. 14-18

Kunstboek (ed.): Switzerland. Landschafts- und Gartenarchitekten und ihre Kreationen, Osstkamp 1999; p. 13-15

Otti, Gmür: «Dieter Kienast gestorben», in: Neue Luzerner Zeitung, Neue Urner Zeitung, Neue Schwyzer Zeitung, Neue Obwaldner Zeitung, Neue Nidwaldner Zeitung, Neue Zuger Zeitung, 5.1.1999

Radziewsky, Elke von: «Et in Arcadia Ego», in: Architektur & Wohnen, 'Schweiz', Special 6, 1999; p. 104-110

Rüegg, Arthur: «Komplexe Gärten aus der Gussform», in: Garten + Landschaft 5/1999; p. 18-21

Schäfer, Robert: «Zeichen setzen», in: Garten + Landschaft 5/1999; p. 1

Stöckli, Peter: «Am Ende der Strasse – ein Nachruf auf Dieter Kienast», in: Anthos 1/1999; p. 58-59

Tremp, Andreas: «Die Allee der Vereinigten Bäume», in: Garten + Landschaft 5/1999; p. 22-25

Weilacher, Udo: «Die Sinnlichkeit architektonischer Strenge. Zum Tod des Landschaftsarchitekten Dieter Kienast», in: Archithese 1/1999; p. 74-75

Weilacher, Udo: «Friedhof Fürstenwald bei Chur», in: Garten + Landschaft 5/1999; p. 14-17

Weilacher, Udo: «Poetische Sinnlichkeit», in: ETH Intern 7.98/99; p. 13

Weilacher, Udo: «Architektonische Gärten jenseits ökologischer Klischees», in: Gartenpraxis 9/1999; p. 38-43

Weilacher, Udo: «Zum Tod des Landschaftsarchitekten Dieter Kienast», in: Basler Magazin 3/23, january 1999; p. 11

Weilacher, Udo: «Natur und Architektur im Dialog», in: NZZ-Folio, march 1999; p. 64-65

Weilacher, Udo: «Poetische Sinnlichkeit in minimalistischer Komposition», in: Stichting Schäfer, Robert: «Dieter Kienast: quality is in being definite», in: Topos 26/1999; p. 131

Wullschleger, Peter: «Ein letzter Garten: Zum Tod des Landschaftsarchitekten Dieter Kienast», in: Der Gartenbau 2/99; p. 13

Wullschleger, Peter: «Ein letzter Garten: Zum Tod des Landschaftsarchitekten Dieter Kienast», in: BSLA Journal 1/1999; p. 1-2 (cf. Der Gartenbau 2/1999)

Wullschleger, Peter: «Ein letzter Garten: Zum Tod des Landschaftsarchitekten Dieter Kienast», in: Werk, Bauen + Wohnen 4/1999; p. 62-63 (cf. Der Gartenbau 2/1999)

Zinsli, Urs; Erhard, Konrad: «Friedhofsanlage bei Chur», in: Baumeister 6/1999; p. 32.

anonymous, «Natura e communicazione», in: Archi 4/1999; p. 16-19

2000

Kienast, Dieter: Kienast Vogt Aussenräume – Open Spaces, Basel, Boston, Berlin 2000

Herzog & De Meuron / Kienast, Dieter: «Aufwertung einer gebauten Leere durch Neuordnung», in: Werk, Bauen + Wohnen 4/2000; p. 10-14

Aeberhard, Beat: «Der Garten der Sinne. Dieter Kienast – Lob der Sinnlichkeit in der ETH Zürich», in: Archithese 1/2000; p. 90

Jenni, Bruno; Noseda, Irma: «Höfe im Hauptsitz der Swisscom, Worblaufen», in: Werk Bauen + Wohnen 9/2000; p. 61.

Proksch, Thomas: «Dieter Kienast und seine Gärten», in: Agrarverlag (ed.): Zauber der Gärten. Leopoldsdorf 2000; p. 15-17

Schmid, André: «Internationale Gartenschau Steiermark 2000», in: Anthos 1/2000; p. 34-37

Weilacher, Udo: «Ein Garten in abstrakter Faltung», in: NZZ-Folio September 2000

Weilacher, Udo: : «Abstrakter Totenbezirk und Gegenwärtigkeit von Landschaft» (Der Friedhof Fürstenwald bei Chur), in: Werk, Bauen + Wohnen 10/2000; p. 40-42.

anonymous, The Garden Book, London 2000; p. 241

2002

Kienast, Dieter: Kienast Vogt Parks und Friedhöfe – Parks and Cemeteries, Basel, Boston, Berlin 2002

Almqvist, Paula: «Solitär am See» (Garden M.), in: Architektur & Wohnen 2/2002; p. 128ff.

Hill, Penelope: Jardins d'aujourd'hui en Eurpoe. Entre art et architecture, Anvers 2002; p. 231-232

Professur für Landschaftsarchitektur ETH Zürich (ed.): Dieter Kienast – Die Poetik des Gartenp. Über Chaos und Ordnung in der Landschaftsarchitektur, Basel, Berlin, Boston 2002.

2003

Treib, Marc: «The Hedge and the Void. The landscapes of Dieter Kienast and an overview of his career», in: Landscape architecture (Magazine of the American Society of Landscape Architectures) 1/2003; p. 79 ff.

2004

Stoffler, Johannes: «Gegen die Vereinfachung der Gartenbotschaft», in: Stadt + Grün 1/2004, p. 16ff.

Günther Vogt, geboren 1957; nach Gärtnerlehre und Studium am Interkantonalen Technikum Rapperswil, Mitarbeiter bei Stöckli Kienast & Koeppel, seit 1987. Ab 1995 Mitinhaber von Kienast Vogt Partner. Seit 2000 Inhaber von Vogt Landschaftsarchitekten.

Christian Vogt, geboren 1946; arbeitet seit 1969 selbständig als Fotograf; zahlreiche Gruppen- und Einzelausstellungen in Europa und Nordamerika. Verschiedene Buchpublikationen.

Marc Schwarz, geboren 1967 in Zürich, Architekt und Filmemacher. Studium an der Eidgenössischen Technischen Hochschule Zürich und der Technischen Universität Graz. Seit 1996 selbständiger Cineast; zahlreiche Filmprojekte und Beiträge für Galerien und Museen in Luzern, Zürich und Lausanne. 1997-99 wissenschaftlicher Mitarbeiter von Prof. Dieter Kienast in Zürich. Seit 2002 Partner bei VUES, «Atelier für eine andere Sicht auf Stadt und Landschaft», Zürich.

Udo Weilacher, geboren 1963; Gärtnerlehre, Studium der Landschaftsarchitektur an der Technischen Universität München-Weihenstephan und an der California State Polytechnic University Pomona/Los Angeles. 1993-98 wissenschaftlicher Mitarbeiter bei Dieter Kienast an der Universität Karlsruhe und an der Eidgenössischen Technischen Hochschule Zürich, danach Lehrbeauftragter an der ETH Zürich. Dissertation an der ETH Zürich 2001. Zahlreiche Publikationen. Seit 2002 Professor für Landschaftsarchitektur und Entwerfen am Institut für Grünplanung und Gartenarchitektur der Universität Hannover.

Martin R. Dean, geboren 1955 in Menziken (Schweiz); Studium der Germanistik, Philosophie und Ethnologie in Basel. Arbeit als Autor, Journalist, Essayist. 1989 Aufenthalt im Istituto Svizzero di Roma. 1992-93 Stadtbeobachter von Zug. 1997-98 Poet in Residence an der Universität Essen. Veröffentlichte zahlreiche Erzählungen, Theaterstücke und Romane, etwa «Die verborgenen Gärten» 1982 und «Meine Väter» 2003.

Günther Vogt, born in 1957; after apprenticeship as a gardener and studies at the Technical College in Rapperswil he became a collaborator at Stöckli Kienast & Koeppel in 1987. Since 1995 partner of Kienast Vogt Partner. The owner of Vogt landscape architects since 2000.

Christian Vogt, born in 1946, has been working as a freelance photographer since 1969. His work has been shown in numerous exhibitions in Europe and North America. He is also the author of several books.

Marc Schwarz, born in Zurich in 1967, architect and filmmaker. He studied at the Swiss Federal Institute of Technology (ETH) in Zurich and at the Technical University in Graz. He has been a free-lance cineaste since 1996; numerous film projects and contributions for galleries and museums in Lucerne, Zurich, and Lausanne. Research assistant of Prof. Dieter Kienast in Zurich from 1997-99. A partner of VUES, "Studio for a different view of the city and the landscape", Zurich, since 2002.

Udo Weilacher, born in 1963; apprenticeship as a gardener, studied landscape architecture at the Munich-Weihenstephan Technical University and at the California State Polytechnic University Pomona/Los Angeles. Research assistant to Dieter Kienast at the University of Karlsruhe and the Swiss Federal Institute of Technology in Zurich (ETH). Doctorate at the ETH Zurich in 2001. A wide range of publications. Professor of landscape architecture and design at the Institute for Planning of Green Space and Garden Architecture since 2002.

Martin R. Dean, born in Menziken, Switzerland, in 1955; studied German language and literature, philosophy and ethnology in Basel. Author, journalist and essayist at the Istituto Svizzero di Roma in 1989. Writer in residence for Zug, 1992-93; Poet in residence at the University of Essen, 1997-98. Has published numerous stories, plays and novels, for example «Die verborgenen Gärten», 1982, and «Meine Väter», 2003.

Übersetzung vom Deutschen ins Englische / Translation from German into English:
Felicity Gloth, Berlin: 4-9, 84-304
Bruce Almberg, Katja Steiner, Ehingen: 12-81

Umschlaggestaltung / Cover design: Erika Kienast, Christoph Kloetzli
Layout: Karin Weisener, Christoph Kloetzli

Die Projektbeschreibungen in diesem Band (Texte und Abbildungen) wurden
den folgenden Publikationen entnommen / The projects described in this book
(texts and illustrations) have been taken from the following publications:
Dieter Kienast: Kienast Gärten – Gardens, ISBN 3-7643-5609-X
Dieter Kienast: Kienast Vogt Aussenräume – Open Spaces, ISBN 3-7643-6030-5
Dieter Kienast: Kienast Vogt Parks und Friedhöfe – Parks and Cemeteries, ISBN 3-7643-6434-3

Die Essays «Sehnsucht nach dem Paradies» und «Zwischen Poesie und Geschwätzigkeit» von
Dieter Kienast wurden folgendem Band entnommen / The Essays "Sehnsucht nach dem
Paradies" (Longing for Paradise) and "Zwischen Poesie und Geschwätzigkeit" (Between Poetry
and Garrulousness) have been taken from the following publication:
Professur für Landschaftsarchitektur ETH Zürich (Hg.) Dieter Kienast – Die Poetik des Gartens.
Über Chaos und Ordnung in der Landschaftsarchitektur, ISBN 3-7643-6578-1

Die Essays von Martin R. Dean und Udo Weilacher wurden als Originalbeiträge für den
vorliegenden Band verfaßt. / The essays by Martin R. Dean and Udo Weilacher have been written
especially for this publication.

Seite 6: Kurt Tucholsky, aus: «Park Monceau»
In: Kurt Tucholsky, Gesammelte Werke ©1960 by Rowohlt Verlag GmbH, Reinbek bei Hamburg
Page 6: Verse taken from the poem "Park Monceau" by Kurt Tucholsky from "Germany? Germany!"
published by Carcanet Press, Manchester 1990. Translation into English by Karl F. Ross.

Bildrechte / Illustration Copyrights
Photos: Christian Vogt, Basel
außer / except:
Herzog & de Meuron / Allianz-Arena München: 285 rechts / right
Margit Schild: 290 links / left
Marc Schwarz: 142, 143
Markus Tretter: 287
Rita Weilacher: 288, 292 rechts / right
Udo Weilacher: 284, 285 links / left, 286, 290 rechts / right, 292 links / left, 294, 295

A CIP catalogue record for this book is available from the Library of Congress,
Washington D.C., USA

Bibliographic information published by Die Deutsche Bibliothek
Die Deutsche Bibliothek lists this publication in the Deutsche Nationalbibliografie;
detailed bibliographic data is available in the internet at http://dnb.ddb.de.

This work is subject to copyright. All rights are reserved, whether the whole or part of the
material is concerned, specifically the rights of translation, reprinting, re-use of illustrations,
recitation, broadcasting, reproduction on microfilms or in other ways, and storage
in data banks. For any kind of use, permission of the copyright owner must be obtained.

© 2004 Birkhäuser – Verlag für Architektur, Postfach 133, CH-4010 Basel, Schweiz
Ein Unternehmen von Springer Science+Business Media
Printed on acid-free paper produced from chlorine-free pulp. TCF ∞

Printed in Germany
ISBN 3-7643-6847-0

9 8 7 6 5 4 3 2 1

www.birkhauser.ch